"Very few writers can take a complex subject—over two hundred years of history with bewildering, bemoaning, and belligerent claims by Americans about whether this nation is Christian or not—hold it up for inspection, and make its utter complexity clear; but John Fea accomplishes this and more. Informed, judicious, insightful, and genuinely delightful."
　　—Scot McKnight, North Park University; author of *The Jesus Creed*

"This is a wonderful book—fascinating, timely, carefully researched, clearly written, and deeply helpful. It examines the Christian nation idea as expressed by the founders and also as it has shaped the country ever since (and still does). As a scholar, Professor Fea leaves no doubt of his disdain for those who 'cherry pick' the historical record to support contemporary arguments. Rather, he presents such a balanced view of the hard facts that neither the Christian nation advocates nor their critics can feel totally vindicated."
　　—Bob Abernethy, executive editor and host of PBS's *Religion & Ethics Newsweekly;* coeditor of *The Life of Meaning*

"With careful research and judicious scholarship, John Fea has produced a remarkably useful guide for navigating the arguments about America's 'Christian' origins. His reluctance to dictate conclusions is a measure of his evenhandedness."
　　—Randall Balmer, Barnard College; author of *God in the White House: How Faith Shaped the Presidency from John F. Kennedy to George W. Bush*

"This is a book for readers who want a credible account of how religion affected the settlement and founding of the United States. It brings out the indisputable importance of religion without claiming more than sound historical scholarship can support. Its most original feature is the fascinating history of the long campaign to define the United States as a Christian nation."
　　—Richard Bushman, emeritus, Columbia University; author of *From Puritan to Yankee* and *The Refinement of America*

"This book is required reading for everyone interested in the question of America's Christian origins—especially for those who think they already have the answer. If I could recommend but one source on the Christian America thesis, this would be it."
　　—Douglas A. Sweeney, Trinity Evangelical Divinity School; author of *The American Evangelical Story*

"This is a timely book that will help make sense of one of the most important divides in American politics. John Fea does more than simply point out the shortcomings of arguments on either side of the debate over Christian America. He offers a clear and balanced reinterpretation of how this debate has shaped American culture and society for more than two hundred years."

—John Wigger, University of Missouri; author
of *American Saint* and *Taking Heaven by Storm*

"John Fea's learned and accessible study documents the surprisingly diverse views of the founders on religion and tells the fascinating story of how Americans have remembered them in later generations."

—Beth Barton Schweiger, University of Arkansas;
coeditor of *Religion in the American South*

"Fea avoids the polarizing polemics of contemporary political debate over the religious beliefs of the founders and instead focuses on the revolutionary generation's spirituality and the ways in which Christian faith shaped understanding during that momentous upheaval. A worthwhile read for scholars as well as the general public."

—Brendan McConville, Boston University;
author of *The King's Three Faces*

"With clarity, wisdom, and precision, John Fea probes the question posed in the title of this book. It is a complex question, yielding complex responses that are not amenable to a sound-bite culture."

—Dennis P. Hollinger, President,
Gordon-Conwell Theological Seminary

"John Fea has produced a carefully balanced and thought-provoking addition to the long-running debate about the role of religion in America's founding. It is particularly strong in its treatment of the anti-Catholicism of some of the founders."

—Ira Stoll, author of *Samuel Adams: A Life*

Was America Founded as a Christian Nation?

Revised Edition

Was America Founded as a Christian Nation?

Revised Edition

A Historical Introduction

John Fea

WESTMINSTER
JOHN KNOX PRESS
LOUISVILLE · KENTUCKY

Revised edition
Published by Westminster John Knox Press
Louisville, Kentucky

16 17 18 19 20 21 22 23 24 25—10 9 8 7 6 5 4 3 2 1

Book design by Sharon Adams
Cover design by Marc Whitaker/MTWDesign.net
Cover art: The First Prayer in Congress, *painted by T. H. Matteson,*
engraved on steel by H. S. Sadd, public domain.

Library of Congress Cataloging-in-Publication Data

Names: Fea, John, author.
Title: Was America founded as a Christian nation? : a historical introduction
  / John Fea.
Description: Second edition. | Louisville, KY : Westminster John Knox Press,
  2016. | Includes bibliographical references and index.
Identifiers: LCCN 2016011998 (print) | LCCN 2016013230 (ebook) | ISBN
  9780664262495 (alk. paper) | ISBN 9781611646931 (ebk.)
Subjects: LCSH: Christianity and politics--United States--History. | United
  States--Church history.
Classification: LCC BR515 .F43 2016 (print) | LCC BR515 (ebook) | DDC
  261.70973--dc23
LC record available at http://lccn.loc.gov/2016011998

♾ The paper used in this publication meets the minimum requirements
of the American National Standard for Information Sciences—Permanence
of Paper for Printed Library Materials, ANSI Z39.48-1992.

Most Westminster John Knox Press books are available at special quantity discounts when purchased in bulk by corporations, organizations, and special-interest groups. For more information, please e-mail SpecialSales@wjkbooks.com.

For my parents, John and Joan Fea

Contents

List of Illustrations

Preface to the Revised Edition

When *Was America Founded as a Christian Nation: A Historical Intro-duction* was released in 2011, I spent some time on the road and on the radio waves promoting it. In the process I learned a lot about what Americans think about the founding of the United States. Many of the people I encountered have been thoughtful, open-minded, and willing to listen to my interpretation of the relationship between Christianity and the American founding. Others have not.

As I traveled I kept a journal about my experiences. I titled it "On the Road with Christian America." I used the journal to reflect on what my encounters with Christian America tell us about how American evan-gelicals, and Americans more broadly, engage the past. In *Was Amer-ica Founded as a Christian Nation?* I tried to bring some complexity and nuance to this politically charged question. In fact, I have often said that the question in the title of my book is a bad historical question, because to answer it requires one to superimpose a late-twentieth-century question on eighteenth-century historical actors who, for the most part, were not asking it. Some people I met while on the road could embrace my histori-cal approach to this topic, but others seemed incapable of thinking about this issue in any way other than through the lens of politics. I found that when I gave a talk on the book, most people who showed up came with their minds already made up about how they would answer the question in the title. Thus they looked to me for evidence to bolster their pre-conceived convictions. Unfortunately, these people often returned home disappointed and dissatisfied. When radio hosts asked me to provide a clear yes or no answer to the question and I answered by saying "it's com-plicated," the interview might as well have ended at that point. If I was not going to take a definitive side in this debate, then what was the point of talking to me? Most radio hosts pegged me as a typical professor trying to make the smooth places rough. I plead guilty.

Here are a few of the more interesting things that have happened to me since the publication of the first edition of *Was America Founded as a Christian Nation*:

- In a talk to a group of mainline Protestant clergy, I was accused of anti-Catholicism for quoting John Adams. Fortunately, cooler heads prevailed, and the other ministers in attendance explained to their colleague that I was not personally endorsing anti-Catholic views but only trying to make the point that the worldview of some founders, particularly Adams, was profoundly anti-Catholic.

- A conservative talk radio host in Orange County, California, asked me if the founding fathers would have opposed the placing of American flags near gravestones at Arlington National Cemetery. (There was apparently a news story dealing with this issue at the time of my interview.) When I said that I did not know, he went off on a tirade about how liberal history professors were destroying this country. At one of the commercial breaks (off the air), he changed to a friendly tone of voice and praised my answer to his question. He said that the interview was "going well" and called it "one of the best I have done in a long time." When we returned from the break, he continued his tirade.

- A syndicated Christian radio host asked me if I thought Thomas Jefferson was a Christian. When I said that it is hard to label a person "Christian" who rejects the resurrection of Jesus Christ, he responded, "Well, he may not have been a Christian, but he was a believer!" I am still trying to get my head around this one.

- A Christian radio host asked me to define George Washington's position on abortion.

- During the Q&A following a talk to a group of youth workers in Minneapolis, a man said that he would not buy my book unless I told him what I thought of David Barton. (No sale was made.)

- After hearing me talk about *Was America Founded as a Christian Nation?* at Colonial Williamsburg, a man asked me if Messiah College, the school where I teach, "was still a Christian college?"

- A host of a Christian radio station spent the entire thirty-minute interview reading to me quotes from the Founding Fathers, Supreme Court decisions, the Star-Spangled Banner, and John Winthrop's "A Modell of Christian Charity." I think my voice was heard on the program for a total of two minutes. Following the interview, he invited me back on the show so that we could continue "this stimulating conversation."

- I began a talk at an Arizona mega-church by asking the audience of two hundred plus evangelicals to raise a hand if they thought that America was "founded as a Christian nation." Nearly every hand in the room went up. (I have since learned not to start my talks in this fashion.)
- A caller to a Pittsburgh Christian radio station who identified himself as a "minister of the Gospel" said that my suggestion that history is "complex" was "wishy-washy." He went on to tell me that "everyone knows that history is black and white."
- During a Q&A at a public lecture, someone asked me what Thomas Jefferson, if he were alive, would say about the election of a black president. When I probed a bit deeper, I realized that she assumed Jefferson would have opposed an Obama presidency because he had said in *Notes on the State of Virginia* that Africans were inferior to white people.
- One Christian radio host introduced me as a history professor at Messiah College. He then caught me completely off guard when he proceeded to ask, "Do you believe in *the* Messiah?" When I said "yes," he responded by saying, "OK then, hallelujah, praise Jesus, we can now continue with this interview."

But through it all I have been blessed by the fact that *Was America Founded as a Christian Nation?* has found its way into the hands of college students, pastors, laypersons in book groups, history buffs, scholars, politicians, and political pundits. If the e-mails I receive are any indication, it has helped people make sense of this controversial topic that still serves as a battleground in our present-day culture wars. Shortly after the book was published, I learned that it was chosen as one of three finalists for the George Washington Book Prize, an important literary prize that honors books that broaden public understanding of American history. It did not win the prize, but it did make for a an evening at Mount Vernon with my wife, Joy, and the editor of the first edition, Jana Reiss, that I will never forget.

I hope you enjoy the second edition. It includes a few corrections from the original edition, a new cover, and a short epilogue that brings the debate over the Christian roots of the United States up to the present.

John Fea
Mechanicsburg, PA

Preface to the First Edition

During the week of June 11, 2007, four thousand Christians converged on Williamsburg, Virginia, to celebrate the four hundredth anniversary of the founding of Jamestown—the first successful English colony in North America. The event was sponsored by Vision Forum Ministries, an organization that, among other things, is committed to "teaching history as the providence of God." The "Jamestown Quadricentennial: A Celebration of America's Providential History" was a gala event. For the cost of admission visitors were treated to lectures on various themes in early American history, historical reenactments, "faith and freedom" tours of Williamsburg and Yorktown, and hot-air-balloon rides over the site of the Jamestown settlement. One of the highlights of the week was a children's parade. Led by a Pocahontas reenactor, a thousand boys and girls dressed in period clothing marched in a one-mile procession to commemorate the planting of this historic colony. The week came to an end for the American Christian pilgrims with a Sunday morning worship service.

The Vision Forum gathering differed markedly from the celebration planned by the national government and its Jamestown 400th Commemoration Commission. While both events featured activities for families and an array of educational opportunities, the government-sponsored commemoration did not include lectures and seminars with titles such as "Jamestown's Legacy of Christ, Liberty, and Common Law" or "Refuting the Revisionists on America's 400th Birthday." Nor did the brochures advertising various tours of Jamestown read like the one being promoted by a popular Christian radio host and theologian: "Join Gary DeMar as he presents well-documented facts which will change your perspective about what it means to be a Christian in America. . . . If you are tired of the revisionism of the politically correct crowd trying to whitewash our Christian history, you will not want to miss this tour."[1]

The providential historians' quadricentennial was part of an attempt by some evangelicals to reclaim what they believe to be America's Christian heritage. They have made the relationship between religion and the creation of the American Republic a dominant topic of debate in our recent culture wars. Many well-meaning Christians, like those associated with the Vision Forum, believe that America was founded as a uniquely Christian nation. These evangelicals have used this historical claim to justify policy on a host of moral and cultural issues facing the United States today. The study of the past, they argue, has been held hostage by secularists who have rejected the notion that the American founders sought to forge a country that was Christian. Instead, these revisionists wrongly claim that the American Revolutionary era was informed by Enlightenment ideals about toleration and pluralism.

In their attempt to counter these arguments, some believers in a Christian America have supported House Resolution 888, an attempt by Christian lawmakers in Congress to establish an "American Religious History Week" that celebrates "the rich spiritual and religious history of our Nation's founding."[2] Others have taken control of the Texas State Board of Education in an attempt to change the state's social studies curriculum to better represent the Christian themes that they believe all schoolchildren should study and learn. Since Texas is the nation's second-largest market for textbook publishers, and these publishers craft their textbooks to suit the needs of their best customers, it is likely that the decisions made by the Texas State Board of Education will influence what students learn in other states as well.[3]

Was America founded as a Christian nation? In my experience as a Christian and a Christian college history professor, I have found that many average churchgoers are confused about this topic. Unfortunately, those who dominate our public discourse tend to make matters worse. For example, during the 2008 presidential campaign, Republican candidate John McCain announced that "the Constitution established the United States of America as a Christian nation," but the Constitution says nothing about the relationship between Christianity and the United States. Former Arkansas governor and fellow presidential candidate Mike Huckabee said on the campaign trail that "most" of the fifty-six men who signed the Declaration of Independence were clergymen.[4] In fact, only one member of the clergy signed the Declaration—College of New Jersey president John Witherspoon. Recently, television personality Glenn Beck has devoted his Friday afternoon shows to the religious beliefs of the founders.

We live in a sound-bite culture that makes it difficult to have any sustained dialogue on these historical issues. It is easy for those who argue that America is a Christian nation (and those who do not) to appear on radio or television programs, quote from one of the founders or one of the nation's founding documents, and sway people to their positions. These kinds of arguments, which can often be contentious, do nothing to help us unravel a very complicated historical puzzle about the relationship between Christianity and America's founding.

It is not just the secularists and Christians who disagree. Evangelicals have legitimate differences over these issues as well. In 2005, when *Time* announced the twenty-five most influential evangelicals in America, the list included both David Barton and Mark A. Noll.[5] Barton, the founder of an organization called "Wallbuilders," is, as we will see in chapter 4, one of the country's foremost proponents of the theory that America is a Christian nation. Noll, a scholar of American religious history at the University of Notre Dame (and a longtime member of the faculty at evangelical Wheaton College), has spent a good portion of his career attempting to debunk, both directly and indirectly, the notion that America is a Christian nation. Barton has suggested that Noll, and scholars like him, rely too much on the work of other historians and not enough on primary documents. Noll has offered careful and nuanced arguments to refute the Christian America defenders, but as a scholar his works lack the immense popularity among ordinary evangelicals that Barton enjoys.

All of this, of course, still leaves us with the question at hand: Was America founded as a Christian nation? I have written this book for the historically minded and thoughtful reader who is looking for help in sorting it all out. I have tried to avoid polemics as much as possible, although I am sure that my treatment of these controversial issues will not please everyone. This book should be viewed as a historical primer for students, churchgoers, and anyone who wants to make sense of the American past and its relationship to Christianity. I hope it might be read and discussed in schools and congregations where people are serious about considering how the history of the American founding era might help them to become more informed citizens in the present.

Defining Our Terms

Was America founded as a Christian nation? The answer to this question depends on how we define our terms. What do we mean when we use terms such as "Christian," "founding," and "nation"? A close examination of these words and their relationship to one another in the context of early American history suggests that the very question, "Was America *founded* as a *Christian nation*?" or even its more contemporary rephrasing, "Is America a Christian nation?" does not do justice to the complexity of the past. When we think about the many ways in which the words in this sentence can be defined, we come to the conclusion that the question itself is not very helpful. This book attempts to make sense of a difficult and complex issue.

Was America founded as a *Christian* nation? How should we define the label "Christian" as it relates to the time of the American founding? We can define "Christian" as a body of doctrine—a collection of theological truths that the church through the ages has described as Christian "orthodoxy." Such an approach would require us to examine either the nation's founding documents or the religious beliefs of the founders to see if those beliefs measure up to the standards of Christian orthodoxy as found in ancient formulations of faith such as the Apostles' Creed or the Nicene Creed. We could, for example, ask whether a particular signer of the Declaration of Independence or member of the Constitutional Convention believed in God, the Trinity, the deity of Christ, the resurrection of Jesus Christ, or the second coming of Jesus Christ. We might examine the earliest forms of national and state government to see if conformity to standards of Christian orthodoxy were required to vote or hold political office. Or perhaps we could explore the intellectual roots of the values for which the Revolution was fought to see if these values—liberty, freedom, natural rights—were grounded in Christian beliefs.

Another way of defining the meaning of the word "Christian" is through orthopraxy. In other words, did the behavior, practice, and decisions of the founders and the governments that they established conform to the spiritual and moral teachings of Christianity as taught in the Bible? Are the actions of the founders consistent with the teachings of Jesus? Do they reflect biblical standards of Christian justice and compassion? Do they institute policies that respect outsiders and neighbors as human beings created in God's image and thus worthy of dignity and honor? Such an approach would require a close examination of specific policies and decisions made at the time of the American founding. For example, we might ask whether a nation that condones the institution of slavery can be honestly called "Christian."

We may also want to examine the Christian character of the people who make up the nation. Though I am skeptical of the idea that any society on this side of eternity can be truly called Christian, it does seem that a society can reflect, in a limited sense, Christian principles if the vast majority of its members are doing their best, through the power of God's grace and the work of the Holy Spirit, to live authentic Christian lives. Such an approach takes the focus away from the founders and the founding documents and places it squarely upon the religious behavior and practice of ordinary early Americans. Those who argue this way might examine church membership, church attendance, or the number of communicants in a particular congregation or denomination. Such popular piety is often difficult to quantify, but there do exist some signposts that can give us a general sense of the spiritual commitments of people living during this period. For example, church membership was a sign of personal commitment to the religious life of a Christian congregation. Similarly, becoming a communicant (partaking of the sacrament of the Lord's Supper) demonstrated devotion to the Christian gospel. By partaking of the bread and the wine, communicants celebrated the death of Jesus Christ for the sins of the world.

This book also sets out to complicate terms such as "nation" and "founded." At what point did the United States of America become a nation? Was it in 1776, when the Continental Congress declared its independence from England? Was it 1789, when the United States Constitution became the official frame of American government? Or was it sometime later? How we define "nation" will have a profound influence on whether we can truly say the United States was "Christian." And at what point was the United States of America "founded"? Was it 1776 or 1787? Was it founded when the Pilgrims arrived on American shores aboard the *Mayflower* in 1620? Again, how we define our terms will affect how we answer the question posed in the title of this book.

One of my goals in writing *Was America Founded as a Christian Nation?* is to get Christians to see the danger of cherry-picking from the past as a means of promoting a political or cultural agenda in the present. I thus begin the book with a short essay on what it means to think historically. Here I lay the theoretical groundwork for much of what will follow and offer historical thinking as a way of preserving the integrity of the past in the midst of the culture wars over the meaning of the American founding.

Following this introductory chapter, I have divided the book into three major parts. Each one of these sections can stand alone, allowing the reader to pick up the book at any point. Part one provides a four-chapter history of the idea that the United States is a "Christian nation." A Christian understanding of American nationalism has been around since the first days of the Republic, but today's advocates of this idea might be surprised to learn the various ways in which a Christian America was defended between 1789 and the present. The last chapter of this section—chapter 4—delves into the contemporary writers and historians who have tried to make the case for a Christian America.

After tracing the idea of Christian nationhood through the course of American history, I turn in the rest of the book to the age of the American Revolution to see if the advocates of Christian America—both past and present—have been right in their belief that the founders set out to create a nation that was distinctively Christian. Part two asks whether the Revolution can be understood as a Christian event. It focuses on the relationship between Christianity and the coming of the American Revolution, the Continental Congress and the Declaration of Independence, and the Articles of Confederation and the Constitution. Part three deals with the specific religious beliefs of the founders. Which ones were Christians and which ones were not? What is the relationship, if any, between the beliefs of the founders and the construction of a Christian nation?

Over the past five years I have given several talks about Christianity and the American founding to all kinds of audiences—both secular and Christian. What I have found is that most ordinary people come to a talk on this topic with their minds already made up. They expect me, the speaker, to confirm what they already hold to be true. Whether you believe that America was founded as a Christian nation or not, I hope that you will come to this book with an open mind. I tell my students that education always requires risk and wisdom. Risk demands willingness, to use the words of historian Mark Schwehn, to "surrender ourselves for the sake of a better opinion," while wisdom "is the discernment of when it is reasonable to do so."[6] My hope and prayer is that those who read this book might be truly educated in the process.

Acknowledgments

My students inspired me to write this book. I assigned drafts of some of the initial chapters in my spring 2009 "Religion and the American Founding" seminar at Messiah College. I want to thank Amanda Delessio, Tommy DeShong, Dillon Keeks, Melinda Maslin, Kacie Morrell, Renae Paulson, Ali Steed, Courtney Weller, Matt Wicks, Thomas Williams, and Marty Zimmerman for their insights during that semester. I have been blessed to have a wonderful team of student research assistants. Katherine Garland proofread every chapter, conducted research, helped with copy-editing, and prepared the "Suggested Reading" sections. Cali McCullough has been a trusted research assistant for several years and her fingerprints are all over this book. In addition to proofreading and editing, she conducted much of the early research. Valerie Weaver, my 2010 Messiah College Smith Intern, helped me bring the book to completion by tracking down sources and checking notes. Jonathan Den Hartog, Jonathan Rowe, and Ray Soller read parts of the manuscript and offered suggestions for improvement. Mary V. Thompson, Ira Stoll, Thomas Fleming, and especially Daniel Walker Howe provided comments on the manuscript that improved my arguments.

I also owe a debt of gratitude to the Louisville Institute for providing me with a summer stipend to complete the writing of the manuscript. Thanks to James Lewis and his staff for supporting my work in this regard. The scholars and pastors present at the Institute's Winter Meeting provided a much-needed critique of my ideas. Messiah College continues to be a great place to be a scholar and teacher. I am thankful to Kim Phipps and Randy Basinger for helping me find time to write. Jana Riess, my editor at Westminster John Knox Press, has been a pleasure to work with. A fine scholar of American religion in her own right, Jana's patience, encouragement, and keen eye for detail made this a much better book. I hope we get to work together again.

Allyson, Caroline, and Joy Fea are always a source of inspiration for me. They also remained wonderfully curious about how this book was progressing. Joy remains a source of strength and stability in my life that I could not live without. I have dedicated this book to my parents, John and Joan Fea. They have never failed to support me in life and I know that they have eagerly awaited the arrival of this book so they can debate with their friends whether America was founded as a Christian nation.

Introduction

How to Think Historically

At the heart of the debate over whether the United States was founded as a Christian nation is the relationship between history and American life. It is thus important to think about the nature of history and identify the difference between good history and bad history. What is the purpose of studying history? What do historians do? Does everyone who conducts a serious study of the past qualify as a historian? "In my opinion," writes Pulitzer Prize–winning historian Gordon Wood, "not everyone who writes about the past is a historian. Sociologists, anthropologists, political scientists, and economists frequently work in the past without really thinking historically."[1] What does Wood mean? Is there a difference between "the past" and "history," two terms that we often assume are synonymous?

The Search for a Usable Past

Sadly, most people have no use for the past. The United States has always been a nation that has looked forward rather than backward. As the first major nation-state born during the Enlightenment, America has attached itself to the train of progress. In some respects U.S. history is the story of the relentless efforts of ordinary Americans to break away from the tyranny of the past. Walt Whitman summed it up best in his tribute to American pioneers:

> All the past we leave behind;
> We debouch upon a newer, mightier world, varied world,
> Fresh and strong the world we seize, world of labor and the march,
> Pioneers! O pioneers![2]

I regularly encounter college students who wonder why they are required to take a history course when it will probably have no direct bearing on their postgraduation job prospects. And, in most cases, they are right. I have yet to meet a graduate who landed a job because a potential employer was impressed with a grade in "History 101." For many the past is foreign and irrelevant. We all remember the high school history teacher—perhaps we called him "coach"—who stood before the class and recited, in the words of historian Arnold Toynbee, "one damned thing after another."

Of course not everyone thinks this way about the past. One will always find history books near or at the top of the *New York Times* bestseller list (think David McCullough or Doris Kearns Goodwin). If we ask the average history buff why we should study history, she will probably talk about its relevance to life today. This should not surprise us. It is our natural instinct to find something useful in the past. We are creatures of the "here and now." The kind of relevance we look for in the past can take several forms, but let me suggest three. First, the past can inspire us. Second, the familiarity of the past helps us to see our common humanity with others who have lived before us. Third, the past gives us a better understanding of our civic identity.

The past can inspire. Christians have made good use of this benefit of studying history. Our lives are enriched by learning about great leaders of the Christian faith—Francis of Assisi, Joan of Arc, Martin Luther, Dietrich Bonhoeffer, William Wilberforce, Dorothy Day, Martin Luther King Jr., Mother Teresa, and Billy Graham. If by learning the stories of great religious leaders we gain insight into how to live faithfully, we can also become inspired by the examples of early Americans who fought for freedom, liberty, and independence in 1776. These men, the so-called founders, put their lives on the line in order to stage one of the greatest revolutions in the history of the world. Whether it was George Washington sneaking across the East River in the fog on an August 1776 evening, or the Continental Army enduring hard winters in Morristown and Valley Forge, or Patrick Henry proclaiming "Give me liberty or give me death!"—something about their heroics makes us proud and gives us an emotional connection to the past. It is easy to be moved by the fact that the men who founded the United States often used religious language and saw their revolution as a sacred cause. Indeed, the past inspires.

When we think about the way the past might be relevant for our lives, familiarity is also important. We tend to search the past for people like us. We want to learn about those in the past who felt the way we do, who endured the same trials and tribulations, and who experienced the same joys and triumphs. Though societies change over time, there is much about the human experience that does not.

I recently completed a biography of Philip Vickers Fithian, a farmer from New Jersey who lived during the age of the American Revolution.[3] Fithian was not one of the founders, nor did he achieve any degree of fame in his lifetime. But it was his obscurity that first attracted me to him. My goal in writing that book was to explore the American Revolution through the eyes of an ordinary person who lived during the period. I spent several years reading and interpreting Philip's diaries in an attempt to reconstruct the eighteenth-century world in which he lived. At the same time I believed that Philip's story would resonate with twenty-first-century readers. I hoped that my readers might relate to Philip's struggles between personal ambition and homesick longings, his desire to improve his life and remain true to what he believed was a call from God, his quest to educate himself for the purpose of overcoming his passions, his willingness to sacrifice his life for his country, and his love affair with the woman he would marry. I wanted my readers to see something familiar in the past and to realize that they were not the first people to experience such things.

The past can also help us understand our place in the communities and nation we call home. As soon as the United States was founded, historians began writing about the meaning of the American Revolution in an attempt to remind us of the values and ideals for which it was waged.[4] History is a tool for strengthening the nation. It reminds us of where we came from and helps us chart where we are going. American history has always been a way of teaching children lessons in patriotism.[5] History helps produce good citizens. We need the stories of our past to sustain us as a people. In America we study it to understand the values and beliefs that we as a people are willing to fight for and die for. We wish that our children and their children would learn the stories of the past and in the process embrace the beliefs that have defined the American experiment since its birth over two hundred years ago. This is why historical debates, such as the one currently being waged over whether the United States of America is a Christian nation, are so intense. The identity of the country is at stake.

What Do Historians Do? The Five Cs

While many of us look to the past for inspiration, continuity with the present, and a sense of civic identity, historians do not approach the past with the *primary* goal of finding something relevant. Those who pursue the past for the purpose of inspiration, familiarity, and civic identity *alone* are not really practicing history at all. Historians know that there exists a constant tension between the familiarity of the past and the strangeness of the past. They must always operate with this tension in mind. Historians Thomas Andrews and Flannery Burke have boiled down the task of historical interpretation into what they call the "5 Cs of Historical Thinking."[6]

Historians must see *change over time*. While some things stay the same over the course of generations, many things change. The historian's task is to chronicle these changes. As historian John Tosh puts it, "There may be a gulf between 'us' and 'them,' but that gulf is actually composed of processes of growth, decay and change which it is the business of the historian to uncover."[7]

Historians must interpret the past in *context*. They examine the documents of the past in light of the time and the place in which they were written. Words ripped from their cultural and chronological context provide useful material for the compilers of quotation books, but they are useless to the historian. The words of the founders, for example, must always be interpreted from the perspective of the eighteenth-century world in which they were uttered or written. There is a wide chasm that separates the past from the present. Context helps us to realize that more often than not people in the past do not think and behave the same way that we do.

Historians are always interested in *causality*. I remember a few years ago when the talk radio host Rush Limbaugh announced that "history is real simple. You know what history is? It's what happened. Now if you want to get into why what happened, that's probably valid too, but why what happened shouldn't have much of anything to do with what happened."[8] Limbaugh could not have been more wrong about what historians do. They are not only interested in facts, but always ask why a particular event in the past happened the way it did.

Historians are concerned with *contingency*. This is the notion that "every historical outcome depends upon a number of prior conditions."[9] Contingency celebrates the ability of humans to shape their own destiny. Every historical moment is contingent upon another historical moment, which in turn is contingent upon yet another moment. Historians are thus concerned about the big picture—how events are influenced by other events.

Finally, historians realize that the past is *complex*. It often resists our efforts to simplify it or to cut it up into easily digestible pieces. Most students of history are exposed to the past through textbooks that offer rather straightforward narratives of how a particular era unfolded. While often necessary for overviews and syntheses of the past, textbooks often fail to reveal that the past can be messy, complicated, and not easily summarized in a neatly constructed paragraph or two. Once again, the debate over whether America is a Christian nation is instructive here. On one hand, the opponents of Christian America draw the conclusion that just because the Constitution does not mention God then it must hold true that the framers did not believe that religion was important to the success of the Republic. On the other hand, defenders of Christian America conclude that if the founders were people of Christian faith, then they must have set out to establish a uniquely Christian nation. Logicians call these assertions "non sequiturs." Historians would argue that those who draw such conclusions lack an appreciation for the complexity of the past.

The task of historians is to use these five Cs to reconstruct the past and make their findings available to the public. Historians make the dead live. They bring the past to an audience in the present. If we think about the vocation of the historian in this way, then we must distinguish between "history" and "the past." The past is the past—a record of events that occurred in bygone eras. But history is a discipline—the art of reconstructing the past.

Most human beings tend to be present-minded when it comes to confronting the past. The discipline of history was never meant to function as a means of getting one's political point across or convincing people to join a cause. Yet Americans use the past for these purposes all the time. Such an approach to the past can easily degenerate into a form of propaganda or, as the historian Bernard Bailyn described it, "indoctrination by historical example."[10]

This sort of present-mindedness is very common among those Christian writers and preachers who defend the idea that America was founded as a Christian nation. They enter the past with the preconceived purpose of trying to find the religious roots of the United States. If they are indeed able to gather evidence suggesting that the founders were Christians or believed that the promotion of religion was important to the success of the Republic, then they have gotten all that they need from the past. It has served them adequately as a tool for promoting a particular twenty-first-century political agenda. It has provided ammunition to win the cultural war in which they are engaged. Gordon Wood has said that if someone wants to use the study of the past to change the world he should forgo a career as a historian and run for office![11]

Such an approach to the past is more suitable for a lawyer than for a historian. In fact, David Barton, one of the leading proponents of "Christian America," counters his opponents by suggesting that his research is done in accordance with the practices of the legal profession. Barton "lets the Founders speak for themselves in accordance with the legal rules of evidence."[12] The difference between how a lawyer uses the past and how a historian interprets the past is huge. The lawyer cares about the past only to the degree that he or she can use a legal decision in the past to win a case in the present. A lawyer does not reconstruct the past in all its complexity, but rather cherry-picks from the past in order to obtain a positive result for his or her client. Context, change over time, causality, contingency, and complexity are not as important as letting the "Founders speak for themselves," even if such speaking violates every rule of historical inquiry. The historian, however, does not encounter the past in this way.

It is the very strangeness of the past that has the best potential to change our lives in positive ways. Those who are willing to acknowledge that the past is a foreign country—a place where they do things differently than we do in the present—set off on a journey of personal transformation. "It is this past," writes historian Sam Wineburg, "one that initially leaves us befuddled, or worse, just plain bored, that we need most if we are to achieve the understanding that each of us is more than the handful of labels ascribed to us at birth."[13]

An encounter with the past in all of its fullness, void as much as possible of present-minded agendas, can cultivate virtue in our lives. Such an encounter teaches us empathy, humility, selflessness, and hospitality. By studying history we learn to listen to voices that differ from our own. We lay aside our moral condemnation about a person, idea, or event from the past in order to understand it. This is the essence of intellectual hospitality. By taking the time to listen to people from a "foreign country," we rid ourselves of the selfish quest to make the past serve our needs. The study of the past reminds us that we are not autonomous individuals, but part of a human story that is larger than ourselves. Wineburg sums it up well:

> For the narcissist sees the world—both the past and the present—in his own image. Mature historical understanding teaches us to do the opposite: to go beyond our own image, to go beyond our brief life, and to go beyond the fleeting moment in human history into which we have been born. History educates ("leads outward" in the Latin) in the deepest sense. Of the subjects in the secular curriculum, it

is the best at teaching those virtues once reserved for theology—humility in the face of our limited ability to know, and awe in the face of the expanse of human history.[14]

Are we willing to allow history to "educate" us—to lead us outward? We need to practice history not because it can win us political points or help us push our social and cultural agendas forward, but because it has the amazing potential to transform our lives.

Part One

The United States Is a Christian Nation

The History of an Idea

Chapter One

Evangelical America, 1789–1865

As the Government of the United States of America is not, in any sense, founded on the Christian religion; as it has in itself no character of enmity against the laws, religion, or tranquility, of Mussulmen; and as the said States never entered into any war or act of hostility against any Mahometan nation, it is declared by the parties that no pretext arising from religious opinions shall ever produce an interruption of the harmony existing between the two countries.

So begins Article 11 of the Treaty of Tripoli, a 1797 agreement between the United States and Tripoli, a Muslim nation located on the Barbary Coast of northern Africa. The treaty was necessary because Barbary pirates, under the sanction of Tripoli, were capturing American ships and selling crew members into slavery. The Muslim states of the Barbary Coast (Tripoli, Algiers, Morocco, and Tunis) had long used piracy to control Mediterranean trade routes. Any nation that wanted to trade freely in the region was forced to negotiate a peace treaty with the Barbary States, which usually included some kind of monetary tribute. During the colonial era, American vessels were protected from the Barbary pirates by British warships, but after the Revolution the United States would need to work out its own treaty with these countries. The Treaty of Tripoli, which included the assertion that the United States was not founded on the Christian religion, was signed by President John Adams and ratified unanimously by the Senate. The text of the treaty was published in several newspapers, and there was no public opposition to it.

The American negotiators of this treaty did not want the religious differences between the United States and Tripoli to hinder attempts at reaching a trade agreement. Claiming that the United States was not "founded on the Christian religion" probably made negotiations proceed more smoothly. But today this brief religious reference in a rather obscure treaty in the history of American diplomacy has played a prominent role

3

in the debate over whether the United States was founded as a Christian nation. It has become one of the most deadly arrows in the quiver of those who oppose the idea that the country was founded on Christian principles.[1]

If the Treaty of Tripoli is correct, and the United States was not "founded on the Christian religion," then someone forgot to tell the American people. Most Americans who followed events in the Mediterranean viewed the struggle between the United States and the Barbary nations—a struggle that would last well into the nineteenth century—as a kind of holy war. Americans published poems and books describing Muslims as "children of Ishmael" who posed a threat to Christian civilization. Captivity narratives describing Christians who were forced to convert to Islam only heightened these popular beliefs.[2] In fact, the sentiment expressed in the Treaty of Tripoli—that the United States was not "founded on the Christian religion"—can hardly be reconciled with the way that politicians, historians, clergy, educators, and other writers perceived the United States in the first one hundred years of its existence. The idea that the United States was a "Christian nation" was central to American identity in the years between the Revolution and the Civil War.

Nineteenth-century Americans who believed that the United States was a Christian nation made their case in at least three different ways. First, they appealed to divine providence. The United States had a special place in God's plan for the world. The success of the American Revolution confirmed it. Second, they argued that the founders were Christians and thus set out to create a nation that reflected their personal beliefs. Third, they made the case that the U.S. government and the documents upon which it was founded were rooted in Christian ideas. Today's Christian nationalists have a good portion of American history on their side.

Christian Nationalism in the Early American Republic

If the United States was ever a "Christian nation," it was so during the period between the ratification of the Constitution (1789) and the start of the Civil War (1861). While the Constitution made clear that there would be no official or established religion in America, and the states were gradually removing religious requirements for officeholders, Christianity, and particularly Protestant evangelicalism, defined the culture.

When ministers, politicians, and writers during these years described the United States as a "Christian nation," they were usually referring to the beliefs and character of the majority of its citizens. The United States was populated by Christians. This meant that it was not a "Muslim nation" or a "Buddhist nation" or a "Hindu nation." Indeed, the people of most Western European nations in the nineteenth century would have used the phrase "Christian nation" to describe the countries to which they belonged. But in America the phrase "Christian nation" could also carry a deeper meaning. It was often used as a way of describing the uniqueness of the American experiment. It was freighted with the idea that the United States had a special role to play in the plan of God, thus making it a special or privileged Christian nation. Moreover, when nineteenth-century Americans talked about living in a "Christian nation" they rarely used the term in a polemical way. In other words, they were not trying to defend the label against those who did not believe the United States was a Christian nation. Instead, they used the phrase as if it were a well-known, generally accepted fact.[3]

One of the main reasons that people could describe the United States as a Christian nation during this period was because the country was experiencing a massive revival of Protestant evangelicalism.[4] Known as the Second Great Awakening, this religious revival stressed salvation through faith in the atoning work of Jesus Christ and was quite compatible with the democratic spirit of the early nineteenth century. Humans were no longer perceived as waiting passively for a sovereign and distant God who, on his own terms and in his own timing, offered select individuals the gift of eternal life. Instead, ordinary American citizens took an active role in their own salvation. Theology moved away from a Calvinism that stressed humankind's inability to save itself and toward a free-will or democratic theology, preached most powerfully and popularly by revivalist Charles Finney. The new theology empowered individuals to decide their own religious fate by accepting or rejecting the gospel message.[5]

This revival of religion owed a lot to the First Amendment (1791). By forbidding Congress from making laws "respecting an establishment of religion, or prohibiting the free exercise thereof," religion became voluntary. If churches could no longer rely on state support, they would need to craft their message in such a way that would attract people to their pews. Long-established denominations such as Episcopalians, Presbyterians, and Congregationalists gave way to more democratic, enthusiastic, and evangelical groups such as Baptists and Methodists. New sects such as the Mormons and the Disciples of Christ emerged with force. Religious services continued to be conducted in churches, but they were also being held in camp meetings like the one in Cane Ridge, Kentucky, in 1801. Writing in 1855, church historian Philip Schaff quoted an Austrian writer who observed, "The United States are by far the most religious and Christian country in the world . . . because religion is there most free."[6] When Thomas Jefferson claimed smugly in 1822 that Unitarianism would soon be "the religion of the majority from north and south," he could not have been more wrong.[7] Apparently Jefferson did not leave Monticello very much during the final years of his life, for America was fast becoming the most evangelical Christian country on the face of the earth.

The Election of 1800

Christianity merged with politics on many fronts during the early nineteenth century. This was especially the case in the presidential election of 1800. The incumbent president, John Adams, represented the Federalists, a political faction with particular strength in New England. Federalist strongholds such as Connecticut and Massachusetts had a long tradition of government-sponsored religion. The Federalists in New England worked closely with the Congregationalist clergy in order to ensure that the region would remain Christian in character and be governed by Christian political leaders.[8] Ironically, John Adams was a Unitarian. As we will see in chapter 12, he rejected many essential Christian doctrines. But he was also a son of New England—a descendant of Puritans who understood that religion was needed to sustain a virtuous society.

Adams's opponent was Thomas Jefferson, the vice president of the United States. Adams had defeated Jefferson in the presidential election of 1796, but the margin of victory was slim. As the population of the United States began to spread out beyond the Appalachian Mountains, and the religious sentiments of the country turned against state-sponsored churches, Jefferson would attract more and more Americans. His commitment to ordinary farmers and his strong defense of religious liberty meant that Baptists and Methodists—the catalysts of the Second Great Awakening, which was just getting underway—rallied to his cause. But Jefferson's religious beliefs, or lack thereof, would present a problem for him in the Federalist-dominated northeast. As we will see in chapter 13, Jefferson was not a Christian. He was skeptical about doctrines such as the Trinity, the resurrection of Jesus Christ, and the divine inspiration of the Bible. He was not the kind of godly president that many New England Federalists thought should be leading a Christian nation.

The attacks on Jefferson's supposed godlessness were fierce. William Linn, a Dutch Reformed minister from New York, wrote that he was forced to oppose Jefferson's candidacy because of the Virginian's "disbelief of the Holy Scriptures . . . his rejection of the Christian Religion and open profession of Deism." He feared that the United States, under Jefferson's rule, would become a "nation of Atheists." Linn made clear that "no professed deists, be his talents and acquirements what they may, ought to be promoted to this place [the presidency] by the suffrages of a Christian nation." He went as far as to argue that the act of "calling a deist to the first office must be construed into no less than rebellion against God." Linn was fully aware that there was "nothing in the constitution to restrict our choice" of a president with religious beliefs akin to Jefferson's, but he warned his readers that if they elected "a manifest enemy to the religion of Christ, in a Christian nation," it would be "an awful symptom of the degeneracy of that nation."[9]

Whig Christian Nationalism

The Federalist attack on Jefferson's beliefs was unsuccessful. Jefferson won the election and became the third president of the United States. The Federalists would fade from the national stage, but their demise did not mean that Christian nationalism would disappear from American politics. Much of the Christian political vision of the Federalists would resurface in the 1830s and 1840s in the voices of the politicians and clergy who would make up the constituency of the Whig Party.

Most Whigs were ardent nationalists. They favored a nation of markets and Protestant religion. Whigs championed infrastructure improvements—roads, canals, and bridges—to connect small and isolated communities to a national economic system shaped by capitalism. Many of the nation's great revivalists, such as Charles Finney and Lyman Beecher, were Whig supporters. These reformers established voluntary societies to promote the Christianization of America. Unlike their Democratic opponents, who favored individual liberty on moral issues, the Whigs dreamed of a homogenous Protestant culture where slavery did not exist, alcohol use was under control, and Sunday was kept as a day of Sabbath rest. In 1851 historian Robert Baird wrote that laws requiring the observance of the Christian Sabbath were based on the "avowed principle that we are a Christian nation."[10] The Whigs merged their economic and moral commitments. Roads, bridges, and canals could provide ordinary farmers with easier access to markets and liberate them from their isolated locales. In the process they would begin to see themselves as citizens of a nation rather than of a particular community, county, or state. There was something providential, the Whigs believed, about these kinds of national infrastructure improvements. God was using them to fashion a nation. Some even believed that American economic and moral progress would usher in the second coming of Christ.[11]

Lyman Beecher provides a good example of the way that Whig political principles and evangelical Christianity came together in this era. In 1832 Beecher, a well-known New England Congregationalist minister, became the first president of Lane Theological Seminary in Cincinnati. Shortly after he was appointed to his new post he embarked on a tour of eastern cities to raise funds for the seminary. As he traveled from town to town, Beecher delivered a speech that he called "A Plea for the West." Beecher was an evangelical minister, but his speech was not designed to recruit missionaries to evangelize the vast American territory between the Allegheny and Rocky mountains. Instead, he believed that it was necessary to civilize this region through the establishment of seminaries of learning—like Lane Seminary—that would train an educated clergy committed to spreading Protestant culture. If such a plan were to be carried out, then American Protestants would need to act quickly. The West, Beecher feared, would soon be populated by Roman Catholic immigrants who had a stronger allegiance to their church than to the nation. Slavery was also on the move westward. Beecher feared that the region would be overrun by slaveholders unless something was done soon. "A Plea for the West" was Beecher's call to extend the Whig and evangelical idea of a Christian nation to the unsettled regions of the country. As Beecher concluded, "perseverance can accomplish any thing, and wherever the urgency of the necessity shall put in requisition the benevolent energy of this Christian nation—the work under the auspices of heaven will be done." Beecher was a nationalist in the sense that he wanted to integrate the unruly West into the United States. He was a *Christian* nationalist in the sense that his vision of the country was a distinctly Protestant one. He was the perfect Whig.[12]

A Christian Nation in Print

The early nineteenth century also saw a revolution in print—newspapers, magazines, books—that would be used to advance the idea that the United States was a Christian nation.[13] Some of the nation's first American historians began to write and publish during this period. Though they seldom described the United States as a "Christian nation," they did not shy away from trying to discern the hand of God in American history. Many of these historians believed that God had intervened on behalf of the United States during the American Revolution. David Ramsay, the author of *History of the American Revolution* (1789), described the events of the Revolutionary War through the grid of divine providence. Mercy Otis Warren, in *History of the Rise, Progress and Termination of the American Revolution* (1805), was also overtly providential in her approach. She thought that the overthrow of English dominion by a band of colonial soldiers, and the creation of a government based on freedom, was so momentous that it could only be attributed to a "superintending Providence" or the "finger of divine Providence."[14] Warren believed that the *"religious and moral character of Americans yet stands* on a higher grade of excellence and purity, then that of most of other nations."[15] She called the American people to live up to the gift of independence that God had given them.

As the nineteenth century rolled on, more histories of the United States were written, perhaps none more magisterial than George Bancroft's multivolume *History of the United States: From the Discovery of the American Continent* (1834–1874). Bancroft was the first historian from the United States to be trained in Germany, the hub of professional historical scholarship in the West. His *History* was an attempt to write American history using footnotes and primary sources. Bancroft was a devout Unitarian Christian who believed in the role of God's providence in shaping the American past. He thought that America was a Christian nation established and sustained by God for the purpose of spreading liberty and democracy to the world.[16]

God's providence in American history was also a dominant theme in school textbooks. Historian Jonathan Boyd's close study of nine of the early nineteenth century's most popular American history schoolbooks confirms that authors used providential language to teach students how to be good citizens of a Christian nation.[17] In this sense, they look very different from the kinds of American history textbooks that schoolchildren read today. Charles Goodrich's *History of the United States* started with a brief lesson on history: "History displays the dealings of God with mankind. . . . It cultivates a sense of dependence on him; strengthens our confidence in his benevolence; and impresses us with a conviction of his justice."[18]

Other schoolbooks chronicled the way that God orchestrated events in history, including the founding of the British colonies, the American Revolution, the 1793 yellow fever epidemic in Philadelphia, and the American invasion of Fort Detroit.[19] Emma Willard's *History of the United States* (1826) describes the "wonderful coincidence of events" that led to the death of Native Americans:

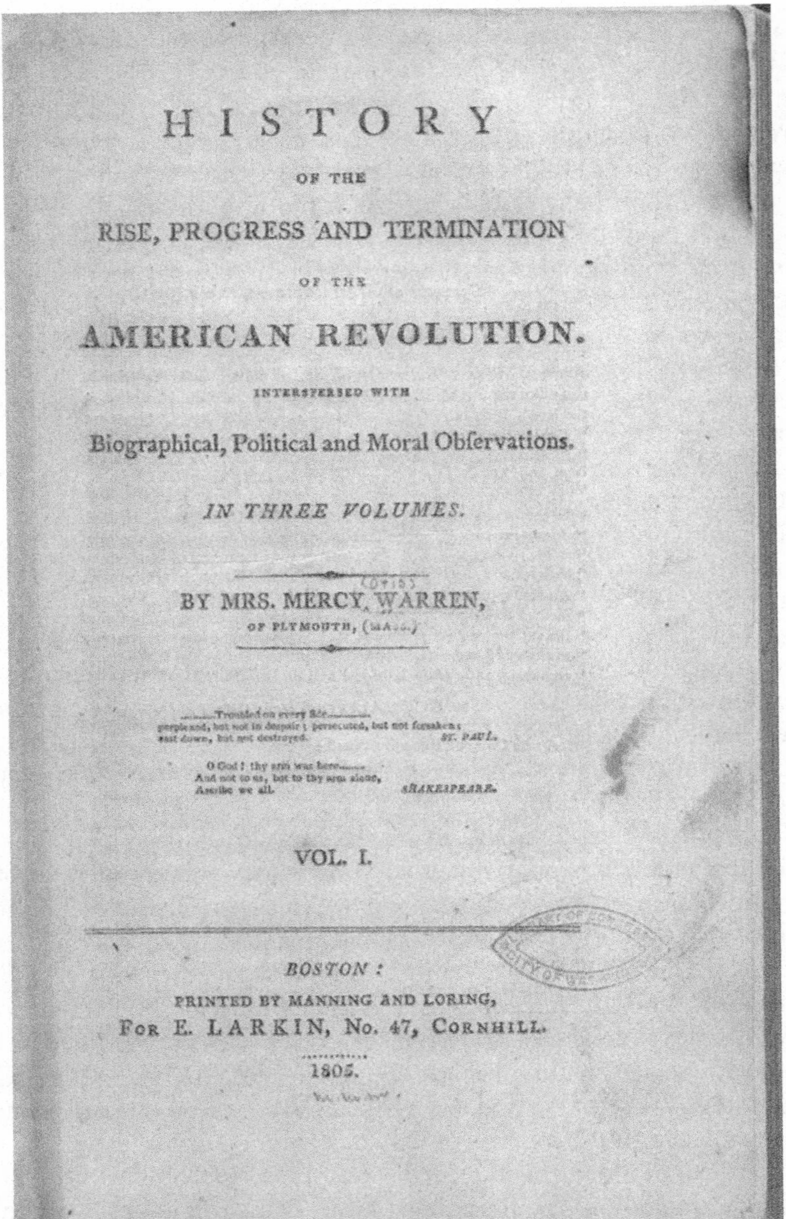

HISTORY

OF THE

RISE, PROGRESS AND TERMINATION

OF THE

AMERICAN REVOLUTION.

INTERSPERSED WITH

Biographical, Political and Moral Obſervations.

IN THREE VOLUMES.

BY MRS. MERCY WARREN,
OF PLYMOUTH, (MASS.)

———Troubled on every ſide———
perplexed, but not in deſpair ; perſecuted, but not forſaken ;
caſt down, but not deſtroyed.   *ST. PAUL.*

O God ! thy arm was here———
And not to us, but to thy arm alone,
Aſcribe we all.   *SHAKESPEARE.*

VOL. I.

BOSTON :
PRINTED BY MANNING AND LORING,
For E. LARKIN, No. 47, CORNHILL.

1805.

Fig. 1.1   Cover page of Mercy Otis Warren's *History of the Rise, Progress and Termination of the American Revolution* (1805).

Had they remained in their full strength, it is evident, that with the small means which the first European emigrants possessed, they could not have effected a settlement. In this the undevout will perceive nothing but a happy fortuity; but the pious heart will delight to recognise and acknowledge a superintending Providence, whose time for exchanging, upon these shores, a savage for a civilized people, had now fully come.[20]

Noah Webster's *History of the United States* (1832) begins with a chapter called "Origins of the Human Race" that provides an exposition of the Genesis creation story. The book ends with an appendix titled "Advice to the Young." A modern observer might wonder why a history textbook would include a chapter exhorting readers to obey their parents, read the Bible, avoid sin, love their neighbors, and disdain luxury, but in the early nineteenth century the story of the American past was used as a source for the religious and moral improvement of young people. This blend of history and morality was considered a foundational part of any good education.[21]

Some writers used the press to refashion some of the founders into evangelical Christians. If America was a Christian nation, then it needed to be "fathered" by Christian statesmen. No one did this kind of refashioning better than Mason Locke Weems, an Anglican minister and traveling book salesman. Weems's biography of George Washington, *Life of Washington*, ran through forty editions between 1799 and 1825. The tales Weems told about Washington, including the story of him cutting down his father's cherry tree, were published over and over again. His stories were included in more than twenty-five nineteenth-century schoolbooks, including the famous *McGuffey's Eclectic Readers*.[22]

While Weems is well known for inventing the story of the cherry tree, it is another story he tells about Washington that is most revealing. This is the account of Washington's father spelling young George's name with cabbage seeds. Augustine Washington secretly planted cabbage seeds in the family garden and patterned them after the letters in his son's name. After the cabbage had grown tall enough for George to see his name spelled out on the ground, his father used the experiment as a means of introducing George to his "true Father." George realized that it was not mere chance that caused these seeds to grow in such a way. The seeds had to be set in place by someone. Weems brought the lesson home through the words of Augustine Washington: "Well, then, and as my son could not believe that *chance* had made and put together so exactly the *letters* of his name . . . then how can he believe that *chance* could have made and put together all those millions and millions of things that are now so exactly fitted to his good?"[23]

But Weems did not stop there. The spiritual lesson of the cabbage patch made George Washington into the kind of evangelical statesman who was needed to build a Christian republic in America. This was Washington's conversion experience. After describing the completion of Augustine's lesson, Weems writes: "At this, George fell into a profound silence, while his pensive looks showed that his youthful soul was labouring with some idea never felt before. Perhaps it was at that moment, that the good Spirit of God ingrafted on his heart that germ of piety, which filled him after life with so many precious fruits of morality."[24] The Spirit had descended on young George. He would now be ready to stake his rightful claim as the Christian savior of the United States.

Christian Nationalism in the Civil War North

Well over a century later Abraham Lincoln would also have a chance to be the savior of the United States. Lincoln understood the meaning of the Civil War better than anyone in America. It was a war over slavery. It was a war over how the U.S. Constitution should be properly interpreted in regard to the rights of individual states. But it was also a religious war—a "theological crisis," as historian Mark Noll has described it.[25] In his second inaugural address, he made it clear: "Both [sides] read the same Bible, and pray to the same God; and each invokes His aid against the other."[26] Both the Union and the Confederacy thought that their societies were blessed by God and supported by his providence. They both claimed to be Christian nations.

Northern politicians and clergy argued against Southern secession by appealing to national unity. The United States was one nation, created by God and thus indivisible. As former Massachusetts Senator Rufus Choate put it in 1858, God "wills our national life." It was the responsibility of its citizens to work hard at keeping this "UNITED, LOVING AND CHRISTIAN AMERICA" together at all costs.[27] The idea that God favored a strong national union could be found in the sermons of many Christian ministers of the day. Both Horace Bushnell, one of the most prominent Christian leaders of the mid-nineteenth century, and Albert Barnes, pastor of Philadelphia's First Presbyterian Church, argued that Christians had a responsibility to obey the national government because it was established by God. "Civil government," Bushnell wrote, must

Fig. 1.2 Abraham Lincoln's second inaugural address (March 4, 1865) asked the nation to work together for reconciliation after the Civil War.

be "accepted as a kind of Providential creation." Barnes added, "Government is to be regarded as of Divine appointment, and as deriving its authority from God." Bushnell, a Protestant liberal, and Barnes, an evangelical Presbyterian, would have had many theological differences, but they could agree that good government was God's government.[28]

In their arguments on behalf of a Christian America, Northern clergy claimed to have the past on their side. Few appealed to history more forcefully than did John F. Bigelow, the pastor of the Baptist Church of Reesville, New York. In his sermon "The Hand of God in American History" (1861), Bigelow wrote that "God through Christ is in all history; and He is in it working out great *principles*." God planted "the seeds of this great nation" in the British colonies and kept America free from the "Roman hierarchy" of its French-Canadian neighbors. The American Revolution, Bigelow argued, was part of God's plan for the "highest interests of the human race for the Ages, and: the whole Kingdom of God on earth." He praised George Washington, a man whom "Divine

Providence had, for years, been giving . . . special training for his work."
Washington was a "second Moses" with a divine mission "to lead our
American tribes from the Egypt of Colonial bondage through the . . . Sea
and wilderness of the Revolutionary struggle, to the Canaan of liberty."[29]

If the Union was ordained by God, then Christians were required to
submit to it. Northern clergy invoked New Testament passages to counter the beliefs of Southern secessionists. Francis Vinton began his sermon
"The Christian Idea of Civil Government" by quoting Romans 13:1–8,
the Pauline passage urging the church in Rome to submit to the authority
of the empire. If the Union was established by God, then "Disloyalty to
the Constitution is, therefore, impiety toward God. . . . To destroy this
Union, therefore, is to commit a sin, which God will righteously punish
by evils which no prescience can forsee, and no wisdom can repair." Like
Vinton, Bushnell also used Romans 13 to take a direct shot at Southern
rebellion: "Let every soul be subject unto the higher powers; for there
is no power but of God." E. E. Adams, the pastor of the North Broad
Street Presbyterian Church in Philadelphia, reminded the South that
"God never overlooks rebellion against his throne—never pardons the
rebel until he repent and submit."[30]

Early in the war Northern clergy railed relentlessly on the sin of secession and defended the idea that the purpose of the war was to keep the
Christian Union intact. In 1861 Albert Barnes told his listeners that the
Civil War was not "a war for liberating by force the four millions of men
which are held in bondage at the South." Barnes believed that slavery was
an "evil," but the emancipation of the slaves was "*not* the object of the
war," nor should it in "any way become the object of the War to secure
this result by force of arms."[31] Yet, in the wake of Abraham Lincoln's
Emancipation Proclamation, the ministerial response to the war began to
change. Most historians agree that Lincoln's decision to issue this decree
gave the North a moral cause for which to fight that was more urgent
than the preservation of the Union. After 1863 more and more clergy
began to conceive the conflict as a war against the evil of slavery.[32]

It would be wrong to give the impression that Northern clergymen only
became interested in the emancipation of Southern slaves after 1863. The
early-nineteenth-century abolitionist movement had its roots in the Second Great Awakening. William Lloyd Garrison, one of the most radical of
the abolitionists, was an evangelical Christian who believed that America
could not truly call itself a Christian nation unless slavery was abolished.
He proposed that the North secede from the Union in order to remain
free from the sinful stain of slavery. Revivalist Charles Finney concurred

with Garrison about the need for separation: "To adopt the maxim, 'Our Union even with perpetual slavery,' is an abomination so execrable as not to be named by a just mind without indignation." Similarly, about a week before the bombing of Fort Sumter, New England clergyman Zachery Eddy told his congregation to separate from the South so that the North could "develop all those forces of a high, Christian civilization."[33]

But it was after the announcement of the Emancipation Proclamation that Northern clergy began to more fully embrace the belief that the Civil War was a war to end slavery. No one took up this cause more strongly than Henry Ward Beecher, the son of Lyman Beecher, the brother of Harriet Beecher Stowe, and the man whom historian Debby Applegate has recently called "The Most Famous Man in America."[34] But Beecher's tirade against slavery lacked any real theological sophistication. In the 1863 sermon "National Prejudice and Penalty," he concluded that slavery violated human rights, and since God was always on the side of human rights, then slavery must be a violation against God. Though one could certainly make an argument that slavery was sinful because it violated the dignity of human beings who were created in the image of God, Beecher did not argue this way. Instead, he concluded that "if God is just, and if he rewards or punishes nations in this world, it is not possible for a nation systematically to violate every natural right of four millions of people, and go unpunished."

Beecher was also a bit hesitant about making biblical arguments to support his opposition to slavery. He made clear that he would not go as far as some abolitionists (such as Garrison) who claimed "if the Bible does not condemn slavery, I will throw the Bible away." But this did not mean that his arguments against slavery were based on an explication of biblical principles. In the end, he appealed to the "voice of God" for his justification of slavery's sinfulness:

> There are plenty of men who believe in Genesis, and Chronicles, and the Psalms, and Isaiah, and Daniel, and Ezekiel, and Matthew, and the other Evangelists, and the rest of the New Testament, clear down to the Apocalypse; there are plenty of men who believe in the letter of Scripture; and there are plenty of men who believe everything God said four thousand years ago; but the Lord God Almighty is walking forth at this time in clouds and thunder such as never rocked Sinai. His voice is in all the land, and in all the earth, and those men that refuse to hear God in his own time, and in the language of the events that are taking place, are infidels.[35]

"Men who believe in the letter of Scripture" was a reference to Southern evangelicals who employed a literal interpretation of the Bible to defend their belief that slavery was sanctioned by God. As a Northern Protestant liberal, Beecher dismissed these Southern literalists and asked his hearers to end slavery regardless of what the Bible said. For Beecher, the United States was a Christian nation not because it followed the teaching of the Bible or church tradition, but because of the moral voice of God—the conscience—that could be found in every human being.

In his second inaugural address, delivered in March 1865 at a time when it appeared that the war would be won by the North, Lincoln was careful to remind the American people to be cautious about judging the South (he cited Matthew 7:1: "but let us judge not that we be not judged"). He urged them to have "malice toward none" and "charity for all." Lincoln asked the nation to work together in an act of reconciliation—to "bind up the nation's wounds; to care for him who shall have borne the battle, and for his widow, and his orphan." While Lincoln believed that the South was responsible for starting the war, he also believed that anger or vengeance would not bring the Union back together in an expedient and peaceful fashion. "The Almighty has his own purposes," Lincoln affirmed, and when he did venture to discern the spiritual meaning of the war he put the blame on both North and South for the "two hundred and fifty years of unrequited toil" that blacks had suffered under slavery.

Lincoln showed much humility in his attempt at understanding the will of God. By asking Americans to lay aside their malice and replace it with love, Lincoln, who was a skeptic for most of his life, spoke in a manner that was fully compatible with Christian values. Yet very few of the North's self-proclaimed Christian professionals heeded Lincoln's call for reconciliation. Most Northern ministers used God-language to condemn Southern secession, Southern slavery, and the war itself. If it is indeed true that vengeance belongs only to God, then it appears that many Northern clergy must have missed that lesson in their divinity training.[36]

Northern clergy were especially ready to call down God's judgment on the South. Secession represented a sinful break from a divinely ordained political Union. It deserved punishment. E. E. Adams wrote that whoever resisted the "good government of the United States resisteth the ordinance of God; and they that resist shall receive to themselves damnation." John Bigelow had similar things to say about anyone who was unwilling to recognize "the teachings of God's Providence in History, which are the same with those of His Word." He prayed that the Confederacy would "lay down their bloody arms, and come into line [with]

Thy great purposes of History." But if the South continued in its rebellion against the Christian Union, Bigelow prayed that God would "with the breath of Thy nostrils, their infernal designs, scattering them to the winds of Heaven; and let the curse of Meroz, scathing with fires of Perdition, fall upon that man, or that class of men, whoever they may be, whether from the South or the North, from East or the West, who shall lift the hand for the overthrow, or the rupture of this *God founded* Republic."[37] So much for "malice toward none" and "charity for all."

Christian Nationalism and the Confederate States of America

As Northern propagandists extolled the Christian virtues of their national Union and the spiritual superiority of their society over a sinful South in need of God's repentance, the religious and political leaders of the Confederacy were building what they perceived to be their own Christian civilization. Indeed, the "Christian nation" theme was even more prominent in the South than it was in the North. Southerners were convinced that the Confederate States of America was a Christian nation. They viewed the Confederacy as a refuge for the godly amid the "infidelity" of the Union to which they once belonged. Southerners were now ready to engage in a war that would prove that God was on their side. This mentality is clear in the Confederacy's decision to adopt the Latin phrase *Deo Vindice* ("With God as our defender") as its national motto.

Southerners looking for evidence that the Confederacy was a Christian nation needed to look no further than their Constitution. Unlike the U.S. Constitution, which does not mention God, the preamble of the Constitution of the Confederate States of America made a direct appeal to "Almighty God":

> We, the people of the Confederate States, each State acting in its sovereign and independent character, in order to form a permanent and federal government, establish justice, insure domestic tranquility, and secure the blessings of liberty to ourselves and our posterity—invoking the favor and guidance of Almighty God—do ordain and establish this Constitution for the Confederate States of America.[38]

Southern clergy were absolutely giddy over the insertion of such God-language. Benjamin Morgan Palmer, the minister of the First Presbyterian Church of New Orleans, called it "a truly Christian patriot's prayer." He blasted the "perilous atheism" of the U.S. Constitution, adding that its framers had been too tinctured with the kind of "free-thinking" and "infidel spirit" that was often associated with the "horror of the French Revolution." Palmer described the ratification of the Constitution in these terms: "The American nation stood up before the world, a helpless orphan and entered upon a career without a God." The Confederacy, however, was charting a godlier path. Its framers had made a conscious effort to avoid the scandalous secularism of the U.S. Constitution. When Palmer read the preamble of the Confederate Constitution, with its "clear, solemn, official recognition of Almighty God," he claimed that his "heart swelled with unutterable emotions of gratitude and joy. . . . At length, the nation has a God: Alleluia! 'the Lord reigneth let the earth rejoice.'"[39]

With a Constitution that recognized "Almighty God," it was not much of a leap for Southern clergy and politicians to affirm that the citizens of the Confederacy were the new chosen people of God. References to the Old Testament "covenant" between God and Israel were a staple of Confederate writings. O. S. Barten, the rector at St. James Church in Warrenton, Virginia, invoked this theme in 1861: "In the gradual unrolling of the mighty scroll, on which God has written the story of our future, as fold after fold is spread before the nation, may there stand, emblazoned in letters of living light, but this one testimony: 'They are my people, and I am their God.'"[40] In an 1861 sermon to a group of Georgia militiamen, J. Jones began his defense of the Confederacy as God's chosen people with an appeal to the Old Testament book of Jeremiah, the prophet of the "New Covenant." Other clergy connected the Confederacy to similar claims made by seventeenth-century Puritans, even going so far as to reference John Winthrop's famous call for the Massachusetts Bay Colony to be a "city set upon a hill."[41] The Confederate government, under the leadership of Jefferson Davis, affirmed this special covenant with regular days of fasting and prayer.[42]

Yet for many northerners, especially abolitionists, the question remained: How could the Confederacy claim to be a Christian nation and still keep four million slaves in bondage? The North asked this question relentlessly during the Civil War era, and in response the South developed an increasingly sophisticated answer. The political and religious leaders of the Confederacy had little problem reconciling slavery with their claim to be a Christian civilization. The nineteenth-century South always understood itself to be a society informed by the teachings of the Bible. And nowhere in the New Testament, they claimed, did the Bible condemn slavery.[43]

Southern clergy justified slavery with a host of biblical passages. In the book of Philemon, for example, the apostle Paul urged Onesimus, Philemon's runaway slave, to return to his master. Romans 13, a passage employed by many Northerners in their arguments against Southern secession, could also be used by Southerners as a biblical injunction for the submission of slaves to their masters. And, of course, there were always passages such as Ephesians 6:5: "Slaves, obey your earthly masters with respect and fear, and with sincerity of heart, just as you would obey Christ." Thomas Dew, a professor of political science at the College of William and Mary, used the Bible to defend the idea that all societies had a fixed and natural social structure. Citing 1 Corinthians 7:20–21, he argued that slaves should remain slaves because God had made them to fulfill such a role in society. They had been given a divine "calling" and, in Paul's words, "each one should remain in the condition in which he was called."[44]

Southerners reserved harsh judgment for what they believed to be the unbiblical approach to slavery taken by Northern abolitionists. In claiming that slaves should be set free, abolitionists violated the explicit teachings of Scripture. Robert L. Dabney, a Virginia Presbyterian clergyman and one of the strongest defenders of slavery in the South, argued that Christianity had always taught that slavery was a permissible institution. The notion that slaves had "rights" and thus deserved freedom was a modern idea that had been introduced in the eighteenth century by the progressive thinkers of the Enlightenment. As Dabney put it: "Neither primitive, nor reformed, nor Romanist, nor modern divines taught the doctrine of the intrinsic sinfulness of slaveholding. The church as a body never dreamed of it." Instead, it was the "political agitators of atheistic, Jacobin France" and a few misguided Christians, such as John Wesley, who first popularized abolitionism, "almost eighteen hundred years after Christ's birth." Dabney represented the traditional culture of the nineteenth-century South—a culture that distrusted the kind of progress that defined modern life. Dabney preferred to cling to nearly two thousand years of biblical scholarship defending the validity of slavery.[45]

Southerners thought that abolitionism had no biblical legs to stand on. Anyone who believed that slavery was wrong would have to abandon a high view of the Bible's authority. William Lloyd Garrison was a prime example of this trend. When Garrison came to terms with the fact that the Bible seemed to support slavery, he rejected the Bible—or at least its literal interpretation. Writing in his abolitionist magazine, *The Liberator*,

Garrison said: "To say that everything contained within the lids of the bible is divinely inspired, and to insist upon the dogma as fundamentally important, is to give utterance to a bold fiction, and to require the suspension of the reasoning faculties. To say that everything in the bible is to be believed, simply because it is found in that volume, is equally absurd and pernicious."[46] As already mentioned, Henry Ward Beecher made a similar argument.

These kinds of public declarations concerning the Bible became fodder for Southern attacks on Northern infidelity. James Henry Thornwell, another powerful theological voice in support of slavery, understood the Civil War as a clash between atheist abolitionists and virtuous slaveholders: "The parties in this conflict are not merely abolitionists and slaveholders—they are atheists, socialists, communists, red republicans, Jacobins, on the one side, and friends of order and regulated freedom on the other." Stephen Elliott, the bishop of the Episcopal Diocese of Georgia, described the "philanthropy" of the North as being opposed "to the word and the will of God." Abolitionists were too optimistic and progressive. According to Southerners they rejected "the curse of God upon sin, which manifested itself in poverty, in suffering, in slavery, in a thousand forms which made the world as miserable as it is. . . . Instead of bowing before the word of God," which clearly taught that slavery was a result of the fall of humankind in the garden of Eden, abolitionists and other opponents of slavery were more content to appeal to "the echo of the French revolution" and ideals such as "liberty, equality, fraternity." In the process the North "defied God." One Southern preacher even suggested that abolitionists should be denied the sacrament of Communion because of their infidelity.[47]

The people of the Confederate States of America believed that they were citizens of a Christian nation *precisely because* they upheld the institution of slavery. Benjamin Palmer thought that the South had a divine mission to support this biblically sanctioned institution. The South had been called "to conserve and to perpetuate the institution of slavery as now existing." It was a duty to "ourselves, to our slaves, to the world, and to Almighty God." No one was more forceful in promoting this view than Robert Dabney. Reflecting on the Civil War, he argued that slaveholders were doing the will of God by lifting the nation's four million slaves "out of idolatrous debasement." By Christianizing slaves the South had brought "more than a half million adult communicants in Christian churches!" In other words, Christian slave masters did more to benefit slaves than any abolitionist ever could. Through their regular attendance at Christian churches, Dabney argued, slaves learned how be obedient to the Bible's teachings on slavery and were thus able to live in a manner that was pleasing to God. The motives behind the mission to Christianize slaves were "not carnal, but evangelical." They stemmed from a "sense of duty" and a "love for Christ and his doctrine."[48] If the Bible supported slavery, as the South believed that it did, then the people of a truly Christian nation must support it too.

Between 1789 and 1865 Americans—North and South, Union and Confederate—understood themselves to be citizens of a Christian nation. The religious, political, and print culture of early national America reinforced the notion that God had a special plan for the United States. Despite the religious skepticism of many of the founders, evangelical Protestantism, which manifested itself in the Second Great Awakening, defined the culture. The real debates in this era were not over whether God was on the side of the United States—that was a well-accepted belief. Rather, the conflict centered on what kind of Christian nation the United States would be. By 1860 there were two visions of Christian America. Many Northerners believed that the national Union was sacred because it was created and blessed by God. Many Southerners argued that the Confederate States of America was a Christian nation because the Bible's teachings were compatible with a Southern way of life.

The Union victory in the Civil War meant that a Northern vision of Christian America would prevail. God was moving his nation forward by ushering in a "new birth of freedom." As the North tried to remake the defeated South in its own image, it would come to embrace progress and modernity in such a way that threatened the very idea of a Christian civilization. Yet the vision of a Christian America persisted. It is to this story that we now turn.

Chapter Two

Evangelicals, Liberals, and Christian America, 1865–1925

The decades following the Civil War brought profound changes to American life. Industrialization led to a host of social problems in American cities. Millions of new immigrants—many of them Catholics and Jews from eastern and southern Europe—flooded into the country. Traditional beliefs were challenged by new ideas such as Darwinism, biblical criticism, and religious pluralism. Yet through it all Christian nationalism proved to be resilient.

There were, however, some significant differences between the Christian nationalism of the post–Civil War years and the Christian golden age of the early Republic. Evangelicals, no longer operating from the center of American culture, became more polemical. They defended Christian civilization as a means of resisting social and cultural change. Liberal Protestants adapted to these changes and developed their own spin on the Christian America theme. In the South, Christian nationalism died with the Confederacy. The region remained strongly evangelical well into the twentieth century, but it was not until the 1980s, when southerners joined the Reagan Revolution, that it came to embrace a view of religion and public life that was national in scope. This chapter provides a sweeping overview of the way that Americans—particularly American Protestants—remained advocates of a Christian America in a time of change.

A Christian Amendment to the Constitution

As we saw in the last chapter, much of the religious debate between North and South during the Civil War focused on the "Christian" nature of the

U.S. Constitution. The South reveled in the fact that the Constitution of the Confederate States of America invoked "the favor and guidance of Almighty God," while the U.S. Constitution did not. Many Northern clergy were bothered by this. In 1861 George Duffield Jr., the minister of the First Presbyterian Church of Detroit, described the framers' decision to exclude a reference to God in the Constitution as a "national sin."[1] Henry Boardman, pastor of Philadelphia's Tenth Presbyterian Church, explained Union military defeats as part of God's punishment on the nation because "our national charter pays no homage to the Deity."[2]

In 1863 several ministers decided to do something to change this godless Constitution. They met in Xenia, Ohio, and proposed the following amendment to the U.S. Constitution:

> WE, THE PEOPLE OF THE UNITED STATES, [recognizing the being and attributes of Almighty God, the Divine Authority of the Holy Scriptures, the law of God as the paramount rule, and Jesus, the Messiah, the Saviour and Lord of all] in order to form a more perfect union, establish justice, insure domestic tranquility, provide for the common defense, promote the general welfare, and secure the blessings of liberty to ourselves and to our posterity, do ordain and establish this Constitution for the United States of America.

This group of ministers eventually became known as the National Reform Association (NRA). In 1864 its leaders brought their proposal for a Christian amendment to the White House. According to an annual report of the NRA, Abraham Lincoln gave his approval to their mission, but asked for "time to deliberate, as the work of amending the Constitution should not be done hastily." By 1874 the organization was holding national gatherings attended by several thousand people, mostly clergy.[3]

The NRA made several arguments on behalf of a Christian amendment. From a religious point of view, the decision to leave references to Christianity out of the Constitution was an "error and an evil" that "dishonors God." Some believed that God had used the Civil War to punish the Union because of its godless Constitution. Others argued that the Constitution did not reflect the religious sentiments of a "great majority" of the American people. In the wake of the Civil War, Protestantism remained the dominant religion in the United States. If most Americans were Protestants, then the Constitution should reflect this reality. The NRA also noted that the Constitution "was inconsistent with the character of nearly all our state Constitutions." Indeed, most state constitutions in the late nineteenth century invoked God in one way or another. As we will see in later chapters, many still required religious (Christian) tests for officeholding.[4]

The NRA also put forth a historical argument for why the Constitution should include a Christian amendment. Not only was the U.S. population in the late nineteenth century predominantly Christian, but its people had always been Christian and its government was founded on Christian principles. Charles Blanchard, a professor at Wheaton College in Illinois, argued that a Christian amendment was an "an act of justice to the past." The Pilgrims and Puritans had come to the shores of the New World to establish a "Christian Commonwealth." The 1874 NRA national convention affirmed, "This country was settled and its institutions founded by those who believed in God and accepted His Word as the law of their lives." Such faith was manifested in the colonial charters, the Declaration of Independence, the state constitutions, and the colonial and state criminal codes. "These Christian features of our American civilization," the NRA claimed, "were indispensable forces for the restraint of vice, the development of virtue, and the unification of the people; and we desire to maintain and perpetuate the same."[5]

A prominent concern of the NRA was the place of the Bible in education. Some states were considering laws to prohibit the reading of the Bible in public schools. The NRA argued that if the Constitution acknowledged God it would make it a lot easier to fend off secular attacks on Bible reading and Christian education. America had a choice. It could "obliterate every Christian feature from existing institutions" or it could "make the Constitution explicitly Christian." The NRA continued: "Shall we thrust out the Bible from our schools to make them conform to the Constitution? Patriotism and true Statesmanship answer, No! But let the acknowledgment of God and the Bible be inserted in the Constitution to make it conform to the Common Schools."[6] The Constitution needed to be changed to give credence and authority to Christian practices already in place and to protect the culture from the forces of secularism.

The NRA was also motivated, in part, by nativism, the belief that immigration posed a threat to the "native" population of the country. In 1874 A. A. Hodge, a theology professor from Western Seminary in Pittsburgh, feared the "multitudes of disappointed political and social theorists" who had "recently immigrated to our land." Hodge did not specifically identity the views of these new immigrants, but his use of the phrase "political and social theorists" was an obvious reference to the growing number of refugees from European revolutions arriving on American shores armed with Marxist or socialist beliefs. These immigrants, Hodge noted, were "disseminating theories of human rights and of man's relation to God which are inconsistent with the facts and traditions of our government as with the Christian religion." A Christian amendment would make clear to these radicals that the United States was a nation of faith, and if they wanted to find a home here, they would need to share in this "heritage." A formal recognition of Christianity as the national religion was a means of guarding against such immigrant threats.[7]

The NRA maintained a commitment to the separation of church and state. "All agree," the Fifth National Reform Convention affirmed, "that the "civil establishment and endowment of any ecclesiastical body would be an evil." Any such establishment would violate the First Amendment. The NRA distinguished the "separation of Church and State," which was forbidden by the Constitution, from the "separation of religion and state," which was not. Its members were very careful to affirm that they were not opposing religious liberty and were not interested in creating a "theocracy." But they did want to give Christianity a privileged place in America. This meant the promotion of Bible reading in schools, the preservation of the Christian Sabbath, and the public recognition of the teachings of Christianity as the country's moral guide.[8] The NRA never specified how the government would strike such a balance between the separation of church and state on the one hand and the privileging of the Christian religion on the other. There is nothing in their formal statements resembling our current debates over prayer in schools or public demonstrations of Christianity during the Advent season.

The movement to add a Christian amendment to the Constitution failed. If Lincoln did endorse the idea, as the NRA claimed he did, his assassination ended any further hope of presidential support. While a few prominent congressmen backed the amendment, it had little support in the House and Senate. Opposition to the Christian amendment movement was strong, particularly among Seventh-day Adventists, Unitarians, and Jews. The NRA amendment never came to a vote in Congress, but this did not derail the movement. The organization revived its platform again in 1894 and 1910, and continued to meet through World War II.[9]

An Evangelical Alliance: 1873

As the National Reform Association gathered in 1873 to promote a Christian amendment to the Constitution, evangelicals from all over the world met in New York City at the Sixth General Conference of the Evangelical

Alliance. The Evangelical Alliance was an international organization with a nondenominational focus. Anyone was invited to participate who could affirm a belief in the inspiration of the Bible, the Trinity, the depravity of human nature, the incarnation of Jesus Christ and his atonement for sins, justification by faith alone, the work of the Holy Spirit in the world, and the resurrection of the body. Since this was an international gathering that met only every few years, it was the equivalent of an evangelical Olympic Games. The minutes of this gathering and the host of addresses delivered by the participants provide a revealing snapshot of American evangelicalism in the wake of the Civil War.

Many of the speakers at the 1873 meeting of the Evangelical Alliance came from the United States. They lectured on topics that had particular relevance for evangelical attempts at sustaining the country's Christian identity. Sessions were devoted to the labor problem, church and state, temperance, the Sabbath, atheism, Catholicism, the family, theology, Christian unity, philosophy, world religions, wealth, literature, education, preaching, religious liberty, missions, philanthropy, caring for the sick, crime, and industry. Few topics (with the exception of race and immigration) escaped coverage during this eleven-day meeting. There was even a session on cruelty to animals.

Theodore Dwight Woolsey, a former president of Yale College and current president of the Evangelical Alliance, asked the convention whether the United States should be considered a "Christian nation." He answered in the affirmative. The United States was a "Christian country" because

> the vast majority of the people believe in Christ and the Gospel, that Christian influences are universal, that our civilization and intellectual culture are built on that foundation, and that the institutions are so adjusted as, in the opinion of most Christians, to furnish the best hope for spreading and carrying down to posterity our faith and our morality.

In another address, William Warren, the president of Boston University, concluded that George Whitefield, the eighteenth-century revivalist of the First Great Awakening, was the "spiritual father of a great Christian nation."[10]

The speakers at this gathering defined "Christian nation" in an overwhelmingly evangelical Protestant way. Non-Christians and Catholics were not capable of contributing to it. The attendees spent an entire day listening to lectures that affirmed long-standing Protestant anxieties about Roman Catholics. The so-called backward ways of "Romanism" were portrayed as a threat to American individualism and progress. According to George P. Fisher, the Titus Street Professor of Ecclesiastical History at Yale Divinity School, Catholicism represented a "dictatorial attitude toward civil authority . . . an exorbitant demand upon the credulity of mankind by unverified miracles and prodigies, an attempt to revive pilgrimages and other obsolete or obsolescent superstitions," and an "increased devotion to the Virgin Mary, which borders on idolatry." Those who believed in such superstition needed to be converted, through organized efforts of evangelism, to the "true" Protestant faith.[11]

If the United States was a Christian nation, then, for the sake of "posterity," it was up to evangelicals to make sure it stayed that way. Attendees spent days listening to talks on topics related to social and moral reform. Speakers from the United States offered lectures on temperance, Sabbath legislation, and the "labor question." Evangelicals believed that all three of these moral issues needed to be addressed as part of an agenda to forge a Christian civilization, both in America and abroad.

Today's evangelicals might be surprised to learn that their nineteenth-century spiritual ancestors were concerned about the plight of workers in the ever-burgeoning industrial world of the West. If America was going to be a Christian nation, then the tensions and hostilities between labor and business needed to be resolved in a Christian manner. William G. Allen, the president of Girard College in Philadelphia, called upon labor interests to stop their violent strikes and use their power to "promote peace on earth and good-will among men." The resources devoted to waging "war" against big business might be better used to "feed the hungry and clothe the naked." Was it too much to ask "nations professing of Christ" to be "imbued with something of the spirit of Christ"? Labor, of course, was only part of the problem. Allen urged the U.S. government to support the eight-hour workday, require that labor disputes be decided through arbitration rather than strikes, design equitable apprenticeship laws, reserve public lands for settlers rather than railroad companies and speculators, and establish a bureau of labor statistics. While Allen believed that evangelicals could support many of the reforms advocated by the labor movement, he rejected the movement's attempts at preventing the importation of immigrants from China. If unions were willing to promote "the solidarity of labor and co-operation of working men everywhere," they should not make distinctions between European and Asian workers. His address both supported capitalism and defended labor. The goal was reconciliation, a virtue fitting of "nations professing Christ."[12]

Labor reform and Sabbath reform went hand in hand at this meeting of the Evangelical Alliance. An address by Reverend Mark Hopkins, the former president of Williams College, urged the federal government to pass laws protecting the observance of the Christian Sabbath (Sunday). Hopkins argued that the Fourth Commandment ("Remember the Sabbath day, and keep it holy") should be embedded in American law in much the same way that commandments prohibiting murder, stealing, and "bearing false witness" were staples of the legal system. If that was not enough to convince naysayers, Hopkins emphasized Jesus' words in Mark 2:27—"The Sabbath was made for man, not man for the Sabbath"—to argue that the human body was created by God in such a way that it required a day of rest. "Men and animals," Hopkins argued, "will have better health and live longer; will do more work, and do it better, if they rest one day in seven, than if they work continuously." Rest was a human right endowed by God. If this were true, then how could a nation with Christian roots not endorse the Sabbath?[13]

Like the movement to preserve the Christian Sabbath, temperance reform had long been part of the social consciousness of American evangelicals. Though slavery had been the most prominent Northern evangelical reform effort in the early national period, it was now time, with the Civil War over and the Thirteenth Amendment passed, to focus once again on temperance. This was the sentiment of Lane Theological Seminary professor Henry A. Nelson in his address "Intemperance and Its Suppression." Nelson's arguments were typical of evangelical crusades against the use of alcohol. The "drunkard" was a "sinner against God" and a "criminal also toward civil society." He disrespected his body, debased his intellect, desolated his home and family, loaded society with the "burdens of taxation," and contributed to national vices that led to the "hopeless ruin of souls by rendering them incapable of receiving the Gospel." Much of Nelson's argument countered those libertarian-minded Americans who believed that government enforcement of morality in this area was a violation of their civil rights. While Nelson admitted that this was indeed a thorny issue, he concluded that the practice of giving Americans the right to drink excessively would ultimately violate the rights of others. "Shall the rum-sellers' rights of property be held more sacred, be treated more tenderly, be guarded more carefully," he argued, than "the right of the mother to rear her boy unexposed to the enticements of the grog-shop?" Any attempt to defend the right to abuse alcohol was driven by selfish and materialistic motives. By following "the calm voice of Christianity, which affirms the higher sacredness of the right to rear children in virtue and piety, and to dwell in peaceful homes," Americans might make a better society for themselves.[14]

Nelson's address on intemperance was similar to many of the speeches on social reform delivered at the Sixth General Conference of the Evangelical Alliance. It was the task of evangelical churches to "educate the State in the Christian ethics of government," whether the issue was labor-capital relations, the preservation of the Sabbath, or the crusade against intemperance. "The questions of legislation and civil administration," Nelson urged, "can never be rightly settled in communities which are not pervaded by spiritual, Christian influences . . . the State must have the Christian temper, tone, spirit, or it can never give its people a truly Christian regulation."[15] Nelson and all of his fellow evangelicals meeting during the fall of 1873 were arguing for nothing less than a "Christian America."

Fundamentalism and Christian Civilization

Not all late nineteenth-century evangelicals were interested in building a Christian civilization in America. As the century came to a close, many evangelicals found comfort in changing times by attending "prophecy conferences." Speakers at these conferences were devoted to interpreting the prophetic books and passages of the Bible as a means of predicting how the plan of God would unfold in the so-called last days. Not unlike Tim LaHaye and Jerry Jenkins, the authors of today's popular *Left Behind* novels, these speakers entertained and edified their audiences with lectures on the "rapture," the second coming of Christ, the "tribulation," and the meaning of the various creatures and events in the book of Revelation.

Those who attended these conferences left with a renewed sense of optimism that God would end human history in a way that was favorable to believers. Christians needed to wait for Jesus Christ's return in the clouds. He would then, in the blink of an eye, rapture them to heaven. Eventually the forces of evil would be defeated and Christ would return again, with those who had been raptured, to establish his earthly kingdom. No one knew when the "end times" would begin, so evangelicals were exhorted to cultivate a right relationship with God through Bible reading, prayer, church attendance, and evangelism. They needed to be ready because "no one knows the day or the hour." Those who defended this view of biblical prophecy were known as "premillennialists." The word comes from the idea that Jesus would rapture all true believers *before* he established his one-thousand-year reign on the earth. Premillennialists had no particular interest in advancing the cause of a Christian nation.[16] Why should Christians invest their energies into making *this* world a better place when they could, at any moment, be transported to the *next* world? For those who believed that they lived in this kind of fallen and temporal world, salvation of souls was all that mattered. Christians should be preparing their neighbors for the "new heavens" and the "new earth." As the nationally known evangelist Dwight L. Moody put it: "God has given me a lifeboat and said 'Moody, save all you can.'"[17]

Other evangelicals were not as dour about this world. William Jennings Bryan, arguably the era's most famous evangelical, never ceased his crusade to make the United States a Christian nation. In the 1890s, as a representative of the populist wing of the Democratic Party, he fought for common farmers, supporting legislation that would give them relief from what he deemed to be the evils of corporate America. Though he failed three times to win the presidency, he became a hero to evangelicals throughout the South and Midwest. Bryan represented a vision of the kingdom of God often described as "postmillennialism." Unlike premillennialists, who believed that God would gather the faithful, defeat the forces of darkness in the world, and return triumphantly to establish his millennial kingdom on earth, postmillennialists thought that they were already living in God's kingdom. Only the conversion of people to the gospel and the Christianization of civilization would precipitate the second coming of Christ. Bryan used his extraordinary oratorical skills at Bible conferences and Chautauqua meetings for the purpose of furthering a society of Bible-believing evangelicals. His faith led him to fight for the dignity of all human beings, to oppose war, and, as we will see below, to protect schoolchildren from Darwinian evolution.[18]

Another evangelical, Billy Sunday, shared many of Bryan's commitments. Sunday was a premillennialist, but he did not act like one. A former professional baseball player, he converted to evangelical Christianity and became a full-time evangelist. Sunday is probably best described by the words on a popular t-shirt depicting his image: "Evangelical with an attitude." Not only did he try to win his audience to Christ with his theatrical preaching, but he crusaded relentlessly against what he deemed to be the evils of the saloon. His sermons fused the traditional evangelical gospel with rants against alcohol. Sunday was an urban reformer driven by a passion to win souls, end the sale and consumption of alcohol, and

Fig. 2.1 Billy Sunday was an evangelical revivalist who fought the "evils" of alcohol as a means of building a Christian civilization.

transform cities into bastions of moral order. He often timed his evangelistic crusades to end just days before voters went to the polls to vote up or down on Prohibition. While his precise impact in this regard is difficult to document, several states went dry through referenda or legislation shortly after Sunday had passed through town.

In almost every crusade, Sunday preached what became known as his "Booze" sermon (the official title of the sermon was "Get on the Water Wagon"). It was a straightforward moral and political attack on what he and millions of others believed to be a threat to Christian America. A staple of this sermon was Sunday's description of a conversation he once had with his wife concerning his crusade on behalf of Prohibition: "Nell, when I am dead, send for the butcher and skin me, and have my hide tanned and made into drum heads, and hire men to go up and down the land and beat the drums and say 'My husband, "Bill" Sunday still lives and gives the whiskey gang a run for its money.'"[19] He was also known to make belligerent and sensational statements against the liquor trade, such as, "I'll fight them until hell freezes over then I'll buy a pair of skates and fight 'em on ice!"[20] William Jennings Bryan would occasionally make appearances at Sunday's crusades. Thousands showed up to hear these two prominent evangelicals talk about Christian America.[21]

According to historian George Marsden, World War I was the decisive moment that turned evangelicals into fundamentalists. Many evangelicals were cautious about throwing their support behind America's entrance into the war. Bryan, the secretary of state in Woodrow Wilson's administration, resigned his position because he opposed U.S. involvement. But as it turned out, Bryan was an exception to the rule. Most evangelicals, despite initial hesitations, chose to support the war. Billy Sunday, for example, wrote in 1917 that "Christianity and Patriotism are synonymous terms and hell and traitors are synonymous." Other evangelicals linked German higher criticism—the belief that the Bible was not God-inspired and should be read and interpreted much like any other piece of literature—with the German war machine. They viewed World War I as a battle against both the Kaiser and the German university. Even premillennialists were able to rid themselves of their otherworldliness for a time in order to support the American war effort.[22]

Following the war, American evangelicals transferred their militant opposition to Germany into a fight for control of their denominations. In 1920 Baptist editor Curtis Lee Laws coined the term "fundamentalist" to describe any evangelical who was willing "to do battle royal for the Fundamentals [of Christian faith]." Marsden has described a fundamentalist as an "evangelical who is mad about something."[23] Evangelicals were angry because their denominations were in danger of being taken over by Protestant liberals who denied traditional Christian doctrines such as the inerrancy of the Bible and the virgin birth of Jesus. They believed that theological liberals undermined a "Christian America"; here the adjective "Christian" was understood to refer to orthodox evangelical doctrine. As Marsden writes, "in the minds of most fundamentalists the theological crisis came to be inextricably wedded to the very survival of Christian civilization—by which they meant a Bible-based civilization. One cannot comprehend the character of the movement without recognizing this social and political dimension."[24]

Darwinian evolution—the belief that human beings came into existence not by the hand of God but by the process of natural selection and the "survival of the fittest"—was a prime example of an issue that fundamentalists rallied around. The fight against Darwinism was important for fundamentalists because it affected the education of their children. If the next generation of Americans were convinced that human beings descended from monkeys and were not created by God, what would happen to Christian civilization in the United States? Fundamentalists put a lot of energy into winning this fight. William Jennings Bryan would be their champion.

The most famous evangelical in America began crusading against evolution around the turn of the twentieth century. In 1925, when Bryan heard that John Scopes, a schoolteacher in Dayton, Tennessee, had violated state law by teaching evolution to his science classes, he could not resist getting himself into the mix. The American Civil Liberties Union chose Dayton as a test case in their crusade to banish laws forbidding the teaching of evolution in schools. They hired famed trial lawyer Clarence Darrow to defend Scopes. Bryan volunteered his services to the prosecution. In the end, Bryan would win the case against Scopes, but the trial was an utter disaster for the fundamentalist movement. Darrow called Bryan to the stand as an expert witness and proceeded to embarrass him before a room of national print and radio reporters. Bryan was not a theologian or a scientist. He thus sounded foolish trying to answer Darrow's well-placed zingers.[25] Bryan passed away five days after the trial ended, and the fundamentalist movement went with him. These militant evangelicals lost control of their denominations and their hold on American culture. Their mission to sustain a Christian nation had come to end, at least for the moment.

Liberal Protestantism and Christian America

Evangelicals and fundamentalists were not the only Protestants in America between the Civil War and the 1920s. Liberal Protestants were much more open to adapting their faith to the spirit of the age. They would engage in "battle royal" with the fundamentalists for control of Protestant denominations, but in the process they never abandoned their ardent belief that the United States was a Christian nation and needed to be defended as such. Indeed, the rhetoric that liberal Protestants used to defend Christian America was considerably stronger than that employed by the fundamentalists.

For the purpose of our study, a liberal Protestant can be defined as a Protestant who questions certain core doctrines affirmed by the historic Christian church. Protestant liberals were often described as "modernists" because of their willingness to conform their theological convictions to modern culture. Many believed in the authority of the Bible for matters of faith and practice, but understood it more as a *witness to God* than as the *word of God*. Some liberals believed in a Creator-God, but thought that this God worked through the science of evolution. They tended to reject the doctrine of original sin, the existence of Satan or hell, and the virgin birth of Jesus Christ. Ultimately, they tied their theological wagons to the train of progress. Society was advancing toward the kingdom of God and Christians needed to play a part in its coming.[26]

The responsibility of liberal Christians to usher in the kingdom of God played itself out in a variety of ways. Henry Ward Beecher, whom we met in the last chapter, was a strong supporter of a Christian America defined by social progress. On Thanksgiving Day 1870, Beecher preached a sermon entitled "The Tendencies of American Progress." On a day like this, Beecher focused on what was good about the United States of America. He praised America's wide-open spaces, its commitment to self-government, the level of economic comfort afforded to its workers, and the way in which immigrants easily assimilated. As his cheery sermon continued he talked about the "golden future" that was "opening before us." The message would have drawn applause from patriots everywhere.

Beecher focused much of his attention in this sermon on the American fascination with wealth. His intention was not to condemn the accumulation of wealth, as many of his Puritan ancestors had done, but to extol its benefits. The opportunity Americans had to improve their lives economically was a clear sign of God's blessing on the United States. Beecher's sermon also defended big business. Corporations could be "dangerous,"

Fig. 2.2   Henry Ward Beecher was one of the nineteenth century's greatest Protestant preachers and a strong promoter of the idea that the United States was a Christian nation.

but they "do not need to be," especially if business tycoons were involved in philanthropy. Capitalism and industrialization powered the train of American progress, and Beecher was on board.[27]

Almost thirty years later, William Lawrence, the Episcopal bishop of Massachusetts, delivered a similar sermon: "The Relation of Wealth to Morals." Lawrence's sermon could have been written by Benjamin Franklin, Andrew Carnegie, Horatio Alger, or any other peddler of the American Dream. He described a poor Irish immigrant coming to American shores and working his way up the ladder of success through hard work and ambition before making a comfortable life for his family. Lawrence asked his readers if "the material prosperity of this nation" were "favorable or unfavorable to the morality of the people." His answer, as one might expect, was "by all means favorable." Or, in other words, "to seek . . . wealth is a sign of a natural, vigorous, and strong character." The material "bounty" that God had lavished on the people of the United States made "the national character sweeter, more joyous, more unselfish, more Christlike."[28] Like Beecher, Lawrence was more than willing to accommodate his theology to the progressive values of American culture. The United States was a land of great opportunity where ordinary people could pursue wealth and material success. And God willed it all.

Not all liberal Protestants connected America's Christian identity to the accumulation of wealth or economic ambition. Around the turn of the twentieth century a group of Protestants put forward a new brand of Christianity concerned more with improving *this* world than preparing one's soul for the next world. Known as the "social gospel," the leaders of this movement believed that by meeting social needs through Christ-like behavior, the United States could build a Christian civilization that would herald the second coming of Christ. Social gospel advocates set out to Christianize America through reforms, government programs, and voluntary societies designed to tackle the social problems—poverty, disease, and immorality—resulting from industrialization, urbanization, and immigration.[29]

These Protestants thought that the Christian identity of the United States should be defined by the way society and the government *behaved*. The citizens of a Christian nation followed the social teaching of Jesus. This approach was obviously different from that of the National Reform Association, whose members understood America as a Christian nation based upon the wording of the Constitution. The social gospel was also different from the way evangelicals tended to approach social issues.

Evangelicals were convinced that the best way for the church to address the problems of society was by saving more souls.

Those who championed the social gospel sought to advance the cause of justice and love throughout the nation and the world. Washington Gladden, the pastor of the First Congregational Church in Columbus, Ohio, described the connection between this mission and the advancement of a Christian nation:

> Every department of human life—the families, the schools, amusements, art, business, politics, industry, national politics, international relations—will be governed by the Christian law and controlled by Christian influences. When we are bidden to seek first the kingdom of God, we are bidden to set our hearts on this great commission; to keep this always before us as the object of our endeavors; to be satisfied with nothing less than this. The complete Christianization of all life is what we pray and work for, when we work and pray for the coming of the kingdom of heaven.

He would later declare: "If we want the nations on the earth to understand Christianity, we have to have a Christian nation to show them." Though the United States would never be a Christian nation in any legal sense, Gladden believed that "It must be, in spirit and purpose and character, a Christian nation." One writer accused Gladden of being a theocrat.[30]

Other leaders of the social gospel movement expressed similar thoughts about America's identity as a Christian nation. The man most historians consider the leader of the movement, Walter Rauschenbusch, a professor at Rochester (NY) Theological Seminary, claimed that his goal was to Christianize every sector of American life, including the family, the church, politics, the schools, and business. Richard T. Ely, an Episcopal layman and professor of economics, claimed that the "main purpose of the State is the religious purpose." If Christians would "put as much as possible, not of doctrine or creed into the State [United States] constitution, but of Christian life and practice into the activity of the State. . . . The nation must be recognized fully as a Christian nation." Similarly, Baptist leader Samuel Zane Batten wrote that "since the Christian ideal is absolute in its requirements, and the Christian law is universal in its sweep, it follows that Christian citizenship is confronted with the task of creating a truly Christian civilization."[31]

In 1908 several liberal clergy established an ecumenical fellowship of Protestant churches known as the Federal Council of Churches. The churches of the Federal Council would work together in a variety of projects related to missions and the promotion of Protestantism in the United States. At an early planning meeting of the Federal Council, William H. Roberts, the clerk of the Presbyterian Church in the U.S.A., noted that "the essential spirit of our Nation is thus that of Jesus Christ, and it is the duty of the American Churches to make that spirit more Christian." The goal of this new fellowship of Protestant religious bodies was to let the United States know that "this world is a lost world apart from Jesus Christ." Its vision for a Christian nation was not a legal one, but it was certainly a political one:

> It is not the province of the church as an organized body to dominate the state politically, or to control specific legislative action; but it is its province to set forth and interpret the principles of the gospel of the kingdom of God so clearly to the entire life of the nation that its citizens shall be moved to make the state, its politics and its legislation, the practical expression and realization of those principles.[32]

The Federal Council of Churches, which would be the umbrella organization for all the major Protestant denominations for decades to come, affirmed its goal of advancing "a Christian civilization organized upon the ethical teachings and controlled by the spirit of Jesus Christ."[33] David Barton could not have put it any better a century later.

The liberal Protestant crusade for a Christian America reached its height during World War I. Though there were many pacifists in their ranks, the majority of liberal Protestants at the turn of the twentieth century saw war as a means of securing a peaceful world—the kind of world that would spread God-inspired democracy and precipitate the second coming of Christ. For example, Lyman Abbott, Henry Ward Beecher's successor at the Plymouth Congregational Church in Brooklyn, believed that the U.S. victory in the Spanish-American War was a harbinger of the kingdom of God. It demonstrated the nation's compassion and care for the suffering and oppressed of Cuba and the Philippines.[34] Abbott offered a spiritualized version of American imperialism not unlike Rudyard Kipling's poem "The White Man's Burden."

While evangelical clergy eased into their support for World War I, Protestant liberals understood it as a "war for righteousness." It pitted the forces of God, in the form of the United States of America and its commitment to democracy and social justice, against the forces of evil, as embodied in the religious tribalism and antidemocratic tendencies of

Germany. Progressive ministers led their churches in patriotic hymns such as "Onward Christian Soldiers" and "The Battle Hymn of the Republic." They described the war as "redemptive" and did not hesitate in portraying it as a holy war designed to usher in the kingdom of God on earth.

Historian Richard Gamble has described the liberal Protestant response to World War I as nothing short of messianic in nature. Frederick Lynch, who held the rather ironic position of secretary of the Federal Council of Churches' Commission on Peace and Arbitration, called the United States a "Christ nation to the other nations of the world." Harold Bell Wright, a best-selling novelist and former Disciples of Christ minister, described American troops in Europe as "the army of the liberty-loving world. Its blood is the blood of humanity, the humanity of Jesus, the humanity for which Jesus lived and died."[35] The patriotism of these liberal ministers and theologians make the religious rhetoric of George W. Bush during the lead-up to the American wars in Afghanistan and Iraq seem mild.

These liberal Protestants found support for their messianic vision from President Woodrow Wilson. A liberal Presbyterian elder himself, Wilson often told audiences of clergy and religious laypersons that the United States was a nation with a special destiny to spread Christianity to the world. As the president of Princeton University, he set out to uphold the institution's long-standing commitment to Christianize America.[36] Like most liberal Protestants, he understood the progress of society in religious terms—as a battle between the forces of God and the forces of evil. Christians had a duty to engage in this battle. The survival of Christian civilization was at stake. As president of the United States, Wilson blended Christianity and patriotism. Both taught people how to sacrifice their lives for something larger than themselves. There was little difference in Wilson's mind between the United States of America and the kingdom of God. This kind of religious idealism naturally found its way into Wilson's foreign policy.[37]

Before the American entrance into World War I, Wilson was an advocate of peace. He ran for reelection in 1916 on a peace platform ("He Kept Us Out of War") and tried to negotiate with European leaders for an end to the war. But these efforts at global reconciliation did not please many liberal Protestant clergy. One group of progressive ministers, which included New York pastor Harry Emerson Fosdick, Princeton University president John Grier Hibben, and Lyman Abbott, formally criticized Wilson's efforts on behalf of peace, claiming that an end to the war in

1917 would fail to fulfill God's plan to punish Germany for the sinking of the British ocean liner *Lusitania* (which had more than a hundred U.S. civilians on board), the invasion of Belgium, and the general instigation of the conflict. "The just God who withheld not his own Son from the cross, would not look with favor upon a people who put their fear of pain and death, their dread of suffering and loss, their concern for comfort and ease, above the holy claims of righteousness and justice and freedom and mercy and truth."[38] It is unclear what kind of impact this statement had on Wilson's foreign policy, but later in the year the United States entered World War I. The progressives finally got their holy war. The cause of Christian America would go forward.

The Supreme Court and the *Church of the Holy Trinity* Case

As evangelical and liberal Protestants preached their various versions of Christian nationalism, the U.S. Supreme Court also weighed in, albeit indirectly, on this topic. In *Church of the Holy Trinity v. United States* (1892) the Supreme Court concluded that an 1885 immigration law passed by Congress did not apply to churches. The act, which was largely meant to target Chinese immigrants who were coming to America and allegedly taking jobs from U.S. citizens, was passed "to prohibit the importation and migration of foreigners and aliens under contract or agreement to perform labor in the United States." In 1887 the historic Holy Trinity Church in New York City violated the letter of this law when it paid the travel costs from England incurred by the congregation's new minister, Reverend E. Walpole Warren. Since Warren was an immigrant, it was illegal for his employer, Holy Trinity Church, to cover his expenses for the trip to New York. When the case came to the Supreme Court, it ruled unanimously that the 1885 act "does not apply to a contract between an alien, residing out of the United States, and a religious society incorporated under the laws of a state, whereby he engages to remove to the United States and enter into the service of the society as its rector or minister."[39]

The author of the *Church of the Holy Trinity* opinion, Associate Justice David J. Brewer, argued that Congress never meant the 1885 law to apply to churches. In other words, Holy Trinity may have been violating the "letter of the statute," but was not violating the "spirit" of the Congress that passed the law. Brewer concluded that "the thought expressed in this reaches only to the work of the manual laborer, as distinguished from that of the professional man"; and "no one reading such a title would suppose that Congress had in its mind any purpose of staying the coming into this country of ministers of the gospel, or indeed, of any class whose toil is that of the brain. The common understanding of the terms 'labor' and 'laborers' does not include preaching and preachers."

But Brewer went even further in his analysis of the case. He also concluded that Congress could not have meant for this statute to apply to churches because "no purpose of action against religion can be imputed to any legislation, state or national, because this is a religious people." He then proceeded to make a historical case in support of the idea that the United States was a Christian nation. Brewer pointed to Christopher Columbus sailing westward in the name of God. He noted the references to God's providence in the earliest colonial charters, the first state constitutions, and in the Declaration of Independence. Brewer concluded that "these, and many other matters which might be noticed, add a volume of unofficial declarations to the mass of organic utterances that this is a Christian nation." If indeed the United States was a Christian nation, then it was absurd to think that Congress would pass a law preventing a clergyman to come to American shores for the purpose of promoting and sustaining such a nation.

It is important to remember that *Church of the Holy Trinity v. United States* was a case about immigration policy. It was not a case about whether the United States was a Christian nation. Yet the court *did* formally declare the United States to be a "Christian nation." What exactly did it mean by this? Part of the answer may lie in the religious views of Justice Brewer. In the wake of the *Holy Trinity* case Brewer took to the lecture circuit to speak about America's Christian roots. In 1905 he published a series of talks on the subject under the title *The United States: A Christian Nation*. Brewer argued that the United States was not a "Christian nation" in "the sense that Christianity is the established religion or that the people are in any manner compelled to support it." Neither, Brewer wrote, was the United States Christian "in the sense that all its citizens are either in fact or name Christians." Nor, he continued, is the United States Christian "in the sense that a profession of Christianity is a condition of holding office or otherwise engaging in public service." Yet America *was* a "Christian nation" in a historical sense. Brewer began by expanding upon the points he made in his *Church of the Holy Trinity* decision, once again pointing out references to Christianity in colonial charters and state governments. He appealed to the 1890 census to suggest that nearly two-thirds of Americans attended Christian churches. He also argued that the U.S. legal code was rooted in the "laws of Moses and the teachings of Christ."[40] While the United States should never be perceived as a "Christian nation" in any formal or official sense, it was certainly a "Christian nation" in terms of culture and history.

As the people of the United States entered the twentieth century, they never abandoned their commitment, dating back over one hundred years, to the proposition that the United States was a Christian nation. Some ministers tried to defend this position through efforts to amend the U.S. Constitution. Evangelicals and fundamentalists fought hard for a Christian civilization in America rooted in the spirit of early-nineteenth-century revivalism and the essentials of Protestant orthodoxy. Liberal Protestants, perhaps the most ardent of the Christian nationalists in this period, envisioned a nation, defined by justice and love, that would usher in the second coming of Christ. All of these nationalists got a boost from the Supreme Court when it declared the United States to be a "Christian nation."

The remainder of the twentieth century would pose some formidable challenges to Christian nationalists. Immigration, economic depression, World War II, the Cold War, and the civil rights movement influenced how Americans understood their identity as a Christian nation. By the end of the century, evangelicals and fundamentalists would reclaim a vision of a Christian America that continues to shape American political and religious life today.

Chapter Three

Christian America in a Modern Age, 1925–1980

Christian nationalism persisted during the twentieth century. While there was no universal agreement over how to define the United States as a Christian nation, all Christians could agree that American culture needed to be protected from the encroaching forces of secularism. The threat of atheistic communism abroad reinforced such a conviction. In the wake of World War I, mainline Protestants struggled to maintain their standing as the new guardians of American religious life, a position secured through their victory over the fundamentalists in the 1920s. Former fundamentalists, now choosing to describe themselves again with the less combative label "evangelicals," continued to prosper within their own networks of churches and parachurch organizations. In the 1950s both Protestant groups would experience a significant religious revival. As the so-called new immigrants came of age in America, Catholics began to stake their own claim on American culture. For Protestants, this Catholic resurgence was a matter of grave concern. Meanwhile the leaders of the civil rights movement, especially Martin Luther King Jr., envisioned a Christian nation defined by equality among the races. King's Christian nationalism provided a powerful critique of the localism of the southern clergy. This chapter explores briefly how all of these groups defended the belief that the United States was a Christian nation. It concludes with the 1970s and the forceful return of evangelicals into American political life.

The Persistence of the Evangelical Pursuit of a Christian Nation

As we saw in the last chapter, the 1920s proved to be a disaster for American evangelicalism. Not only had evangelicals lost control of their denominations, but whatever cultural power they enjoyed in the nine-teenth century was lost. The Scopes trial represented what was happen-ing to evangelicals in this regard. When ACLU lawyer Clarence Darrow embarrassed William Jennings Bryan before a national radio audience in Dayton, Tennessee, conservative evangelicalism was embarrassed with him. In the half-century between 1925 and 1975 evangelicals—with a few exceptions—withdrew from public and political life. But as historian Joel Carpenter has shown, this turn away from mainstream American culture did not mean that evangelicals were abandoning their desire to bring the culture into conformity with the teachings of Christianity. Evangelicals continued to dream of a Christian nation and sought to fulfill these long-ings through the creation of an evangelical subculture made up of Chris-tian schools, colleges, publications, radio programs, youth agencies, and other parachurch organizations.[1]

In the wake of the Scopes trial American evangelicals returned to their revivalist roots. If evangelicals were no longer custodians of the culture, they could still forge a Christian America by winning people to Christ. A nation of born-again Christians who practiced their faith in everyday life would lead to the restoration of an evangelical culture in the United States. Evangelicals prayed for a return to the golden era of the early nineteenth century, a time when evangelicalism defined the cultural mainstream. They relied upon the power of the Holy Spirit to awaken the churches amid this season of cultural impotence. Evangelicals believed God remained active in the course of their lives, a belief that enabled them to accept their new religious status as outsiders.[2]

This focus on revivalism was promoted heavily by the National Asso-ciation of Evangelicals (NAE), a fellowship of evangelical denominations founded in 1943. At the first meeting of the NAE, Harold John Ockenga, the organization's first president, delivered a presidential address entitled "Christ for America." Ockenga called upon the long-standing American belief, dating back to the seventeenth-century Puritans, that the United States had a mission on the earth akin to that of Old Testament Israel. America, Ockenga believed, was on the verge of a great religious revival. He urged the members of the NAE to "become the vanguard for the reconstruction of society's foundations." The NAE also became a strong supporter of a "Christian amendment" to the U.S. Constitution. In 1947 and 1954 the organization promoted an effort to add the following words to the Constitution: "This nation divinely recognizes the authority and law of Jesus Christ, Savior and Ruler of Nations through whom are bestowed the blessings of Almighty God."[3]

During the 1940s and 1950s evangelicals wed their hopes for the preservation of Christian America to revival meetings conducted by charismatic preachers. No one was better suited to fulfill this role than Billy Graham. The young preacher, who began his career as an itinerant youth evangelist with the evangelical parachurch organization Youth for Christ, crusaded throughout the United States and the world delivering the message of salvation through faith in Jesus Christ. Graham always understood his ministry to be more about winning souls than forging a cultural agenda for the nation, but he probably did more to contribute to the evangelical vision of a Christian America than any other figure. Graham used his sermons to rail against what he believed to be America's pressing moral problems. His messages were filled with jeremiads against divorce, promiscuous sex, materialism, alcohol abuse, and crime. The only way to overcome these social problems eroding the moral fabric of the United States was for individuals to turn to Jesus Christ. The Cold War often served as a backdrop for Graham's sermons, many of which included anticommunist rants. Unlike the atheistic Soviet Union, the United States was a Christian nation, or at least had the potential to become one if more people would accept Jesus as their personal Savior.[4]

According to Carpenter, evangelical Christians in the middle decades of the twentieth century continued to believe that they were the moral and religious "custodians" of American culture. They thus never lost their commitment, "despite their alienation" from the larger culture, to restoring America to its Christian roots. While all evangelicals believed that such cultural transformation must happen through revivalism and evangelism, others devised more subtle ways of winning the culture for Christ. A group of young, educated evangelicals sought to bring conservative theology into the mainstream of American intellectual and religious life. These so-called neo-evangelicals, who included Ockenga and theologians Carl F. H. Henry and Edward J. Carnell, had a deep concern for what they perceived to be the decline of Christian culture in the West. They set out to construct institutions, establish publications, and develop intellectual networks to cultivate an evangelical vision of cultural transformation. Neo-evangelicals founded Fuller Theological Seminary in Pasadena, California, in 1947 as an evangelical divinity school that would reject the separatist tendencies of fundamentalism by engaging in theological and religious dialogue with mainline and liberal Protestantism. The periodical *Christianity Today*, founded in 1956, was originally designed as a magazine that would bring evangelical theology to bear on American culture.[5] Though Fuller Seminary, *Christianity Today*, and other similar initiatives were never as successful as the neo-evangelicals had hoped they would be at moving the country in a Christian direction, they did represent significant evangelical attempts to Christianize America.

Mainline Protestantism and Christian America

As evangelicals focused on revivalism as a means of reclaiming America for Christ, mainline Protestants—the descendants of the Protestants who gained control of the denominations during the fundamentalist-modernist controversy of the 1920s—struggled to "win America." While evangelicals prospered within their own subculture during the 1930s and 1940s, mainliners suffered through what Carpenter has called a "religious depression."[6] The liberal Protestant dream of ushering in the second coming of Christ through efforts at moral reform seemed utopian and out of touch with the economic woes of American life. Enthusiasm for missionary activity was waning and financial contributions to churches were declining. This religious depression can be explained in a variety of ways. Many optimistic Protestants became disillusioned by the horrors of World War I. The war had discredited liberal Protestant ideas about wedding Christianity and progress. Of course, the economic depression of the 1930s had a lot to do with declines in financial contributions. And some have suggested that the decline is explained best by Protestant accommodation to American culture.[7]

Despite these difficulties, mainline Protestants fought doggedly to maintain their place as the religious custodians of American culture. The fight was no longer against the fundamentalists for control of Protestant denominations. Mainliners now saw themselves engaged in a larger culture war against two emerging forces in American life: secularism and Catholicism. In 1946 *The Christian Century*, the flagship periodical of mainline Protestantism, ran a thirteen-part series by retiring editor Charles Clayton Morrison entitled, "Can Protestantism Win America?"

Morrison noted that membership in mainline churches was growing, but Protestants were losing the battle for cultural influence. The mission of American Protestantism was not only to win souls and bring spiritual nourishment to the faithful, but to win the culture. Morrison lamented that Protestants were abandoning their "ascendant position in the American community" to the forces of secularism and the rising Catholic threat. Secularism was seen most prominently in three areas of American life: education, science, and popular entertainment.[8] Protestants had a responsibility, Morrison argued, to "incorporate the teaching of religion in the public school system, as an integral part of the curriculum." He did not advocate "indoctrination" or the "inculcation of religious devotion," but did urge school districts to consider the study of religion—all religions—as an essential academic subject. Science, Morrison believed, was a threat to Protestant cultural influence. He called for mainliners to integrate faith and science in ways that did not make scientific inquiry hostile to Christian faith. Commercial entertainment—the third prong of the secular assault on America—was producing a "cultural mentality" in young people that made it difficult for them to "respond to the truth of Christian faith." Such entertainment dulled the mind and prevented the cultivation of a "Protestant conscience."[9]

Morrison argued that mainline Protestantism was particularly poised to win back America. Evangelicals could not serve as a model for Protestant resurgence because they remained too isolated from modern culture. At the same time, liberal Protestantism had accommodated to culture to such an extent that it "played into the hands of secularism," creating an "adjusted Christianity" that was "conspicuously sterile."[10] He chided the leaders of the ecumenical movement within Protestantism for being more concerned with the ideas they shared with other world religions than with the uniqueness of Protestantism and the role it might play in Christianizing the United States. Furthermore, Protestants were too concerned with the politics and preservation of their specific denominations and as a result failed to express "either the richness or the power of the Christian faith." Any renewal of cultural Protestantism needed to be undergirded by the teachings of the Bible. According to Morrison, Protestants misused the Bible when they employed it solely to support their own distinctive views of Christianity. The Bible must always be subordinated to Christ's call for Christian unity and his lordship over the church. Morrison challenged local churches to see themselves as part of a biblically rooted ecumenical Protestant movement that transcended denominational identities and differences. He believed that if mainline Protestant churches would rally around these ideas they might have a chance to "win America."[11]

Catholic Resurgence

In 1895 Pope Leo XIII wrote a papal encyclical to the archbishops and bishops of the United States entitled "Longinqua" or "On Catholicism in the United States." The encyclical laid out a Catholic vision for the United States as the nation entered what would later be called "the

American Century." Leo reminded the American bishops that Catholicism had played an important role in the creation of the United States. Columbus had opened "a pathway for the Christian faith into new lands and new seas." Catholic priests—Dominicans, Franciscans, and Jesuits—had converted American Indians to Christianity. The many towns, rivers, and mountains named after Catholic missionaries and explorers pointed to the nation's rich Catholic past. Puritans were not the only group to claim a special place in God's plan for America. According to Leo, the advancement of the Catholic Church in North America was the "design of divine Providence." Even George Washington had struck up a close friendship with John Carroll, the first bishop of the Catholic Church in the United States. As Leo put it, "the well-known friendship and familiar intercourse which subsisted between these two men seems to be evidence that the United States ought to be conjoined in concord and amity with the Catholic Church." The church, Leo believed, offered the United States the kind of Christian virtue necessary for the Republic to survive.[12]

Leo painted a rather rosy picture of Catholicism in eighteenth- and nineteenth-century America. He failed to mention the overt anti-Catholicism of many of the founders and the attempts by Protestants to keep Catholics out of mainstream American culture. We have already examined some of this anti-Catholicism and will return to it again in our discussion of the religious beliefs of the founders in the third part of this book. But this encyclical suggests that Leo was conscious of some profound changes taking place in American life that might lead to a Catholic revival. Catholic immigrants were flooding American shores. In addition to the large number of German and Irish Catholics who had arrived just prior to the Civil War, massive numbers of southern and eastern Europeans were coming to America as part of what has been called the "new immigration." The demographic makeup of the country was changing, and the Catholic Church was ready to exert its power to Christianize America. As Leo put it, "America seems destined for greater things. Now it is Our wish that the Catholic Church should not only share in, but help bring about, this prospective greatness."[13]

As the United States grew and prospered, Leo urged his American bishops to make sure Catholicism grew and prospered with it. Leo praised the work that Catholics had already done in securing a foothold in American culture through the establishment of churches, colleges, hospitals, monasteries, and convents. The number of Catholic priests was growing and parochial schools were training a new generation of Catholics. Leo wanted to build from this success. He praised the work of Catholic University in Washington, D.C. Founded by Leo and the American bishops in 1887, Catholic University would be at the forefront of advancing Catholic learning. Leo believed that Catholic leadership in the field of science was a tangible way of contributing to American progress. He also encouraged Catholic labor unions, but warned against the kind of violence and rioting often associated with working-class resistance to low wages. Leo encouraged Catholics to pursue vocations in journalism in order to bring Catholic voices to the public sphere. And, of course, Catholics should be actively engaged in evangelism. "With mildness and charity," he instructed the bishops, "draw them to us, using every means of persuasion to induce them to examine closely every part of Catholic doctrine." Leo called attention to the mission field among American "Indians and the negroes" in the hopes that those who "have not yet dispelled the darkness of superstition" might find a home in the Catholic Church.[14]

Leo's charge was heeded by twentieth-century American Catholics. Historian Jay Dolan writes: "Catholics emerged from the experience of World War I confident and optimistic about the future. . . . Priests and lay people became involved in highly publicized convert crusades to win America to Christ." Such tactics bore fruit in the interwar period and post–World War II years; from 1945 to 1960 the Catholic population in the United States grew by 90 percent. Similar growth was seen in the number of bishops, priests, women religious, seminarians, hospitals, parochial schools, and colleges. Catholicism set out to build a "Christian culture" in the United States and in doing so seemed to pay little attention to the nation's dominant Protestant ethos. The Catholic attempt at Christianizing America required doing battle against the forces of secularism. Catholics led assaults against the secular and anti-Christian nature of popular culture, defended the family and condemned divorce, criticized the materialism of American capitalism, and excoriated communism's failure to respect the dignity of humanity. Dolan sums this resurgence up well: "Catholic intellectuals believed that Catholicism was more than just a religion, it was an 'important cultural reality.'" It should pervade every inch of American culture, including "literature, politics, philosophy, indeed even athletics."[15]

Needless to say, some Protestants were alarmed by this bold Catholic vision for a Christian nation. Harold Fey, a Protestant minister, editor, and writer, had an eight-part series in *The Christian Century* entitled, "Can Catholicism Win America?" Fey described in detail Rome's efforts to turn the United States into a Catholic nation. He described a change in American Catholicism that he believed should cause all good Protestants to take notice. Catholics were no longer content as religious outsiders in a predominantly Protestant culture. They were now acting "as a national church" with an agenda to reshape American character along Catholic lines. Using Robert S. and Helen Merrell Lynd's famed studies of Muncie, Indiana, or "Middletown," as a model, Fey showed the subtle ways in which Roman Catholicism might use "certain instruments of power" to take over an average American town. Catholics could call upon the National Catholic Church Extension Society to build more churches in Middletown. The National Confraternity of Christian Doctrine would fund the establishment of daily vacation Bible schools. Catholics could recruit "hundreds of orders of teaching nuns" to staff a host of new Catholic schools, and the Catholic Press Association could aid in the creation of a Catholic newspaper. Soon the Catholics in Middletown would want their own hospital and would call upon the National Catholic Hospital Association to build one. Catholic workers would appeal for support through the National Catholic Welfare Conference. Fey alerted his Protestant readers to Catholic initiatives to convert African Americans, defend the rights of workers, fight communism, and infiltrate rural America. He described a Catholic institutional machine on a mission to turn the United States into a Catholic nation. Was such a Catholic takeover possible? Fey concluded that it certainly was.[16]

The Revival of Christian America: The 1950s

As Morrison, Fey, and others expressed concerns in the 1940s over the rise of Catholicism, by the 1950s evangelical and mainline Protestants were experiencing growth of their own. The nation experienced nothing short of a religious revival. President Dwight D. Eisenhower set the agenda for this new awakening when he wrote, "Without God there could be no American form of government, nor an American way of life."[17] During the 1950s the U.S. population grew by 19 percent, but church attendance grew by 30 percent. Between 1951 and 1961 Protestants added over twelve million people to their ranks. Church giving also boomed. Between 1950 and 1955 financial contributions to some Protestant churches rose by close to 50 percent.[18]

What was most striking about this new revival of American religion was the sense of Protestant unity that it fostered. Differences between evangelicals and mainline Protestants did not disappear during this decade, but Protestants of all stripes shared a common purpose of responding to perceived threats from Catholics and Communists. Both groups actively pursued the goal of Protestant nationalism. Much to the chagrin of some evangelicals, Billy Graham reached out to mainline Protestant clergy by bringing them onto the platform during his crusades and giving them the opportunity to speak and pray. As we have seen, *The Christian Century*, the unofficial voice of the Protestant mainline, devoted much space to its concern over the rise of Catholicism in American life. The National Association of Evangelicals shared this fear of a Catholic takeover. At its 1950 meeting its members expressed its "grave concern" over the "militant and aggressive tactics of the Roman Catholic hierarchy within and upon our government."[19]

The 1950s also saw a close link between Christianity and the federal government. In November 1950 the National Council of Churches was formed in Cleveland. Those present at this meeting witnessed a ten-foot-high banner over the main platform that said, "This Nation Under God." In 1954 Congress approved an act to add the words "under God" to the Pledge of Allegiance. Once again, it was important during the Cold War for the United States to define itself as a God-fearing nation. Louis Rabaut, a Democratic congressman from Michigan and a supporter of the change to the pledge, wrote: "You may argue from dawn to dusk about differing political, economic, and social systems but the fundamental issue which is the unbridgeable gap between America and Communist Russia is a belief in Almighty God."[20] In 1955 this connection between God and the United States was further strengthened when Congress opted to put the words "In God We Trust" on all United States coins and currency. The following year it changed the national motto from "E pluribus unum" to "In God We Trust." Eisenhower was a strong supporter of what has been called America's "civil religion." He opened his cabinet meetings with prayer and even read a prayer at his inauguration ceremony. The Supreme Court in the case *Zorach v. Clauson* declared, "We are a religious people whose institutions presuppose a Supreme Being." If the United States was not a distinctively "Christian" nation in the 1950s, it was certainly a Judeo-Christian nation. This was the argument made by sociologist Will Herberg in his popular and influential book, *Protestant, Catholic, Jew*.[21]

Martin Luther King Jr.'s Vision for a Christian Nation

As white Protestants and Catholics waged war against each other and against the forces of secularism and communism, African Americans were engaged in their own battle for a Christian nation. Theirs was not a battle over amending the Constitution to make it more Christian or promoting crusades to have the name of God inserted into the Pledge of Allegiance. It was instead a battle against injustice and, for many, an attempt to promote a national community defined by Christian ideals of equality and respect for human dignity. Most historians now agree that this powerful social movement in American life was driven by the Christian faith of its proponents. As historian David Chappell has recently argued, the story of the civil rights movement is less about the triumph of progressive and liberal ideals and more about a revival of an Old Testament prophetic tradition that led African Americans to hold their nation accountable for the decidedly unchristian behavior it showed to many of its citizens.[22]

There was no more powerful leader for this kind of Christian America than Martin Luther King Jr., and no greater statement of this vision for America than his famous "Letter from a Birmingham Jail." King arrived in Birmingham in April 1963 and led demonstrations calling for an end to racist hiring practices and segregated public facilities. When King refused to end his protests, he was arrested by Eugene "Bull" Connor, the city's Public Safety Commissioner. During several days of solitary confinement, King wrote a letter to the Birmingham clergy who were opposed to the civil rights protests in the city. The "Letter from a Birmingham Jail," which was published in pamphlet form and circulated widely, offered a vision of Christian nationalism that challenged the localism and parochialism of the Birmingham clergy and called into question their own version of Christian America.

A fierce localism pervaded much of the South in the mid-twentieth century. For Southerners, nationalism conjured up memories of the Civil War and Reconstruction, a period when Northern nationalists—Abraham Lincoln, the "Radical Republican" Congress, and the so-called carpetbaggers—invaded the South in an attempt to force the region to bring its localism in line with a national vision informed by racial equality. When he arrived in Birmingham from Atlanta in the spring of 1963, King was perceived as an outside agitator intent upon disrupting the order of everyday life in the city. Many Birmingham clergy believed that segregation was a local issue and should thus be addressed at the local level. King rejected this kind of parochialism. He fought for moral and religious ideas such as liberty and freedom that were universal in nature. Such universal truths, King believed, should always trump local beliefs, traditions, and customs. As he put it, "I am in Birmingham because injustice is here." Justice was a universal concept that defined America. King reminded the Birmingham clergy that Thomas Jefferson and Abraham Lincoln had defended equality as a national creed, a creed to which he believed the local traditions of the Jim Crow South must conform. In his mind, all "communities and states" were interrelated. "Injustice anywhere," he famously wrote, "is a threat to justice everywhere." He added: "Anyone who lives inside the United States can never be considered an outsider anywhere within its bounds." This was King the nationalist at his rhetorical best.

King understood justice in Christian terms. The rights granted to all citizens of the United States were "God given." Segregation laws were unjust not only because they violated the principles of the Declaration of Independence ("all men are created equal") but because they did not conform to the laws of God. King argued, using the views of Augustine, Thomas Aquinas, and theologian Paul Tillich, that segregation was "morally wrong and sinful" because it degraded "human personality." Such a statement was grounded in the biblical idea that all human beings were created in the image of God and as a result possess inherent dignity and worth. King also used biblical examples of civil disobedience to make his point. Shadrach, Meshach, and Abednego took a stand for God's law over the law of King Nebuchadnezzar. Paul was willing to "bear in my body the marks of the Lord Jesus." And, of course, Jesus Christ was "an extremist for love, truth, and goodness" who "rose above his environment."

In the end, Birmingham's destiny was connected to the destiny of the entire nation—a nation with a "sacred heritage" influenced by the "eternal will of God." By fighting against segregation, King reminded the Birmingham clergy that he was standing up for "what is best in the American dream and for the most sacred values in our Judeo-Christian heritage, thereby bringing our nation back to those great wells of democracy which were dug deep by the founding fathers in their formulation of the Constitution and the Declaration of Independence." The civil rights movement, as King understood it, was in essence an attempt to construct a new kind of Christian nation—a beloved community of love, harmony, and equality.[23]

The Religious Right and Christian Nationalism

The 1960s were not good years for American evangelicals concerned about the Christian identity of the United States. The counterculture seemed to be challenging the kind of morality necessary for a Christian republic to survive. The feminist movement empowered women in a way that led them to reject what some evangelicals saw as women's God-given place in society. Rock and roll music and the culture that came with it glorified drugs, alcohol, and free sex. In 1962 the Supreme Court, in *Engel v. Vitale*, made prayer in school unconstitutional. A year later, in *Abington Township School District v. Schempp*, the high court declared Bible reading in public schools to be unconstitutional. Though a "silent majority" of conservatives would manage to vote Richard Nixon into office in 1968, the culture had apparently given way to forces intent upon undermining the idea of a "Christian America."

In the early 1970s two significant Supreme Court cases galvanized evangelicals who were concerned about the fate of Christian America. In *Green v. Connally* (1971) the Supreme Court ruled that a private school or college that discriminated on the basis of race would no longer be considered for tax-exempt status. At the heart of this controversy was Bob Jones University, a school that banned interracial dating and denied admission to unmarried African Americans. In 1975 the IRS moved to revoke the tax-exempt status of the university. *Green v. Connally* would also have implications for the hundreds of private Christian schools cropping up all over the United States. Many of these schools were in the South and had discriminatory admissions policies. When Jimmy Carter, a self-proclaimed "born-again Christian," threw his support behind *Green v. Connally*, he alienated many conservative evangelicals, including Virginia Baptist pastor Jerry Falwell, Christian psychologist James Dobson, and Christian Right activist Paul Weyrich. These conservatives believed that the president and the Supreme Court were undermining the liberty of Christians to form their own schools in their own way, without interference from the federal government. By 1976, the year that *Newsweek* declared to be "The Year of the Evangelical," the so-called Christian Right had organized into a full-blown political movement.[24]

The second major Supreme Court case that mobilized the Christian Right was *Roe v. Wade*, which legalized certain types of abortion in the United States in 1973. Prior to *Roe v. Wade* abortion had never been an important issue for evangelicals. Most evangelicals believed abortion was morally suspect, but thought of opposition to abortion as a distinctly Catholic cause. This all changed, however, after 1973. More and more evangelicals began to publicly oppose abortion and *Roe v. Wade*. Many of them were awakened to a belief that abortion was equivalent to legalized murder.

The leaders of this new "Christian Right" found theological and philosophical support for their views from the teachings of Christian intellectual Francis Schaeffer. From his chalet in the Swiss Alps called L'Abri, Schaeffer had developed a reputation as a thoughtful evangelical at a time when the movement lacked serious intellectual depth. He attracted hundreds of bright young evangelical minds to L'Abri, where he taught them how to formulate a "Christian world view." By the mid-1970s Schaeffer was a household name among American evangelicals. Following *Roe v. Wade* he also became convinced that the fight against abortion was worth his time and energy. In a popular film series entitled *How Should We Then Live*, Schaeffer challenged *Roe v. Wade* on legal and philosophical grounds and defended the dignity of all human life. His ideas were soon being used by Falwell and other members of the Christian Right.[25]

As the leaders of the Christian Right continued their battles against the IRS and abortion, they also began to dabble in the field of history. The American Bicentennial offered an ideal moment for the Christian Right to put forward a revisionist narrative of the founding of the United States that placed God at the center. In his book *Listen, America!* (1980), written in the wake of the bicentennial, Falwell argued that the American founders "were not all Christians, but they were guided by biblical principles. They developed a nation predicated on Holy Writ. The religious foundations of America find their roots in the Bible." Like many of today's Christian nationalist writers who appeal to the past, Falwell worked his way through early American history—from the Pilgrims to the American Revolution—noting whenever an early settler or founder invoked the name of God in public discourse, made reference to the providential destiny of the United States, or defended the belief that religion was essential to the survival of the Republic.[26] According to the leaders of the Christian Right, history proved that the United States was a Christian nation. Somewhere along the way Americans had failed to learn this important civics lesson.

Francis Schaeffer played an important role in shaping the Christian Right's belief in a Christian America. As Schaeffer's prolific writings began to take on a more activist tone, he became interested in the writings of Christian Reconstructionist Rousas John Rushdoony. Reconstructionists like Rushdoony believed that Old Testament civil law should be binding on the people of the United States. Though Schaeffer did not agree with all of Rushdoony's ideas, he was influenced by the Reconstructionist view that the United States was founded upon biblical principles. In 1981 Schaeffer argued in *A Christian Manifesto* that American democracy was founded upon biblical ideas passed along in a direct line from the Protestant Reformation, to the works of seventeenth-century

writer Samuel Rutherford, to eighteenth-century Christian minister and
Founding Father John Witherspoon, to the writing of the Declaration of
Independence. He also used this book to criticize a liberal understanding
of the First Amendment, arguing that the amendment was being used
to "silence the church" whereas it was originally written to protect the
church from government interference. As historian Barry Hankins has
shown, Schaeffer engaged in an extended private debate on these issues
with evangelical historians Mark Noll and George Marsden, who, in
1983, would join Nathan Hatch in writing *The Search for Christian America*, a work that was in many ways a direct response to Schaeffer and the
members of the Christian Right who relied upon his writings about the
American founding.[27]

We will explore the writings of some of these Christian nationalists
in the next chapter, but we should note that this view of American history got a great boost from the presidency of Ronald Reagan. Reagan
was fond of talking about the Christian roots of American freedom,
often mentioning the seventeenth-century Puritan belief that the United
States was a "city upon a hill." Reagan was not only successful in merg-
ing American exceptionalism with Christian ideals, but he managed to
win many over to an understanding of American nationalism based upon
these ideals. Even the South, a region that largely rejected this kind of
nationalism, turned away from its Democratic roots and joined the Reagan Revolution. By the time Reagan would leave office the people of
the South would be transformed into some of the strongest defenders of
Christian nationalism.

In conclusion, those who want to argue that the United States is a Christian nation have some strong historical evidence on which to rely, but
they also must realize that Christian nationalism took many different
forms during the twentieth century. Evangelicals, mainline Protestants,
African American Protestants, and Roman Catholics were united in their
desire to make the United States a Christian country, but they were
divided on just what such a nation might look like. By the 1970s the man-
tle of Christian America had been taken up by the Christian Right, and
they have used it as a tool to promote their moral and political agenda
ever since. Our next chapter turns to those contemporary defenders of
Christian America and explores the way they have managed to articulate
a historical narrative that has won the hearts and the minds of millions of
conservative evangelicals.

Chapter Four

History for the Faithful

The Contemporary Defenders of Christian America

In the twenty-first century the idea that the United States was founded as a Christian nation is alive and well. One might even say that this view of the American past is thriving. There are millions of Christian nationalists in the United States today. We watch them preach every Sunday morning, we sit next to them in Sunday school, we meet them at homeschooling co-ops and Christian school parents' association meetings, we see them on our television screens, and we may even elect them to political office. Perhaps you are one of them. Those who believe that America is a Christian nation are serious about their faith in God and country. They have an earnest and commendable desire to influence the nation for Christ and celebrate the freedoms we enjoy as citizens of the United States. They find the study of history as one way of promoting this belief.

Most of what the general public knows about those who embrace this view of American history comes from the mouths and words of pundits who see a "Christian" view of the nation's past as a threat. These commentators often paint with broad strokes, using words like "fascists" or "theocrats" to describe evangelicals who believe that the United States is a Christian nation. They quote selectively from the writings of their subjects and tend to cite the most controversial, inflammatory, or egregious passages from their work. (Of course, the Christian America defenders often fall into the same trap in criticizing their opponents.) There has yet to be a sustained and thorough attempt to understand this view of the American past and the agenda of those who propagate it. How, specifically, do these Christians interpret the founding of the United States? Why is it so important that they prove that the founders were Christian believers who set out to create a Christian nation? Why do they fear "revisionist history"? This chapter provides some answers to these questions.

As we saw in the previous three chapters, the belief that the United States was founded as a Christian nation has a long history that dates back to the beginning of the Republic. But recently strong and tireless voices have championed the Christian America cause. They have been influential in convincing members of the evangelical rank and file that such an interpretation of American history is correct. The most prolific of these voices is David Barton, the founder of WallBuilders, a ministry devoted to "presenting America's forgotten history and heroes with an emphasis on our moral, religious, and constitutional heritage."[1] It is hard to separate Barton's historical work from his political passions. He served eight years as the vice chair of the Texas Republic Party, the same political organization whose 2004 platform included the line: "the United States of America is a Christian nation." Barton's books and videos about America's Christian heritage have sold thousands of copies, and he speaks widely on the subject to large evangelical audiences, both in person and through his radio and television ministry. In 2005 *Time* named Barton one of the twenty-five most influential evangelicals in America.

Peter Marshall and David Manuel are also defenders of the idea that America was founded as a Christian nation. Their work may even be more popular than Barton's. They are the authors of *The Light and the Glory*, a providential history of early America. This book has sold close to one million copies, and for many evangelicals it is the only history book they have ever read. Though it was first published over thirty years ago, *The Light and the Glory* continues to be a fixture on the bookshelves of American evangelicals. A new edition appeared in 2009.

Before his death in 2007, D. James Kennedy, the former pastor of the Coral Ridge Presbyterian Church in Fort Lauderdale, Florida, and the creator of the "Evangelism Explosion" method of evangelism, was churning out books and DVDs extolling the Christian America position. Much of his nationally syndicated television program, "The Coral Ridge Hour," is devoted to promoting these views of America's past. In 1996 he founded the Center for Reclaiming America with a mission to "renew the vision of our Founding Fathers, as expressed in America's founding documents." The center recently shut down operations, but it still maintains a Web site and holds conferences related to its mission.

Other significant promoters of the Christian America viewpoint include Vision Forum Ministries, the organization behind the "Jamestown Quadricentennial" celebration discussed briefly at the beginning of this book.

Based in San Antonio, one of Vision Forum's stated goals is "Teaching History as the Providence of God." Tim LaHaye, a Christian writer known today for the best-selling *Left Behind* series of apocalyptic novels, has also made this theme part of his eclectic and productive ministry. So has Gary DeMar, a radio host and author who has written extensively on the Christian roots of America under the umbrella of his organization, "The American Vision." Finally, this interpretation of American history reaches hundreds of thousands of elementary and high school students through the writers of American history textbooks published by A Beka Publishers and Bob Jones University Press, two of the nation's most successful distributors of Christian school and Christian homeschooling materials.

After reading extensively in these writings I have boiled today's Christian nation view of early American history down to five central themes. The defenders of Christian America teach that:

1. *God is sovereign over history.* God has acted providentially to shape the course of human affairs, and he has a special destiny for the United States that can be accurately discerned and explained by historians.
2. *The seventeenth-century settlement of the American colonies should be interpreted in light of the eighteenth-century American Revolution.* In other words, they search the colonial (pre-1763) record— with a particular emphasis on the Puritans and Pilgrims of New England—in an attempt to find the antecedents of the Christian nation that they believe was founded in 1776.
3. *Most of the signers of the Declaration of Independence and the framers of the U.S. Constitution were men of deep Christian faith.* At the very least, they argue, the founders believed that Christianity was essential and necessary to the survival of the American Republic.
4. *The Constitution of the United States is a Christian document, rooted in biblical and theological truth.* Some argue that it was designed to create a Christian establishment of religion in America.
5. *Historical revisionism, especially as it relates to school textbooks, is irresponsible and dangerous.* Revisionists, they argue, have removed Christianity from the stories of the nation's past taught to children in public schools. This trend has had serious moral and social consequences for the nation.

Let's explore more fully some of these historical arguments, beginning with the belief in "providence."

Providence

Marshall and Manuel begin *The Light and the Glory* by informing their readers, "In truth, this book is not intended to be a history textbook, but rather a search for the hand of God in the different periods of our nation's beginnings."[2] This is an interesting statement in light of the fact that thousands of Christians have taken this book to be a definitive account of early American history and have not hesitated in using it as a textbook in Christian schools and home schools. *The Light and the Glory*, by its own authors' admission, is more theology than history, but other defenders of Christian America do not seem to be bothered by the distinction between these two different approaches to knowing. Those who have "searched for the hand of God in . . . our nation's beginnings" often market their books as authoritative historical studies.

Writers extolling a providential view of American history begin with the theological premise that God is sovereign over his creation and continues to order the universe that he has created. There are no coincidences. Nothing that has happened in the past can be explained by random chance. God has intervened in human history in miraculous ways in order to accomplish his purposes. President George W. Bush, a favorite of the Christian America defenders, reflected this view when he reminded the nation in his first inaugural address that "an angel rides in the whirlwind and directs this storm."[3]

Many history textbooks written from the Christian America perspective thus begin with the assumption that God is in control of history, God's plan for history has Jesus Christ at the center, and history is best understood as a "battle of the ages" between God and Satan.[4] A Bob Jones textbook starts by reminding students that "nothing in history is accidental; our sovereign God directs the affairs of men and nations to accomplish His will. As you begin your study of the history of the United States, keep in mind that God has likewise directed—and is still directing—America's history." History is indeed "His Story."[5]

The specific study of American history illuminates best God's true plan for the ages. The history of the United States is more important than any other era or region on the globe, save that of ancient Israel. This is because God has given the United States of America a unique destiny. In the seventeenth century he chose America to be his new Israel in the North American wilderness and has ever since reserved for it a special place in his design for his creation. The growth of the United States as a twentieth-century superpower and the world's great defender of democracy and freedom confirm this assertion.

Behind all of this is the idea that God establishes covenants with nations much in the same way he made Israel his chosen people. When things have gone wrong in America—as they have on numerous occasions in the nation's past—it is because the people of the United States have not remained obedient to God. As Barton writes, "The Founders understood that the principle of Divine rewards and punishments applied not only to individual leaders but also to the nation and its policies. The primary difference was that rewards and punishments for nations occurred in *this* world rather than the next." Marshall and Manuel ask: "What if, in addition to the intimate relationship with the individual through Jesus Christ the Savior, God continued to deal with nations corporately, as He had throughout Old Testament history? What if, in particular, He had a plan for those He would bring to America, a plan which saw this continent as the stage for the next act in the drama of mankind's redemption?"[6] Such a view of the relationship between God and the United States has been an important part of America's self-identity ever since John Winthrop, the first Puritan governor of the Massachusetts Bay Colony, described this settlement of devout English Calvinists as a "City upon a Hill."[7]

Writers in this vein are quick to call attention to the fact that some of America's greatest revolutionary statesmen shared this sense of the nation's uniqueness. One Christian textbook cites John Adams, who, in the wake of the signing of the Declaration of Independence, wrote, "I always consider the settlement of America with reverence and wonder, as the opening of a grand scheme and design in Providence for the illumination and emancipation of the slavish part of mankind over all the earth." Though Adams's remark was not overtly Christian in nature (it did not mention Jesus Christ), it is the kind of comment that offers a rationale for America's long history of spreading democracy across the world. Again, the words of George W. Bush, written by evangelical speechwriter Michael Gerson, are instructive here. Though careful not to describe America as a "Christian nation," Bush echoed Adams's sense of American destiny in his second inaugural address when he spoke of America's divine mandate to spread freedom all over the world. Other Christian writers have been more overt about this view of America's global purpose. Tim LaHaye describes the United States as a "miracle nation" that God raised up to "preach the gospel to the ends of the earth." D. James

Kennedy adds: "God established this land of America, a nation in His providence, a nation unique in the history of the world."[8]

If God is indeed ordering the universe according to his plan, then the job of the historian, according to the defenders of Christian America, is to identify and proclaim his purposes as it played out in the past. The historian has a prophetic role. She is not unlike the Old Testament prophets who reminded Israel of God's history of faithfulness to them in the hopes that the people might turn to God and repent of their sins in the present and the future. These Christian writers are confident in their ability to explain God's purposes in American history, and they fuse the stories they tell about the American past with this kind of prophetic insight. This is seen clearly in a student exercise included in the teacher's manual for Bob Jones University Press's *The American Republic for Christian Schools*. The exercise asks students to consider what might have been different had the Pilgrims landed in the already established Jamestown colony rather than in Plymouth (what today is the Cape Cod region of Massachusetts). The guide then asks teachers to encourage their students to "find other evidences of God's sovereignty in the success of the Pilgrim colony." Possible answers include God's sending of the Indian Squanto to help the settlers and his provision of outstanding leaders in the early years of the colony's founding. Later in the text, students are asked to contemplate the reasons that God allowed the American Revolution to take place at the time that it did.[9] The idea, of course, is that teachers and students, working together in a Christian classroom, might be able to fathom the specific will of God in human history.

What does this type of providential history look like in the historical narratives written by the defenders of Christian America? How do providential themes intersect with the details of the American past? Some of these textbooks begin their journey through American history with coverage of the tribes who inhabited North American soil before European exploration, but most of them bypass Native American history and start with Christopher Columbus. These writers have found a special place for Columbus in God's plan for the United States. God anointed Columbus's mission and providentially sustained him along the way. Marshall and Manuel suggest that Columbus's "accidental" founding of America was not an accident at all, but an event that opened the "curtain of an extraordinary drama." God saved Columbus from storms and Indian attacks, but the explorer's arrogance, lust for power, and greed for gold (the "devil's tool") drew him away from the "original purpose of his mission—and his life." God had used Columbus—but only up to a point. His sin, and the sin of the explorers who followed him, meant that the Spanish "were destined not to thrive or come into the mainstream of what God had planned for America."[10]

Any student who reads these works carefully would learn that God is a Protestant, and probably an Anglo-Saxon. There is an anti-Catholic bias in much of the discussion of Columbus's voyages. Though Marshall and Manuel are willing to admit that God worked his will through Columbus, most writers in this genre are quick to imply that God, following the initial phase of exploration in the Americas, had ceased using Roman Catholics to carry out his plans. God's designs for America were Protestant in nature. Those familiar with conservative evangelicalism should not be surprised that this is the case. Though evangelicals and Catholics have made great strides in recent years toward bridging their Reformation-era differences, pockets of anti-Catholic sentiment continue to exist in American Protestantism, and the defenders of Christian America make up one of the strongest of these bastions.

For example, in recounting Columbus's first voyage, D. James Kennedy describes a moment when a flock of birds led the explorer's fleet to land at San Salvador. Had the birds—a sign that land was near—not appeared, the ships would have continued on their course until they hit what today is northern Florida. Kennedy concludes that if it were not for the providential appearance of these birds, Columbus and his crew would have ended up founding land that today is part of the United States. He puts it this way: "And to think, if it had not been for the flight of some birds, America would probably have the same culture and religion as that of South and Central America today. . . . I believe that just as God used a talking donkey to set Balaam straight (Num. 22:21–31), so He used a cloud and a flight of birds to change Columbus's destination." It is not difficult to read between the lines of Kennedy's remarks: God intervened in human history to make sure that the United States would not be a Spanish-Catholic nation. But just to make sure that no one misses his point, Kennedy concludes by adding: "Therefore, Anglo-Saxons and Celtics rather than Spaniards became the dominant force in Europe and in America. The hand of God? Or mere coincidence?"[11]

When it comes to the earliest English settlement of the North American colonies, New England has a privileged place in these historical narratives. This makes perfect sense, since it was the colonies of Plymouth and Massachusetts Bay that most openly set out to construct a Christian society. New England was the place where the notion of America as God's new Israel began. For Marshall and Manuel, the Pilgrims who arrived on the *Mayflower* in 1620 were "The Army of Light" that "established a beachhead in the new Promised Land." Those "who had eyes to see it recognized it as a miracle from God, of a magnitude which had seldom been equaled in the previous sixteen hundred years of the Church's history." An A Beka high school American history textbook describes Plymouth as the place where God instituted representative democracy, religious toleration, political freedom, and government based upon biblical principles.[12]

God is everywhere in the stories told by Christian nationalists about the Plymouth and Massachusetts Bay colonies. When the English ship *Speedwell*, the vessel that was originally designed to carry the Pilgrims to the New World, had trouble with its masts, forcing it to turn back after three days at sea, several Pilgrims had second thoughts about taking the voyage to America and chose instead to stay home in England. According to Marshall and Manuel, the *Speedwell*'s difficulties were part of God's plan to "separate the wheat from the chaff," to remove those individuals whom he did not want to be part of the settler community at Plymouth. D. James Kennedy interprets the epidemic that killed off most of the local Wampanoag Indians of Cape Cod several years prior to the anchoring of the *Mayflower* as a scourge from God to protect the Pilgrims. If God did not intervene, Kennedy argues, the natives "would have slaughtered those Pilgrims in the first few days of their arrival." One textbook attributes James I's persecution of the Pilgrims in England as a blessing in disguise and attributes the Indian guide Squanto's pre-Plymouth exposure to European Christianity as a direct sign of God's care for the settlers.[13]

But if Plymouth and Massachusetts Bay were the soil where the seeds of God's plan for a new nation devoted to democracy and religious freedom could grow, then how do the Christian nationalists explain the long history of religious intolerance that characterized these colonies? What about people like Roger Williams, Anne Hutchinson, and a host of Quakers and Baptists who were removed from the colony, and in a few cases even executed, for their lack of conformity to Puritan theology and a government based upon that theology? Marshall and Manuel analyze these dissenters to the "Puritan Way" in a chapter entitled "The Pruning of the Lord's Vineyard." Roger Williams, America's first defender of liberty of conscience in matters of religion, is portrayed in *The Light and the Glory* as a sinner who refused to submit to the authority of the Puritan magistrates. Anne Hutchinson, a woman Bible teacher who was ousted from the Massachusetts Bay Colony for, among other things, her claim to speak directly to God, is described as a tool of Satan. According to Marshall and Manuel, the voices that Hutchinson claimed to have heard, and that she attributed to God, were actually of Satan, who can deceive people into believing that their "inner voices" are the voice of God. When Hutchinson gave birth to a deformed baby after she left Massachusetts Bay, Marshall and Manuel, like most of the Puritans of the day, suggest that this may have been a sign of Satan's work and a confirmation that her religious views were wrong. In the end, Williams and Hutchinson stood in the way of God's plan for America. As a result, "the Vinedresser" was forced to "remove two aberrant shoots that were producing wild grapes."[14]

Of course the ultimate moment in God's plan for America occurred in 1776. The defenders of Christian America see the hand of God in almost every major event surrounding the American Revolution—from the meetings of the Continental Congress to the battles of the Continental Army. It was God's will for America to "break forcibly" with England. This was an event comparable to the ancient Israelites' desire to break free from Egypt during the time of the exodus. One Vision Forum textbook suggests that George III's rejection of American petitions of protest against English taxes was like the "hardening of Pharaoh's heart." These writers believe that God raised up Christian men to lead the nation to independence against the sinful and tyrannical British.[15]

The most important of these men was George Washington, the general of the Continental Army. God had not only preserved Washington's life in several military campaigns during the French and Indian War, but had now given him a divine mission to bring freedom to the colonies. God watched over his chosen vessel at every moment of battle, directing the outcome toward his sovereign plan. The examples of this kind of divine protection addressed in Christian nation textbooks are too abundant to chronicle here, but one event is worth mentioning: Washington's late-night retreat from Long Island in the wake of the Battle of Brooklyn. The description of this event is providential history at its best. On the evening of August 29, following a day of defeat at the Battle of Long Island, the American troops found themselves healing their wounds and trying to regroup. The British army was entrenched in the earth only yards away from the American fortifications on Brooklyn Heights, hoping to deal the final blow to this so-called war for independence. As nightfall came, Washington's troops began to abandon their posts in order to parade to ferries that would take them across the East River and to the safety of Manhattan. Between 7:00 p.m. and the following morning Washington had evacuated nearly ten thousand Continental troops. The commander was aided by a dense fog that lingered over the East River long enough to shield the American ferries from the sight of the British navy. For Marshall and Manuel, that fog was a sign of God's providence. It was "the most amazing episode of divine intervention in the Revolutionary War." The lesson learned from this event was an obvious one: God had intervened on behalf of the American army. Washington may have suffered a defeat at Long Island, but God, through the storm, had saved the Continental Army.

Christian Whig History

For these Christian nationalists, the American Revolution was the penultimate event in the history of the world. They celebrate an approach to the study of the past known as "Whig history." The term was coined in 1931 by British historian Herbert Butterfield to describe the practice of interpreting the past as an ever-constant progression toward freedom and democracy. In the context of Butterfield's Britain, Whig historians emphasized moments in England's past that would help the British explain the rise of Parliament and the limits it placed on monarchy. The task of the Whig historian is to mine the past for events that foreshadow the kinds of constitutional reforms that led to greater liberties. The name "Whig" comes from the eighteenth-century English party that supported Parliament and liberty against their "Tory" opponents, who supported the monarchy and order. Whig historians of the early American past have been inclined to interpret the colonial period through the grid of the Revolution. For these historians the purpose of studying the history of the British-American colonies is to locate the intellectual and political antecedents of the United States. While most professional early American historians have abandoned a Whig approach to the past, leaving it to older nineteenth-century historians of the Revolutionary era, the defenders of Christian America continue to embrace it. These writers study America's pre-1776 history in order to find examples of nascent democracy. They interpret every significant event in colonial life to show how it served, in some way, as a forerunner to the American Revolution and the Christian nation that the Revolution would create.

This kind of Whig history is applied to events that occurred as far back as the Age of Exploration. Marshall and Manuel describe the martyrdom of sixteenth- and seventeenth-century Spanish and French priests at the hands of Native American tribes as part of God's design for the United

States: "In soil watered with the blood of their sacrifice, God could now plant the seeds of the nation which was to become the New Promised Land." Rather than interpreting Spanish and French missionary activity as an attempt to convert the American Indians to Catholicism and advance the cause of the mother country in the mercantile work of the seventeenth-century West, the Christian nationalist thinks that the stories of these missionaries are important for the way they provide a historical precursor to the creation of the United States. A Bob Jones University Press textbook describes a "stubborn streak of independence that ran through the colonies," which, as we find later in the story, reached its full potential in 1776. Gary DeMar asserts, "Our nation begins not in 1776, but more than one hundred fifty years earlier."[16]

Some events in colonial America are more suitable to a Whig interpretation than others. Once again, seventeenth-century Plymouth and Massachusetts Bay serve as fertile ground in the historical search for the seeds of a Christian nation. Marshall and Manuel make a direct connection between the Mayflower Compact, the first governing document of the Plymouth colony, and the Declaration of Independence, composed 156 years later: "Such ringing affirmations as 'We hold these truths to be self-evident, that all men were created equal' would have to wait another century and a half, but here was their introduction onto American soil." Michael R. Lowman, the author of an A Beka American history textbook, describes the government of Plymouth as a representative government dominated by "Scriptural concepts." Over in Massachusetts Bay, Lowman adds, the Puritans "endowed America with a rich heritage, promoting Biblical morality, individual responsibility, industry, frugality and education." In emphasizing these seventeenth-century forms of government and cultural practices, these authors are claiming to have found the Christian roots of the United States as it was formed between 1776 and 1787.[17]

The First Great Awakening is another moment in colonial history that fits nicely with the Whig view of early America. Nearly all defenders of a Christian America make a direct connection between this religious revival and the coming of the American Revolution. Marshall and Manuel write that George Whitefield, the chief propagator of the revival through his extensive evangelical preaching ministry throughout the British Empire, came to America because he wanted to unite the thirteen colonies and help to create "one nation under God." Since the theological message of the Great Awakening was based on the individual's equality before God, it must have had a direct effect on the fight for equality taken up by American patriots a generation or so later. The revival created the kind of liberty and spiritual fraternity that would come to full maturity when the colonies became a nation. Lowman suggests something similar: "In his providential mercy, God brought spiritual revival to America through the Great Awakening, giving the colonists a strong moral foundation on which to build a new nation." The Awakening "prepared people's hearts for religious and political freedom." It drew the colonists together "and prepared them for independence by creating a kindred spirit among people of different denominations and colonies." A textbook published by the Vision Forum takes this a step further, asserting, "Without the Great Awakening there would have been no American Revolution. . . . The Godly environment of the Awakening deeply affected and helped prepare them for their destiny."[18]

The Founders and Christian Belief

It is absolutely essential for the defenders of Christian America to prove that the majority of the so-called founders—the signers of Declaration of Independence, the members of the Constitutional Convention, the early members of Congress, the first justices of the Supreme Court, and the members of George Washington's presidential cabinet—were believers.[19] These writers assume that if the founders were Christians, then they must have opposed the separation of church and state and favored the establishment of Christianity as the official national religion. David Barton puts it this way: "If the Founders were generally men of faith, then it is inconceivable that they would establish policies to limit expressions of that faith. However, if the contemporary portrayal is correct, and if, as many claim, the Founders were by and large a collective group of atheists, agnostics, and deists, then it is logical that they would not want religious activities as a part of official public life." According to Barton and other writers like him, the United States has lost its way. A return to the founders' beliefs—especially their religious vision for the nation—is the only way to get it back on the right track.[20]

We have little space to examine the immense list of founders' quotations that these writers use to defend the notion that America was founded as a Christian nation (I discuss the faith of the individual founders in part 3), but a few general observations are worth noting. Tim LaHaye argues that the members of the Constitutional Convention were elected because of their Christian faith and would not have been chosen if they were not orthodox believers. George Washington, he adds with an evangelical flourish, "was a devout believer in Jesus Christ and had accepted Him as

His Lord and Savior." As evidence to prove Washington was a Christian, some defenders of Christian America appeal to the story of his prayer while leading the Continental Army during the winter of 1777–1778 at Valley Forge. Many of their books include the popular late-nineteenth-century print of the event with Washington kneeling in the snow, hands clasped in prayer. (The image graces the cover of Barton's book *America's Godly Heritage*.) Other textbooks place emphasis on Benjamin Franklin's call for prayer at a particularly contentious moment in the Constitutional Convention or fill the pages of their books with quotations dug from the papers of the founders that offer positive references to God, Jesus Christ, or Christianity. Many of these writers have found a most valuable resource in William J. Federer's book *America's God and Country: Encyclopedia of Quotations*. On some occasions, however, the defenders of Christian America uncover words attributed to the founders that, in fact, they never uttered. Barton has listed several "unconfirmed quotations" on his Web site that critics have discovered were fabricated or drawn from secondary sources that inaccurately attributed them to founders.[21]

Some of the founders openly rejected many of the tenets of historic Christianity, making it very difficult to cast them as orthodox Christian believers. Advocates of the Christian America view of history have a hard time placing statesmen such as Thomas Jefferson or Benjamin Franklin in the evangelical fold. Yet, they argue, even these heterodox founders still saw the importance of Christianity for the health and welfare of the American Republic. According to Barton, the founders believed that the teachings of Christ (over that of other religious teachers in history) provided the greatest means of cultivating a civil society. LaHaye argues that though Benjamin Franklin was not an orthodox Christian, he did have a clear sense that a providential God—even a God who answered prayer—was ordering the universe. D. James Kennedy reminds his readers that the founders wanted to promote Christian virtue as the best check to the kinds of vices, passions, and license that could destroy a democracy. As the argument goes, some of the founders may not have been Christians, but they certainly respected Christianity and understood it, to use the words of Washington, as an "indispensable support" of popular government.[22]

Religion and the Constitution

No argument defending the idea that America was founded as a Christian nation would be complete without a sustained treatment of the U.S. Constitution. These writers are strong adherents to an "original intent" interpretation of this foundational American document. The supporters of original intent believe that in order to understand what the Constitution means for us today we must grasp what the framers of the document had in mind when they wrote it and then apply their views to the contemporary issues under consideration. The defenders of a Christian America have little tolerance for progressive Supreme Court justices who treat the Constitution as a "living" document that must be amended and interpreted to meet the challenges of a given era.

How then, according to these writers, should we understand the original intent of the constitutional framers? First, the Constitution is a document with deep roots in Christian theology, particularly Calvinism. Marshall and Manuel describe it as the "culmination of nearly two hundred years of Puritan political thought." LaHaye writes that the Constitution was rooted in a Calvinist view of humankind. Michael Lowman's *United States History* textbook echoes LaHaye, suggesting that James Madison, the primary architect of the document, brought a Calvinist view of human nature to the Constitution that he learned from his college teacher John Witherspoon, the evangelical president of the College of New Jersey at Princeton. Most of the members of the Constitutional Convention, Lowman suggests, believed in creating "a strong government based upon sound Biblical principles which recognized man's rights and responsibilities." If the advocates of original intent can prove that the Constitution was rooted in Christian beliefs, then they can argue that the political and social order it brought to the nation in the wake of the American Revolution was definitively Christian.[23]

Of particular interest to the defenders of Christian America is the First Amendment's religion clause: "Congress shall make no law respecting an establishment of religion, or prohibiting the free exercise thereof." This clause, they argue, does not teach a full-blown separation of church and state in the way suggested by organizations like the American Civil Liberties Union. They insist that the Constitution allows for open expressions of faith in public life. Christian America writers are quick to note that the phrase, a "wall of separation between church and state," does not appear in the Constitution, but comes instead, as we will see in chapter 10, from an 1802 letter that Thomas Jefferson wrote to a group of Baptists in Danbury, Connecticut.

The villain behind the view of separation of church and state currently peddled by liberal organizations and politicians is the 1947 Supreme Court. This was the Court that handed down the verdict in the now famous *Everson v. Board of Education* case. In that decision the Court declared, borrowing from Jefferson's letter to the Danbury Baptists (and not the words of the Constitution itself), that there should be a "wall" of separation between church and state. The court concluded that this wall should be "high and impregnable" (Jefferson did not use these words in his letter). According to the defenders of Christian America, this case provides a perfect example of what happens when the high court strays from the original intent of the framers of the Constitution and allows other sources to shape its decisions about how the meaning of the document should be applied.[24]

As one might expect, the Christian America advocates have their own way of interpreting the First Amendment, one that differs fundamentally from the 1947 Court. This interpretation focuses on two interrelated points. The first addresses the phrase, "Congress shall make no law respecting an establishment of religion." In the context of the eighteenth century, they assert, this phrase means that the framers rejected the idea of a religious establishment of one specific *Christian* denomination. In other words, the framers did not want one denomination or sect to have a special relationship with the federal government in the way that church and state were so closely connected in Europe. It was wrong, they believed, for Christians to be forced to pay taxes to a denomination to which they were not affiliated just because that denomination enjoyed the special privilege of being an "established" church.

But these writers do not stop there. If the framers did reject the idea of one established Christian sect, they did not reject the idea that there should be a general "Christian" establishment made up of denominations of all stripes. The United States was a Christian nation, defined by Christian pluralism. (It may be more accurate to say that it was a Protestant nation defined by Protestant pluralism.) The beliefs of Christianity would shape the moral fabric of the nation and the Christian faith would hold a special position in society. This means that Christian expressions of faith should be not only permitted but encouraged throughout the nation. It also means that those of non-Christian faiths would be tolerated, but would need to learn how to live with the Christian culture that defined the country.

This notion of a Christian establishment is everywhere in the works of these writers. David Barton is perhaps its strongest supporter. According to him, "The Founders intended only to prevent the establishment of a single national denomination, not to restrain public religious expression." He later adds that the founders "never intended the First Amendment to become a vehicle to promote a pluralism of other religions."

Here Barton quotes commentaries on the Constitution written by the early-nineteenth-century Supreme Court justice Joseph Story (one of the Christian Right's favorite Supreme Court justices), who argues: "The real object of the [First A]mendment was not to countenance, much less to advance, Mahometanism, or Judaism, or infidelity, by prostrating Christianity; but to exclude all rivalry among *Christian* sects." Gary DeMar, in commenting on the same quote from Story, concludes that "Christianity was the accepted religion of the colonies, but that no single sect should be mandated by law. The amendment was not designed to make all religions equal, only to make all *Christian* denominations (sects) equal in the eyes of the Constitution and the law."[25]

The second point that these writers make is that the First Amendment was meant to prohibit only the federal government, not the states, from establishing a particular brand of Christian religion. As Barton puts it, "it was well established that the States were free to do as they pleased." This view—which places the decisions related to certain aspects of American life in the hands of the states—is often referred to as "federalism." The result of this, of course, is that the Supreme Court, in its role as the interpreter of the Constitution, has no right to strike down state laws that allow the public expression of religious belief. By taking this view, Barton can argue that the Virginia Statute for Religious Freedom (1786), a bill authored by Thomas Jefferson calling for complete religious freedom for all individuals in Virginia, must not be understood as a "prototype" for the rest of the nation. Virginia was perfectly within its constitutional rights to pass this bill, but this does not mean that other states could not pass bills that were more restrictive of religious liberty. This federalist view also explains why the Constitution does not mention God. If the question of the relationship between religion and public life was to be handled at the level of the states, then it did not need to be addressed in a national document such as the Constitution. The implication is that the federal government has no authority to meddle in the religious affairs of individual states. It also means that the states did not need to abide by the Constitution's prohibition of religious tests for office, because this applied only to federal officials.[26]

Revisionism

Christian nationalists believe that professional historians, through the textbooks that they write, are out to indoctrinate American children in a secular humanist view of the American past. Barton defines "historical revisionism" as "a process by which historical fact is intentionally ignored, distorted, or misportrayed in order to maneuver public opinion toward a specific political agenda or philosophy." Historical revisionists, he argues, accomplish their goals by (1) "Ignoring those aspects of American heritage which they deem to be politically incorrect and overemphasizing those portions which they find acceptable"; (2) "Vilifying the historical figures who embraced a position they reject"; and (3) "Concocting the appearance of widespread historical approval for a generally unpopular social policy." His Web site includes examples taken from school textbooks in which the name of God or Jesus Christ has been removed—usually by the careful use of ellipses—by an author quoting the words of one of the founders. As Gary DeMar puts it, "For some time secular historians have steadily chopped away at the historical record, denying the impact Christianity had on the moral and political character of the United States."[27]

For these writers revisionism is not only about the practice of removing references to God from the narratives historians tell about the past, but also about the way that historians treat their sources. Revisionism is dangerous because it implies looking critically at primary sources rather than simply accepting them at face value. For example, if the Puritans believed that they were God's new Israel, and this assertion can be supported by primary documents, then it must be true that the Puritans were indeed God's new Israel. Good historians must always believe what the primary sources tell them. Such an approach does not allow a place for any type of theological critique of those sources. If John Witherspoon, the only minister to sign the Declaration of Independence, wrote that God was on the side of the patriots in the American Revolution, then it must be true—a theological certainty—that God was on the side of America. To suggest that Witherspoon was wrong or misguided is the kind of interpretive work that these writers shun as a mark of dangerous revisionism.

The fear of revisionism is why the defenders of Christian America make such a big deal about grounding their research in primary sources. If a historian makes an argument based upon the ideas of another historian's work, rather than the primary sources, then she has succumbed to revisionism. Barton calls his historical method a "best evidence" approach. This way of dealing with evidence allows him to let the founders speak for themselves, but it rarely explores deeply the context in which such words were uttered.[28]

The attack on historical revisionism is most intense when discussing the American history textbooks used in the nation's public schools. This has been a pet issue for Tim LaHaye, who has suggested that "a whole generation of school children is being robbed of its country's religious heritage in the learning process." He calls this the "deliberate rape of history" by "left-wing scholars for hire." A Vision Forum textbook sums this view up well:

> Many modern educators deny the Providential view of history and would have us believe that their promotion of one of several "secular" views of history is simply the recounting of brute facts. They fail to tell their students that their own humanistic presuppositions and religious doctrines determine their choice of people, principles, and events. . . . Even as there are not many interpretations of Scripture (2 Pet. 1:20–21), neither are there of history—there is really one correct view; that which is the Author's interpretation and perspective. God is the Author of Scripture and History.[29]

For Christian nationalists there is a lot at stake in getting history—"His story"—correct. The removal of God from public life and the ensuing tragedy associated with the failure to teach children about the Christian roots of America have profound consequences for the social and moral fabric of the nation. LaHaye believes that the removal of America's religious heritage from textbooks encourages "humanism's antimoral philosophy." It has led to a rise in sexual permissiveness, unwed pregnancies, venereal disease, and a decline in academic achievement. Barton adds to this list a rise in violent crime, lower SAT scores, and the growth of single-parent households. The only solution to these problems is to confront historical revisionism head on by producing textbooks that tell the story of America's founding as the founders would have wanted it to be told.

These, in a nutshell, are some of the fundamental arguments of those writers who defend and promote the idea that America was founded as a Christian nation. They are committed to a theological position that affirms that humans can be reasonably sure about what God is up to in the course of history, particularly American history. Therefore they are not shy about pointing their readers to the hand of God in the events of the past. They combine this providentialism with a Whig view of American history that connects the history of the colonies to the success of the American Revolution. The colonies are not worthy of study in their own right, but are only important as a means of foreshadowing God's plan for 1776. These Christian nationalists also believe that God gave the responsibility for founding the United States to Christian men who then applied their faith directly to the creation of the Constitution. According to these nationalists, it would be clear to anyone with common sense that if we interpret the Constitution carefully, and get a clear sense of what the framers originally meant when they wrote it, America should have a Christian establishment of religion with a very small, and certainly pregnable, wall between church and state. Unfortunately, the Supreme Court, in pivotal moments in the last seventy-five years, has turned its back on this view of the Constitution and has made this wall higher than it should be. This has resulted, the Christian nationalists argue, in the disappearance of providence and Christianity from history textbooks, a change that has led to the moral and social decline of the Republic.

In this chapter I have tried to explain the arguments made by those Christians who believe that the United States was founded as, and continues to be, a Christian nation. But we have yet to ask just how much we should we rely on the likes of Barton, DeMar, LaHaye, or Kennedy to teach us our American history. Should we entrust our young people's history education to A Beka Publishing, Peter Marshall and David Manuel, Bob Jones University Press, or Vision Forum ministries? How do we begin to think about the question of whether America was founded as a Christian nation? Parts two and three will take up these issues in the hope of helping Christians think more clearly about the past and their relationship to it.

Suggested Reading for Part One

Balmer, Randall. *Thy Kingdom Come: An Evangelical's Lament*. New York: Basic Books, 2006.

Barton, David. *Original Intent: The Courts, the Constitution, & Religion*. 3rd ed. Aledo, TX: WallBuilder, 2000.

Carpenter, Joel. *Revive Us Again: The Reawakening of American Fundamentalism*. New York: Oxford University Press, 1997.

Curtis, Susan. *A Consuming Faith: The Social Gospel and Modern American Culture*. Baltimore: Johns Hopkins University Press, 1991.

DeMar, Gary. *America's Christian Heritage*. Nashville: Broadman & Holman, 2003.

Dolan, Jay P. *The American Catholic Experience: A History from Colonial Times to the Present*. New York: Doubleday, 1985.

Green, Steven K. *Inventing Christian America: The Myth of the Religious Founding*. New York: Oxford University Press, 2015.

Handy, Robert T. *A Christian America: Protestant Hopes and Historical Realities*. 2nd ed. New York: Oxford University Press, 1984.

Haselby, Sam. *The Origins of American Religious Nationalism*. New York: Oxford University Press, 2015.

Hatch, Nathan. *The Democratization of American Christianity*. New Haven: Yale University Press, 1991.

Haynes, Stephen R. *Noah's Curse: The Biblical Justification of American Slavery*. New York: Oxford University Press, 2002.

Kazin, Michael. *A Godly Hero: The Life of William Jennings Bryan*. New York: Knopf, 2006.

Kennedy, D. James, and Jerry Newcombe. *What if America Were a Christian Nation Again?* Nashville: Nelson, 2005.

Marsden, George M. *Fundamentalism and American Culture: The Shaping of Twentieth-Century Evangelicalism, 1870–1925*. New York: Oxford University Press, 1980.

Marshall, Peter, and David Manuel. *The Light and the Glory*. Old Tappan, NJ: Revell, 1977.

Noll, Mark A. *America's God: From Jonathan Edwards to Abraham Lincoln*. New York: Oxford University Press, 2002.

Noll, Mark A., Nathan O. Hatch, and George Marsden. *The Search for Christian America*. 2nd ed. Colorado Springs: Helmers & Howard, 1989.

Stout, Harry S. *Upon the Altar of the Nation: A Moral History of the Civil War*. New York: Viking, 2006.

White, Ronald W. *Lincoln's Greatest Speech: The Second Inaugural*. New York: Simon & Schuster, 2002.

Wilsey, John. *One Nation Under God: An Evangelical Critique of Christian America*. Eugene, OR: Wipf and Stock Publishers, 2011.

Wuthnow, Robert. *The Restructuring of American Religion*. Princeton: Princeton University Press, 1988.

Part Two

Was the American Revolution
a Christian Event?

Chapter Five

Were the British Colonies Christian Societies?

"Planting" versus "Founding"

In describing the seventeenth-century settling of New England, the late D. James Kennedy, a once-prominent defender of the notion that America was founded as a Christian nation, wrote: "Here God established a certain sort of nation, a nation that was founded by the Pilgrims and the Puritans and others who came with evangelical Christianity." Similarly, Christians who gathered at Jamestown in 2007 to celebrate the four hundredth anniversary of the first English settlement in America announced that they were there to recognize "the importance of commemorating the providential goodness of the Lord through our nation's birth at Jamestown." Radio personality Gary DeMar affirms without reservation: "Our nation begins not in 1776, but more than one hundred fifty years earlier."[1]

Many defenders of Christian America argue that the United States, as a "nation," was founded when the first English migrants brought Christianity to North America in the seventeenth century. Such assertions read history backward. They confuse the *planting* of British colonies on the Atlantic seaboard with the *founding* of the United States of America. The nation that we know today as the United States of America was not founded by Pilgrims, Puritans, or Jamestown adventurers. These earliest English settlers in North America did not come for the purpose of creating a new nation. Indeed, many of them, especially those who came to Jamestown, had no real interest in staying for any length of time. Those who did stay long enough to establish colonies planted *English* colonies. As we will see in the next chapter, these colonies remained fiercely loyal to the English monarchy until a few years prior to the American Revolution.

In fact, the English often referred to these North American settlements as "plantations."

This chapter examines the religious culture and societal values of these early English plantations in North America. Were they Christian societies? Were the seeds of a Christian nation somehow planted in the soil of Plymouth, Massachusetts Bay, or Jamestown? As we begin our investigation we must remember that seventeenth-century English-America was made up of distinct colonies with distinct governments and cultures. There was no sense of intercolonial unity. Each colony was more connected to London than to the other colonies. This was particularly the case in terms of the religious makeup of the colonies and the ways in which the people of each colony understood themselves as "Christian." I have chosen to focus here on two of the earliest and most prominent English settlements in the New World: Jamestown and Massachusetts Bay.

Did the earliest English settlers come to Jamestown and Massachusetts Bay to establish Christian societies? Yes. Did they succeed in making their vision for a Christian society a reality? Not really. Let us start with the settlement at Jamestown.

Jamestown

In April 1606, King James I of England issued a charter to a group of investors known as the London Company to settle what would become Jamestown, the first successful English colony in America. In addition to providing the legal right to settle a colony in the New World, the charter also affirmed the London Company's

> Desires for the Furtherance of so noble a Work, which may, by the Providence of Almighty God, hereafter tend to the Glory of his Divine Majesty, in propagating of Christian Religion to such People, [who] as yet live in Darkness and miserable Ignorance of the true Knowledge and Worship of God, and may in time bring the Infidels and Savages, living in those parts, to human Civility, and to a settled and quiet Government.[2]

In November of the same year, James I issued "Instructions for the Government of Virginia." These orders required the first settlers to develop a series of governing councils to provide some stability and structure to the colony. One of the primary duties of these councils was to make sure that the "true word and service of God, according to the rites and services of the Church of England, be preached, planted, and used in the colonies and among the neighboring savages."[3]

In April 1607, 105 settlers on three ships arrived at the cape of the southern entrance to the Chesapeake Bay, near present-day Virginia Beach. They decided to name their landing point "Cape Henry," after Henry Frederick, King James I's eldest son. After the so-called First Landing on Cape Henry, the settlers would explore further inland until they eventually decided to build their settlement—Jamestown—on the banks of what would become the James River.

Aboard one of those ships—*Susan Constant*—arriving at Cape Henry was an Anglican priest named Robert Hunt. After the passengers and crew of the expedition planted a cross in the soil, Hunt led the group in a public prayer of thanksgiving to God. He would continue to serve as the Anglican chaplain to the settlers at Jamestown until his death about one year later. Hunt's work did not go unnoticed in Jamestown. John Smith described him as our "honest, religious, and courageous divine." During the first year of the Jamestown settlement Hunt led the colonists in twice-daily prayer, preached two sermons every Sunday, and administered the Lord's Supper once every three months.

Christianity was important to some of the Jamestown settlers. A church building was constructed before the end of 1607 and was rebuilt after it was destroyed by a fire in 1608. When Lord de la Warr arrived at Jamestown in 1610 to institute martial law and enforce discipline, church attendance was required of all colonists. Those who failed to attend were subject to punishment. In 1617 a third church was built at the settlement, the foundation of which can still be seen by tourists visiting Historic Jamestown. It was in this church that the first meeting of the House of Burgesses was held in July 1619.

Mandatory church attendance continued in Jamestown well into the seventeenth century. Soldiers were required to bring their "pieces, swords, poulder and shuttle" with them to church.[4] In 1624 failure to attend church services could result in a fine of fifty pounds of tobacco.[5] The Church of England was established as the colony's official denomination. Settlers were forced to pay tithes to support the salaries of Anglican ministers. Catholic or "popish" priests were not permitted in the colony for a period of time longer than five days. When a group of Puritans from New England arrived in Virginia in 1643 and petitioned the government for a Congregational minister, a law was passed forbidding any ministers other than those from the Church of England to preside over services in the colony. Eventually these Puritan settlers were also required by law to conduct church services using the Book of Common Prayer. When Quakers, a religious group that the House of Burgesses described as "an unreasonable and turbulent sort of people," began to arrive in Virginia in 1660, a law was passed to apprehend them, imprison them without bail, and remove them from the colony.[6]

The government was actively involved in promoting Christian morality. In addition to the punishments doled out for lax church attendance, the House of Burgesses passed laws punishing adulterers, fornicators, and slanderers.[7] Ministers were required by law to "catechize, and instruct the youth and ignorant persons of his parrish, in the ten commandments the articles of the beliefe and in the Lord's prayer; and shall diligentlie here, instruct and teach the catechisme, sett forth in booke of common prayer." Parents were required to make sure that their children and their servants were catechized.[8]

Christianity, in the form of the rituals of the Anglican Church, was important in Jamestown and the surrounding Virginia colony. As historian Edward Bond has shown, the colonial leaders of Virginia made regular appeals to God for support in governing the colony. They invoked the Almighty in prayer for the colony's survival amid periods of starvation and disunity. They used the fear of divine judgment to enforce their laws and decrees. As Bond notes, colonial Virginians were very much connected to a "spiritual world."[9]

Yet this is not the entire story of the Jamestown settlement or colonial Virginia as a whole. While Christianity was present everywhere in the laws of the settlement, there is little evidence to suggest that Christianity permeated the culture and value system of the colony. Freedom of religion was not the reason people came to Jamestown. The most cursory look at the literature promoting the colony in England shows that the real appeal of Jamestown was economic opportunity and the very real possibility of striking it rich. Few came to Jamestown with any sense of establishing a permanent colony there. The goal was to find gold, or perhaps a natural resource that might serve as the equivalent of gold in the European mercantile market, and get out. As a result, the colony tended to attract the kind of person that one would not normally find in attendance at church in England. When Sir Thomas Dale, an early governor of the colony, arrived at Jamestown in 1611, he described the inhabitants as "so prophane, so rioutous, so full of Mutenie and treasonable Intendments" that they provided "little testimonie besides their names that they are Christians."[10]

The settlers of Jamestown could best be defined as individualistic, greedy, and selfish. They were, as historian T. H. Breen has described them, "Looking Out for Number One." Because of the abundant and rich soil of Jamestown and the surrounding countryside, the settlers tended to spread out on small plantations generally located five miles or so from one another. Since these plantations were necessary for the growth of tobacco, the colony never developed a communal center or any sense of common mission. As Breen notes, people became "increasingly distrustful of whatever lay beyond the perimeter of their own few acres." The House of Burgesses was notorious for its factionalism and failure to bring order to the colony. The settlers were so driven by their self-interests that most of them were unwilling to contribute to the colony's defense against the neighboring Indians. There were few churches outside Jamestown, and those ministers who did come to the settlement had a difficult time collecting funds for their own support.[11]

As the seventeenth century progressed, stability came to the Jamestown colony. But this stability could hardly be attributed to the emergence of a Christian social order. Jamestown survived because of tobacco. This crop fueled the self-interested cultural values already in place in Virginia and profoundly influenced the kind of settlers who populated the colony. Until the last few decades of the seventeenth century, Virginia was largely populated by white indentured servants. These young men (and a few women) were brought to Virginia by plantation owners for the purpose of working the tobacco fields. They signed contracts or "indentures" that required them to work for a tobacco grower for a period of years (usually 5–7 years) before being set free to pursue their own fortune in the Old Dominion. These servants composed about 75 percent of the emigrants to Virginia (and Maryland) in the seventeenth century. Because most of these servants were young men, the colony was home to few traditional families. Servants did not fare well. Many succumbed to a combination of the harsh labor they were forced to endure and the disease-ridden climate in which they labored. Others were beaten and abused like slaves. Those that were eventually set free found themselves on frontier lands with poor soil. They lived with a constant threat of Indian attack.[12]

In 1676 a group of former indentured servants, or "freemen," led by Virginia landholder Nathaniel Bacon, responded to the Virginia government's failure to protect them from Indian invasion by marching on the colonial capital at Jamestown in protest. Their action drove royal governor William Berkeley into hiding. "Bacon's Rebellion" was a defining moment in the history of the colony. It taught the colonial leaders that something needed to be done to calm the ever-growing number of former indentured servants living on the Virginia frontier.

This problem was solved for the Virginia government by the institution of African slavery. Though Africans had been present in Virginia since 1619, they made up a small portion of the population. By roughly 1680, however, slaves became more affordable, and as the death rate in Virginia decreased, they became a much better investment for tobacco planters. As Virginia entered the eighteenth century, slavery became the dominant system of labor in the colony. Unlike indentured servants, slaves did not have to be set free after a term of service. All Virginia citizens, including freemen, could aspire to owning slaves to aid them in their accumulation of wealth and prosperity. Slavery would go a long way toward solving the social conflicts that culminated in Bacon's Rebellion. Since slaves were a permanent underclass defined by their racial difference, freemen realized that they had more in common with the white men in charge of the colony than they did with these new laborers from Africa. Freemen were also no longer on the bottom rung of society. Relations between the freemen and the government improved, thanks to the introduction of slavery, and the colony finally reached a level of stability and order that was absent during the first fifty or so years of settlement.

The seventeenth-century development of the Jamestown colony raises some very interesting questions about the "Christian" character of this society. Tobacco and slavery allowed Virginians—especially the wealthy families who could trace their roots to the earliest decades of settlement—to prosper. Freemen were able to pursue the agricultural ambitions with the help of slave labor. As slaveholding tobacco growers accumulated wealth, they were able to build impressive plantations and surround themselves with the finest of English luxuries. The sons, grandsons, and great-grandsons of these tobacco growers were sent to college—in England or Scotland or at the College of William and Mary in the new colonial capital of Williamsburg. Through their studies they were exposed to Enlightenment learning and would soon emerge as some of the great leaders of the Revolutionary generation. This scenario, as historian Edmund Morgan has shown, is one of the great moral paradoxes in American history. Only with the arrival of slaves was Virginia able to become a prosperous and stable society. Ironically, it was some of the greatest spokesmen of freedom—Thomas Jefferson, George Washington, and George Mason, to name a few—who benefited the most from the seventeenth-century introduction of black chattel slavery into Virginia society.[13]

In the end Jamestown, and eventually the colony of Virginia as a whole, set out with high aspirations of creating a society in which the Anglican

Church would provide the necessary religious and moral order needed for the colony to survive. While this vision looked good on paper, it never materialized. Jamestown almost did not survive due to the selfishness and materialism of its earliest settlers. When it did turn the corner toward stability, it was not Christianity that led the way. It was the introduction of slavery that brought prosperity to the colony. Slavery brought wealth to the colony and made it possible for some of the leading lights of the American Revolution to protest against their own enslavement under British tyranny.

Massachusetts Bay

The defenders of a Christian America love to talk about colonial New England. The roots of the United States, they argue, go back directly to the Pilgrims who arrived on the *Mayflower* in 1620 and the Puritans who established Massachusetts Bay Colony about a decade later. The colonies established by the Calvinist settlers of Plymouth, Massachusetts Bay, and Connecticut were designed to be Christian societies. The first settlers of these colonies were English Calvinists who were dissatisfied with the slow progress of the Protestant Reformation in England. They wanted the Church of England purified from what they perceived to be Catholic abuses. These Calvinists, or "Puritans" as they became known, believed that God had predestined them for eternal life with him. They taught that all individuals, in order to obtain eternal life, must be able to testify to a conversion experience. Conversion was an intensely personal moment. It came when an individual understood the depths of his or her sinful nature and realized that salvation would come only through God's grace. Puritans believed that the most important part of a Sunday service was the proclamation of the Word of God through the preaching of an ordained minister. The Puritans rejected the priesthood, the Christian calendar of holy days, elaborate church decorations, the practice of kneeling during the service, and every other practice in the Church of England that they associated with Catholicism. As Congregationalists, these Calvinists wanted to rid the Church of England of its hierarchy of bishops. Power in the church, they believed, belonged to the laypersons who made up each individual congregation.

Some of these Puritans—who eventually became known as Separatists—believed that the Church of England had grown so corrupt that it was not worth saving. These Separatists, true to their name, believed that the only way to have a pure church was to leave the Church of England. Many of them left England physically as well, establishing a small settlement in Holland. Some of them eventually found their way to America, arriving on Cape Cod in 1620 aboard the *Mayflower*. Known today as the "Pilgrims," these New World travelers established the colony of Plymouth.

Most English Puritans, however, were not willing to abandon the Church of England. Believing separation from the mother church to be sinful, they attempted to purify it from within. This proved difficult, especially when Anglican authorities, under the leadership of King Charles I and Charles Laud, the archbishop of Canterbury, set out to remove whatever influence Puritans had in the Church of England. Puritan ministers were removed from office for refusing to use the Book of Common Prayer in their worship. Church courts fined and excommunicated Puritan laypersons. These religious struggles, coupled with an economic downturn in England during the late 1620s, prompted many Puritans to leave England in search of religious freedom and access to more land. Throughout the 1630s, in what became known as "the Great Puritan Migration," more than twenty thousand English Calvinists came to America. Most of them tried to establish colonies in the West Indies, but some of them came to the Chesapeake Bay region and New England. One of the more successful of these settlements was founded by Puritans who arrived in present-day Boston in 1630 under the leadership of soon-to-be colonial governor John Winthrop.[14]

Winthrop knew exactly what kind of colony he wanted to build in America. On the voyage across the Atlantic, on a ship called *Arbella*, Winthrop delivered one of the best-known sermons in American history, "A Model of Christian Charity." This sermon called for the Puritans to build a Christian civilization that would stand as a "city on a hill"—a Christian utopia that would be a beacon of spiritual light to the rest of the world. The Massachusetts Bay Colony tried to construct its society on the tenets of Christian orthodoxy as the colonists understood it. At the core of this society would be what the Puritans called "visible saints." These were individuals who could testify to a conversion experience. Visible sainthood was required for church membership, a privilege that gave people the right to participate in local congregational governance (for adult males), partake of Communion, and have their children baptized.[15]

The right to vote and hold office in Massachusetts Bay was based entirely on whether one was a visible saint. In theory, religious and political power was held not by the wealthy or those who owned large amounts of property, but by those who could claim a conversion experience. The church and the state functioned as two separate entities in Massachu-

Fig. 5.1   John Winthrop, first governor of Massachusetts Bay

setts Bay, but since both were run by saints, they tended to work closely together in the creation and enforcement of laws. Since the Puritans believed themselves to be God's chosen people (a new Israel), the laws of the colony were often grounded in Old Testament decrees. For example, adultery, kidnapping, and the worship of other gods were crimes punishable by death. Public displays of affection, long hair on men, and short sleeves on women's dresses were also against the law.

While the Puritan leaders were clearly interested in creating a pure and holy Christian society, it is hard to tell if they had the demographic base of committed Christians to sustain it. In the early years of settlement, attendance at religious services was required of all inhabitants, making the number of people in church on Sunday rather large. Church membership, however, was never very high in seventeenth-century Puritan churches. Membership was a mark of true Christian commitment, and one could obtain it only through a conversion experience. As the seventeenth century progressed, all indications suggest that church membership gradually declined throughout New England society.

We also know that many inhabitants of the New England colonies practiced forms of spirituality that did not necessarily conform to Puritan teachings. They were lukewarm adherents to the Puritan way who tended to practice their Christianity on their own terms and in their own manner. One historian has described these Puritans as "horse-shed" Christians for their propensity to spend the long intermission between services on Sunday morning behind the horse shed discussing secular matters. It is thus fair to say that while New England was governed as a Christian society, the majority of those living in that early settlement following the first generation of settlers did not necessarily conform to Puritan practice.[16]

The Puritans' understanding of a Christian society differed markedly from the Jamestown settlers' view. John Winthrop opposed the kind of economic greed and materialism that characterized commercial society and class divisions in England. Though his vision of a materialism-free society never quite caught on in Massachusetts, settlers did try to establish small towns and communities to protect themselves from the greed of the marketplace. Puritans arrived to the New World in families and made every effort to keep those families healthy, strong, and together. They taught their children to read the Bible, making Massachusetts Bay one of the most literate places in the world. And, of course, their everyday lives centered on the meetinghouse and the worship of God. Modern-day observers often rail on the limits of this Christian society. Women had virtually no civil rights, fathers tended to be patriarchal, and the wealthy still tended to dominate local life. But by seventeenth-century standards the Puritans did make some serious attempts to apply their Christian beliefs to the social fabric of their society.

Another way of evaluating whether the Puritans of New England measured up to standards of Christian practice is to examine how they treated their neighbors, specifically those with whom they had theological disagreements. Dissenters to Puritan orthodoxy did not fare well in colonial New England. The very same Puritans who came to the New World to practice their religion freely were not very interested, once they arrived on America's shores, in granting this liberty to others. Non-Puritans were free to practice orthodoxy as defined by the Puritans in charge. If they failed to conform, they would be forced to leave. Some dissenters, such as the Quaker Mary Dyer, were even killed for their obstinate lack of submission to Puritan authority.

Roger Williams was one of the first to challenge Puritan authority in New England. Williams arrived in Massachusetts in 1631 and quickly became a popular minister among the settlers. He ran into trouble with colonial officials when he insisted that church and state remain completely separate in Massachusetts. This idea challenged the Puritan belief that Congregational churches and the colonial government—both of which were ruled by visible saints—should work closely together. Williams believed that the government had no authority to intervene in the affairs of the church. He argued, for example, that government had no right to fine people for not attending church or refusing to swear an oath on the Bible in court.

Williams's primary concern was with the purity of the church. He feared that if government remained in the business of regulating congregational life then it could only lead to the worldly contamination of the church. His views were quite radical for his day, and the colonial leaders feared that they would undermine the religious utopia that they had hoped to create in Massachusetts Bay. In 1635, after much debate, they decided to banish Williams from the colony. The ousted Williams traveled south, bought land from the Narragansett Indians, and founded a new settlement at a place called Providence.[17]

Anne Hutchinson was another dissenter who ran afoul of Puritan orthodoxy. Hutchinson challenged the authority of the Puritan ministers, and by extension the government of Massachusetts, by affirming that the Puritan way of salvation was the equivalent of a form of works righteousness. Puritans believed that one was "saved" by faith in Jesus Christ, but a conversion was deemed authentic only if the one converted continued a life of good works. Hutchinson, however, believed that works had nothing to do with the conversion process. She claimed that salvation came through faith alone. Puritans leaders believed that Hutchinson's position, which was becoming popular through a small group of followers that gathered regularly in her home, would undermine the good works necessary to sustain a well-ordered and moral society. They thus put her on trial and labeled her views "Antinomian" (anti-law). It did not help matters that Hutchinson was a woman in a patriarchal society. It is worth noting that her mentor, the esteemed Puritan divine John Cotton, held similar theological views but was not deemed enough of a threat to prosecute.

During her trial Hutchinson argued for freedom of conscience in matters of religion and alienated the council by claiming to have received direct revelation from God. This pronouncement served as the last straw for the leadership of a society that believed God's revelation to humans came only through the Bible. Hutchinson, like Williams, was banished from the colony and settled in Rhode Island, a colony that would quickly develop a reputation as a haven for Puritan outcasts.[18]

If people today are looking for the supposed roots of modern American convictions concerning the relationship between church and state, they would be more likely to find those values in the ideas of Williams and Hutchinson than in the leadership of the Christian civilization of Massachusetts Bay. But does the removal of all religious dissent make the Puritan leaders of Massachusetts Bay less Christian? From the perspective of the seventeenth century, these colonial leaders were doing whatever it took to preserve what they believed to be the purity of God's chosen people in the wilderness—the "city on a hill." They firmly believed that by removing dissenters such as Williams and Hutchinson they were maintaining the integrity of their Christian society. If dissenters were bound to undermine what the Puritan leaders believed God had created, then it was only logical that they be removed from the colony.

Yet, as we look back on the behavior of the Puritans toward their dissenting neighbors, it should raise some questions about the "Christian" identity of this society. Any good society needs to maintain law and order, but in Massachusetts Bay this was sustained by government interference in the religious beliefs of its people. Williams and Hutchinson were Christians who happened to have some theological disagreements with the Puritan leadership. Williams acted out of a deep love for the church, Hutchinson out of a commitment to liberty of conscience. While the attempts to remove these dissenters are certainly understandable in light of the kind of society the Puritans had hoped to construct in Massachusetts Bay, one should be hesitant to see them as necessarily "Christian" in character. Sometimes rigid commitment to doctrinal orthodoxy can get in the way of showing compassion and Christian charity.

But it seems that the Massachusetts Bay Puritans failed to act in a Christian fashion in a more obvious way, namely in their treatment of their Native American neighbors. In addition to his belief in the separation of church and state, Roger Williams criticized the government of Massachusetts Bay for taking Indian land without paying for it. Since they understood themselves to be the new Israel, Puritans believed that it was their God-ordained right to usurp this Indian land.

In theory, the Puritans took Indian land for religious reasons. They needed to expand their "city on a hill" westward, and Native Americans were in the way. As Massachusetts settlers moved into the Connecticut River Valley in the 1630s, tensions developed with the Pequots, the Indians who controlled the region's fur trade. In 1637 the settlers, with the help of their Narragansett allies, burned the Pequot village in Mystic, Connecticut, killing several hundred Pequot women and children. This is how Plymouth's Governor William Bradford described the massacre:

> It was a fearful sight to see them [the Pequots] thus frying in the fire and the streams of blood quenching the same, and horrible was the stink and scent thereof; but the victory seemed a sweet sacrifice, and they [the English] gave the praise to God, who had wrought so wonderfully for them, thus to enclose their enemies in their hands and give them so speedy a victory over so proud and insulting an enemy.[19]

With the Pequots out of the way, the New England settlers were free to extend their settlement into Connecticut with little resistance. They would continue to push forward with what they perceived to be the will of God.

But not all of these Indian fighters and western settlers were motivated by spiritual goals. Many drove west to obtain more land and political power. Indeed, this was the primary reason why seventeenth-century New Englanders were so mobile. Land grew scarce rather quickly in the New England coastal towns. Settlers with ambition knew that by starting a new community they could become "town fathers"—respected members of society with influence in church and society. If the American Indians needed to be removed so these ambitious dreams could be achieved, then so be it.

The Puritans made every effort to try to convert the American Indians to Christianity, and some missionaries were successful in these attempts. But in the end the Puritan approach to Indians living in their midst must be viewed as embarrassing for a society that claimed to be Christian in orientation. There was no attempt, for example, to treat the Indians as fellow human beings, created in the image of the same God that the Puritans worshiped. There were few attempts to treat the Indians fairly and justly. Instead, Puritan-Indian relations reveal the selfishness and greed of the Puritans and their attempts to extend their society westward at all costs. Is this the behavior of a Christian society?

As we have seen in this chapter, two of the earliest colonial settlements in America—Jamestown and Massachusetts Bay—began with high hopes that a truly Christian civilization was possible. Both societies did their best to embed the teachings of the Bible, as its leaders understood them, into their laws and statutes. In this sense, one might call them "Christian" societies. But we also must acknowledge that in other ways—what we might call orthopraxy—both of these colonies failed, and in some cases failed miserably, in their attempts at maintaining societies in which public behavior was guided by the dictates of Christianity. In Jamestown greed and the pursuit of wealth among white settlers resulted in the human bondage of thousands of Africans. By the time of the Revolution, the leaders of colonial Virginia were crying out for freedom and liberty even as they glanced out the windows of their plantations to see slaves laboring in their fields. The Christian society in Massachusetts Bay was defined so narrowly that believers who deviated from Puritan orthodoxy were forced to leave the colony or, in some cases, were imprisoned, fined, or even executed for their beliefs. Native Americans were slaughtered and removed from their homes to advance the "city on a hill."

Christians today can debate whether these societies were truly Christian, but it is hard to ignore the fact that Jamestown and Massachusetts Bay failed, in many respects, to model Christian behavior. This reality should not surprise contemporary Christians who believe that human beings are inherently flawed by sin. While there will always be individuals within society trying to live godly lives to the best of their ability, there will also be those who are apathetic to such pursuits. Those searching for a historic golden age of colonial Christianity will, if they look hard enough, end up disappointed.[20]

Chapter Six

Christianity and the Coming of the American Revolution

W as the American Revolution a Christian event? This question has been answered in a variety of ways by historians, scholars, and Christian leaders. If indeed the Revolution was somehow "Christian" in nature, one might expect formal statements of resistance to British tyranny to be loaded with references to the Bible and Christian doctrine. But when one examines the specific arguments made by colonial political leaders in the years leading up to 1776, one is hard-pressed to find any Christian or biblical language apart from a few passing references to God. This chapter provides a brief political history of the years between 1763 and the calling of the First Continental Congress in September 1774. Our particular focus is on whether those leading the Revolution employed Christian arguments to counter what they perceived to be the unfair taxation schemes of the British Empire.

A Snapshot of the British-American Colonies in 1763

Most historians point to the French and Indian War (1754–1763) as an important precursor to the American Revolution. The British victory over France was a decisive one. As a result of the Treaty of Paris (1763), England obtained all of the North American territory east of the Mississippi River and much of present-day Canada. The war with France was a costly one for the British, making the prospect of governing all of this new North American territory difficult. As the story goes, the British decided to place some of the burden of governing and defending this territory on the colonists. Soon after the French and Indian War ended, the British initiated a series of taxes in the colonies to raise the revenue needed to maintain order over their North American empire. The rest, as they say, is history. The colonists bristled under these new taxes until things finally came to a head in 1776 when they decided to break political relations with England and declare independence. This story will be developed more fully in the rest of this chapter, but first it is worth providing a brief snapshot of life in the British-American colonies on the brink of revolution.

One common misconception is that the American Revolution was a climactic event triggered by over 150 years of British oppression heaped upon the colonies. According to this interpretation, the people of British North America, since the planting of their first colony at Jamestown in 1607, or perhaps the settlement of Plymouth Colony by the Pilgrims in 1620, had grown more and more hostile to the way they had been treated by the Crown until things finally came to the point of outright rebellion. To put it differently, the seeds of the American Revolution were planted in the soil of Jamestown and Plymouth, watered during the colonial period, and eventually blossomed, around 1776, into the United States of America.

Such an interpretation of colonial life works very well for nationalists who want to make the story of the British colonies connect seamlessly to the story of the American Revolution. But it fails to capture the spirit of the colonial people in 1763. For as the colonies developed from remote New World outposts in the seventeenth century to mature provinces of the British Empire in the eighteenth, their economic, cultural, political, and religious connections to London grew stronger, not weaker. By 1763 the colonies were more *British* than they had ever been. Historians have called this process of "becoming British" *Anglicization*. Let's develop this idea further.

The purpose of any colony was to serve its mother country. In the seventeenth and eighteenth centuries, colonies played an important role in the economic system known as mercantilism. Mercantilism required that a nation's economy remain under the strict control of the mother country. A nation's wealth was measured by the quantity of precious metals or "specie" (gold and silver) that it possessed. In order to be successful in a mercantile economy, a nation needed to have a favorable balance of trade, or export more goods than it imported. The goal was thus to find some kind of product or crop that could be traded with other countries. If such a product or crop created a demand among the other European powers, then perhaps those nations might be willing to sacrifice specie in order to obtain it. Since Europeans mostly grew grain, they needed to rely on colonies to provide the kinds of goods, crops, or services that would make them successful in this mercantile economy.

By 1763 all thirteen of the colonies on the eastern seaboard of North America had been effectively integrated into the British mercantile system. The planters of South Carolina were growing rice that the British could trade on European markets. The Virginians had a place of honor within this system because of their tobacco plantations. In the mid-Atlantic (New York, New Jersey, Pennsylvania) farmers grew grains that were shipped to the West Indies in order to feed the slaves working in the lucrative British sugar colonies. New England made similar food contributions to West Indian sugar plantations and also added shipbuilding to the mix. The colonies prospered under this system. They had steady markets for their goods and their commerce was protected by the most powerful navy in the world.

The Navigation Acts, a series of laws that made sure that the British alone would benefit from American trade, brought law and order to this entire system. Because the Navigation Acts prevented the colonies from participating in a global market that would allow them to get the best price for their crops, many have interpreted these acts as just another example of the tyrannical hold that England had over the economic livelihood of their colonies. We need to be careful, however, about interpreting economic life in the eighteenth century through the capitalist lens of the twenty-first century. The Navigation Acts may not have allowed the colonists access to the "free" market, but they did offer the kind of security and trade protection that was conducive to the colonial pursuit of happiness and comfort.

The colonists also benefited economically from their relationship with the mother country through their access to British consumer products. Very little large-scale manufacturing took place in the American colonies. For the most part, fashions (clothing), furniture, china, and other household items were obtained directly from England. The colonies participated in a consumer revolution. Between 1750 and 1773 English exports of consumer goods to the colonies increased 120 percent. The colonists now had unprecedented access to British products, and the standard of living in most places was quite high as compared to the rest of the world. Luxury items had, by the eve of the American Revolution, become necessities of life in the colonies. Through purchasing these goods, people's everyday lives—their dresses, dining room tables, and leisure activities—began to resemble the everyday lives of people living in England. These goods brought the colonists more fully into the British Empire. In terms of refinement and culture, none of the colonial cities of America could compare to London. But Philadelphia, Boston, New York, and Charleston were getting close.[1]

Politically, England was the freest country in the world. While most of its European neighbors on the Continent had absolute monarchs, England's monarchy was generally held in check by the people as represented in Parliament. Balanced government meant that the people's rights as English subjects would always be protected. These included the right to a trial by jury, the right to petition the monarch, freedom from a standing army in a time of peace, freedom for Protestants to take up arms in their own defense, freedom to elect members of Parliament without government interference, and freedom of speech. All of the colonies had established governments that, in one way or another, embodied these British ideals. Looking backward from our perch in the twenty-first century, it is hard to imagine England as such a champion of liberty. After all, we know what happened in 1776. But as historian Gordon Wood has put it, "the eighteenth-century colonists were freer, had less inequality, were more prosperous and less burdened with cumbersome feudal restraints, than any other part of mankind in the eighteenth century, and more important, they knew it."[2] Whatever the colonies understood about the meaning of liberty, they learned from the British.

Religiously, the thirteen colonies were overwhelmingly Protestant, and Protestantism was always understood to be a religion of liberty. Individual Protestants were free to read the Bible for themselves, in their own language, and draw theological conclusions. This kind of freedom fit very well with British political liberties. Civil liberty and Protestant liberty went hand in hand in the British Empire.

Religious freedom in England was limited to Protestants. The 1689 Act of Toleration, which allowed certain religious groups that dissented from the established Church of England (Anglican) to worship in peace, did not apply to Catholics, Quakers, or the members of any sect that could not affirm a belief in the Trinity. For the most part, the colonists had more religious freedoms than those living in England. For example, Quakers enjoyed unprecedented liberty in Pennsylvania, New Jersey, and Rhode Island. Puritans, who were not permitted to hold political office or attend English universities under the Act of Toleration, had the liberty to build their own religious colonies in New England. Yet even in the colonies it was rare that Roman Catholics or non-Christian settlers were given the right to vote or run for office. Freedom—both religious and civil—was a Protestant idea.[3]

By 1763 an intense spirit of patriotism had emerged in the colonies, but it was not directed toward the creation of an independent nation. Very few colonists would have even contemplated such an idea. This sense of nationalism was focused on the glories of being part of Great Britain—the freest, economically strongest, and most Protestant empire in the world. In 1764 an anonymous author, writing in the *New York Mercury*, exuded this sense of patriotism: "We think of ourselves at present the happiest people (with respect to government) of any people under the sun, and really are so."[4] Such patriotism reached its height in the immediate aftermath of the French and Indian War. The British victory over the "tyrannical" and Roman Catholic France brought a renewed appreciation for the colonists' British identity.

The Stamp Act Crisis—1765

The above snapshot of life in the British colonies in 1763 prompts the question: How, in the course of thirteen years, did the colonies move from being satisfied, if not exuberant, members of the British Empire to declaring independence from their beloved mother country? Ironically, the American Revolution was the high point of colonial "Britishness." As historian John Murrin has written, "In a word, America was Britain's idea." At one level, "the Revolution was . . . the culminating moment in the process of Anglicization."[5] The colonists, who were upset by a series of revenue-raising taxes issued by Parliament, took long-standing lessons they had learned about the freedom and rights provided to all Englishmen and used them against the mother country. The time had come for the colonists to teach England how to be "British." If the colonies had not been so deeply ensconced in British ideas and culture, the American Revolution, ironically, would never have happened.

The coming of the Revolution is a familiar story to many students of American history, but it is worth recapping some of the highlights. Colonial protests began in earnest with the passing of the Stamp Act in 1765. The act was part of a series of policy decisions by British Prime Minister George Grenville for the purpose of raising revenue that would contribute to the defense of the North American colonies. The Stamp Act required colonists to purchase newspapers and legal documents on specially stamped paper. It also taxed land grants, pamphlets, playing cards, and calendars. This was not a particularly onerous tax. The money raised by the act would go directly to the British troops commissioned to protect the colonies against invaders. In other words, the money would be used to benefit the colonies. But even then the revenue that was raised through the Stamp Act and another tax, the Molasses Act (1764), would cover only one-third of the cost of maintaining an army in the colonies. England was prepared to pay for the rest. From the perspective of Grenville, the Stamp Act was not oppressive. Indeed, Benjamin Franklin, who was living in England at the time, did not expect much colonial resistance to the act. During the process of writing the Stamp Act, Grenville solicited the opinion of colonial leaders. He gave them the opportunity to make changes to the act or even provide an alternative means of raising revenue. No colonies took Grenville up on his offer.[6]

If the colonists were to agree to help Grenville modify the Stamp Act, they would essentially have been agreeing to the idea that Britain had the right to tax them. Colonial leaders were not as much bothered by the way that the tax would affect their pocketbooks as much as they were by the fact that Parliament claimed the right to issue the tax in the first place. Since the colonists were not represented in Parliament, they held the belief that only their colonial assemblies had the power to issue direct taxes. The Virginia House of Burgesses, inspired by the impassioned rhetoric of Patrick Henry, responded first with a document called the "Virginia Resolves." This document, which would become a template for many similar documents that would appear over the course of the next decade, claimed that the people of Virginia had rights and privileges as British subjects based upon the language in the colony's original charter. It affirmed the idea that the British government did not have the right to tax the colonies without the consent of the people as represented in the General Assembly of the colony. When the Virginia Resolves were published in colonial newspapers, two more points—the right to resist any taxes imposed by England and the right to consider those who impose unfair taxes as enemies of the colony of Virginia—were added to the list of grievances, but neither of these more radical proposals had been adopted by the House of Burgesses.[7] It is worth noting, for our purposes, that the Virginia Resolves made no reference to God, the Bible, Christianity, or any religious reason why resistance to the Stamp Act was necessary.

In October 1765, nine of the thirteen colonies sent delegates to New York to defend the idea of "no taxation without representation." The delegates to this "Stamp Act Congress" claimed that they would not accept any taxes placed on them "without their consent" and called for the immediate repeal of the Stamp Act.[8] Grenville, on the other hand, argued that the colonies were represented by Parliament in a "virtual" fashion. What right did the colonies have to claim direct representation when only about 5 percent of the people of Great Britain were represented in this way? The battle thus became less over a particular tax and more over whether the Parliament had the right to tax the colonies in the first place. For Grenville, the tax was a fair one. The money it garnered would go directly toward the defense of the colonies. For the colonists, Parliament had no right to tax them whatsoever.

The Stamp Act served as an incubator for the revolutionary ideas that would define colonial resistance to England over the course of the next decade. A language of liberty would come to dominate public discourse in the British-American colonies. Referred to as "Whig" or "republican" thought, this language centered on a common vocabulary that includes words and phrases such as "tyranny," "liberty," "slavery," "freedom," "natural rights," "arbitrary government," and "power." This line of political thinking was associated with the English "Whig" or "Country" party, an emerging faction in eighteenth-century England whose mission was to oppose monarchial power. Whigs defended political and Protestant liberty against the ever-present threat of political and religious tyranny. There were several variations on Whig political thought, but all of its defenders believed that a government that undermined the natural liberties of its people was enacting a form of political slavery upon them. Such power needed to be resisted, and, in some cases, this resistance might even result in the overthrow of the government.

Many Whigs were strong believers in the teachings of John Locke as put forward in his famous *Second Treatise of Government* (1689). In this book, written to explain why it was right for the English to remove King James II from office in 1688, Locke argued that when a government broke its contract with its people—a contract that required submission to government as long as government was protecting natural rights to life, liberty, and property—revolution was justified. Though the revolutionary implications of Locke's ideas would not become prevalent in colonial life for several decades following the publication of the *Second Treatise*, much of this Enlightenment-based Whig political thought was used to resist the Stamp Act.

The Stamp Act Congress and the Virginia Resolves, with their rational Whig arguments, were not the only way that the colonies protested this tax. Many, including the now infamous members of the Sons of Liberty, believed that violence was the only way to get Parliament's attention and bring about repeal. In Boston, opponents of the Stamp Act did everything in their power to make sure that the tax was not collected. Andrew Oliver, who was responsible for administering the Stamp Act in Massachusetts, was hung in effigy on a giant elm tree that would soon be called the "Liberty Tree." Patriots destroyed his office and his stable house and burned his coach. He was eventually paraded through the streets of Boston and forced to publicly resign his post. When Lieutenant Governor Thomas Hutchinson tried to stop the mob, he was stoned by the crowd. The Boston mobs did not hesitate to damage the homes of anyone connected with the tax. Hutchinson's house was ransacked. His furniture was destroyed, his wine cellar emptied, and the interior walls of the house torn down. He and his family barely escaped with their lives. Similar events occurred throughout the colonies, and stamp officials began resigning in droves. Partially in response to the violence, the Stamp Act was repealed.[9]

From a purely political point of view, the colonists had a legitimate argument against the Stamp Act. They demanded the right to levy taxes through their own colonial legislatures. There was logic to this argument, although it was not the kind of logic that the Parliament was willing to accept. For our purposes, it is worth asking whether the resistance to the Stamp Act was decidedly "Christian" in nature. There is no evidence of Christian motivations behind the deliberations of the Virginia Resolves or the Stamp Act Congress. All fourteen of the points put forth in the "Declaration of Rights of the Stamp Act Congress" were informed by long-standing British or Whig ideas about rights and liberties. The colonies argued that they had "inherent rights and privileges" not because they were Christian or even believed in God, but because they were "natural born subjects within the kingdom of Britain."[10] This was not a religious fight, but a political and constitutional one. And what should we make of the mob violence and the blatant destruction of property that ultimately led to the repeal of the Stamp Act? Who was acting tyrannically here? The mobs responded to a mild Parliamentary revenue-raising scheme with violence that was well out of proportion to the tax levied against them. Even the many Christian ministers who opposed the Stamp Act condemned the violence that appeared to be necessary for its repeal.

The Townshend Duties

With the repeal of the Stamp Act came the infamous Declaratory Act (1766), which announced that Parliament had the right to make laws for the colonies in "all cases whatsoever." Parliament did not waste any time in fulfilling that promise. In 1767 a new set of taxes, known as the Townshend Acts (proposed by Charles Townshend, chancellor of the exchequer), were levied on the colonies. Unlike the Stamp Act, which taxed

Fig. 6.1 *The Repeal of the Stamp Act* in 1766 represented the American colonists' first political victory over Parliament.

documents that were essential to colonial life, the Townshend duties were taxes on luxury items such as wine, fruit, glass, lead, paint, and tea. The colonists once again protested these taxes based on the idea that Parliament had no legal right to tax them for the sole purpose of raising revenue. John Dickinson, in his famous *Letters from a Farmer in Pennsylvania*, urged the colonists to boycott British goods until the Townshend duties were repealed. He repeated what by now had become a common political mantra related to the Crown's threat to British liberties in the colonies: taxes such as the Townshend duties could be levied only by colonial assemblies. He warned of the potential of similar taxes unless the colonists resisted. Dickinson made four references to God in *Letters*, but they were largely tangential to his dominant political argument.[11]

The Massachusetts House of Representatives also responded to the Townshend Acts. In February 1768 it issued a "Circular Letter" to the legislatures of the British-American colonies opposing the tyrannical nature of this new round of taxes. Written by Samuel Adams, it began with an assertion of colonial rights. These rights, which assured freedom and liberty for members of the British Empire, were "sacred and irrevocable" and could not be removed without the consent of the people. The "sacredness" of these rights, according to Adams and the House of Representatives, came from the fact that they were part of the British constitution. The letter went on, as might be expected, to argue that the Townshend duties were a violation of these "natural and constitutional rights" because the colonists did not have direct representation in Parliament. Since colonial representation in a political body (Parliament) separated by "an ocean of a thousand leagues" would never be practical, taxes of this nature, the letter argued, must stem from local or "subordinate" assemblies in the colonies.[12]

The Tea Act and the Boston Tea Party

Although the Townshend duties were repealed in 1770, the tax on tea continued and the colonial boycotts persisted. In 1773 Parliament added to the controversy over this potable with the passing of the dreaded Tea Act. What is ironic about the Tea Act is that it *lowered* the price of tea in the colonies. It was an attempt by Parliament to save the British East India Company from bankruptcy. The company's warehouses were full of tea, but the strength of the boycotts was making it difficult to sell the beverage in America. In order to aid the company with its financial difficulties, Parliament allowed it to sell tea in the colonies at very low prices in the hope that sales would increase. It would be difficult, however, to sell cheap East India tea at the same time that Parliament was enforcing a tax on the commodity. Repeal of the tax on tea would have meant caving in to colonial protests and boycotts.

The English government thus needed to come up with a creative way of reducing the price of tea without repealing the tax. The problem was solved in a relatively simple fashion. Under the British Navigation Acts, any product shipped to the colonies had to pass first through England. Upon receiving the tea from the East Indies, English merchants were required to pay a tax on their purchase. The merchants normally made up for this tax by raising the price of tea sold to colonial importers. The importers then passed it along to American consumers through higher tea prices. The Tea Act altered this arrangement by offering a rebate to English merchants to be used to cover the cost of the tax. As a result, they were able to sell tea to colonial merchants at lower prices. The merchants could then pass the savings along to the average tea-drinking colonist. But there was a catch: only a few American retailers would be able to benefit from the plan. The Tea Act allowed the East India Company to choose a select group of colonial merchants who would be permitted to sell this specially discounted tea.

Opposition to the Tea Act came from three different segments of the colonial population. First, some believed that the lower price on tea was a clever attempt by England to trick the colonists into forgetting about the already existing tax on tea. Parliament, they argued, may have been helping American consumers, but it was still taxing the colonies without representation much in the same way that it had tried to do with earlier taxes such as the Stamp Act and Townshend duties. Second, merchants who were not chosen to sell the cheap East India Company tea were unhappy about being left out of what they saw as an excellent business opportunity. Third, the reduced tea prices hurt smugglers, who now found it difficult to compete with the legitimate merchants selling East India Company tea.[13]

The first attempts to ship East India Company tea to America occurred in the summer of 1773. Patriots in New York and Philadelphia would not allow the tea to be unloaded, but there was very little confrontation. The resistance reached violent proportions, however, in Boston. When a shipment of East India Company tea arrived in Boston Harbor, Thomas Hutchinson, now the colonial governor, demanded that the cargo be unloaded and refused to allow the ships to leave port until it was safely stored. Local patriots had other ideas. On December 16, 1773, a group of men dressed as Indians—and probably inspired by the inveterate patriot Samuel Adams—climbed aboard the ships and threw over 340 casks of tea into the water. Like the violent response to the Stamp Act crisis, the Boston Tea Party was an act of resistance that resulted in the blatant destruction of property. While some opposed the Tea Act for the same reasons that they opposed the Stamp Act, namely the belief that Parliament did not have the right to tax them, others destroyed massive quantities of tea because they could not make money through its sale or because the low prices on tea hurt illegal smuggling operations.

The Coercive Acts

The British response to this act of rebellion was harsh. In a series of Coercive Acts, the English closed Boston Harbor, limited the number and scope of town meetings in Massachusetts, raised the number of British troops in the colony, and required that the trials of British provincials indicted of a crime be held in communities where those Loyalists might find a sympathetic jury. One of the most troubling of the acts passed in the wake of the Boston Tea Party was the Quebec Act. While this was technically not one of the so-called Coercive Acts, many of the colonists grouped it together with the laws being enforced in Boston. The Quebec Act allowed the Catholic Church to remain the established religion of the British-owned colony of Quebec and permitted French civil law to continue in the province. What angered the colonists about this decision was that Quebec, which England had acquired after defeating France in the French and Indian War, would not be required to have an elected legislature or a system of trial by jury. The colonists, with their fears of French religious and political tyranny, thought that the British endorsement of Quebec undermined British religious (Protestant) and political liberties and thus posed a threat to a liberty-based Protestant civilization in North America.

As news of the Coercive Acts spread down the eastern seaboard, patriots in other colonies rallied to the support of their fellow revolutionaries in Massachusetts. The acts went a long way toward developing a community of resistance to what were believed to be the tyrannical acts of Parliament. The very cause of British liberty was at stake. Several local communities responded with their own resolves opposing the Coercive Acts as violations of their rights and liberties as English subjects. These resolves were largely devoid of religious language. The Suffolk Resolves, published by patriots in Suffolk County, Massachusetts, noted that the people of Massachusetts had a duty to "God, our country, ourselves, and posterity" to fight for their civil and religious liberties, but most of the document was driven by traditional Whig concerns about British tyranny.[14]

Were the Coercive Acts a sinister plot by the Crown to take liberties away from the people of Boston? Perhaps. But they were also designed as a punishment for the violence and destruction of property propagated by colonists—many of whom would have identified themselves as Christians—who were unhappy with the economic decision of Parliament to flood the colonies with East India tea. The Tea Act would affect their wallets more than their civil liberties or religious faith. Indeed, colonial responses to the Coercive Acts among those who led the political opposition were largely secular in nature. They relied heavily upon Whig political thought and the preservation of English liberties. If such British liberties or rights were seen as stemming from Christian sources or somehow ordained by God, this is not the way that they were explained in the many documents of resistance to British tyranny.

The First Continental Congress

In September 1774, as local communities continued their boycotts and wrote their resolves, some of the finest political minds in the colonies gathered in Philadelphia for a meeting that would soon be called the First Continental Congress. The primary goal of this Congress was to form a proper response to the Coercive Acts. Fifty-five delegates from every colony except Georgia participated in the meetings. They were not in Philadelphia to consider independence, but to remedy the differences between the colonies and England and to convince the Crown to address their colonial grievances. In October the Congress issued a "Declaration and Resolves" that reaffirmed the colonists' rights to "life, liberty, and property"; their status as "free and natural-born citizens" of England; their right not to be taxed without representation; their right to trial by jury; and their right to assemble freely and to petition the king. The Declaration and Resolves echoed traditional fears of a standing army in times of peace and condemned the Crown for interfering in the work of colonial assemblies. Finally, the Congress complained about the establishment of the "Roman Catholic religion" in Quebec and the failure to uphold an "equitable system of English laws." The Congress wanted England to restore the colonies to the state of "happiness and prosperity" that existed prior to the French and Indian War. In order to accomplish this, it announced that it would "enter into a non-importation, non-consumption, and non-exportation agreement or association" and petition the king in an attempt to get him to agree to their demands.[15]

The Congress's nonimportation, nonconsumption, and nonexportation proposal was explained six days later in the text of a document called the "Continental Association," or simply "the Association." The document, which would be enacted by local governments in the colonies, forbade the importation of "goods, wares, and manufactures" from Great Britain and Ireland, tea from East India, molasses, syrup, and coffee from the West Indies, wine from the Madeira Islands, and slaves from British slave traders. The articles of the Association specifically noted that the sale, purchase, or consumption of tea was forbidden. It also called for colonial farmers to kill their sheep in moderation in order to improve breeding and conserve wool. The Congress asked the colonies, in general, to "encourage Frugality, Economy, and Industry," and to promote "Agriculture, Arts, and Manufacturing of this Country, especially that of Wool." The Association also called on the colonists to behave in a moral fashion by ceasing the kind of "extravagance and dissipation" associated with horse racing, gaming, cockfighting, and attendance at plays. It demanded that the style of dress at funerals and the quality of funeral gifts be modest. Those who failed to abide by these rules were to have their names "published in the Gazette, to the end that all such foes to the rights of *British America* may be publickly known, and universally condemned as the enemies of *American* Liberty, and thenceforth we respectively will break off all dealing with him or her."[16] The Revolution was underway.

In conclusion, we return to the question posed at the start of this chapter. Was the American Revolution a Christian event? While we still have some more history to explore in relationship to this question, it is clear that the political leaders who wrote resolves and served as delegates to the Continental Congress between 1765 and 1774 seldom explained their views in religious terms. The most important documents connected to the coming of the American Revolution focused more on Enlightenment political theory about the constitutional and natural rights of British subjects than on any Christian or biblical reason why resistance to the Crown was necessary. Indeed, as the research of political scientist Donald S. Lutz has shown, during the 1760s the founders cited from Enlightenment, Whig, and classical authors more than twice as much as they cited the Bible. And though the founders cited the Bible more than any other source during the 1770s, when one compares the combined number of citations to Enlightenment, Whig, and classical authors during this decade, the number exceeds that of the Bible. The same could be said for the 1780s.[17]

Yet we should not dismiss this lack of religious language too quickly. Though references to God seldom found their way into the formal documents produced by those challenging British tyranny, the Bible and Christian themes were often used in their private writings and by members of the clergy as a justification for the Revolution. Such themes were also used by those who opposed the American Revolution. And, as we will see in chapter 7, the Continental Congress did not hesitate to invoke the Almighty on behalf of its cause. Let's explore this history more fully.

Chapter Seven

The Revolutionary Pulpit

As we saw in the last chapter, the major colonial statements written to resist British taxation schemes between 1765 and 1774 relied more upon Whig political thought and the long history of English liberties than the Bible or Christian theology. The colonial cry of "no taxation without representation" was informed by a political vocabulary that included words such as "tyranny," "liberty," "rights," "slavery," and "power." But political leaders were not the only ones articulating revolutionary ideas during this period. Clergy were also active in the patriotic cause. It was not uncommon during this era to hear sermons justifying American independence and resistance to England. Some of these sermons were little more than a rehashing of Whig ideas, while others tried to integrate Whig politics with a belief in the providence of God. Still others used the Bible to support their political convictions. Very few patriot sermons noted the differences between civil liberty as taught by patriots and spiritual liberty as taught in the Bible. Some even reinterpreted passages teaching submission to government to make them fit better with the revolutionary spirit pervading the colonies. This chapter explores the way that the colonial clergy used their pulpits to give a biblical and theological meaning to the American Revolution.

Whig Sermons

Colonial clergy were consumed with the political issues of the day. It was quite common for ministers to blend Whig politics with biblical themes. In 1773 Baptist clergyman John Allen, preaching to the Second Baptist Church in Boston, fashioned himself as a modern-day Micah, the Old Testament prophet who challenged the tyrannical reign of King Ahaz of Judah. Referring to 2 Chronicles 28, Allen showed how Ahaz "did not that which was right in the sight of the Lord." Ahaz's failure to conform to the moral standards that God required of all monarchs prompted Micah to stand up for the "liberties and happiness of the people above the authority of the King." At one point in the sermon Allen even described Micah as a "son of liberty." Based on this interpretation of 2 Chronicles and other episodes in Israel's history, Allen concluded that God had indeed established monarchs to rule over Israel, but such kings—including David, Saul, and Solomon—were "made for the people, and the people for them." Allen did not hesitate to make the comparison between this view of Old Testament monarchy and the reign of George III of England. By unfairly taxing the people of the colonies and taking away their liberties, George III was departing from the "royal standard" that God had placed on all kings throughout history. With such a view of monarchy affirmed, Allen concluded his sermon with a healthy dose of Whig politics: "The Parliament of England cannot justly make any laws to oppress, or defend the Americans, for they are not the representatives of America, and therefore they have no legislative power either for them or against them."[1] This was a bold, but common, interpretive leap. Allen moved from the sins of Ahaz, to a lesson on a king's responsibility to serve the people, to a political plea for "no taxation without representation."

In a 1776 sermon on the occasion of his appointment as a chaplain to a New Jersey militia, Enoch Green, the minister of the Deerfield Presbyterian Church, grounded his understanding of colonial rebellion in the history of British liberties, arguing that the "King derives his power from the people." He continued with a history lesson on the English civil war and the Puritan resistance to Charles I: "Little better than a century ago," he preached, the people "resisted and opposed a Tyrant, King Charles . . . and they took . . . their rights and vanquished the Tyrant." George III's newfound "Tory" sentiments prompted Green to encourage his listeners to begin making gunpowder in preparation for war. The language Green employed in this sermon was similar to a message on tyranny and liberty he had preached at Deerfield six years earlier. In this sermon Green noted, "Because we were enslaved" and had become "Slaves to Sin—to ye Tyrant Satan . . . we are all fond of Liberty." He added, "as long as we are out of Christ, we are enslaved to ye worst kind of Bondage, enthralled by ye Tyrant of Hell." By the time of the American Revolution, Green's theological and biblical understanding of tyranny and liberty had taken on a new political meaning. The enslaver and tyrant was no longer Satan but George III and his army. Liberty was no longer the freedom from sin and the right to enjoy God's presence forever in heaven, but the individual rights secured to all people. The champion of liberty was not Christ but the New Jersey militia, for which Green would serve as chaplain.[2]

Many clergy were more explicit in their use of the Bible to justify rebellion against England. Two such sermons are worth treating in some depth. The first, Abraham Keteltas's "God Arising and Pleading His People's Cause," was preached in 1777 to Dutch and Huguenot Christians in Jamaica, New York. Based on Psalm 74:22: "Arise O God! Plead thine own Cause," Keteltas's sermon is a classic example of the way ministers made the Bible conform to Whig ideas. Keteltas began by reminding his hearers that God demands righteousness of his people. God requires Christians to love, worship, and please him, and to obey his "will and commandments." Christians are to show their love for God by leading lives of benevolence, justice, charity, integrity, truth, and kindness. They are to love their neighbors and hate sin. A society that practices this kind of righteousness will always be pleasing to God. Keteltas assumed that colonial America was this kind of Christian society.

Keteltas affirmed that "the righteous" would always have God's protection. "When the true believer is injured, oppressed, persecuted, plundered, imprisoned, tormented, and murdered," he argued, God will "look upon their cause as his own." God views injuries and threats to his righteous followers as if they were done to him. This is why, for example, God punished Nebuchadnezzar, the Babylonian king who persecuted the Hebrew people. Keteltas offered several other biblical and theological reasons as to why God will punish those who persecute his righteous people. He concluded that God has proven throughout biblical history to intercede "in behalf of his elect." Jesus is "our merciful High Priest" and will always make intercession on behalf of the righteous who call to him for aid.

Based on this biblical and theological evidence, Keteltas asserted that "the cause of this American continent, against the measure of cruel, bloody, and vindictive ministry, is the cause of God." If the colonies were indeed God's "elect" people, as Keteltas believed, then any such war carried out against them must be "unjust and unwarrantable." His conclusion was a powerful one:

> Be therefore of good courage, it is a glorious cause: It is the cause of
> truth, against error and falsehood; the cause of righteousness against
> the oppressor; the cause of pure and undefiled religion, against big-

otry, superstition, & human inventions. It is the cause of the reformation, against popery; of liberty, against arbitrary power, of benevolence, against barbarity, and of virtue against vice. It is the cause of justice and integrity, against bribery, venality, and corruption. In short, it is the cause of heaven against hell—of the kind Parent of the universe, against the prince of darkness, and destroyer of the human race.

If this was not enough to convince his hearers, Keteltas added that the cause of the American Revolution was the cause "for which the Son of God came down from his celestial throne, and expired on a cross."[3] There was little difference between the gospel and the resistance to English tyranny, or between the church and the colonies.

The second sermon worth discussing at length is Samuel Sherwood's "The Church's Flight into the Wilderness: An Address on the Times." Sherwood, the Congregational minister in Weston, Connecticut, blended millennial themes from the book of Revelation with contemporary political ideas. His sermon was based on Revelation 12:14–17, the story of a woman who, with the help of eagle's wings, flies into the wilderness to find protection from an evil serpent (dragon). When the serpent cannot drown the woman with the flood pouring from its mouth, it decides instead to make war on the woman's "seed" who "keep the commandment of God, and have the testimony of Jesus Christ." Like most commentators on the book of Revelation—past and present—Sherwood interpreted this story as a metaphor. The serpent is an agent of Satan, who from the beginning of time has used his "subtlety and malice to defeat the purposes of divine grace, and to destroy Christ's kingdom on earth." But for Sherwood this evil dragon is a very specific manifestation of Satan's minions: "Among all his crafty and subtle interventions, *popery*, which exalts the principal leaders and abettors of it . . . seems most cunningly devised, and best adapted to answer his purpose; and has proved the most formidable engine of terror and cruelty to the true members of Christ's church."[4]

What exactly did Sherwood mean when he equated the dragon of Revelation 12 with "popery"? Ever since the Reformation, Protestants have connected the evil forces of the book of Revelation with the leader of the Roman Catholic Church. It was especially common for Protestant Bible commentators to declare that the pope was the "great whore of Babylon" from Revelation 17. As Protestantism grew, especially in the English-speaking world, it became convenient for clergy to define themselves politically and religiously against the so-called papists who were loyal to Rome. By the eighteenth century, Protestant nations such as England saw themselves as "free" nations. Religiously, they could read the Bible and interpret it as they saw fit without any interference from popes, bishops, or priests. They quickly connected this kind of religious liberty with the civil rights they enjoyed as British subjects and, as we have seen, compared the freedom of England to the religious and political tyranny of Catholic France.

Sherwood expanded this definition of "popery" beyond the Catholic Church to include any government or power that threatens civil and religious freedom: "This popish mysterious leaven of iniquity and absurdity . . . has not been confined to the boundaries of the Roman empire, nor strictly to the territory of the Pope's usurped authority and jurisdiction; but has spread in a greater or less degree, among almost all the nations of the earth; especially amongst the chief rulers, the princes and noblemen thereof."[5] In other words, "popery" was synonymous with religious and political tyranny. It was not merely confined to France, but could also be applied to some of the seventeenth-century Stuart monarchs (Charles I and James II) who threatened the religious liberties of England. Popery could be found anywhere that a "corrupt system of tyranny and oppression" was in place.

Such a broad definition of "popery" allowed Sherwood to apply the lessons of Revelation 12 to the cause of the American Revolution: "I am of the opinion that the Church of Christ in every age, may find something in this book applicable to her case and circumstances; and all such passages that are so, may lawfully be applied and improved by us accordingly." Sherwood was prepared to put an American spin on Revelation 12. The woman, whom Sherwood now identified as the "Church of Christ," fled to a "wilderness," which he now identified as the English-American colonies. Here the woman would be nourished by God in the "quiet enjoyment of her liberties and privileges, civil and religious." But the serpent, or Parliament, was threatening. In a strange blend of political vocabulary and biblical interpretation, Sherwood described the "despotism," "arbitrary power," "dominion," "tyranny," and "corruption" that this English "serpent" was enforcing on the woman in the wilderness. The woman was representative of some combination of the "Church of Christ" and the English colonies as a whole. Sherwood's conclusion brought it all home:

> Liberty has been planted here; and the more it is attacked, the more it grows and flourishes. The time is coming and hastening on, when

Babylon the great shall fall to rise no more; when all wicked tyrants and oppressors shall be destroyed for ever. These violent attacks upon the woman in the wilderness, may possibly be some of the last efforts, and dying struggles of the man of sin. These commotions and convulsions in the British empire, may be leading to the fulfillment of such prophecies as relate to his downfall and overthrow, and to the future glory and prosperity of Christ's church. It will soon be said and acknowledged, that the kingdoms of this world, are become the kingdoms of our Lord, and of his Christ. The vials of God's wrath begin to be poured out on his enemies and adversaries; and there is falling on them a noisome and grievous sore.[6]

For Sherwood, there was little difference between the coming kingdom of God as described in the book of Revelation and the emergence of a new nation defined by liberty and justice for all.

In writing about the use of the Bible in Revolutionary America, historian Mark Noll has suggested: "To be sure, patriotic ministers often applied biblical texts to support their cause. But now, after the passage of time, these efforts look more like comical propaganda than serious biblical exposition."[7] Many clergy took great liberties with biblical passages in order to make them fit with the dominant political ideas of the day. Few patriot clergy offered deep theological reflection on the political climate in which they found themselves.[8]

A Biblical Argument for Revolution

Was the American Revolution a "just war"? Many patriotic clergy answered this question with a resounding yes. Reverend David Jones, the pastor of the Great Valley Baptist Church in Chester County, Pennsylvania, told a group of Pennsylvania militia that "when a people are oppressed, insulted and abused, and can have no other redress, it then becomes our duty as men, with our eyes to GOD, to fight for our liberties and properties." Jones added: "a defensive war is sinless before GOD; consequently to engage therein, is consistent with the purest religion."[9] Similarly, John Carmichael, a Presbyterian minister in Lancaster County, Pennsylvania, told local troops in 1775: "although war is in itself a very great evil, and one of those sore judgments, by which a holy God punishes the world for sin, therefore to be deprecated, and avoided as much as possible; yet is, at times, by reason of certain circumstances, so unavoidable, that it is our duty to enter into it."[10]

Clergy such as Jones and Carmichael used the Bible extensively to argue for the justness of the War for Independence. Jones began with Abraham (Abram), who, as recorded in Genesis 14, used "martial weapons" to rescue his nephew Lot from enemy tribes. Abram's exploits, Jones continued, were praised by Melchizedek, the high priest described by modern biblical interpreters as a "type of Christ." The Old Testament examples of defensive wars abound, and Jones did not hesitate to refer to as many as possible. Moses engaged in a bloody defensive war against the Amorites; Joshua was forced to fight multiple battles to secure the promised land; and similar wars were waged in the age of the judges and by King David.[11] For anyone hearing or reading this sermon in 1775, the comparison to the revolutionary crisis of England was clear.

While it was rather easy to invoke examples from the Old Testament to justify war, the violence of armed conflict would be more difficult to square with the New Testament, particularly the teachings of Jesus. By providing a few creative interpretations of Jesus' teaching, Carmichael offered a sophisticated response to those who argued that Jesus condemned war and violence. For example, when Jesus told his followers to "turn the other cheek," he did "not mean to forbid us to use lawful and proper means of self-preservation." Indeed, Carmichael argued, this command from the Sermon on the Mount should be interpreted as "proverbial." It teaches that "we should be ready to put up with a good deal of ill-usage, before we would create disturbance, yea that we should do anything consistent with our own safety." The message fit well with the contemporary political crisis in America. The colonies had been patient with England for long enough. It was now time to engage in a violent act of self-preservation. Related to this was Carmichael's interpretation of Jesus' command to "love our enemies." Carmichael argued that Jesus "can't possibly [have] meant that we should love them better than ourselves—that we should put it in the enemy's power to kill us, when we have it in our power to save our own life, by killing the enemy." Finally, Carmichael noted that Jesus, in Matthew 17:27, encouraged his disciples to pay the proper amount of tribute money to Emperor Tiberius Caesar, despite the fact that Tiberius was engaged in wars throughout the world and was presumably using taxes to fund those wars. As Carmichael put it: "Tiberius was a Pagan; but as the Jews were tributaries to the Romans, and our Lord was a Jew by birth, he paid his tax as a peaceable member of the commonwealth; but had our Lord been a Mennonist [*sic*] he would have refused to pay tribute, to support war, which shews the absurdity of these people's conduct."[12] Carmichael, of course, said nothing about the fact that such a passage might also be interpreted to mean that all good followers of Jesus should pay their taxes, including angry American patriots.

Romans 13 and 1 Peter 2

While the Old Testament and the Gospels were used frequently to argue on behalf of a just war, it was the Epistles, especially Romans 13:1–7 and 1 Peter 2:13–17, that drew the most discussion and debate among clergy during the time of the American Revolution:

> Let every soul be subject unto the higher powers. For there is no power but of God: the powers that be are ordained of God. Whosoever therefore resisteth the power, resisteth the ordinance of God: and they that resist shall receive to themselves damnation. For rulers are not a terror to good works, but to the evil. Wilt thou then not be afraid of the power? do that which is good, and thou shalt have praise of the same: For he is the minister of God to thee for good. But if thou do that which is evil, be afraid; for he beareth not the sword in vain: for he is the minister of God, a revenger to execute wrath upon him that doeth evil. Wherefore ye must needs be subject, not only for wrath, but also for conscience sake. For this cause pay ye tribute also: for they are God's ministers, attending continually upon this very thing. Render therefore to all their dues: tribute to whom tribute is due; custom to whom custom; fear to whom fear; honour to whom honour. Owe no man any thing, but to love one another: for he that loveth another hath fulfilled the law. *Romans 13:1–7*

> Submit yourselves to every ordinance of man for the Lord's sake: whether it be to the king, as supreme; Or unto governors, as unto them that are sent by him for the punishment of evildoers, and for the praise of them that do well. For so is the will of God, that with well doing ye may put to silence the ignorance of foolish men: As free, and not using your liberty for a cloke of maliciousness, but as servants of God. Honour all men. Love the brotherhood. Fear God. Honour the king. *1 Peter 2:13–17*

When taken at face value, these passages suggest that all rulers are "ordained by God" and are worthy of "Honour." Romans 13 states clearly that one who resists such authority will receive "damnation." These passages also require Christians to pay their taxes ("tribute"). When taken at face value, they seem to be teaching complete submission to government authorities with no exceptions or caveats.

This is exactly the way in which many Loyalists, mostly Anglican ministers, interpreted the meaning of these passages of Scripture. Jonathan Boucher no doubt had Romans 13 in mind when he wrote: "To resist and to rebel against a lawful government, is to oppose *the ordinance of God*, and to injure or destroy institutions most essential to human happiness."[13] New York Anglican Samuel Seabury thought his sermon on 1 Peter 2:17 was necessary "to wipe off those Asperations and ill Impressions which the Ignorance and foolish Men had brought upon the Christian Religion, by pretending that their Christian Liberty set them free from Subjection to civil Government."[14] Another New York Anglican, Charles Inglis, believed that the Christians' obedience to government was what "distinguish[ed] themselves from others and manifest[ed] the native Excellence and Spirit of their Religion."[15]

These Anglican Loyalists affirmed that obedience to civil authority was required of Christians regardless of the form of government or behavior of the government. Christians must obey the government, Seabury argued, "whether it be exercised by KINGS as Supreme, or by Governors sent by them and acting by their Authority." He reminded his readers:

> When St. Peter and St. Paul wrote their Epistles, they were under the Government of Heathen Emperors and Magistrates, who persecuted them, and the other Christians—depriving them of their Possessions, beating and banishing and killing them—without any Crime proved against them, but merely because they were Christians. And yet it was to these Emperors and Magistrates—even to *Nero and Caligula*—that the Apostles commanded Honor and Respect, at all Times; and whenever it could be done consistently with Obedience to God, Duty and Submission.[16]

Similarly, Inglis noted that Peter wrote his epistle at a time when Nero was the emperor of Rome. He stressed that "the personal Character of the Magistrate was not to interfere with the Civil Duty of the Subject. Even when bad, it did not dissolve the Obligation of the latter."[17]

The patriots used phrases such as "passive obedience" and "unlimited submission" to describe this Anglican view of the relationship between Christians and civil authority. They spent hundreds of pages trying to counter it. The most outspoken defender of such a patriotic interpretation of Romans 13 and 1 Peter 2 was Jonathan Mayhew, the minister at Boston's West Church. Mayhew was a liberal Congregationalist and forerunner of the Unitarian movement in New England. He was committed to interpreting the Bible predominantly through the grid of natural law and reason. His sermon on Romans 13, "A Discourse Concerning Unlimited Submission and Non-Resistance to the Higher Powers," was preached in 1750 on the celebration of the one hundredth anniversary of the execution of Charles I during the English Civil War. Despite the fact that Mayhew's sermon was published a quarter-century prior to the outbreak of revolutionary hostility in Boston, John Adams, reflecting on the causes of the Revolution, wrote in 1818, "If the orators on the fourth of July really wish to investigate the principles and feelings which produced the Revolution, they out to study . . . Dr. Mayhew's sermon on passive obedience and non-resistance."[18]

Mayhew began his sermon by affirming that Romans 13 required Christians to be obedient to government, regardless of whether the government was a monarchy, republic, or aristocracy. But the real issue at hand was the *extent* to which such "subjection to higher powers" should be practiced. Mayhew concluded that sometimes resistance to civil authority might be justified. According to Mayhew, Romans 13 could not be advocating unlimited submission to government because such a practice did not conform either to the true meaning of the passage or to the dictates of reason. Paul's primary audience in this passage was those in the first-century Roman church who did not show proper respect to civil authority and were of a "licentious opinion and character." Moreover, Romans 13 could not conceivably require submission to all rulers, but only to those rulers who were "good." Rulers who "attend continually upon the gratification of their own lust and pride and ambition, to the destruction of the public welfare," were not worthy of a Christian's submission. Mayhew argued, "Rulers have no authority from God to do mischief." It is "blasphemy," he continued, to "call tyrants and oppressors God's ministers." It follows that when a ruler becomes tyrannical, Christians "are bound to throw off our allegiance to him, and to resist; and that according to the tenor of the apostle's argument in this passage." Perhaps the most ironic thing about Mayhew's argument is the way he managed to transform Romans 13 from a verse teaching submission to authority into a verse justifying the execution of Charles I and, for that matter, all rebellion against tyrannical government. Charles I, he concluded, had failed to respect the "natural and legal rights of the people, against the unnatural and illegal encroachments of arbitrary power." As a result, resistance was absolutely necessary in order to preserve the nation from "slavery, misery, and ruin."[19]

For Mayhew, it was "obvious" to any rational person exercising common sense that Romans 13 and 1 Peter 2 did not teach submission to a government perceived to be tyrannical. How could God require his people to live under oppression? God had promised his people freedom. But such an interpretation required ministers like Mayhew to move beyond a plain reading of these texts. In order to turn these passages into revolutionary manifestos, Mayhew needed to interpret them with a strong dose of the ideas of political philosophers such as John Locke. In his famous *Two Treatises on Government* (1689), a pamphlet designed to explain why the Glorious Revolution (the removal of English monarch James II from the throne) was justified, Locke taught that individuals had the right to overthrow tyrannical governments that violated their natural rights to life, liberty, and property. His justification for resistance to government had a profound influence on the leaders of the American Revolution, but it ran counter to the teachings of Romans 13 and 1 Peter 2. This tension did not stop clergy from interpreting these passages through the grid of Locke's revolutionary teachings.[20]

The liberal or "Lockean" interpretation of these biblical passages was a minority position in the history of the Christian church and was relatively new in the history of Protestantism. According to political scientist Steven Dworetz: "Basing revolutionary teaching on the scriptural authority of chapter 13 of St. Paul's Epistle to the Romans must rank as one of the greatest ironies in the history of political thought." Romans 13 served as "the touchstone for passive obedience and unconditional submission from Augustine and Gregory to Luther and Calvin." Martin Luther, the father of the Protestant Reformation, wrote that resistance to civil rulers is "a greater sin than murder, unchastity, theft, and dishonesty, and all that these may include."[21]

John Calvin, the Genevan reformer who had the most influence on the theology of the colonial clergy, taught that rebellion against civil government was never justified: "If we keep firmly in mind that even the worst kings are appointed by this same decree which establishes the authority of kings, then we will never permit ourselves the seditious idea that a king is to be treated according to his deserts, or that we need not obey a kind who does not conduct himself towards us like a king." Calvin added: "we must honour the worst tyrant in the office in which the Lord has seen fit to set him," and "if you go on to infer that only just governments are to be repaid by obedience, your reasoning is stupid." He taught that Christians must "venerate" even those rulers who were "unworthy" of veneration.[22] As political scientist Gregg Frazer has argued, "One cannot legitimately employ Calvin to justify rebellion, which is why the patriotic preachers argued in terms of 'Mr. Locke's doctrine' rather than Calvin's."[23] In the end, today's Christians who are interested in understanding the relationship between Romans 13 and 1 Peter 2 and the American Revolution must come to grips with the fact that many patriotic clergy may have been more influenced in their political positions by John Locke than the Bible.

The Revolution as a "Just War"

If ministerial arguments for independence favored Enlightenment political ideas over the teachings of Scripture, it is also true that Christian arguments for war against England failed to conform to classic Christian arguments used to support a "just war." In fact, such just war arguments, often associated with historic church leaders such as Augustine and Aquinas, were rarely if ever employed by Revolutionary-era Protestant ministers.[24] The just war tradition affirms that government is ordained of God to preserve peace and to maintain justice. War is to be avoided whenever possible, but at times the desire for peace might make war necessary. War is thus justified only as a last resort. It must be declared by a legitimate government and have an attainable goal, namely the restoration of peace. It must protect the lives of noncombatants.[25]

The closest any patriotic clergyman came to arguing on behalf of traditional just war theory was John Carmichael in "A Self-Defensive War Lawful." In this sermon he laid out what he perceived to be the parameters of a "lawful war." First, he argued that a lawful war required that any combatant believe he was "called by God" to fight and that "with a good conscience and courage, he may rely on God for strength and protection." Second, Carmichael believed that every soldier should make sure that "his peace is made with God, by believing in his Son Jesus Christ for salvation," before entering battle. Third, Christian soldiers engaged in war "must set out in the fear of God" and rely on the "justice and righteousness of the superintendency of Jehovah, over all the fates." Fourth, soldiers were to avoid doing violence to those who are unable to defend themselves. Fifth, they are not to accuse others falsely.[26] With the exception of Carmichael's fourth point, which conforms to just war teaching that noncombatants must always be protected during battle, none of his points defending a "lawful war" complies with classic Christian teaching about what makes a war "just."

Of course, from the perspective of the colonial ministers we have examined in this chapter, the American Revolutionary War was clearly a war that was ordained by God. Others, however, were not so sure. As we saw in the previous chapter, the American colonies were part of Great Britain, the freest and most liberty-loving nation on the face of the earth. As citizens of the empire the colonists enjoyed a great deal of economic prosperity and political freedom. John Wesley, the famed eighteenth-century English evangelical, could not understand why the colonists demanded more liberty than they already had as members of the British Empire. The colonists, he wrote, "enjoyed their liberty in as full manner as I do, or any reasonable man can desire." Wesley ticked off a litany of colonial sins: they refused to pay their taxes, they had destroyed property ("Ship-loads of tea"), and, most importantly, they held African slaves even as they cried for their own freedom from English tyranny. For Wesley, the cry of "no taxation without representation" was absurd: "I reply, they are now taxed by themselves, in the very same sense that nine-tenths of us are. We have not only no vote in parliament, but none in electing the members." Lack of representation in Parliament did not mean that the colonists were exempted from "subjection to the government and laws."[27] As one might imagine, Wesley did not think the American Revolutionary War was justified.

Christians today who want to argue that the Revolutionary War was "just" must offer concrete evidence to suggest that this war was indeed a "last resort." They must also make a compelling case that the colonists' grievances against the Crown merited military resistance. Here are a few questions that one might ask in this regard: Do high taxes justify a military rebellion against the government, even if such a rebellion is conducted in direct violation of passages such as Romans 13 that command Christians to pay their taxes? Was the English government as "tyrannical" as the colonists claimed? And if it was, did the level of tyranny justify armed conflict? After all, Great Britain offered more freedom to the inhabitants of their empire than any other nation in the world. Did the revolutionaries have a moral case to make for their own freedom when many had denied freedom to the slaves in their midst? (Perhaps, as Mark Noll has argued, it was only the enslaved African Americans who could legitimately "justify taking up arms to defend themselves."[28])

In conclusion, American patriotic clergy used their pulpits to promote the cause for independence by infusing biblical interpretation with the predominant Whig political thinking of the day. Biblical terms such as "slavery" and "freedom" took on new political meanings. Clergy protested against British taxation using political language that was baptized with the conviction that God was always on the side of liberty. The long-standing Puritan view that the people of America were the chosen people of God—a new Israel—was used to show that God must be on the side of the patriots. Bible passages that had historically been employed to teach the importance of submission to governmental authorities were now being interpreted to justify revolution. And there was no attempt to reflect on classic Christian understandings of what constituted a "just war."

Did the Bible, as proclaimed from American pulpits, play a prominent role in the coming of the American Revolution? Yes. But those who argue that the American Revolution was a Christian event need to reflect deeply on the ways in which the Bible was interpreted by those responsible for teaching it to ordinary Christians in this time of political crisis.[29]

Chapter Eight

Nature's God

Is the Declaration of Independence a Christian Document?

In September 1774 some of the greatest political minds in British America gathered in Philadelphia for the opening meeting of the First Continental Congress. The Congress was called in the wake of the dreaded Coercive Acts, a series of British decrees designed to punish the colony of Massachusetts for the destruction of a shipload of tea in Boston Harbor the previous December. As news of the Coercive Acts spread down the eastern seaboard, patriots in other colonies rallied to the support of their fellow revolutionaries in Massachusetts. The response to the Coercive Acts went a long way toward developing a community of resistance to what many believed to be the tyrannical acts of Parliament. The very cause of British liberty was at stake, and the men in Philadelphia met to decide the best way to respond to the crisis.

On the second day of the Continental Congress, a Massachusetts delegate named Thomas Cushing put forth a motion that the daily sessions be opened with prayer. The members of Congress were initially divided over the idea. John Jay of New York and either John or Edward Rutledge of South Carolina thought that prayer might undermine unity in Congress since all of the delegates represented different "religious sentiments." Samuel Adams, however, supported Cushing's motion, declaring, "I am no bigot. I can hear a prayer from a man of piety and virtue, who is at the same time a friend of his country. I am a stranger in Philadelphia, but I have heard that Mr. Duché deserves that character; and therefore I move that Mr. Duché, an Episcopalian clergyman, be desired to rend prayers to the Congress tomorrow morning." Eventually the motion passed and Duché was appointed the first chaplain of the Continental Congress.[1]

The following day Duché read from Psalm 35 and prayed for about ten minutes. John Adams described the new chaplain's devotional words to his wife, Abigail:

> [Duché] read several prayers in the established form; and then read the Collect for the seventh day of September, which was the thirty-fifth Psalm. You must remember that this was the next morning after we heard the horrible rumor of the cannonade of Boston. I never saw a greater effect upon the audience. It seemed as if Heaven had ordained that Psalm to be read on that morning.
>
> After this, Mr. Duché, unexpected to everybody, struck out into an extemporary prayer, which filled the bosom of every man present. I must confess I never heard a better prayer, or one so well pronounced, Episcopalian as he is. Dr. Cooper himself never prayed with such fervor, such earnestness and pathos, and in language so elegant and sublime—for America, for Congress, for the Province of Massachusetts Bay, and especially the town of Boston. It has had an excellent effect upon everybody here.[2]

Duché made clear that England's cause was "malicious," "cruel," and "unrighteous." Most in the room that day believed that the Continental Congress was doing the Lord's work.[3]

Religion and the Continental Congress

Though the purpose of the First and Second Continental Congresses was political in nature, religion was often part of the agenda. The delegates to Congress lived in a world that was very different from our own—a world in which most people were Christians or at least affiliated in one way or another with a Christian church or denomination. As historian Derek Davis has noted, "The Continental Congress . . . functioned essentially under traditional Western political theory, that is, on the belief that religion is central to a well-ordered polity."[4]

The official statements of the Continental Congress invoked the providence of God on behalf of the revolutionary cause. In 1778 the Congress recorded in their official records that "our dependence was not upon man; it was upon Him who hath commanded us to love our enemies, and to render good for evil." Congress believed that God had delivered them from calamity and aided them in their military efforts. In an address to the "Inhabitants of the United States of America" Congress asked: "How often have we been reduced to distress, and yet been raised up?" Deliverance happened in "such a variety of instances, so peculiarly marked, almost by the direct interposition of Providence, that not to feel and acknowledge his protection would be the height of impious gratitude." Indeed, Congress affirmed that the "God of battles in whom was our trust, hath conducted us through the paths of danger and distress to the thresholds of security."[5] In a letter to the Iroquois, Delaware, and Shawnee Indians, Congress noted that "God Almighty . . . superintends and governs men and their actions." Congress thanked God for military victories and triumphs. In 1779 it affirmed that the "arduous contest with Great Britain in its commencement was sustained under almost every possible disadvantage, and it has been conducted with such success as manifests to us the peculiar favor of Divine Providence." In 1778 Congress put forth a manifesto affirming the justice of their cause and their commitment to "confiding in Him, who disposes of human events."[6]

The Continental Congress appealed publicly to God for help during the most difficult times of the American Revolutionary War. In May 1778, when its attempts to foster reconciliation with England were spurned by the Crown, Congress "made a solemn appeal to the tribunal of unerring wisdom and justice: to that Almighty Ruler of Princes, whose kingdom is over all." If England would not listen, then Congress would appeal solely to "that God who searcheth the hearts of men, for the rectitude of our intentions."[7] On July 6, 1775, in the wake of the battles of Lexington and Concord and Bunker Hill, Congress passed a document entitled "The Necessity for Taking Up Arms." It told the now-familiar story of British tyranny from the end of the French and Indian War to the present day and argued that the cause of the Revolution was just. The document was loaded with religious language. It stated that the "Divine Author of our existence" and the "great Creator" was concerned about the general "welfare of mankind" and consequently was opposed to the "unbounded power" exercised by England over the colonies. It concluded that God had providentially brought this conflict with England precisely at a time when the colonies had grown in size, had some military experience (a reference to the French and Indian War), and were able to defend themselves. It was now up to the colonists to exert "the utmost energy of those powers which our beneficent Creator has graciously bestowed upon us." The statement concluded: "with a humble confidence in the mercies of the supreme and impartial Judge and Ruler of the universe, we most devoutly implore his divine goodness to protect us happily through this great conflict, to dispose our adversaries to reconciliation on reasonable terms, and thereby to relieve the empire from the calamities of a civil war."[8]

Congress's views on God and religion are revealed most fully in the texts of the various fast and thanksgiving proclamations issued during the course of the Revolutionary War. Throughout the war, Congress appointed committees to write resolutions for days of "fasting and humiliation" in which Americans were urged to cease their labor, go to church, and pray for the nation. As might be expected, these resolutions often came with an acknowledgment of God's providence. The proclamation of June 12, 1775, began by affirming that the "great Governor of the World, by his supreme and universal Providence, not only conducts the course of nature with unerring wisdom and rectitude, but frequently influences the minds of men to serve the wise and gracious purposes of his providential government."[9] The God invoked here is an active God who intervenes in the lives of human beings and nations. Many of these proclamations, as in the case of the one issued on March 29, 1779, affirmed that God had brought the colonies into the war as a punishment for the sins and transgressions of their people: "Whereas, in just punishment of our manifold transgressions it hath pleased the Supreme Disposer of all events to visit these United States with a destructive calamitous war, through which his divine Providence hath, hitherto, in a wonderful manner, conducted us. . . ." Or, as the proclamation of March 11, 1780, noted, "It having pleased the righteous Governor of the World, for the punishment of our manifold offences, to permit the sword of war still to harass our country. . . ."[10] The Congress affirmed that God brought war because his people had sinned.

Many of these proclamations urged the colonists to pray for victory, success, and "deliverance" from British tyranny. The proclamation of March 16, 1776, asked colonists to "supplicate his interposition for averting the threatened danger, and prospering our strenuous efforts in the cause of freedom, virtue, and posterity." The same declaration called upon "the Lord of Hosts, the God of Armies, to animate our officers and soldiers with invincible fortitude, to guard and protect them in the day of battle, and to crown them the continental arms, by sea and land, with victory and success."[11] At the heart of these proclamations, particularly the ones calling for days of "fasting" and "humiliation," was the national confession of sins. The delegates to the Continental Congress believed that God would not support their cause unless colonists were willing to admit to their transgressions and repent of their wrongdoings. As Congress declared in 1779, "too few have been sufficiently awakened to a sense of their guilt, or warmed our Bosoms with gratitude, or taught to amend their lives and turn from their sins, that so He might turn from His wrath."[12] Such calls might seem strange to modern readers. Indeed, many of these proclamations seem more fitting for a church than a political body staging a revolution. Yet Congress seemed to have no qualms about leading the nation in national repentance. Some of these calls for repentance were more overtly Christian. For example, in March 1776 Congress asked the colonists to "confess and bewail our manifold sins and transgression, and, by a sincere repentance and amendment of life, appease his righteous displeasure and, through the merits and mediation of Jesus Christ, obtain his pardon and forgiveness; humbly imploring his assistance to frustrate the cruel purposes of our unnatural enemies."[13] Or consider the March 1781 proclamation that called the colonists to "by sincere repentance and amendment of life, appease his righteous displeasure, and through the merits of our blessed Saviour, obtain pardon and forgiveness."[14]

Forgiveness, the members of Congress believed, must lead ultimately to a revival of Christian piety and a reformation of morals. The kind of virtue needed to sustain a successful republic would best be found in the cultivation of Christianity. Congress hoped that "virtue and true religion may revive and flourish throughout our land."[15] It called upon God to "grant us his grace to repent of our sins, and amend our lives, according to his holy word."[16] In 1782, with the war nearly over and Congress now entrusted with the responsibility of leading a new and independent republic, it asked Americans to pray that God would "diffuse a spirit of universal reformation among all ranks and degrees of our citizens; and make us holy, that so we may be an happy people."[17] A similar idea was put forth by Congress in 1780 when it asked for prayer that God would "establish virtue and piety by his divine grace to revive and spread the influence of patriotism, and eradicate that love of pleasure and gain which renders us forgetful of our country and our God."[18] The founders believed that the grace of God was necessary to instill patriotism in the United States and develop a sense of moral nationalism.

As the end of the war approached, calls for fasting and humiliation gave way to calls for thanksgiving and praise. In the midst of victory the Continental Congress did not forget to give credit where credit was due. It continued to call the nation to repentance, but also urged its citizens to gather in churches to remember the "smiles of Heaven" that had brought them military victory and political independence. In addition to their prayers of thanksgiving for these military and political successes, Congress also reminded Americans to be thankful that they were a Christian people. In October 1781 Congress gave thanks for Americans' victory over the enemy, but "above all" they were asked to remember how God "hath diffused the glorious light of the gospel, whereby, through the merits of our gracious Redeemer, we may become the heirs of his eternal glory."[19] Congress prayed that God would "grant to his church the plentiful effusions of divine grace, and pour out his holy spirit on all ministers of the gospel; that he would bless and prosper the means of education, and spread the light of Christian knowledge through the remotest parts of the earth." Similarly, Congress petitioned God to "establish the independence of the United States upon the basis of religion and virtue, and support and protect them in the enjoyment of peace, liberty, and safety."[20]

The Continental Congress did other things, beyond the promotion of fast and thanksgiving days, to promote Christianity and virtue. As we have seen, it appointed Jacob Duché the first chaplain to Congress. Duché's responsibility was to attend the meetings of Congress and offer prayers and Scripture readings every day at 9:00 a.m. Between 1776 and 1787 Congress had five chaplains. The military also had a clergy presence: on July 29, 1775, Congress created the Chaplain Corps in the Continental Army and about a year later decided to appoint a chaplain to each regiment in the Army.[21] Congress monitored chaplains closely. The records of Congress's meetings show a concern with making sure that they were paid appropriately.

In 1777 Congress explored the possibility of publishing an American edition of the Bible, but the idea was shelved due to the cost of publishing, the availability of the appropriate paper, and the pressing demands of war. In Philadelphia, printer Robert Aitken went forward with the publication of his own American Bible. Congress had turned down Aitken's initial request for funds to support his Bible project, but it did give his new Bible an official endorsement. On September 12, 1782, congressional chaplains William White and George Duffield praised the project, and the Congress as a whole recommended Aitken's edition to the inhabitants of the United States.[22]

The Declaration of Independence and "Original Intent"

Of course, the most significant document that came out of the Continental Congress was the Declaration of Independence. Many defenders of Christian America have claimed that the Declaration was a Christian document written to establish a uniquely Christian nation. Gary T. Amos has responded to scholars—some of them fellow Christians—who have questioned the religious roots of the Declaration of Independence and the religious beliefs of the founders generally. There seems to be a lot at stake in such a project. As Amos puts it: "The bleak view of the founding fathers is not only wrong, it is causing devastating results in the Christian community. . . . When Christians accept these mistaken views they begin to feel vulnerable. They become defensive and think that they must continually apologize for America's past. Many feel alienated, as though it is wrong or useless to participate in the public process." Amos then proceeds to defend the Declaration as a document that gives hope to all Christian attempts to be a witness to American culture.[23]

Amos and many Christian commentators like him tend to focus their interpretation of the Declaration of Independence on the document's four references to God. Those passages, which will be treated in detail in the next section of this chapter, include the idea that the right to declare independence from England comes directly from the "Law of Nature and Nature's God"; the notion that the "unalienable rights" of "life, liberty, and the pursuit of happiness" are endowed by the "Creator"; the appeal to the "Supreme Judge of the world for the rectitude of our intentions"; and the closing reference to the "firm reliance on the protection of divine Providence." Focusing too heavily on these passages, however, neglects the eighteenth-century motivation behind the writing of the Declaration. In other words, it misses the "original intent" of the document. For all the effort that Christian conservatives place on discerning and interpreting the "original intent" of the U.S. Constitution, there has been little effort to understand the meaning and the purpose of the Declaration of Independence as the founders intended it.

Most would agree that the Declaration of Independence was not a theological or religious document, but neither was it designed primarily to teach Americans and the world about human rights. Americans have become so taken by the second paragraph of the document that they miss the purpose of the Declaration as understood by the Continental Congress, its team of authors, and its chief writer, Thomas Jefferson. In the context of the American Revolution, the Declaration of Independence was just what it claimed to be—a "declaration" of "independence" from England and an assertion of American sovereignty in the world.

Historian David Armitage has argued convincingly that the Declaration of Independence was written primarily as a document asserting American political sovereignty in the hopes that the newly created United States would secure a place in the international community of nations. In fact,

Armitage asserts, the Declaration was discussed abroad more than it was at home. This meant that the Declaration was "decidedly *un*-revolutionary. It would affirm the maxims of European statecraft, not affront them." To put this differently, the "self-evident truths" and "unalienable rights" of the Declaration's second paragraph would not have been particularly new or groundbreaking in the context of the eighteenth-century British world. These were ideals that all members of the British Empire valued regardless of whether they supported or opposed the American Revolution. The writers of the Declaration of Independence and the members of the Second Continental Congress who endorsed and signed it did not believe that they were advancing, as historian Pauline Maier has put it, "a classic statement of American political principles." This was a foreign policy document.[24]

The writers of the Declaration viewed the document this way. In an 1825 letter to fellow Virginian Henry Lee, Thomas Jefferson explained his motivation behind writing it:

> when forced, therefore, to resort to arms for redress, an appeal to the tribunal of the world was deemed proper for our jurisdiction. This was the object of the Declaration of Independence. Not to find out new principles or new arguments, never before thought of . . . but to place before mankind the common sense of the subject, in terms so plain and firm as to command their assent, and to justify ourselves in the independent stand we are compelled to take.[25]

John Adams, writing five years after he signed it, called the Declaration "that memorable Act by which [the United States] assumed an equal Station among the nations." Adams's son, John Quincy, though not a participant in the Continental Congress, described the Declaration as "merely an *occasional* state paper. It was a solemn exposition to the world, of the *causes* which had *compelled* the people of a small portion of the British empire, to cast off their allegiance and renounce the protection of the British king: and to dissolve their social connection with the British people." There is little in these statements to suggest that the Declaration of Independence was anything other than an announcement to the world that the former British colonies were now free and independent states and thus deserved a place in the international order of nations.[26]

If the original intent of the writers of the Declaration of Independence was to affirm American statehood to the world, then at what point did this revered document become, in the minds of Americans, a statement of individual or human rights? Indeed, as Abraham Lincoln put it, "The assertion that 'all men are created equal' was of no practical use in effecting our separation from Great Britain; and it was placed in the Declaration, not for that, but for our future use."[27] Lincoln was a revisionist. He found the Declaration useful for reasons that were not primarily intended by its writers. Americans like Lincoln took a document that was originally addressed to the world as a "declaration of independence" and turned it into a document that would come to represent American ideals and values related to individual rights. As Armitage writes,

> this effort of domestication would have two equal and opposite effects: first, it would hide from Americans the original meaning of the Declaration as an international, and even a global document; second, it would ensure that within the United States only proponents of slavery, supporters of Southern secession, and anti-individualist critics of rights talk would be able to recall that original meaning.[28]

In the hands of abolitionists, women's suffragists, and especially Lincoln, the Declaration became "American Scripture." The abolitionist William Lloyd Garrison appealed to the Declaration's assertion that "all men are created equal" in his defense of the immediate emancipation of slaves. The Seneca Falls convention of 1848 used it to proclaim the rights of women. And Lincoln, in the opening lines of the Gettysburg Address ("four score and seven years ago") made a direct connection between the Union cause in the Civil War and the Declaration of Independence.[29] These American reformers were in search of a usable past—an interpretation of the American founding that they could employ to promote human rights and equality in their nineteenth-century settings. The original intent of the Declaration was not as useful as the famed second paragraph asserting the "self-evident" truth that people were created equal and possessed certain unalienable rights.

This kind of historical revisionism continues today among those who uphold the belief that the Declaration of Independence was a Christian document. While the Declaration clearly affirms, for example, that human rights come from "the Creator," the original intent of the founders was not to write a theological document, a system of government, a treatise on American values, or even declare that human rights came from God. The "original intent" of the Declaration of Independence was something much more practical. It was written to announce the birth of the United States to the rest of the world.

God and the Declaration of Independence

While the Declaration of Independence was not meant to be an official statement of American values, a document affirming universal human rights, or a theological treatise on the source of those rights, we cannot ignore the fact that by the nineteenth and twentieth centuries it had become all of these things. Unlike the U.S. Constitution, the Declaration *does* make appeals and references to God. A close examination of that God-language sheds light on the religious worldview of its writers and its endorsers. We will close this chapter by examining the four references to God in the Declaration of Independence in an attempt to grasp how the founders understood the relationship between religion and the American founding.

The first paragraph of the Declaration of Independence begins:

> When in the Course of human Events, it becomes necessary for one People to dissolve the Political Bands which have connected them with another, and to assume among the Powers of the Earth, the separate and equal Station to which the Laws of Nature and of Nature's God entitle them, a decent Respect to the Opinions of Mankind requires that they should declare the causes which impel them to the Separation.

Here Jefferson is affirming that the justification for separating from England comes from natural law and from God, the author of such natural law. "Nature's God" was a term used often by eighteenth-century deists who upheld the belief that God created the world, instilled it with natural laws of science, morality, and politics, and allowed it to function based on those laws without any further divine interference. Jefferson, as we will see in chapter 13, was not a deist. He did, at times, believe that God supernaturally intervened into human affairs. Yet his choice of the phrase "Nature's God" is a vague one. It reflects his belief that God is indeed the author of the natural right to separate from tyranny. "Nature's God" is a phrase that all of the founders and most of the American people could accept. Deists, freethinkers, and Enlightenment liberals such as Jefferson would have no problem affirming the idea that natural rights came from God. Though they might prefer to have this reference to God be more explicit, Christians could also affirm this belief.

The next reference to God in the Declaration of Independence, which has become the most oft-cited part of the document, occurs in the second paragraph: "We hold these Truths to be self-evident, that all Men are created equal, that they are endowed by their Creator with certain unalienable Rights, that among these are Life, Liberty, and the Pursuit of Happiness." Actually, the reference to self-evident truths being "endowed by their Creator" was not part of Jefferson's original draft of the Declaration. It was added later by Benjamin Franklin, a member of the writing committee. Jefferson's original wording was: "that from that equal creation they derive rights inherent and inalienable."[30] Franklin's change to the text makes clear that he and the Continental Congress wanted to affirm the belief that the unalienable rights of "Life, Liberty, and the Pursuit of Happiness" found their origin in God. Yet, like Jefferson's use of the phrase "Nature's God" in the first paragraph, Franklin never elaborated on the attributes of this Creator. Such a vague reference to God could be embraced not only by Christians but by deists, Unitarians, and freethinkers as well.

References to God do not appear again in the Declaration until the final paragraph. Here we find the phrase: "We . . . appealing to the Supreme Judge of the World for the Rectitude of our Intentions, do, in the Name, and by Authority of the good People of these Colonies, solemnly Publish and Declare, That these United Colonies are, and of Right ought to be, FREE AND INDEPENDENT STATES." Once again, these words were not included in Jefferson's original draft, but were added on the floor of Congress during the editing process. Unlike the references to "Nature's God" and the "Creator," the phrase "Supreme Judge of the World" moves our understanding of the God of the Declaration of Independence closer to a Christian framework. Unlike the rather passive God of the first two paragraphs, "Supreme Judge of the World" suggests that the God to whom Congress is appealing will one day judge humankind. While we normally think of God judging his creation as part of Christian theology, it was indeed possible for one to reject some of the central tenets of Christianity, such as the deity of Christ or his resurrection, and still believe that human beings would be judged in the next life for their moral conduct in this one. Indeed, all of the non-Christian founders that we will discuss in part three of this book would have believed in a God who judges the good and the bad. So while Congress's use of the phrase "Supreme Judge of the World" certainly tells us a bit more about the attributes of the God of the Declaration, it does not definitively identify this God as uniquely Christian.

The same might be said for the last reference to God in the Declaration: "And for the support of this Declaration, with a firm reliance on the

Protection of divine Providence, we mutually pledge to each other our Lives, our Fortunes, and our sacred Honor." Here we learn even more about the God of the Declaration of Independence. He is not only the author of natural rights and the judge of the world, but he also governs the world by his providence. The term "providence," as it was used in the eighteenth century, implies an active God who is sustaining the world through his sovereign power. This is not the distant God of the deist, but a God who is ordering his creation. By mentioning providence Congress was affirming its belief that God would watch over America and protect it in this time of uncertainty, trial, and war. It reflects a view of God held by most of the representatives seated in the room during the summer of 1776. As we will see, whether they embraced all the tenets of orthodox Christianity or not, most could affirm the providence of God.

In the end, some Christians may be disappointed with the way in which Jefferson, his committee, and the Second Continental Congress refused to be overtly Christian in writing the Declaration of Independence. The Declaration never mentions Jesus Christ, nor does it quote the Old or New Testaments. It fails to move beyond vague descriptions of God. On the other hand, the Declaration of Independence was not a secular, atheistic, or even deistic document. While we would be hard-pressed to describe the Declaration as a uniquely "Christian" source, it is certainly a theistic one.

Yet from a historical perspective we should be very careful to avoid turning this document into something it was never intended to be. Unlike Congress's proclamations for days of fasting and thanksgiving, the Declaration was not a religious document. In fact, it was not even meant to be a document that said something new or uniquely American about human rights. But those who wrote the Declaration and signed it did affirm a God who is the author and creator of those rights, who presides providentially over his world, and who will one day judge humankind.

Chapter Nine

Religion in the Critical Period

W hen did the United States become a "nation"? For many people the answer is obvious: the United States achieved nationhood on July 4, 1776—Independence Day. But those more informed about American history might argue that the United States became a nation when the Constitution was finally ratified in 1789. Or perhaps the United States became a "nation" in the wake of the War of 1812—the so-called Second American Revolution. After winning another war against England and establishing its right to participate in the world of Atlantic trade, an era of "good feelings" pervaded the country. In this view, nationalism would be measured by the emotional sense of connectedness or patriotism or common purpose that its citizens felt toward a given place or polity. We could thus say that the United States was created in 1776 or 1789, but did not become a "nation" until the early nineteenth century. Finally, one might argue that a real sense of nationalism—the kind of patriotism that Americans would come to embrace in the twentieth century—did not emerge until after the Civil War. The Civil War decided that individual states that placed their own interests over the interests of the nation would be punished with military force.

It is not my intention here to debate the meaning of American nationalism or decide when the United States became a nation. I leave that task up to other historians. But it does seem that those who want to claim that the United States was founded as a "Christian nation" must be clear about what exactly they mean by the word "nation." This chapter focuses on the United States during the very early years of the Republic (roughly 1776–1787), when the country was a "nation" in name only. It is difficult to find any sense of national unity in the United States during this period. Political power rested with the thirteen disparate states and their governments.

Religion and the Articles of Confederation

Between 1776 and 1781 the Second Continental Congress was the government of the United States. The members of Congress were not far removed from their Declaration of Independence and were doing what they could to lead their new country in its war with England. Congress faced several challenges during this period, not the least of which was how to bring thirteen colonies—with very different cultures, ethnic populations, religious convictions, and economies—into a unified nation. Was such a union possible? Prior to the Revolution the thirteen British-American colonies had little in common. In 1776 these colonies were able to unite around common political beliefs about liberty and tyranny that they had imbibed from their British heritage, but when the common enemy had been defeated, they were more than willing to return to their own independent enclaves as separate and sovereign entities.

Bringing these thirteen colonies together in the wake of the Revolution would not be easy. Long-standing disagreements between them— such as the establishment of western boundaries—continued to be a problem. Moreover, during the Revolution each colony thought that it had resisted Parliament's taxation schemes individually. They believed that taxes could be levied only by their own colonial assemblies. This commitment to local government would translate into the newly formed state legislatures. None of the colonies was willing to sacrifice its sovereignty to some sort of national American government that had the potential of becoming tyrannical in the same way that England had become during the 1760s and 1770s. All thirteen of these states had long-standing fears of central government and believed that the ideals of the American Revolution—liberty, freedom, even democracy—were best cultivated in small republics. As a result, shortly after 1776, these states went to work on establishing constitutions that would set the ground rules for their new governments and define the rights of citizens.

Members of the Continental Congress, however, believed that some type of governmental structure was needed to hold these states together. In 1777 Congress approved the Articles of Confederation as the basis of the first official government of the United States of America. About four years later the Articles would be ratified by the states and begin to function for the new "national" government. It is worth noting that Congress decided upon a "confederation" as the American form of government. A "confederation" is a group of states or sovereign units that come together for specific and limited purposes usually related to the regulation of trade or protection from foreign invaders.

The Articles of Confederation were intended to form a very weak central government. Indeed, one would be hard-pressed to call it a "central government" at all. This was a government of sovereign states. The Articles did not provide for an executive or judicial branch, and Congress would have very limited powers. The national government under the Articles was described as a "firm league of friendship" among the states. In the years when the Articles were functioning as the basis of government, people often referred to "THESE United States of America" or emphasized "States" over "United" when referring to the "United States of America." Each state would be required to send a delegation to Congress (two to seven members) and would receive one vote.

The weakness of Congress under the Articles of Confederation becomes evident when we examine what it could and could not do. Congress could borrow money, conduct foreign affairs, coin money, establish a postal system, govern westward expansion, and supervise Indian affairs. But it was forbidden to tax, control commerce, or pass any legislation without the approval of nine of the thirteen states. Any amendment to the Articles would require a unanimous vote from the states. Congress under the Articles of Confederation had responsibilities, but very little authority to carry them out.

The Articles of Confederation say very little about religion. There is no mention of religious tests for holding office in Congress, nor did Congress have the power to dictate how an individual state handled the relationship between the church and the government. During the drafting of the Articles, John Dickinson of Pennsylvania proposed that the text make a specific endorsement of religious liberty. His suggestion was rejected because the framers of the document did not want to interfere with the states on any religious matter. Article III does state, as fitting with the nature of a confederation, that all of the states agree to come to the aid of another state that has fallen under "attack" from an outside force "on account of religion." Article XIII refers to the "Great Governor of the World" who has "inclin[ed] the hearts of the legislatures" to ratify the Articles. We should not make too much of this reference. It represents the kind of vague and generic God-language used in the Declaration of Independence. Yet one could also make a legitimate argument that the framers believed that God was somehow watching over the process of ratification.[1] In the end, it is clear that the framers of the Articles were not interested in interfering with the religious traditions of the states. To do so might jeopardize the ratification of the Articles. With that in mind, it is worth looking at the individual state constitutions to see just what they thought about the relationship between church and the state.

Virginia and the Quest for Religious Liberty

As we have already seen in chapter 5, the Church of England was the established church in colonial Virginia. This meant that a portion of the taxes paid by all Virginians was used to fund the salaries of Anglican ministers. The Anglican establishment, which was enforced and maintained by the Virginia House of Burgesses, the colony's legislative assembly, tolerated religious dissenters (Baptists and Presbyterians were the largest dissenting groups), but did not fund their efforts to build meetinghouses or allow them to hold political office. Toleration did not stop the royal government from persecuting dissenters. Baptist laypersons and ministers were often physically attacked or imprisoned for propagating their faith too zealously.

Following American independence, some of the colony's most prominent politicians and statesmen made a concerted effort to topple the Anglican establishment and secure religious liberty for all Virginians. In June 1776 a convention gathered to affirm a document written by George Mason that would eventually become known as the "Virginia Declaration of Rights." Article 16 of Mason's declaration affirmed:

> That religion, or the duty which we owe to our Creator and the manner of discharging it, can be directed by reason and conviction, not by force or violence; and therefore, all men are equally entitled to the free exercise of religion, according to the dictates of conscience; and that it is the mutual duty of all to practice Christian forbearance, love, and charity towards each other.[2]

By the end of the month the convention had written a state constitution that dissolved Virginia's relationship with England and established executive, legislative, and judicial branches of government. It also forbade ministers from holding legislative office. Nowhere in the Virginia constitution were any religious qualifications placed on officeholders, with the exception of the aforementioned prohibition against ministers.[3]

The battle for religious freedom, however, was not done yet. Enlightened defenders of the idea, such as Thomas Jefferson and James Madison, would not stop their crusade until the Anglican Church was separated completely from the new state government. In 1777 Jefferson composed a "Bill for Establishing Religious Freedom." It proposed that the phrase "full and free liberty" be added to the state constitution. For the next two years, as a legislator and governor of the state, Jefferson pushed for the passage of this bill, but it was ultimately rejected by a Virginia Assembly fearful about separating religion from government.[4]

In 1784, with the War for Independence over, the assembly revisited this issue. Several prominent Virginians, led by Patrick Henry, the state's new governor, set out to establish Christianity as Virginia's official religion. The victory in the American Revolutionary War, coupled with the rising number of Protestant dissenters, meant that the Church of England (now the Protestant Episcopal Church) would no longer remain Virginia's established church. But Henry and others, including Richard Henry Lee and Edmund Randolph, thought that Jefferson's proposal for complete religious liberty was too extreme. Throughout Virginia's history the Anglican Church had served as a moral compass for the colony. The English royal government believed that a close relationship between church and state was necessary to maintain good order. As Henry wrote, "the general diffusion of Christian knowledge hath a natural tendency to correct the morals of men, restrain their vices, and preserve the peace of society."[5] Many Virginia statesmen were still influenced by the old belief that religious liberty was the first step toward anarchy.

Henry and his supporters proposed "A Bill for Establishing a Provision for Teachers of the Christian Religion," which has been commonly referred to as the "General Assessment" bill. This bill would tax Virginians for the purpose of supporting ministers and churches of every denomination by "abolishing all distinctions of preeminence amongst the different societies or communities of Christians." Local sheriffs and tax collectors would work closely with church leaders to make sure that taxes would benefit all the religious communities of a particular jurisdiction.[6] The General Assessment bill did not privilege one Christian church over any other, but it did keep the state government in the business of promoting religion. Henry's proposal was not unlike the interpretation of the U.S. Constitution put forth by contemporary Christian nationalists. David Barton, for example, has argued that the framers of the Constitution never intended the federal government to cease promoting Christianity. The First Amendment was meant to prohibit one specific Christian *denomination* from being privileged, in much the same way that Henry thought the Virginia government should privilege all Christian denominations instead of just the Anglican Church.[7]

However, the General Assessment was not what Thomas Jefferson and James Madison had in mind when they thought about religious liberty. With Jefferson serving the country as minister to France, the leadership of the opposition to the General Assessment fell on Madison. During the debates over the bill in the Virginia House of Delegates, Madison argued that any state involvement with religion would give government the power to decide which religions were worthy of support and which ones were not. In other words, the government would decide the validity of the religious convictions of an individual or a community. For defenders of religious freedom and the separation of church and state, this was a recipe for disaster. Madison did not oppose religion or the usefulness of religion to the moral order of Virginia, but he did oppose allowing the government to interfere in its practice.[8]

The Virginia House of Delegates voted in favor of Henry's General Assessment, but concluded that more details needed to be worked out before it was officially passed. While debate continued over these details (debate that the opponents of the General Assessment helped to prolong), Madison returned to his study and composed a document called the "Memorial and Remonstrance Against Religious Assessments." In one of the most important American documents ever written about religious liberty, Madison offered fifteen reasons why the Virginia House should reject the General Assessment. He described the bill as a "dangerous abuse of power" and demanded that the members of the House "remonstrate against it." As he had done in the earlier debates, Madison concluded, citing article 16 of the Virginia Declaration of Rights, that "Religion or the duty which we owe to our Creator and the manner of discharging it, can be directed only by reason and conviction, not by force or violence." Religion, Madison continued, "must be left to the conviction and conscience of every man; and it is the right of every man to exercise it as these may dictate." Freedom to worship according to conscience was an "unalienable right" and thus needed to be protected from a government that might try to dictate how one should exercise that right. Madison compared the fight for religious liberty in Virginia to the cause of the American Revolution— a battle over basic human rights. He challenged a European tradition of church-state relations that was over a thousand years old.[9]

The Memorial and Remonstrance garnered 1,552 signatures and found widespread support among Baptists, the representatives of a religious tradition that had always defended the separation of church and state. Many of today's conservative Virginia Baptists, such as those affiliated with Jerry Falwell's fundamentalist Baptist empire in Lynchburg, Virginia, might be surprised to learn that in their attempts to promote a "Christian America" they are actually breaking with, rather than carrying on, the legacy of their Baptist past.[10] Madison also had the support of George Washington, who hoped the General Assessment would "die an easy death." In the end, Washington got his wish—and so did Madison. The Memorial and Remonstrance led to multiple petitions to the assembly in support of religious liberty as Madison defined it. In the end, Henry's General Assessment was never brought to a final vote.

In the wake of the battle over the General Assessment, the champions of religious liberty in Virginia saw the opportunity to revisit Jefferson's 1777 Bill for Establishing Religious Freedom. After some minor changes, Jefferson's bill was passed in January 1786 as "The Virginia Statute for Religious Freedom."[11] Like the Declaration of Independence, the statute reflects the theistic worldview of eighteenth-century America. It begins by affirming that "Almighty God hath created the mind free" and any attempt to limit that freedom would be considered "a departure from the plan of the Holy author of our religion." It rejects wholeheartedly the colonial practice of paying taxes to support an established state church, calling this tradition both "sinful and tyrannical."

Jefferson then moved to a discussion of the relationship between civil rights and religious conviction: "our civil rights have no dependence on our religious opinions any more than our opinions in physics or geometry." Religious belief, Jefferson continued, should have no bearing whatsoever on whether or not a person is qualified to hold political office. This was a radical proposal for the eighteenth century. As we will see below, nearly every other state in America would limit political participation to Christians. The general thrust of the statute is summarized in section II:

> Be it enacted by the General Assembly that no man shall be compelled to frequent or support any religious worship, place, or ministry whatsoever, nor shall be enforced, restrained, molested, or burthened in his body or goods, nor shall otherwise suffer, on account of his religious opinions or belief; but that all men shall be free to profess, and by argument to maintain, their opinions in matters of religion, and that the same shall in no wise diminish, enlarge, or affect their civil capacities.[12]

Fig. 9.1   Thomas Jefferson's tombstone at Monticello. Jefferson believed the Virginia Statute for Religious Freedom was one of his greatest achievements.

Massachusetts and Religious Establishment

When it comes to state constitutions promoting religious freedom, Virginia was the exception rather than the rule. Like Virginia, Massachusetts had a long history of government support for Christianity. As we saw in chapter 5, Massachusetts was meant to be a "city upon a hill," a Calvinist utopia in the new world where political leadership would be carried out by true believers in the Puritan way. During the earliest years of settlement in Massachusetts, dissenters were often removed from the colony

for espousing theological views that did not conform to Puritan orthodoxy. Any state constitution in Massachusetts would thus need to reckon
with this history. The chances that the framers of the Massachusetts constitution would endorse the kind of religious liberty enjoyed by Virginia
were slim.

The Massachusetts Constitution of 1780 affirmed that all members of
society had the "right as well as the duty" to "worship the SUPREME
BEING, the great Creator and Preserver of the universe." The framers
of this state constitution—John Adams was the primary drafter—had a
limited understanding of what constituted the religious rights of its citizens. The people of Massachusetts had the right to worship the "Supreme
Being," the "Creator," and the "Preserver of the universe." By implication,
religious rights were not afforded to those who did not worship this God.
The constitution suggests that the worship of God is not only a "right" but
a "duty." This emphasis on duty reflects the historic New England Puritan
ideal that individual rights must always be understood within the context of
the responsibilities one has to the larger Christian community.[13]

The Massachusetts Constitution did, however, affirm liberty of conscience in matters of religion. It states that "no subject shall be hurt,
molested, or restrained, in his person, liberty or estate, for worshipping
GOD in the manner and season most agreeable to the dictates of his own
conscience." Citizens of the state could freely, without any government
interference, practice their religious faith, but the wording of this clause
suggests that such religious freedom applied only to those who worship God. When the framers wrote about worshiping God, they probably had the Protestant God in mind. Unlike Virginia, the government
would collect taxes to support public worship and Protestant teachers
of "piety, religion, and morality." The Congregational Church would
remain the state's established religion, but those who were not part of
this church would be permitted to use their tax dollars for the "support of
the public teacher or teachers of his own religious sect or denomination."
This assumed that there was a minister available from such a dissenting
denomination or sect. Those who did not have a Protestant minister to
support, or who were not affiliated with any congregation, would need to
pay a tax toward the support of the Congregational Church. Thus, while
the Massachusetts Constitution allowed non-Congregationalist Protestants to worship freely and direct their taxes to the salaries of their own
ministers, everyone else was required to pay taxes to support the Congregational Church. John Adams called this "a most mild and equitable
establishment of religion."[14]

Adams and the other framers made sure that anyone serving in the Massachusetts state government was a Christian. The governor of the state was required to "declare himself to be of the Christian religion" and anyone else elected to "State office or to the Legislature" needed to "believe the Christian religion, and have firm persuasion of its truth." The framers of the 1780 Massachusetts Constitution were concerned with promoting Protestant religion as a means of maintaining moral and public order in the state. Though the days of removing dissenters from the colony were long gone, the established Congregational Church was not. The Massachusetts Constitution set out to maintain a "Christian" state.

Other States

The rest of the New England state constitutions, with the exception of Rhode Island, adhered closely to the Massachusetts model of religious liberty. In the period between the American Revolution and the writing of a new constitution in 1818, Connecticut continued to be governed by a seventeenth-century document known as the Fundamental Orders of Connecticut. The Fundamental Orders, an article adopted in 1638 by the earliest settlers to the Connecticut River Valley, ordered a Christian frame of government. It claimed that the colonial government was "established according to God" based upon the teachings of the "word of God."[15] It added that the members of the colony had come together for the purpose of preserving "the liberty and purity of the gospel of our Lord Jesus." The governor of the colony was required to "execute Justice according to the rule of Gods word" in the "name of the Lord Jesus Christ," and magistrates were required to swear a similar oath. The state would become a prime target for champions of religious freedom, such as Thomas Jefferson, who did everything they could to topple the close connection between church and government and encourage the state's growing number of religious dissenters.[16]

Those who view Vermont today as a state on the front lines of social change and civil rights might be shocked to read the Christian language in the 1777 constitution of the independent state of Vermont. (Vermont would not join the United States until 1791.) The constitution affirmed a natural right to "worship ALMIGHTY GOD" as long as that worship was "regulated by the word of GOD." Freedom of religion was a "civil right" afforded only to those who "profess the protestant religion." The constitution also noted that "every sect or denomination of people ought to observe the Sabbath, or the Lord's day, and keep up, and support, some sort of religious worship, which to them shall seem most agreeable to the revealed will of GOD." All members of the Vermont government needed to affirm a belief in God as the "Creator and Governor of the universe, the rewarder of the good and punisher of the wicked." In addition, civil servants had to testify to a belief in the divine inspiration of the Old and New Testaments and "profess the protestant religion."[17]

In the Mid-Atlantic states, where a tradition of religious freedom had existed since the English settlement of the region in the seventeenth century, state constitutions reaffirmed this commitment to religious liberty, but also placed limits on who could benefit from it. In Pennsylvania civil rights were afforded to anyone who "acknowledges the being of a God." Each member of the legislature was required by law to subscribe to a belief in a God who creates and governs the world, a God who rewards the good and punishes the wicked, and the "Divine inspiration" of the Old and New Testaments. The 1776 New Jersey Constitution noted that it would be unlawful for its citizens to pay taxes to support churches. But like Pennsylvania it limited civil rights and government participation to Protestants. New York's Constitution afforded "liberty of conscience" to "all mankind" and forbade ministers or priests from holding office.[18]

In the South the Maryland Constitution (1776) offered religious liberty to "All persons, professing the Christian religion," and allowed the legislature to "lay a general and equal tax, for the support of the Christian religion" that allowed individuals to direct the tax toward either the Christian congregation of their choice or toward the relief of the poor from a particular denomination. Maryland officeholders were expected to declare a belief in the "Christian religion." The South Carolina Constitution of 1778 required all "state officers," members of the "privy council," and state legislators to be Protestants. The right to vote was limited to any free white male who "acknowledges the being of a God" and believed in "the future states of rewards and punishments." Religious toleration in the state was afforded to religious groups and individuals who affirmed the existence of one God who is "to be worshipped" and a "future state of rewards and punishments." The South Carolina Constitution also affirmed that the "Christian Protestant religion shall be deemed, and is hereby constituted and declared to be, the established religion of this State."[19]

Some of these constitutions clearly affirmed what might be called a "Christian state." In Massachusetts, Connecticut, Rhode Island, New Hampshire, Maryland, and South Carolina, the government remained in the business of promoting Christianity through the collection of taxes.

South Carolina openly declared itself a Protestant state. All of the state constitutions affirmed some level of religious freedom for citizens, but many of them limited such toleration to those who believed in God, worshiped God, or believed in an afterlife where individuals would be judged according to their actions in this life. With the exception of Virginia and New York, the power to hold political office in state government was limited to Protestants or, in some cases, those who could affirm basic Christian doctrines like the inspiration of the New Testament. Unlike Jefferson, who wrote in the Declaration of Independence that "all men" were endowed by their Creator with "unalienable rights," many of the state constitutions limited religious rights to those who worshiped "Almighty God."

In the late eighteenth and early nineteenth century several states wrote new constitutions or else made significant amendments to their existing constitutions. Some of these new constitutions modified religious clauses to make them more liberal, while others kept their religious language intact. Delaware's 1792 Constitution, for example, removed the Christian requirements for office embedded within its 1776 Constitution. The new 1789 Georgia Constitution dropped its Protestant requirement for officeholders. The 1798 Georgia Constitution further declared that "no religious society shall ever be established in this State."[20]

In Connecticut a new constitution was written in 1818, bringing an end to the establishment of the Congregational Church. The constitution did, however, include a separate article on religion (Article 7) that extolled the "duty" of inhabitants to "worship the Supreme Being, the great Creator and Preserver of the Universe." The article affirmed religious freedom, but such freedom was to be practiced within the context of Christianity, the most dominant religion in the state. This new constitution also set out specific rules about how church leaders might gain financial support from their congregations, but it made clear that such support would no longer come from the government.[21] In Massachusetts the Congregational establishment would hold on until 1833, when the voters of the state overwhelmingly ratified the eleventh amendment to the 1780 Constitution. From this point forward churches would be supported by the voluntary contributions of their members.[22]

Others state constitutions retained the language of their religious clauses well into the nineteenth century. Maryland's overtly Christian 1776 constitution would remain in place until 1851. The people of South Carolina ratified a new constitution in 1790, but made no substantial changes to their affirmation that the "Christian Protestant religion shall be deemed, and is hereby constituted and declared to be, the established religion of this State." Vermont's 1786 and 1793 constitutions reaffirmed most of the religious provisions of its original 1777 constitution.[23]

As I have tried to suggest in this chapter, the question of whether the United States was founded as a "Christian nation" is a complicated one, especially as it relates to the period between 1781 and 1789 when the Articles of Confederation functioned as the document of America's national government. The phrase "Christian nation" is problematic in this era, since it would be very difficult to call the United States a "nation" in the same way that we might use the term today. Moreover, there was not one unified understanding of the way that religion should function in society or what role, if any, government should have in promoting it. Virginia offered its citizens complete religious liberty and assured that the state government would not interfere in any matters related to how individuals worshiped or how churches functioned. The way in which Virginia decided this question would end up looking, as we will see in the next chapter, quite similar to the way that the framers of the U.S. Constitution handled this issue.

But Virginia was an exception to the rule. Most states made very clear that they were Christian societies, placing Protestant qualifications on officeholding and allowing government to tax citizens for the purpose of promoting the Christian religion. All of these states would eventually remove these qualifications and do away with any suggestion that Christianity was the established religion of their state, but in most cases this did not happen until well into the nineteenth century. So what does this all mean for our understanding of whether the United States was founded as a Christian nation? Many inhabitants of the early American Republic, but not all of them, lived in political communities where Christianity, and in most cases Protestantism, was such an important part of the culture that the framers of government thought it was necessary to sustain that culture by privileging Christianity.

Chapter Ten

A "Godless Constitution"?

W illiam Lloyd Garrison was not a fan of the U.S. Constitution. One of the country's most active abolitionists and a deeply pious evangelical Christian, Garrison devoted his life to bringing an end to slavery. He believed that the Constitution was responsible for the prevalence of this institution in American society. In an 1843 speech to the Massachusetts Anti-Slavery Society, Garrison, drawing from Isaiah 28:15, made his feelings about the Constitution abundantly clear: "the compact which exists between the North and South is 'a covenant with death, and an agreement with hell' involving both parties in this atrocious criminality; and should be immediately annulled." Eleven years later he would burn a copy of the Constitution in protest.[1] Garrison had no patience for pundits and political leaders who described the Constitution as a sacred compact between the free North and the slaveholding South: "We pronounce it [the Constitution] the most bloody and heaven-daring arrangement ever made by men for the continuance and protection of a system of the most atrocious villainy ever exhibited on earth." Writing in *The Liberator*, Garrison minced few words:

> By the infamous bargain which they made between themselves, they virtually dethroned the Most High God, and trampled beneath their feet their own solemn and heaven-attested Declaration, that all men are created equal, and endowed by their Creator with certain unalienable rights—among which are life, liberty, and the pursuit of happiness. They had no lawful power to bind themselves, or their posterity, for one hour—for one moment—by such an unholy alliance. It was not valid then—it is not valid now.

Garrison believed that he was on the "side of God and his dear Son," while the Constitution and its framers were part of the "kingdom of darkness."[2]

Garrison was not the only Christian who had problems with the Constitution. As we saw in chapter 1, many nineteenth-century Christians complained about the "godless" nature of this most important of American founding documents. But we should not forget that there have always been Christians who have thought that the Constitution was a sacred document and its framers blessed by God. This chapter examines the process by which the U.S. Constitution became the country's frame of government and explores what its signers thought about the role that God should play in the Republic forged during that warm Philadelphia summer of 1787.

The "Need" for a Constitution

Not everyone thought that the United States needed a national constitution. Many, including some prominent founders who served on the front lines of the American Revolution, thought that the Articles of Confederation were just fine. The Articles allowed democracy to flourish where it should be flourishing—at the local level. A confederation meant that there would be no strong national government to interfere with the rights of the states. Small republics would give the people more direct representation in government. Many favored town and county governments over large republics, local juries over national judiciaries, and state and local militias over a national standing army.

Yet others believed that the Articles of Confederation needed a serious overhaul. The 1780s had taught them that the United States must have a national government that was able to handle serious foreign policy problems, provide some stability for a struggling economy, and curb the self-interested mind-set of the American people. These nationalists were convinced that Congress under the Articles of Confederation was powerless to address these pressing questions. When the British, in violation of the Treaty of Paris (the treaty that ended the Revolutionary War), continued to maintain their military forts in the American west and refused to provide American ships access to the Great Lakes, the anemic Congress could do nothing about it. Similarly, Spain was instigating Indian raids against American settlers in the Mississippi River Valley and preventing American traders from navigating through the port of New Orleans.

Economically, the colonies were no longer under the thumb of British mercantilism. They now had to fend for themselves in European trading markets. England knew this, and began placing restrictions on American imports. At the same time British merchants poured low-priced consumer goods into the United States, creating an unfavorable balance of trade that led to an economic crisis. Congress did not have the power to levy taxes, making it nearly impossible to raise revenue for the purpose of stabilizing the economy and paying off the country's war debts. In order to solve these problems Congress printed more and more money, little of which was backed up by specie (gold or silver). The "Continental," as the new "national" currency was called, was becoming increasingly worthless, and few American creditors were willing to accept it. To complicate matters further, the states issued their own inflated paper money. In Massachusetts the state government raised taxes to pay off its own war debt, but refused to accept payment in its own paper money, requiring specie instead. Debtors sought tax relief and the publication of more paper currency, but the Massachusetts legislature did not respond to their needs. Finally, in the summer of 1786, Revolutionary War veteran and western Massachusetts farmer Daniel Shays took matters into his own hands. He gathered a small army of farmers and traveled throughout the region to close courts responsible for the collection of debts.

Shays' Rebellion, and other protests like it occurring across the country, led many to wonder whether the local and democratic forms of government prevailing in the states might lead to anarchy and the collapse of the American Republic. With ordinary citizens holding political office and the voice of the people carrying unprecedented weight in local government, many feared a new kind of tyranny—a tyranny of the majority. Shays' Rebellion was a sign that Americans were more concerned with their own interests than the greater good of the nation. More and more people were engaging in land speculation—the process of purchasing land and reselling it for the purpose of making exorbitant profits. To the twenty-first-century eye, such a practice looks like good business, but to the framers of the Constitution land speculation was a sign of greed and selfishness. Many also feared the growing number of political factions emerging in the states. These factions were perceived as bad for the Republic because they symbolized self-interest—people gathering together to support their own agendas. Others talked about a rise in immoral behavior, such as horse racing, gambling, and cardplaying. Some pointed to the fact that many churches were reporting declines in membership.

These moral and political failures led some educated politicians to believe that an earlier vision for the American Republic, grounded in the cultivation of a virtuous citizenry willing to sacrifice its own interests for the common good, was rapidly eroding. It was clear to many that the American people could not be virtuous or "disinterested." The experiment in republican government was falling victim to the tyranny of the American people. Was a virtuous society still possible? Many believed that it was, but not without a drastic change in the country's political culture. Historian Gordon Wood has put it this way: "The move for a stronger national government thus became something more than a response to the obvious weakness of the Articles. It became as well an answer to the problems of the state governments."[3] Democratic self-interest had run amok under the state-dominated Articles of Confederation, and many thought that it was time to fix things. These were the concerns of the fifty-five men who gathered in Philadelphia in the summer of 1787 to write what would become the U.S. Constitution.

Religion and the Constitution

Despite Arizona senator John McCain's claim during the 2008 presidential race that the Constitution established a "Christian nation," the Constitution was never meant to be a religious document, nor did its framers set out to use the document to establish a Christian nation. In fact, with the exception of the mention in Article VII of the "Year of our Lord," a common eighteenth-century way of referring to the date, the Constitution never refers to God. In this sense, the Constitution departs from both the Declaration of Independence and the Articles of Confederation. This prompts the question: Why did the framers leave God out of this most important of all American documents? There has been much historical debate over this issue, but two views have been most popular. Some have said that the framers deliberately omitted references to God in the Constitution because they set out to create a secular nation. Others have argued, based on the political idea of "federalism," that the framers did not mention God because they believed that the relationship between religion and government was a subject that should be addressed at the state, not the national, level.[4]

The Constitutional Convention was, in some ways, a political coup d'état. Those gathered in secret amid the sweltering heat of the summer of 1787 were proposing a radical new alternative to the Articles of Confederation. What is amazing about this meeting, apart from the fact that convention delegates managed to survive in a forty-by-forty-foot room with no ventilation (the windows were boarded for secrecy), is that the framers thought that they could convince the rest of the country to accept their new proposal.

The conversation among the framers was not always civil. For example, debate raged over how to structure the proposed Congress. The delegates from the larger states favored the Virginia Plan, which, among other recommendations, proposed a two-house legislature. Under this plan, the number of representatives to both legislative houses would be based upon the population of the given state. In other words, the larger states would have more representatives and thus more political power. The delegates to the Constitutional Convention who hailed from smaller states favored the New Jersey Plan, which, among other things, proposed a one-house legislature with every state having an equal number of representatives and thus an equal vote.

The New Jersey Plan was defeated in favor of the Virginia Plan, but the discussion over representation in the Virginia Plan's proposed two-house legislature became quite heated. Delegates from small states demanded that they receive an equal number of representatives in both legislative houses.[5] By June 1787 the debates had reached a standstill. It was at this point that Benjamin Franklin suggested that the members of the convention consider the "thought of humbly applying to the Father of lights to illuminate our understandings." In the course of making his proposal, Franklin asked the members of the convention to consider the role that "daily prayer" had played in Congress during the American Revolution. At that time, Franklin reminded his fellow delegates, "our prayers, Sir, were heard, and they were graciously answered." Franklin asked his colleagues if they had "not forgotten that powerful friend? or do we imagine that we no longer need his assistance?"

As we will see in chapter 14, Franklin was a religious skeptic his entire life, but despite his theological disagreements with orthodox Christianity, he could still affirm before the members of the convention that "God governs in the affairs of men. And if a sparrow cannot fall to the ground without his notice, is it probable that an empire can rise without his aid?" (This is a reference to Matthew 10:29.) He followed this up with a reference to Psalm 127:1: "Except the Lord build the House they labour in vain that build it." Franklin then applied this verse more explicitly to the framing of the Constitution: "I firmly . . . believe that without his concurring aid we shall succeed in this political building no better than the Builders of Babel." He concluded by "imploring the assistance of

Heaven, and its blessings on our deliberations, be held in this Assembly every morning before we proceed to business, and that one or more of the Clergy in this City be requested to officiate at this service."[6]

A close reading of the convention minutes during these days of fierce debate suggests that prayer was probably another one of Franklin's many good ideas. Roger Sherman of Connecticut seconded Franklin's motion, opening the floor for discussion. Alexander Hamilton of New York and "several others" argued that "however proper" Franklin's resolution might be, it should have been raised at the start of the convention. Thinking ahead to the ratification process, Hamilton thought that a decision to institute daily prayer at this current stage of deliberation might be seen as a sign of weakness. It might give the impression that the decision to conduct prayers was based on "embarrassments and dissentions within the convention." Hamilton, of course, was absolutely correct, at least about the political climate of the convention. There was a great deal of embarrassing dissension taking place. This, after all, was why Franklin proposed prayer in the first place. Yet for Hamilton and others, giving the impression that the convention was unified was more important than seeking God's blessing on the proceedings.[7]

Roger Sherman argued against Hamilton's remarks, suggesting that the rejection of Franklin's proposal would lead to public criticism of the convention. Hugh Williamson of Pennsylvania offered a more pragmatic answer to Franklin's proposal. He noted that a clergyman was never hired to lead the convention in daily prayer because "the Convention had no funds" to pay his salary. Edmund Randolph of Virginia proposed that a sermon be preached before the convention on July 4th to commemorate the anniversary of American independence and "thenceforth prayers be used in ye Convention every morning." Franklin seconded Randolph's motion, but the majority of the members of the convention successfully postponed the matter by adjourning "without any vote on the motion." In his own account of this incident, Franklin wrote, "The Convention, except three or four persons, thought Prayers unnecessary." The following day debate over representation in the proposed Congress continued as usual and the delegation from Connecticut would offer a version of what would eventually become known as the Connecticut Compromise. Each state would have equal representation in the Senate, but the number of representatives from each state in the House of Representatives would be based on state population.[8]

The Constitution makes one reference to religion. Article VI affirms that "no religious Test shall ever be required as a Qualification to any

Office or public trust under the United States." The framers of the Constitution made clear that a person could not be excluded from serving his or her country in the new national government based solely upon his or her religious convictions. Article VI, as constitutional scholar Akhil Reed Amar has noted, "ran well ahead of contemporary Anglo-American practice."[9] In England monarchs were required to be members of the Anglican Church. And, as we saw in the last chapter, at the time of the Constitutional Convention all but Virginia imposed religious qualifications on state officeholders. The voters of the United States were given the liberty to vote for candidates to federal office who were Protestants, Catholics, Muslims, or atheists.

Slavery and the Constitution

William Lloyd Garrison reminds us that any discussion of the U.S. Constitution as a "Christian" document must consider the subject of slavery. The bottom line is this: the U.S. Constitution, as it was framed in 1787, permitted the practice of black chattel slavery. Article I of the Constitution states, "Representatives and direct Taxes shall be apportioned among the several States . . . by adding to the whole Number of free Persons . . . three-fifths of all other Persons." "Other Persons," of course, refers to the approximately 700,000 men and women experiencing the human bondage of slavery. The so-called Three-Fifths Compromise meant that large slave populations could bolster the number of white representatives that a given state could have in Congress. This could also result in more Electoral College votes. Southern states with roughly the same number of free citizens as northern states often received more representation in the House of Representatives due to their large number of slaves. As a result, the Three-Fifths Compromise gave slave masters in southern states the motivation to import more and more slaves. And this is exactly what they did in the time between the ratification of the Constitution (1789) and 1808, the year when the Constitution mandated an end to American involvement in the international slave trade.[10] There is a common misconception that the Three-Fifths Compromise meant that slaves would be considered only "three-fifths" of a human being. While this is technically true for the purpose of white representation in Congress, to claim that the Constitution reduced the human dignity of slaves to a fraction is giving the framers too much credit. Since slaves were not permitted to participate in Congress, they were actually valued, at least politically, at "zero-fifths"—individuals with no human dignity to speak of.[11]

The framers' decision to compromise with slaveholders for the purpose of keeping the Union together should cause Christians to shudder. One of the fundamental principles of the Christian religion is that all human beings are created in the image of God and thus possess human dignity and worth (Genesis 1:26–27). Historian Mark Noll makes an interesting observation about the way Christians should think about the Three-Fifths Compromise and the framers' acceptance of slavery in general. He compares it to contemporary debates on the subject of abortion:

> Opposition to such practice [abortion] is sometimes based on a questionable view of American traditions. Abortion-on-demand, it is said, violates the heritage of American respect for life and for the legal status of all persons. There is some truth to this, but only some. A realistic view of American history, especially the history of the Revolution, shows that from the beginning of the country, high ideals of liberty for all existed side by side with the systematic denial of legal protection for entire classes of human beings. American governments have never done a good job of protecting the powerless and the unrepresented. Even the Constitution, which often reflects sound views on the restraint of power, treated slaves as less than human and completely avoided the question of their rights.[12]

Of course, the Constitution does allow for amendments, or, in the case of slavery, the opportunity to atone for past sins. Following the Civil War, the Thirteenth Amendment ended the institution of chattel slavery once and for all. Any Christian concerned with the dignity of human life should be grateful for this amendment, but must also balance such gratitude with the fact that a bloody Civil War might have been avoided if the moral issue of slavery had not taken a back seat to the preservation of the Union during negotiations in the summer of 1787.

The Federalist

Once the drafting concluded in September 1787, the advocates of this new proposal for government needed to convince the states to scrap the Articles of Confederation and sign on to the Constitution. The task would not be an easy one. It was especially important to win over the larger states—Virginia, Massachusetts, New York—which had the most to lose by abandoning the Articles. And even if the Constitution was ratified, to what extent would it breed a sense of American nationalism? A localist impulse still pervaded the former colonies, and many still had a basic distrust of strong federal governments.[13] In order to convince the states to ratify the Constitution, three of its strongest supporters—Alexander Hamilton, James Madison, and John Jay—wrote a series of newspaper articles (85 in all) under the pseudonym "Publius" explaining the meaning of the Constitution and advocating ratification. These essays were gathered together, along with eight other essays, and were published as *The Federalist*, also known as the *Federalist Papers*.

There are very few references to God in *The Federalist*. *Federalist #2*, written by Jay, is the most overtly religious in nature. He mentioned "Providence" three times in this article, connecting the will of God to the necessity of national union. Jay wrote how Providence had brought the diverse colonies into "one connected fertile, widespreading country." It was God who had brought the people of the United States together under the new form of government: "Providence has been pleased to give this one connected country to one united people, a people descended from the same ancestors, speaking the same language, professing the same religion, attached to the same principles of government, very similar in their manners and customs." He employed God in the service of convincing Americans to ratify the Constitution. It was the "design of Providence, that an inheritance so proper and convenient for a band of brethren, united to each other by the strongest ties, should never split into a number of unsocial, jealous, and alien sovereignties." Jay was a strong proponent of a God-inspired republicanism that required all citizens—and the states that they inhabited—to sacrifice for the common good of the United States.[14]

The Federalist's perspective on the nature of human beings was compatible with Christian beliefs. The *Federalist Papers*, especially the ones written by James Madison, made clear that the founders' utopian vision of a republic of disinterested citizens was not going to work. In the years between 1776 and 1787, many American statesmen learned some valuable lessons about human nature. This period, as we have seen, taught them that humans were largely incapable of being virtuous or disinterested without help from a strong central government. In other words, as Madison would write in *Federalist #51*, "But what is government itself, but the greatest of all reflections on human nature? If men were angels, no government would be necessary." As a result, a government designed to check the self-interested nature of its citizens was absolutely necessary to maintain at least some commitment to the public good.

This understanding of human nature is seen best in Madison's *Federalist #10*. Here the Virginian argues that a strong federal union was needed to check the self-interested "factions" that he and many others believed were dominating American society. Madison, like many of the other founders, knew from his study of history that republics survive only when their citizens are willing to make sacrifices for the common good. This was the essence of republican virtue and it was the antithesis of self-interested factionalism. Madison defined a "faction" as a group of citizens "united and actuated by some common impulse of passion, or of interest, adverse to the rights of other citizens, or to the permanent and aggregate interests of the community." In other words, factions undermined the common good. Since the cause of such self-interest was "sown in the nature of man," the only way of "curing" this problem was to create a government to control factions so that one faction would not dominate all the other factions. When one faction grew too strong the result would be political tyranny and the destruction of the liberty and rights of individuals.

Madison believed that the Constitution offered a "republican remedy for the diseases most incident to republican government." It would check the selfish will of the people by passing their views "through the medium of a chosen body of citizens, whose wisdom may best discern the true interest of their country, and whose patriotism and love of justice will be least likely to sacrifice it to temporary or partial considerations." He also argued that the large legislative districts (one representative per 30,000 people) proposed by the Constitution would guard citizens against "Men of factious tempers, of local prejudices, or of sinister designs" who might betray the interests of the people through "cabals." In other words, large republics would dilute the power that one cabal or faction may have over all the others. Such "filters" are present throughout the Constitution. They can be seen in the establishment of the Electoral College to choose the president and the creation of an upper legislative house, the Senate, whose members were not chosen directly by the people.[15]

Even a cursory reading of *The Federalist* reveals Madison's dour view of human nature. In *Federalist* #55 Madison goes so far as to say that "there is a degree of depravity in mankind which requires a certain degree of circumspection and distrust." Madison's use of the term "depravity" invokes long-standing Christian beliefs about the inherent sinful nature of human beings. Several historians have suggested that Madison's view of human nature was influenced by traditional Calvinism, a form of Protestantism that emphasized the belief that human beings have inherited a sinful nature as a result of the original sin committed by Adam and Eve (Genesis 3). Others have gone further, claiming that Madison was influenced by the teaching he received as a student at the College of New Jersey at

Princeton, where he studied under Calvinist divine John Witherspoon. These kinds of intellectual connections are hard to make, especially with someone like Madison, who did not leave historians with much information about his religious life or political influences. It is certainly possible that Madison's thoughts in *The Federalist* were influenced by the Calvinist theology he learned at Princeton, but if that were the case he would have been breaking ranks with almost all the framers of the Constitution, who, according to historian John Murrin, did not embrace the doctrine of original sin from Calvinist orthodoxy.[16]

God and the Ratification Debate

With the exception of John Jay's Christian nationalist argument in *Federalist* #2 and Madison's suggestion in *Federalist* #37 that the Constitutional Convention was blessed by the "finger of that Almighty Hand," the Federalists generally did not appeal to God as a means of convincing the states to ratify the Constitution. As we have seen, there was nothing in the Constitution itself that they could appeal to in order to make such an argument. Instead, they extolled the benefits of Article VI and patted themselves on the back for championing religious freedom for office-holders. James Iredell of North Carolina, a future Supreme Court justice, went so far as to argue that he had no problem with Americans choosing political officials who were "pagans," "Mahometans," or had "no religion at all." Baptist leaders, such as John Leland and Isaac Backus, were thrilled that their denomination's 150-year fight for religious liberty in America had finally come to fruition.[17]

This was not the case for the Anti-Federalists, however, who openly opposed ratification. While Anti-Federalist opposition was always more political than it was religious, many Anti-Federalists rejected the Constitution because it did not make any appeals to God. Even some statesmen who were prone to give their support to the Constitution on political grounds wondered why the framers had not made the slightest mention of God in drafting the document. The writings of these constitutional skeptics present an interesting dilemma for those today who want to argue that the Constitution was a Christian document. In the eighteenth century it was those who *opposed* the Constitution who made the strongest arguments in favor of the United States being a Christian nation.

When Luther Martin reported on the events of the Constitutional Convention to the Maryland state legislature, he could not help including some editorial comment about the way that the convention handled

Fig. 10.1   Luther Martin was an Anti-Federalist who believed that the Constitution should "hold out some distinction between the professors of Christianity and downright infidelity or paganism."

the question of religion. According to Martin, "there were some members *so unfashionable* as to think, that a *belief of the existence of a Deity*, and of a *state of future rewards and punishments* would be some security for the good conduct of our rulers." For Martin, the United States was a "Christian country" and the Constitution should "hold out some distinction between the professors of Christianity and downright infidelity or paganism."[18]

One of the more scathing critiques of the godlessness of the Constitution came from William Petrikin, an Anti-Federalist from Carlisle, Pennsylvania. Writing under the pseudonym "Aristocrotis," Petrikin attacked the framers of the Constitution as elitists who preferred a refined religion of "nature" over a religion of "supernatural divine origin." In doing so, he sounded a lot like a twenty-first-century working-class evangelical complaining about the so-called secular liberal elites who had no respect for the Constitution. The difference, of course, was that Petrikin was *attacking* the U.S. Constitution and the men who framed it. Using stinging sarcasm, he argued that the framers believed that the Christian religion was the religion "of the vulgar in this country" and its "precepts are . . . so rigid and severe, as to render it impossible for any gentleman of fashion or good breeding to comply with them in any sense, without a manifest violation of decorum, and an abandonment of every genteel amusement and fashionable accomplishment." Petrikin did not stop there. He chided the members of the Constitutional Convention for denying a belief in God, the "immortality of the soul," the "resurrection of the body," a "day of judgment," and a "future state of rewards and punishments."[19]

Anti-Federalists especially attacked Article VI because it placed no Christian qualifications on officeholders. "Samuel," an Anti-Federalist from Massachusetts, worried that the lack of a religious test for office would mean that a "Pagan" or a "Mahometan" might serve the country in the "most important trusts." "A Watchman," writing from western Massachusetts, feared that the Constitution opened a door for "the Jews, Turks, and Heathen to enter into publick office, and be seated at the head of the government of the United States." A "Friend of the Rights of the People" also feared the possibility that "a Papist, a Mohomatan, a Deist, yea an Atheist" might be elected to the "helm of Government."[20] And a New York Anti-Federalist, writing under the name "Curtopolis," was particularly harsh on Article VI because he feared it would allow the following kinds of people to serve in the national government:

> 1st Quakers, who will make the black saucy and at the same time deprive us of the means of defence—2dly, Mahometans, who ridicule the doctrine of the trinity—3dly. Deists, abominable wretches—4thly, Negroes, the seed of Cain—5thly Beggars, who when set on horseback, will ride to the devil—6thly, Jews & c. & c. It gives the command of the whole militia to the President—should he hereafter be a Jew, our dear posterity may be ordered to rebuild Jerusalem.[21]

The Anti-Federalists wanted to insert an acknowledgment of God or a Christian requirement for officeholding into the Constitution because they took seriously the idea that religion was absolutely essential to a virtuous republic. Charles Turner, a delegate to the Massachusetts ratifying convention, was willing to support the Constitution, but wanted to make clear that the new government would not survive without "the prevalence of *Christian piety and morals.*" He urged the new Congress to make its first order of business a bill requiring all states to promote religious and moral education.[22]

"David," another Massachusetts Anti-Federalist, argued in the *Massachusetts Gazette* that lawlessness in any society could only be constrained "by prepossessing the people in favour of virtue by affording publick protection to religion." He favored governmental support for the clergy, laws for the "due observance of the Sabbath," a continuance of the New England tradition of fast and thanksgiving days, and the "frequent and publick acknowledgements of our dependence on the Deity." David believed that "religion secures our independence as a nation, and attaches the citizens to our own government." Religious tests for office were needed to prevent "Papists" and "Atheists" from serving their country. Atheists, he explained, "have no principles of virtue," while Catholics "acknowledge a foreign head, who can relieve them from the obligation of an oath." Religious tests were essential for securing a Protestant nation.[23]

Religion and the States: The "Federalist" Interpretation of the Constitution

In the end, of course, the Anti-Federalists lost. The Constitution was ratified and remains the foundation of American government today. The framers of this document chose deliberately to reject the notion that the U.S. government was a "Christian" government or that those who served in that government should acknowledge Christianity or even a belief in God. Today, many of the Anti-Federalist ideas about God and government can be found in the arguments made in defense of the notion that the U.S. Constitution was a Christian document that established a Christian nation. As far as history is concerned, the defenders of Christian America today cannot have it both ways. If they continue to defend the Constitution as a Christian document, they must be willing to part ways with some of the strongest eighteenth-century defenders of a Christian America, the Anti-Federalists. On the other hand, if they want to continue to make arguments in favor of a Christian America, then they might find some strong allies in the Anti-Federalists. But this would mean that they would have to be a lot more skeptical and critical of the framers of the Constitution.

There is, however, one way around this quandary, and, for lack of a better term, I will call it the "federalist argument." The Tenth Amendment to the U.S. Constitution states, "The powers not delegated to the United States by the Constitution, nor prohibited by it to the States, are reserved to the States respectively, or to the people." This amendment makes the Constitution a "federalist" document. The Constitution does not give the national government the right to enforce a religious test for officeholders (Article VI) or establish a national religion (First Amendment), but it says nothing about how these issues should be handled at the level of state government.[24] There is plenty of evidence to support this reading of the Constitution. As we have seen in the previous chapter, many of the original state constitutions included very detailed religious tests for holding state office. As the eighteenth century progressed, some of these states loosened religious restrictions on officeholders, but most of them did not. Massachusetts and Connecticut, as we have seen, maintained religious establishments well into the nineteenth century. When South Carolina revised its constitution in 1790, it continued to require officeholders to be Christians who believed in the divine inspiration of the Old and New Testaments. Such a religious test, if applied to a national officeholder, would have violated Article VI of the U.S. Constitution, but it was not a problem in the states. Even those states formed *after* the ratification of the U.S. Constitution included language that would have been in clear violation of Article VI and the First Amendment. Tennessee's 1796 constitution, for example, limited officeholding in the "civil department" of the state to those who believed in God and in a "future state of rewards and punishments."[25]

Thomas Jefferson upheld a similar federalist view on matters of religion. In an 1808 letter to Presbyterian clergyman Samuel Miller, Jefferson wrote:

I consider the government of the United States as interdicted by the Constitution from intermeddling with religious institutions, their doctrines, discipline, or exercises. This results not only from the provision that no law shall be made respecting the establishment or free exercise of religion [1st Amendment], but from that also which reserves to the States the powers not delegated to the United States [10th Amendment]. Certainly, no power to prescribe any religious exercise or to assume authority in any religious discipline has been delegated to the General government. It must then rest with the states.[26]

Jefferson echoed similar federalist ideas in his second inaugural address:

In matters of religion, I have considered that its free exercise is placed by the constitution independent of the powers of the general

government. I have therefore undertaken, on no occasion, to prescribe the religious exercises suited to it, but have left them, as the
constitution found them, under the direction and discipline of State
or Church authorities, acknowledged by several religious societies.[27]

Those who uphold a federalist view of the relationship between church
and state argue convincingly that the Constitution does not mention God
or delve deeper into church-state issues not because the framers were trying to create a secular nation, but because, as a point of federalism, they
believed that religious matters should be left up to the states. The "federalist" nature of the Constitution on matters of religion should force us
to think hard about whether America was founded as a Christian nation.
Again, how we define the word "nation" is important. If the "nation"
represents the national government formed by the U.S. Constitution,
then it is clear that the framers of the Constitution were not interested in
promoting a religious nation of any kind. But if we agree with historian
John Murrin's assertion that the Constitution created a "roof without
walls," or a very limited sense of "national" identity, then we must look
to the state governments as the best reflection of the will of the American
people. In other words, the state governments *were* "the nation." Virginia
was the only state that upheld views on the relationship between church
and state that conformed to the U.S. Constitution. The other original
states constructed republics that were, in one way or another, explicitly
Christian. These states sought to establish constitutions that reflected the
beliefs and values of a Christian people.

Religion and the First Amendment

While some Anti-Federalists opposed the Constitution for its failure to
affirm a religious test for national office or its failure to reference Almighty
God, others opposed it for its failure to affirm liberty of conscience in
matters of religion. Centinel, a Philadelphia Anti-Federalist, wrote that
the Constitution had "no declaration, that all men have a natural and
unalienable right to worship Almighty God, according to the dictates
of their own consciences and understanding." Recalling the long history
of religious persecution in Europe, another Philadelphia Anti-Federalist,
"An Old Whig," demanded a *"bill of rights* to secure, in the first place by
the most express stipulations, the sacred right of conscience." "Sydney," a
New York Anti-Federalist, wondered why the U.S. Constitution did not

include a statement protecting citizens from religious persecution in the way that the New York state constitution had done.[28]

Anti-Federalist demands for a formal statement defending the right to liberty of conscience in matters of religion came to fruition when the First Amendment to the U.S. Constitution went into effect in 1791. The amendment was part of ten amendments, known today as the "Bill of Rights," passed by the first U.S. Congress in 1789 and ratified, as per the Constitution, by three-fourths of the states. The First Amendment stated that "Congress shall make no law respecting an establishment of religion, or prohibiting the free exercise thereof." The amendment's religious clause has drawn much discussion throughout the course of American history. Contemporary debate over the meaning of the amendment has centered on whether the federal government can limit public displays of Christmas manger scenes or the Ten Commandments in federal buildings. While such debates are certainly worthwhile, our intention here is to explore the meaning of the First Amendment in the historical context in which it was written.

Most interpreters of the First Amendment agree that it forbids Congress from passing a law that privileges a particular religious group over any other. Unlike many of the British-American colonies and some of the states, the U.S. government does not promote a specific religious group or use federal funds to support a particular sect. As we saw above, the "no-establishment" clause applied only to the national government. The First Amendment also forbids the national government from inhibiting the "free exercise" of religion. It protects individuals from government intrusion into their religious practices. The First Amendment was written to secure the individual right to worship according to one's conscience. It was not meant as a means of protecting government from the religious beliefs of its citizens.

A Wall of Separation between Church and State?

Most Americans do not realize that the phrase "a wall of separation between church and state" does not appear in the U.S. Constitution. It stems from seventeenth-century religious dissident Roger Williams, who desired "a hedge or wall of separation between the garden of the church and the wilderness of the world." This image appeared again in an 1802 letter written by Thomas Jefferson, then serving as president of the United States, to the Danbury Baptist Association of Connecticut:

> Believing with you that religion is a matter which lies solely between
> Man & his God, that he owes account to none other for his faith or
> his worship, that the legitimate powers of government reach actions
> only, & not opinions, I contemplate with sovereign reverence that
> act of the whole American people which declared that *their* legisla-
> ture should "make no law respecting an establishment of religion, or
> prohibiting the free exercise thereof," thus building a wall of separa-
> tion between Church & State.[29]

Jefferson's "wall" metaphor implies that the First Amendment is meant
to separate or cordon off government from religion and vice versa. In
1947 the Supreme Court, in *Everson v. Board of Education*, interpreted
Jefferson's letter this way and concluded that the First Amendment was
designed to create a "high and impregnable" wall between religion and
the national government.[30]

But what did Jefferson believe when he wrote about a "wall" between
church and state? In order to make sense of this oft-cited phrase, we need
to examine the historical context in which the letter was written. The
Danbury Baptist Association was a group of Connecticut Baptist churches
that might best be described as a disgruntled religious minority in a state
with a Congregational establishment. Though the Baptists in Connecticut no longer had to pay taxes to support the Congregational Church,
they were not happy with their status as dissenters and were engaged in
a battle for complete religious liberty through the disestablishment of
Congregationalism.[31] On October 7, 1801, the Danbury Baptist Association wrote to Jefferson congratulating him on his election to the presidency. The bulk of the letter, however, complained about the Baptists'
status as a religion that was merely tolerated, and not completely free.
The Danbury Baptists knew that Jefferson had no jurisdiction over how
Connecticut chose to handle matters of church and state, but it hoped
that Jefferson's support might boost their attempts at toppling the state's
religious establishment.[32]

Jefferson would carefully craft a proposal to this letter. His first draft
was filled with edits and various deletions. The most convincing interpretation of these edits and deletions comes from historians who have argued
that the letter must be understood in the context of federalism. James H.
Hutson, chief of the Manuscript Division at the Library of Congress,
hired the FBI to examine the edited or blotted-out portions of Jefferson's original draft of the letter in the hope of finding out more about his
motivation for writing it. Hutson concluded that the purpose of the letter

was more political than religious. Jefferson wanted revenge against his political opponents, the Federalists, a faction with strong roots in New England. During the presidential election of 1800 the Federalists, in an attempt to win the votes of pious Americans, publicly portrayed Jefferson as an "atheist" and "infidel." These attacks on Jefferson's religious beliefs continued in the wake of his election.

In November 1801 Britain and France signed the Treaty of Amiens. This treaty was met with much celebration in the United States because it meant that the country would not be drawn into a war between the two European powers. Federalists demanded that Jefferson, in light of the treaty, establish an official day of national thanksgiving, not unlike the kind of proclamation that Federalist presidents George Washington and John Adams had issued on similar occasions. Knowing that Jefferson was opposed to such proclamations, his Federalist opponents used his refusal to issue a day of thanksgiving as yet another political attack against him.[33]

The reply to the Danbury Baptists, Hutson argues, would be Jefferson's opportunity to make a formal statement about the proper relationship between religion and the federal government. In his preliminary draft, Jefferson explained why it was inappropriate for a U.S. president to issue "occasional performances of devotion" (thanksgiving and fast days). Such proclamations were "religious acts." Jefferson was elected to do a job that was "temporal" in nature. Moreover, religious fast days, Jefferson argued, were "practised indeed by the Executive of another nation as the legal head of its church." This was a reference to George III of England. As Hutson notes, by alluding to George III, Jefferson was linking his New England Federalist opponents to the tyranny of the British crown. Jefferson sent a copy of his preliminary draft to Levi Lincoln, his attorney general and a native New Englander. Lincoln advised Jefferson to remove the references to his opposition to fast and thanksgiving days because it might offend New Englanders who were accustomed to these kinds of religious proclamations. Thanks to the FBI, we know that Jefferson took Lincoln's advice. He removed the references to thanksgiving days from the preliminary draft of the letter to the Danbury Baptists.[34]

After deciding that his remarks on thanksgiving days were not politically expedient, Jefferson opted for an alternative way of showing his Federalist opponents that he was not opposed to religion. On January 3, 1802, Jefferson decided to attend religious services at the House of Representatives. The preacher that day was John Leland, a Baptist from Cheshire, Massachusetts, who had come to Washington, D.C., to deliver a 1,235-pound wheel of cheese as a gift commemorating Jefferson's election to the presidency. Thus, two days after he wrote his reply to the Danbury Baptists, which included the infamous "wall of separation" phrase, Jefferson was attending religious worship in, of all places, a federal building. The press publicized Jefferson's visit to the service, even noting that he participated in singing Psalm 100.

Hutson concludes that Jefferson's "action on January 3, 1802, less than forty-eight hours after issuing the Danbury Baptist letter, must be considered a form of symbolic speech that completes the meaning of that letter." In other words, Jefferson did not view the "wall of separation" to mean that religion should not play a role in the national government. Such a view does not account for his worshiping with Leland at the House or the various other times that Jefferson attended services there. While Jefferson clearly believed that religion should stay out of government, he seems to have also believed that there were times that "government, although it could not take coercive initiatives in the religious sphere, might serve as a passive, impartial venue for voluntary religious activities." While Hutson affirms Jefferson's "wall" metaphor, he claims that such a wall was "punctuated by many checkpoints." Jefferson, he argues, "would have had no objection if, at these checkpoints, government invited religion to pass through and make itself at home in the use of its spaces, structures, and facilities, provided that it treated equally everyone who wanted to come along."[35]

Daniel Dreisbach has expanded upon Hutson's view. He argues that the "'wall' constructed by Jefferson separated the federal regime on the one side and ecclesiastical institutions and state governments on the other." He distinguishes between the many religious proclamations Jefferson issued during his tenure as governor of Virginia and his refusal to issue such proclamations as president of the United States. The former were permissible because the Constitution did not interfere with the relationship between religion and government in individual states. The latter were not permissible based upon Jefferson's interpretation of the First Amendment. The "wall" metaphor must be understood in light of these facts. In other words, Jefferson did not propose a wall that separated church and state in all realms of civil government—only at the national level. According to Dreisbach, the twentieth-century Supreme Court has badly misread what Jefferson meant when he used the phrase, "wall of separation between church and state."[36]

However one interprets Jefferson's "wall" metaphor, we can be safe in asserting that the third president of the United States believed that there was a barrier between the church and the national government. While it may not have been as "high" or "impregnable" as Justice Hugo Black made it out to be in the 1947 *Everson v. Board of Education* case, Jefferson did think that it existed. Though there could be some exceptions, Jefferson believed that religion was a private matter that should remain free of government interference. This was the kind of separation of church and state he affirmed in writing the Virginia Statute for Religious Freedom. While, as we will see in chapter 13, Jefferson would have certainly wished that states such as Massachusetts or Connecticut also embraced this kind of religious liberty, he realized that any attempt to interfere with their religious establishments was outside the jurisdiction of the national government and thus in violation of the Constitution.

In conclusion, we return to our original question: Is the U.S. Constitution a "godless" document? If we define "godless" as the absence of any reference to God or the Christian religion in the text, then the answer would be an unqualified yes. The Constitution was written to be a frame for a government, not a treatise on the relationship between Christianity and the state. It never declares the United States to be a "Christian nation," nor does it set forth any specifically Christian ideals. This is why many eighteenth-century advocates of a "Christian America" opposed it.

Yet it is also important to remember that the framers of the Constitution did not exclude God because they wanted to establish a completely secular society devoid of any religion. Rather, they realized that the role of religion and the government should be decided locally, among the individuals who made up the states. Thus, to the degree that the states made up the "nation" in the late eighteenth century, one could make a legitimate argument, based on the explicitly Christian statements in most state constitutions, that the people of the United States did privilege Christianity over other religions. Most states were clear about their desire to set up governments run by Christians and, in most cases, specifically Protestant Christians. In this sense, the U.S. Constitution does not reflect the religious values, however we choose to define them, of the eighteenth-century American people.

Suggested Reading for Part Two

Anderson, Virginia DeJohn. *New England's Generation: The Great Migration and the Formation of Society and Culture in the Seventeenth Century*. New York: Cambridge University Press, 1992.

Bond, Edward L. "Source of Knowledge, Source of Power: The Supernatural World of English Virginia, 1607–1624." *Virginia Magazine of History and Biography* 108, no. 2 (2000): 105–38.

Bonomi, Patricia. *Under the Cope of Heaven: Religion, Society, and Politics in Colonial America*. New York: Oxford University Press, 1986.

Cressy, David. *Coming Over: Migration and Communication between England and New England in the Seventeenth Century*. New York: Cambridge University Press, 1987.

Dworetz, Steven M. *The Unvarnished Doctrine: Locke, Liberalism, and the American Revolution*. Durham: Duke University Press, 1994.

Fea, John. *The Way of Improvement Leads Home: Philip Vickers Fithian and the Rural Enlightenment in Early America*. Philadelphia: University of Pennsylvania Press, 2008.

Gaustad, Edwin. *Roger Williams*. New York: Oxford University Press, 2005.

Hall, David D. *World of Wonder, Days of Judgment: Popular Religious Belief in Early New England*. Cambridge: Harvard University Press, 1990.

Hall, Timothy D. *Anne Hutchinson: Puritan Prophet*. Saddle River, NJ: Prentice-Hall, 2009.

Kidd, Thomas S. *God of Liberty: A Religious History of the American Revolution*. New York: Basic Books, 2010.

Morgan, Edmund. *American Slavery, American Freedom: The Ordeal of Colonial Virginia*. New York: Norton, 1975.

Morgan, Edmund. *Visible Saints: The History of Puritan Idea*. Ithaca, NY: Cornell University Press, 1965.

Noll, Mark A. *Christians in the American Revolution*. Grand Rapids: Eerdmans, 1977.

Noll, Mark A., George M. Marsden, and Nathan O. Hatch. "America's 'Christian' Origins: Puritan New England as a Case Study." Pages 28–47 in *The Search for Christian America*. Expanded ed. Colorado Springs: Helmers & Howard, 1989.

Rhoden, Nancy L. *Revolutionary Anglicanism: The Colonial Church of England Clergy during the American Revolution*. New York: New York University Press, 1999.

Part Three

The Religious Beliefs of the Founders

Chapter Eleven

Did George Washington Pray at Valley Forge?

In the winter of 1777–1778 the Continental Army faced one of its lowest points in the Revolutionary War. British troops under the direction of General William Howe were in control of Philadelphia. George Washington's soldiers were coming off major defeats at Brandywine and Germantown. Amid public criticism stemming from these military failures, Washington took his army to Valley Forge, Pennsylvania, eighteen miles northwest of Philadelphia. Here they would heal their wounds and prepare for the spring campaign. The conditions at Valley Forge, as any elementary school student knows, were not good. The army lacked some of the basic necessities of life. It was cold. Washington, who managed to keep the army together during these trying times, praised the heroic determination of his soldiers: "To see Men without Cloathes to cover their nakedness, without Blankets to lay on, without Shoes, by which their Marches might be traced by the Blood from their feet . . . is a mark of Patience and obedience which in my opinion can scarce be parallel'd."[1]

As the army struggled through the Valley Forge winter, a local man named Isaac Potts, the owner of the house where Washington was staying, walked through the woods near the encampment and heard a voice amid a bower of oak trees. He realized quickly that the voice he heard was Washington himself, who was kneeling on the ground praying to God. Potts was moved. As a Quaker he opposed this war, but his sympathies were with the British. Seeing Washington in prayer, however, changed everything. As Potts arrived back home he announced to his wife, Sarah: "I have this day seen what I never expected. Thee knows that I always thought the sword and the gospel utterly inconsistent; and that no man could be a soldier and a Christian at the same time. But George

Washington has this day convinced me of my mistake." Seeing Washington in prayer transformed Potts into a patriot: "If George Washington be not a man of God, I am greatly deceived—and still more shall I be deceived if God does not, through him, work out a great salvation for America."[2]

Versions of Potts's account of Washington praying at Valley Forge appeared in dozens of nineteenth-century school textbooks, including William Holmes McGuffey's well-known *Eclectic Reader* series. In 1866 Henry Brueckner recaptured this event in a painting, *The Prayer at Valley Forge*. It portrays Washington on his knees in the snow making supplication to God, supposedly on behalf of his army and the American cause. Brueckner's painting has become a well-known piece of Americana. Visitors to the Washington Memorial Chapel at Valley Forge and the prayer chapel in the U.S. Capitol can find a stained-glass rendering of the image. In 1928 it appeared on a U.S. postage stamp.[3]

There is one major problem with Potts's story of Washington praying at Valley Forge—it probably did not happen. While it is likely that Washington prayed while he was with his army at Valley Forge in the winter of 1777–1778, it is unlikely that the story reported by Potts, memorialized in paintings and read to millions of schoolchildren, is anything more than legend. It was first told in the seventeenth edition (1816) of Mason Locke Weems's *Life of Washington*. Weems claimed to have heard it directly from Potts, his "good old FRIEND." Potts may have owned the house where Washington stayed at Valley Forge, but his aunt Deborah Potts Hewes was living there alone at the time. Indeed, Potts was probably not even residing in Valley Forge during the encampment. And he was definitely not married. It would be another twenty-five years before he wed Sarah, making a conversation with her in the wake of the supposed Washington prayer impossible. Another version of the story, which appeared in the diary of Reverend Nathaniel Randolph Snowden, claims that it was John Potts, Isaac's brother, who heard Washington praying. These discrepancies, coupled with the fact that Weems was known for writing stories about Washington based upon scanty evidence, have led historians to discredit it.[4]

The "Prayer at Valley Forge" is one of many events in Washington's life that play a prominent part in the debate over whether he was a Christian. Lest one think that this debate is a new one, it is worth noting that many of Washington's contemporaries also wondered whether he was a true believer. Reverend Timothy Dwight, the president of Yale College and one of the leaders of the evangelical revival known as the Second

Fig. 11.1   Washington praying at Valley Forge. Whether this event actually happened is a subject of historical debate.

Great Awakening, felt confident that Washington was a Christian, but he was also aware that "doubts may and will exist" about the substance of his faith. Reverend Stanley Griswold, the pastor of the Congregational Church in New Milford, Connecticut, knew that there were many who "objected" to the belief that Washington was a Christian.[5] Thomas Jefferson was also fascinated by the question of Washington's religion. In 1800 he recorded in his private diary a bit of gossip surrounding this question:

> Doctor Rush tells me that he had it from Asa Green that when the clergy addressed General Washington on his departure from the Government, it was observed in their consultation, that he had never, on any occasion, said a word to the public which showed a belief in the Christian religion, and they thought they should so pen their address, as to force him at length to declare publicly whether he was a Christian or not. They did so.
>
> However, he observed, the old fox was too cunning for them. He answered every article of their address particularly except that, which he passed over without notice. Rush observes, he never did

say a word on the subject in any of his public papers, except in his valedictory letter to the Governors of the States, when he resigned his commission in the army wherein he speaks of the "benign influence of the Christian religion." I know that Gouvernor Morris, who pretended to be in his secrets and believed himself to be so, has often told me that General Washington believed no more in that system than he himself did.[6]

The debate continues today. Washington's faith has become a minor battlefield in America's ongoing culture wars. Tim LaHaye, a fundamentalist preacher and coauthor of the best-selling *Left Behind* novels, has called Washington "a devout believer in Jesus Christ" who, in good evangelical fashion, "had accepted Him as His Lord and Savior." Peter Lillback, the current president of Westminster Theological Seminary in Philadelphia, has written over 1,100 pages in an attempt to prove that Washington was "an orthodox, Trinity-affirming believer in Jesus Christ, who also affirmed the historic Christian Gospel of a Savior, who died for sinners and was raised to life." In contrast, Joseph Ellis, a historian who won the Pulitzer Prize for his writing about the American founders, has described Washington as a "lukewarm Episcopalian." Historian Edwin Gaustad has called him a "cool deist." Writer Brooke Allen has recently concluded that "there are very real doubts as to whether Washington was a Christian or even whether he was a believer at all."[7]

Who is right? Or, more importantly, what is at stake in deciding who is right? Those on the Christian Right use Washington's supposed Christianity to help promote their cultural agenda for contemporary America. Consider the words of Lillback:

Establishing that George Washington was a Christian helps to substantiate the critical role that Christians and Christian principles played in the founding of our nation. This, in turn, encourages a careful appraisal of our history and founding documents. A nation that forgets its past does not know where it is or where it is headed. We believe such a study would also empower, enable, and defend the presence of a strong Judeo-Christian worldview in the ongoing development of our state and national governments and courts. We set out to provide the necessary foundation for an honest assessment of the faith and values of our founders and the government they instituted. . . . Are today's secularists trying to recreate the faith of our founding father into the unbelief of a Deist in order to rid our nation of Washington's holy flame of faith? Was it a secular flame or a "sacred fire" that Washington ignited to light the lamp for America's future?[8]

Lillback and a host of other writers about Washington—both on the right and the left—are often guilty of the historical fallacies covered in the introduction to this book. Washington's past is used to promote a particular political platform in the present. The argument goes something like this: "If Washington was a Christian, then America must be too"; or, "if Washington was not a Christian, then he must have desired the United States to be a secular nation." My discussion of Washington attempts to lay out as much information as possible about his religion in the hopes that informed Christians and others might use it to draw good historical conclusions about the "Father of Our Country."

Providence

Washington was quiet about his faith. Unlike John Adams, Thomas Jefferson, or Benjamin Franklin, he did not leave behind definitive statements about what he believed. Neither was he particularly curious about theology or other religious matters. His religious reading was confined largely to sermons purchased by his devout wife, Martha.

Any discussion of Washington's religious beliefs must begin with what he called "Providence." According to historian Gary Scott Smith, "arguably no president has stressed the role of Providence in the nation's history more than Washington."[9] He used the term "Providence" 270 times in his writings, usually employing it as a synonym for the Judeo-Christian God. And on occasion, he described "Providence" using the pronouns "who" or "it."[10] This was an omniscient, omnipotent, and loving God who created and ordered the universe, but whose purposes remained mysterious. God, in his providential ordering of the world, could bring war, natural disaster, or other forms of tragedy. Humans were not supposed to question God; they were supposed to trust him.[11]

Washington's God was active in the lives of human beings. He could perform miracles, answer prayer, and intervene in history to carry out his will. It is thus inaccurate to label Washington a "deist," as Edwin Gaustad has done. Eighteenth-century deists believed in a "watchmaker God"—a deity who created the world as we know it and then drew back and let it run on the natural laws that he set in place. The deist God rarely, if ever, intervened in the lives of human beings. Deists believed that all things could be explained by reason, but were also unwilling to abandon a belief in the existence of a Creator-God. Providence and deism were intellectually incompatible doctrines.

Washington believed that God could intervene in history, but he used human beings to carry out his plans. God created humans with free will. Though individuals had the power to shape history, the course of human events moved forward through time in a way that was governed by God.[12] In this sense Washington's view of Providence differed significantly from the kind of providential history advanced by many on the Christian Right today. Washington did not try to predict what God was doing in history. Neither did he try to pinpoint the moments in history when God intervened into human affairs. Instead, he acted in history—often with great valor and determination—and let God's purpose be done.

Washington first began to wonder if Providence was preparing him for something great in the wake of the so-called Massacre on the Monongahela. In the summer of 1755, General Edward Braddock staged a failed attempt to capture Fort Duquesne as part of a larger campaign to drive the French out of the Ohio River Valley. The twenty-three-year-old Washington served as an aide-de-camp on Braddock's staff. Due to a series of tactical errors, Braddock's forces were ambushed by a group of nine hundred French soldiers and Indians as they prepared to cross the Monongahela River. Braddock was killed in the raid, leaving Washington to rally the troops. As he rode among his fellow soldiers, many of whom were crying out in death, French and Indian musket balls killed two of his horses and brushed his uniform. It was an experience he would never forget.

Washington was convinced that he survived this attack because of "the miraculous care of Providence that protected me beyond all human expectation." Following the massacre, he sent a letter to his brother, John Augustine Washington, to let him know he was alive:

> As I have heard since my arriv's at this place, a circumstantial acct. of my death and dying speech, I take this early opportunity of contradicting both, and of assuring you that I now exist and appear in the land of the living by the miraculous care of Providence, that protected me beyond all human expectation; I had 4 Bullets through my Coat, and two Horses shot under me, and yet escaped unhurt.

When the evangelical clergyman Samuel Davies heard about Washington's heroic role in the massacre, he wrote: "As a remarkable instance of this, I may point out to the Public that heroic Youth Col. Washington, who I cannot but hope Providence has hitherto preserved in so signal a Manner for some important Service to his Country."[13]

Washington credited Providence for his successes and failures in battle. During the Philadelphia campaign in the fall of 1777, he wrote to John Augustine: "But for a thick Fog [that] rendered [all] so infinitely dark at times, as not to distinguish friend from Foe at the distance of 30 Yards, we should, I believe, have made a decisive and glorious day of it. But Providence or some unaccountable something, designd it otherwise."[14] Following the Battle of Saratoga, an American victory that prompted the French to support the American Revolution, Washington ordered thanksgiving services to be held: "Let every face brighten, and every heart expand with grateful Joy and praise to the supreme disposer of all events, who granted us this signal success."[15] In his first inaugural address, the newly selected president wrote, "No people can be bound to acknowledge and adore the invisible hand which conducts the affairs of men, more than the people of the United States. Every step by which they have advanced to the character of an independent nation seems to have been distinguished by some token of providential agency."[16]

His use of "Providence," however, does not tell us very much about whether Washington was a Christian. As we will see in the next few chapters, nearly all of the so-called Founding Fathers believed in a God who controlled the world, intervened in the affairs of humankind, and, at times, even answered prayer. A closer look at Washington's religious beliefs and practices is thus in order.

Church Involvement

Washington was born in February 1732 and christened into the Anglican Church that April. His father, Augustine Washington, served briefly as a vestryman in the church before his premature death in 1743 at the age of forty-nine. Mary Ball Washington, who was known for her piety, raised George with knowledge of the Bible and the Book of Common Prayer. He was a product of the dominant religious culture of eighteenth-century Virginia and would remain an Anglican (labeled after the American Revolution an Episcopalian) his entire life.[17]

Washington married Martha Dandridge Custis in 1759. He and Martha attended two churches within the bounds of Virginia's Fairfax Parish. The Pohick Church was in Fairfax County and was located about six miles from Washington's Mount Vernon home. Christ Church was in

Alexandria, about nine or ten miles away. Washington went to Sunday services at these churches about once a month, an attendance pattern that was required by "custom and law." His decision to attend church on any given Sunday was based on a variety of factors, including the weather, the busyness of his schedule (he often wrote letters and entertained friends on Sunday), the availability of a minister in the Fairfax Parish, or the opportunities he had for leisure (mostly foxhunting and cardplaying).[18] Christians today might find Washington's church attendance wanting, but it was actually quite customary for a Virginia plantation owner. Few would have criticized Washington for choosing foxhunting, cardplaying, or business over attendance at church.

If what he chose to record in his diary is any indication, Washington viewed weekly church attendance as an opportunity to discuss the pressing political issues of the day with his fellow members of the Virginia gentry. While attending church at Alexandria on June 26, 1774, Washington appears to have been more interested in meeting with friends and acquaintances in the churchyard following the service than he was in worshiping the Almighty. The following week he was at the Pohick Church, where he recorded his attempts to convince George Mason to run for political office. Washington's church attendance was most consistent during the years he served as president of the United States. Between 1788 and 1796 he attended church almost every Sunday. In New York, the site of the first national capital, he worshiped at St. Paul's Church. After the capital moved to Philadelphia, he attended Christ Church.[19]

Between 1762 and 1784 Washington served his parish in the capacity of a vestryman and churchwarden. (Two vestrymen in every congregation were asked to serve as churchwardens, and Washington was elected to this position for three terms.) Vestrymen were responsible for supervising all church affairs, a job that included caring for the poor in the parish, purchasing wine for Communion, and building new meetinghouses or making repairs to old ones. Washington attended as many of the regular vestry meetings as he possibly could. Between 1762 and the American Revolution he showed up for 23 of the 35 meetings of the Truro vestry and, as historian Mary V. Thompson has found, had legitimate excuses for the twelve meetings that he missed.[20]

Historians who are intent upon criticizing the spiritual depth of Washington's Christianity have been cynical about his leadership in his local Anglican parish. They have suggested that the Anglican Church was little more than an institution used by the elite members of plantation society to control their social inferiors—both poor whites and slaves. It was more of a social club than a "vehicle of personal salvation."[21] It is easy to dismiss Washington's involvement in the Anglican Church as a means of securing his place in the Virginia elite. Everything about the Anglican Church exuded a sense of social order, from the practice of pew renting to the "rituals of entry and exit."[22]

Yet it is also possible to go too far with this line of analysis. Much of the discussion of Washington's faith is tainted by an American evangelical understanding of what constitutes true religion. While it may be true that wealthy Virginians got involved in Anglican churches as a means of finding a place in plantation society, Anglicans did champion a deep Christian faith rooted in the Book of Common Prayer, the liturgy, and the sacraments. However, they did not always express their faith in terms that evangelicals thought appropriate. As a result, Washington's leadership in his parish has been misinterpreted to mean something other than religious commitment. Granted, Washington was no evangelical enthusiast. He was not a "born-again Christian." But his church involvement and participation as a vestryman is no legitimate reason to conclude that his faith was more social than spiritual.[23]

Washington's Beliefs

We now know that Washington believed in Providence and was an active leader, by eighteenth-century Anglican standards, in his parish. But what did he believe about God, the Bible, Jesus Christ, and other doctrines of the Christian faith? These questions are not easy to answer because Washington never described his beliefs in anything close to a systematic way. In 1795 he wrote, "In politics as in religion my tenets are few and simple."[24]

We have seen that Washington often referred to God with the term "Providence," but he also used other words and phrases to describe the Deity. In a 1789 letter to the General Assembly of the Presbyterian Church shortly after his presidential inauguration, Washington wrote of "my dependence on the assistance of Heaven to support me in my arduous undertakings." His list of names for God included: "The Governor of the Universe," "Higher Cause," "Great Ruler of Events," "All Wise Creator," "Great Spirit," and "The Supreme Dispenser of all Good."[25] These references to God are quite vague and nondescript. There is little about them to suggest that Washington believed in the Judeo-Christian God of history.

Washington almost never used the name "Jesus Christ" in his public or private writings—indeed, only once in the entire corpus of his extant work. In 1779 the Delaware Indians agreed to allow three of their children to be educated by white Americans. Washington delivered a speech on the occasion praising the Indians for their willingness to learn Anglo-American culture: "You do well to wish to learn our arts and ways of life, and above all, the religion of Jesus Christ. These will make you a greater and happier people than you are."[26] The reference to Jesus Christ in this speech affirms Washington's belief in the importance of the Christian religion to the civilization of Native Americans, but it says nothing about the nature of his personal commitment to such religion.

Washington also made an indirect reference to Jesus Christ in his 1783 "Circular Letter" to the states. Written upon his retirement from the Continental Army, this public letter was the most explicit theological statement in Washington's writings. In order to be truly happy as a society, Washington believed that America needed to follow the example of the "Divine Author of our blessed Religion":

> I now make it my earnest prayer, that God would have you, and the State over which you preside, in his holy protection, that he would incline the hearts of the Citizens to cultivate a spirit of subordination and obedience to Government, to entertain a brotherly affection and love for one another, for their fellow Citizens of the United States at large, and particularly for their brethren who have served in the Field, and finally, that he would most graciously be pleased to dispose us all, to do Justice, to love mercy, and to demean ourselves with the Charity, humility, and pacific temper of mind, which were the Characteristicks of the Divine Author of our blessed Religion, and without an humble imitations of whose example in these things, we can never hope to be a happy Nation.[27]

While the Circular Letter refers to "the Divine Author" as a source of human happiness, it never affirms any orthodox Christian ideas such as the deity of Christ, his death for the sins of the world, or his resurrection. It is thus hard to claim that this is a uniquely "Christian" document. Even some of the most consistent eighteenth-century deists saw Jesus as a moral teacher who was worthy of imitation by all people.

Washington was biblically literate. He presented his family with Bibles, read the Scriptures publicly and privately, supported the idea of giving a Bible to each of his soldiers at the end of the Revolutionary War, and donated money to get a Bible (*Brown's Self-Interpreting Bible*) published. In his public addresses and private writings Washington quoted and paraphrased from the Bible more than any other book. His speeches regularly included references to biblical phrases such as "the throne of Grace" (Hebrews 4:16), "the race is not to the swift" (Ecclesiastes 9:11), and "swords into ploughshares" (Isaiah 2:4). Peter Lillback has argued convincingly that in one letter to the Jewish congregation in Newport, Rhode Island, Washington alluded to nine passages in the Old and New Testaments. Washington described the Bible as the "Word of God," "revealed" religion, "the pure and benign light of Revelation," and "Holy Writ." He never talked about it as being without error or infallible, but it does seem that he thought it was divinely inspired.[28]

Many of Washington's contemporaries and the people who knew him well had a lot to say about his religious faith. Bishop William White, the Episcopal bishop of Pennsylvania and Washington's pastor while he lived in Philadelphia during his years as president, said that he didn't know anything that would prove Washington believed in Christian revelation. John Marshall, arguably America's greatest Supreme Court justice and a member of Washington's staff during the Revolution, wrote that Washington was quiet about his religious convictions, but he was a "sincere believer in the Christian faith, and a truly devout man." Reverend Samuel Langdon wrote to Washington asking him to publicly identify himself as a "disciple of the Lord Jesus Christ." Washington replied to Langston's request with a reference to "the Great Author of the Universe" whose "divine interposition was so frequently manifested on our behalf." In other words, he skirted the question and refused to identify himself, as Langdon had hoped, with the Christian faith.[29] The story suggests that there were times when Washington went deliberately out of his way to avoid talking about Jesus Christ.

Religious faith seemed to play no role in Washington's death. In the winter of 1799 he grew ill during a snow and sleet storm while making his regular rounds at Mount Vernon. As the sixty-seven-year-old statesman realized that his sickness was more than a cold, he began to prepare himself for death. "Doctor, I die hard," he was reported to have said to his friend and physician, James Craik. He offered final instructions about his burial. Washington had never been decisive about his belief in an afterlife, but he did seem to believe that there was such a place where the good would be rewarded and the bad punished. Yet as he lay on his deathbed at Mount Vernon, Washington did not ask for a minister. He did not ask to pray. He did not talk about heaven, God, or Jesus Christ. Joseph Ellis has suggested that he "died as a Roman stoic rather than a Christian saint." The story of Washington's death prompted Samuel

Miller, a New York Presbyterian minister, to ask how "a true Christian, in the full exercise of his mental faculties [would] die without one expression of distinctive belief, or Christian hope?"[30]

Washington's religion best reflects a belief, popular among eighteenth-century Anglicans, known as latitudinarianism. This was an approach to religion that downplayed doctrinal differences among Christians in favor of ecumenical unity. It emphasized human love and social harmony. Latitudinarians tended to stress religion's contribution to the improvement of society over any eternal rewards it provided to the believer. Doctrinal differences, latitudinarians believed, led to division and strife, the kinds of passions that undermined the common good. (Washington opposed political parties for the same reasons.) Though he was an Anglican, Washington was not interested in the theology that distinguished one denomination from another. This may explain why, during his visit to Philadelphia for the First Continental Congress, he attended services at meetinghouses and churches run by Quakers, Anglicans, Presbyterians, and Catholics. In a 1787 letter to the Marquis de Lafayette, Washington wrote: "Being no bigot myself to any mode of worship, I am disposed to indulge the professors of Christianity in the church, that road to Heaven, which to them shall seem the most direct plainest easiest and least liable to exception." Similarly, in his Farewell Address, he wrote to the American people: "With slight shades of difference, you have the same Religion."[31] Washington was always in search of religious common ground because he believed such harmony and ecumenism would bring unity and order to public life.

Washington's Faith in Practice

We have now looked at what Washington believed, but did his actions—both in the religious realm and otherwise—reflect the life of a Christian? Was he a man of prayer? Did he engage in any other spiritual disciplines? What did he do about slavery?

The Valley Forge story aside, Washington was a man of prayer. God did not always answer prayers in the way his petitioners desired, but Washington believed that he did hear them. As an Anglican, Washington prayed publicly as a member of the body of Christians that met together on Sundays for worship. When he attended church he would have participated in the rituals and liturgies informed by the Book of Common Prayer. This meant that he would have confessed sins, both individually and corporately, and recited or sung psalms. The Anglican prayer book was important to him. In 1771, Washington tried to purchase a "Prayr Book with the New Version of Psalms & good plain Type . . . as thin as possible for the greatr ease of carryg in the Pocket."[32]

Since Washington seldom talked about his own inner devotional life, we can only glean information about how he prayed from those who knew him. His step-granddaughter, Nelly Custis Lewis, said she had never witnessed Washington in "private devotions," but added that he "was not one of those who act or pray, 'that they may be seen of men.' He communed with God in secret." In the same letter to Jared Sparks, the first editor of Washington's papers, Nelly described Washington kneeling and praying "most affectingly" at the deathbed of her dying aunt. One Frenchman who knew Washington said, "Every day of the year, he rises at five in the morning; as soon as he is up, he dresses, then prays reverently to God." Polish traveler Julian Ursyn Niemcewicz confirmed this, noting in his diary that Washington rose early, "dresses himself and prays with great piety."[33] While these eyewitness accounts should be used with caution, they do show that Washington had a reputation as a man of prayer.

Washington also participated in other spiritual disciplines. On June 1, 1774, he "fasted all day" as part of a general day of "fasting, humiliation and prayer" conducted throughout Virginia as a means of entreating God for help during the imperial crisis with England.[34] He and Martha used their money to aid the poor and support the salary of the ministers who served in the Fairfax Parish. Perhaps most telling was Washington's willingness to serve as a godfather to at least eight different children. During the christening ceremony as described in the Book of Common Prayer, the godfather was required to acknowledge Jesus Christ as a "vouchsafe" for the child and pray that God would "release him from sin, to sanctify him with the Holy Ghost, to give him the kingdom of heaven and everlasting life." In addition to this, the godfather was to renounce the devil and all his works, affirm a belief in God's Word, and pledge to remain obedient to God's commandments. Mary V. Thompson reminds us that Thomas Jefferson refused to serve as the godfather of a friend's child because he could not affirm a belief in the Christian doctrine of the Trinity, yet Washington seems to have had no problem with the requirement.[35]

To what extent did Washington integrate his religious convictions into his work as a farmer, landowner, and statesman? Washington has always had a reputation as a distinguished republican citizen. He made many sacrifices for his country and was often willing, when asked, to take up the call in service to the burgeoning United States. He showed restraint and prudence after the war when he resigned from the leadership of a standing army, a clear sign that he was not seeking to gain political power by the sword as was common with many popular and powerful generals in early modern Europe. Washington should be commended for these virtues. He was a man of character, integrity, and honesty.

Of course the biggest blemish on Washington's career, like that of many southern founders, was his ownership of slaves. When forced to decide between ending slavery and preserving the Union, Washington, in good republican fashion, always chose the preservation of the Union. When Marquis de Lafayette approached him for help with a plan to abolish slavery, Washington was sympathetic, but remained concerned about what such a decision might do to the Union. When Quakers had earlier tried to promote the ending of the slave trade in America, Washington called it an "ill-judged piece of business" because it offended the southern plantation owners and thus threatened the stability of the Union.[36] Washington eventually did free all 123 of his slaves when he died. Such an act is commendable. But his decision while he was alive to deny freedom to slaves—human beings created in God's image—is an obvious scar on whatever Christian faith Washington may have upheld.

Communion

Perhaps the most discussed aspect of Washington's religious behavior is his Communion habits. The Lord's Supper is a sacrament in which the partaker identified personally and publicly with the death of Jesus Christ for the sins of the world—a core tenet of all Christian denominations and sects.

Washington seldom wrote about his Communion habits. Much like his prayer life, we can only glean information about them from the witness of others. According to information she received from her mother, who had lived at Mount Vernon for a number of years, Nelly Custis Lewis reported that Washington, prior to the American Revolution, partook of Communion regularly. After the Revolution, Nelly remembered that Washington, on Communion Sundays, would leave church after the priest's blessing and travel home with her, sending the carriage back for his wife, Martha, who stayed to receive the sacrament. Bishop William White wrote that "truth requires me to say, that General Washington never received the communion," but "Mrs. Washington was an habitual communicant."[37] One of the more interesting stories about Washington's Communion habits comes from James Abercrombie, the assistant rector at Christ Church, Philadelphia, where Washington worshiped during his presidency. It is worth quoting Abercrombie's view of the president's Communion habits here in full:

> as pastor of the Episcopal church, observing that, on sacramental Sundays, Gen. Washington, immediately after the desk and pulpit services, went out with the greater part of the congregation— always leaving Mrs. Washington with the other communicants—she invariably being one—I considered it my duty in a sermon on Public Worship, to state the unhappy tendency of example, particularly of those in elevated stations who uniformly turned their backs upon the celebration of the Lord's Supper. I acknowledge the remark was intended for the President; and as such he received it.

Washington apparently acknowledged the rebuke, but never again attended services at Christ Church on Sundays when Communion was served. Abercrombie would later write that Washington may have been a "professing Christian," but the minister could not "consider any man as a real Christian who uniformly disregards an ordinance so solemnly enjoined by the divine Author of our holy religion, and considered as a channel of divine grace."[38]

At first glance, Washington's lack of interest in Communion suggests that he was either a bad Christian or not a Christian at all. Perhaps this is true, but the refusal of Communion was not uncommon among eighteenth-century Anglicans. Historians have shown that about 15 percent of all southern Anglicans partook of the Lord's Supper. In parts of England the percentage of communicants was even lower. Most Anglicans, like Washington, left the service before Communion was served. As a result, complaints by ministers like Abercrombie were not unusual.[39]

Washington may have avoided Communion for several reasons. Perhaps he did not identify himself with one of the most important events in Christian history—the death of Jesus Christ. Or he may have been unwilling to affirm his Christian commitments publicly. It is also possible that Washington did not believe he was worthy to participate in the sacrament, an act that reflected a deep and abiding dedication to Christian faith. None of these reasons, however, explains why, if the testimony of his step-granddaughter Nelly Custis is right, he received Communion before the Revolution and not after it. It is possible that Washington may have refused the sacrament after the American Revolution because he did not want to commune with the king of England (the head of the Anglican

Church) or the new American bishop Samuel Seabury, a staunch supporter of the Crown during the Revolution.[40]

While Washington's refusal to partake of Communion was normal
by eighteenth-century standards, it also raises serious questions about
his Christian commitment. The evidence that suggests he partook of
the sacrament before the American Revolution is weak, but the evidence that he refused to partake of Communion after the Revolution
is strong. It is fair to ask why a Christian statesman would not identify
regularly with the sacrificial death of Jesus Christ for the sins of the
world. Washington may have been a Christian who did not participate in
the Lord's Supper, but such behavior raises questions about the quality
of his faith.

Morality, Ethics, and Public Religion

We are on much firmer evidentiary ground when we discuss Washington's views on the relationship between religion and public life. As a lati-
tudinarian, Washington cared less about particular doctrinal differences
than about the way religion helped to preserve the moral fabric of the
nation.[41] Washington first became involved in these matters when he
was chosen to serve on the Religion Committee of the House of Burgesses in Virginia. This committee, of which Washington was a member
from 1769 to 1774, was given the duty of considering all matters related
to religion in the colony and reporting its proceedings to the House.
Washington's work on this committee included dividing the geographi-
cal bounds of Anglican parishes (a role in which his skill as a surveyor
would have certainly helped him), making decisions about parish poor
relief, and revising policies for the election of vestries. We do not know
a great deal about how he understood his role on the committee, but
Washington clearly believed that the regulation of religion in Virginia
was an important service he could provide to his colony.[42]

Washington's belief that the United States needed to be a religious
republic is evident most clearly in his so-called Farewell Address of 1796,
shortly before he left the presidency. So much attention has been paid to
Washington's statements about religion in this address that it is easy to
forget that his discussion of the topic was only a minor part of a larger
address that made important statements about American foreign policy
and politics. Nevertheless, Washington devoted two paragraphs to religion in the Farewell Address:

Of all the dispositions and habits which lead to political prosperity, religion, and morality are indispensable supports. In vain would that man claim the tribute of patriotism, who should labor to subvert these great pillars of human happiness, these firmest props of the duties of men and citizens. The mere politician, equally with the pious man, ought to respect and to cherish them. A volume could not trace all their connections with private and public felicity. . . . Whatever may be conceded to the influence of refined education on minds of peculiar structure, reason and experience both forbid us to expect that national morality can prevail in exclusion of religious principle.

It is substantially true that virtue or morality is a necessary spring of popular government. The rule, indeed, extends with more or less force to every species of free government. Who that is a sincere friend to it can look with indifference upon attempts to shake the foundation of the fabric?[43]

The Farewell Address was rooted in the traditions of what political philosophers call "classical republicanism." Republicans of the classical variety believed in representative government, but also demanded that representatives and citizens practice virtue as a prerequisite for the survival of any republic. Good republicans often asked the same question that Washington did in his Farewell Address: What makes citizens willing to lay aside their own interests for the greater good of the nation? Washington believed that the best way to accomplish this essential component of a good society was through the promotion of religion.

For Washington, Christianity, or any other religion for that matter, was more important for its role in bringing moral improvement to the nation than it was in helping people get right with God. Washington was a republican before he was a Christian believer. He placed more emphasis in his public and private writings on the place religion would play in the building of the United States than he did on religion as a devotional practice that brought glory to God and salvation to humans.

His belief that religion is essential to republican society explains many of Washington's military orders during the American Revolution. On more than one occasion Washington gave his troops Sundays off from work to attend public worship. He urged ordinary soldiers and officers to go to church whenever it was possible and insisted that each regiment have a chaplain to serve its spiritual needs. Washington also cracked down on his soldiers for immoral behavior such as "profane cursing and swearing." Such immoral behavior, he believed, might deter "the bless-ing of Heaven on our Arms." In May 1778 Washington delivered the following order, which best summarizes his general approach to religion in the army:

> While we are zealously performing the duties of good Citizens and soldiers we certainly ought not to be inattentive to the higher duties of Religion. To the distinguished Character of Patriot, it should be our highest Glory to add the more distinguished Character of Chris-tian. The signal Instances of providential Goodness which we have experienced and which have now almost crowned our labours with complete Success, demand from us in a peculiar manner the warmest returns of Gratitude and Piety to the Supreme Author of all Good.[44]

Religious Freedom

Washington's belief in the importance of religion to public virtue also helps to explain his commitment to religious freedom. Upon his inaugu-ration as president, Washington received dozens of letters from Ameri-can denominations and religious groups congratulating him on his new position. Washington's responses to these letters reveal both his commit-ment to the place of religion in the American Republic and his dogged defense of religious freedom.

In writing to the General Assembly of the Presbyterian Church, Washington stressed how "the general prevalence of piety, philanthropy, honesty, industry, and oeconomy" was essential for "advancing and confirming the happiness of our country."[45] To the Roman Catholics Washington wrote that "under the smiles of a Divine Providence" the "cultivation of manners, morals, and piety" would lead to an "uncommon degree of eminence, in literature, commerce, agriculture, improvements at home and respectability abroad."[46] In a letter to the Protestant clergy of Philadelphia, Washington echoed the same words from his Farewell Address: "Believing, as I do, that Religion and morality are the essential pillars of civic society, I view, with unspeakable pleasure, that harmony and Brotherly Love which characterizes the clergy of different denomi-nations—as well in this, as in other parts of the United States, exhibiting to the world a new and promising spectacle, at once the pride of our Country and the surest basis of universal harmony."[47]

These letters to denominations also reveal Washington's support for any and all religious groups that he believed could contribute to the public good. He used these letters to assure communities of faith that their religious freedom was not in jeopardy. Washington reminded the Hebrew Congregation in Newport, Rhode Island, that everyone in America "shall sit safely under his own vine and fig tree, and there shall be none to make him afraid."[48] To the Swedenborgian congregation in Baltimore Washington wrote: "in this land truth and reason have triumphed over the power of bigotry and superstition, and that every person may here worship God according to the dictates of his own heart."[49] To the Baptists of his home state of Virginia, Washington affirmed that the Constitution would never "endanger the religious rights of any ecclesiastical Society." He let them know that he would never have signed the Constitution if it rendered "liberty of conscience insecure" or allowed the "horrors of spiritual tyranny, and every species of religious persecution."[50]

Washington took several other steps designed to end religious persecution and enhance religious freedom. For example, amid much protest from Christian clergy, he appointed John Murray, the founder of Universalism, as a chaplain in the Continental Army.[51] While the Continental Army was engaged in Boston in 1775 Washington banned his soldiers from participating in Pope's Day, a popular anti-Catholic holiday in New England that featured, among other things, burning effigies of the pope.[52] When Presbyterians complained to Washington that the new U.S. Constitution made no reference to God or Jesus Christ, he answered their complaint with a general statement about how the new government would promote morality, assuring Presbyterians that they could expect "true religion" to be advanced in support of this cause.[53]

When it comes to the religious beliefs of George Washington, historians, as well as Christians, should tread cautiously. Washington was an intensely private man concerning his faith, though he did not hesitate to speak publicly about the role of Providence in the creation of the United States and the importance of religion in sustaining the Republic. Based on the evidence we have, he was not an evangelical Christian, as some have suggested. Those evangelicals that claim him today should realize that Washington would probably not meet the requirements for lay leadership in their own congregations. Washington's lifelong identity as an Anglican could mean many things. The Anglican Church was a big tent that included everyone from deists to warm evangelicals. Most of them did not wear their faith on their sleeves. We must also remember that Washington was a soldier and statesman, not a theologian. He did not devote a great deal of his time to reflect on religious matters.

Having said that, the available evidence points to a man who did not seem particularly interested in the divinity of Jesus Christ or his salvific death for humankind. He tried to live by the Golden Rule and did a pretty good job of it, despite some rather blatant shortcomings. Washington never shared his most intimate spiritual thoughts, but historians will always wonder what his letters to Martha would have said if she had not burned them after his death.

The study of Washington's religion reminds us that the past is distant and the historian is often limited in his or her ability to reconstruct it. Sometimes, based upon the evidence available to us, we must just say "perhaps." It is never good to use the past to promote political and cultural agendas before we fully understand it in all its complexity. There is a lot to celebrate about George Washington—his leadership, his courage, his civility, and his morality. But we must show due prudence in celebrating him as a Christian. His religious life was just too ambiguous.

Chapter Twelve

John Adams

Devout Unitarian

John Adams believed that he was a Christian. The Massachusetts revolutionary, signer of the Declaration of Independence, and second president of the United States was raised in a Christian home. He worshiped God in a Congregational church founded by seventeenth-century Puritans. He considered pursuing a career as a clergyman. He once described himself to Benjamin Rush as a "churchgoing animal."[1] Anyone who has read David McCullough's wildly successful biography of Adams, or watched the HBO miniseries based on McCullough's book, cannot help but admire the man. His personal convictions often led to behavior that one could easily describe as "Christian."

As a young man, John Adams dreamed of living in a godly society. "Suppose a nation in some distant region," he wrote,

> should take the Bible for their only law Book, and every member should regulate his conduct by the precepts there exhibited. Every member would be obliged in Conscience to temperance and frugality and industry, to justice and kindness and Charity towards his fellow men, and to Piety and Love, and reverence towards almighty God. In this Commonwealth, no man would impair his health by Gluttony, drunkenness, or Lust—no man would sacrifice his most precious time to cards, or any other trifling and mean amusement—no man would steal or lie or any way defraud his neighbour, but would live in peace and good will with all men—no man would blaspheme his maker or prophane his Worship, but a rational and manly, a sincere and unaffected Piety and devotion would reign in all hearts. What a Eutopa, what a Paradise would this region be.[2]

"Justice, Kindness, Piety, Charity"—Adams did his best to make his life conform to the ideals of such a godly paradise. He placed his life and family in the hands of a providential God who ordered the world according to his own good purposes. Adams was a loving father who cared deeply for the spiritual well-being of his children. His relationship with his wife, Abigail, was characterized by love, mutual respect, and honor. He often worried about how his entrance into politics would affect the general well-being of his family.[3] Adams believed in forgiveness—even for the British government during the American Revolution. He railed against the luxury and materialism of the society in which he lived and worried about what the self-interested inclinations of ambitious men would do to the American Republic. Though he ultimately rejected the Calvinist doctrine of total depravity, he did believe that human beings were limited in their capacity to understand God and comprehend his plan for the universe.[4] Based upon the way he conducted his life and his own understanding of his religious identity, Adams appears to have been a Christian.

Adams and Christian Orthodoxy

Adams may have often behaved in a Christian fashion and lived a life guided by the moral principles of the Bible, but his personal beliefs, especially as they relate to the person of Jesus Christ, fell well short of conforming to the historic doctrines of Christian orthodoxy. If we return to the categories used in the preface to the first edition of this book to define the meaning of the term "Christian," we might say that Adams passes the "orthopraxy" test, but fails—and fails miserably—the "orthodoxy" test. Even as he referred to himself as a Christian in his personal writings and letters, Adams was well aware of the fact that his religious beliefs were "not exactly conformable to that of the greater Part of the Christian World."[5]

On several occasions Adams described his personal religious creed. While serving as vice president of the United States he wrote: "The Christian Religion is, above all the Religions that ever prevailed or existed in ancient or modern Times, The Religion of Wisdom, Virtue, Equity and Humanity. . . . It is resignation to God—it is Goodness itself to Man."[6] A few years later he described his religious convictions more succinctly and personally: "Benevolence and Beneficence, Industry, Equity and Humanity, Resignation and Submission, Repentance and Reformation are the Essence of my Religion."[7] In a letter to Benjamin Rush, Adams noted that his religious convictions could be found in John 5:29: "But after all that has been said of doctrines, they only who *have done good* shall come forth to the resurrection unto life, and they only who *have done evil* to the resurrection of damnation."[8] In 1816 he informed Thomas Jefferson, "The Ten Commandments and the Sermon on the Mount contain my Religion."[9] As these statements make clear, Adams was interested primarily in the way religion was practiced in everyday life. A godly person cultivated benevolence, performed good deeds, and obeyed the moral law as set forth in the Bible.

As his reference to the Sermon on the Mount indicates, Adams had much respect and reverence for the life and teachings of Jesus Christ. By studying the words of Jesus one could learn much about the nature of God and the "future state" of rewards and punishments. Adams described the ethical teaching of Jesus as the "most benevolent and sublime, probably that has been ever taught and more perfect than those of any of the ancient Philosophers." Yet he could not accept the historic Christian belief that Jesus Christ was God or that his death atoned for the sins of the world: "An incarnate God!!! An eternal, self-existent omnipresent omniscient Author of this stupendous Universe suffering on a Cross!!! My Soul starts with horror, at the Idea." Adams thought the notion of "a mere creature, or finite Being," making "Satisfaction to infinite justice for the sins of the world" was a "convenient Cover for absurdity." These doctrines were not part of the pure and undefiled teachings of Jesus as found in the Gospels, but were rather created by the leaders of the early Christian church who "misunderstood" Jesus' message and thus presented it in "very paradoxical Shapes."[10]

In denying the deity of Jesus Christ, Adams was also casting aside the traditional Christian belief in the Trinity. Indeed, he thought that anyone who believed in the Trinity violated the First Commandment, which "forbids the worship of but one God." His son, John Quincy Adams, was considerably more conservative and orthodox in his Christian beliefs, a fact that often drove his father crazy. John Adams could not fathom how his son could possibly embrace the teaching of the Athanasian Creed, the first ancient Christian confession to affirm the deity and equality of the three persons of the Trinity.[11]

Adams's devout belief in one God and his disdain for the Christian doctrine of the Trinity made him a Unitarian. New England Unitarianism grew out of the premise, which was gaining ground among some Congregational ministers in the region, that God was understood best through the power of reason. Since the Trinity could not be explained rationally, it was discarded in favor of a unitary God. By the turn of the nineteenth century Unitarian thinkers had gained control of Harvard

College, and Unitarian clergy trained at Harvard were presenting a serious threat to Christian orthodoxy in this Calvinist stronghold.[12] Adams claimed that the First Parish Church of Quincy, Massachusetts, the congregation in which he held lifelong membership, had embraced Unitarian teaching in 1750. The close connection between historic New England Congregationalism and Unitarianism explains why Adams could claim that he was both a "Christian" and a "Unitarian." He had been raised in a Puritan household, but by the time he reached adulthood he had developed convictions more in sympathy with the liberal wing of New England Congregationalism.[13]

Clergy, Catholics, and Calvinists

Adams's liberal religious commitments and his propensity for stubborn independent thinking could result in a harsh disdain for the defenders of Christian orthodoxy. Throughout his life he maintained a strong distrust of clergy. He did not like the authority that ministers held over the lives of ordinary people and remained especially suspect of their complex theological systems. Adams's disgust with the clergy is best illustrated by an 1804 entry in his autobiography in which he described why he chose not to pursue a career in the ministry. Shortly after he graduated from Harvard, Adams was exposed to a religious controversy that divided Quincy's First Parish Church. The minister of the church, Lemuel Briant, was accused of teaching Arminian doctrines and behaving in a way that was "too gay and light if not immoral." Arminianism, a theological view that asserted the free will of individuals, posed a direct challenge to a New England Calvinism that emphasized the depravity of the human will and the inability of individuals to experience God apart from a divine work of grace. These debates were part of the theological shift from Calvinism to Unitarianism taking place in Adams's congregation during the mid-eighteenth century. When a church council was held in the Adams home John saw firsthand what he called the "Spirit of Dogmatism and Bigotry of the Clergy and Laity." Adams never forgot what he witnessed during these years (1751–1755) of local religious controversy. He knew that if he pursued a ministerial path he would be urged to take sides in a whole host of theological squabbles not unlike the one he observed in Quincy. In the end, Adams concluded that "the Study of Theology and the pursuit of it as a Profession would involve me in endless Altercations and make my Life miserable, without any prospect of doing any good to my fellow Men."[14]

Adams's description of this church controversy also illustrates his lifelong conviction that the purpose of religion was to make "good men, good majestrates, good Subjects, good Husbands and good Wives, good Parents and good Children, good masters and good servants."[15] Such a belief was consistent with New England Unitarianism, which stressed ethical living over a strict adherence to religious dogma. The New England clergy were "good Riddle Solvers or good mystery mongers," but they largely failed, in Adams's view, to cultivate a benevolent, moral, and harmonious society. He challenged his Calvinist neighbors to find anything in the teachings of Jesus related to the "Ecclesiastical Synods, Convocations, Councils, Decrees, Creeds, Confessions, Oaths, Subscriptions and whole Cartloads of other trumpery, that we find Religion incumbered with in these Days."

Adams used the phrase "Protestant Popedom" to describe the authority that the clergy held over the members of their congregations.[16] Religion, as it was practiced in the eighteenth-century Western world, was so driven by rituals and "theatrical ceremonies" that it could "delude and terrify men out of all their knowledge, virtue, liberty, piety, and happiness."[17] Clergy were too motivated by ambition and power to take seriously the true religion of Jesus. Ultimately, Adams declared, "true Religion is from the Heart, between Man and his Creator and not the Imposition of Man or creeds and tests."[18] He compared the "unchangeable and eternal Foundation of Religion" found in all human beings with the "fungous growth or spurious sprout" resulting from sermons preached by "the grossest Blockheads and most atrocious Villains." Adams pulled no punches in his attack on the established clergy of New England Congregationalism. As far as he was concerned, ministers had a power that bordered on tyranny. They were "able to cultivate into Systems and Sects to deceive millions and cheat and pillage hundreds and thousands of their fellow Creatures."[19]

Adams's ire against the religious formalism of the clergy and institutional religion in general was targeted specifically at two groups: Roman Catholics and Calvinists. He understood Catholicism to be the ultimate form of superstitious and irrational religion. Adams attended several Catholic masses during his lifetime and visited the sites of Catholic shrines and monasteries when traveling in Europe. He never described Catholic worship and practice in a positive light and often spewed the kind of anti-Catholic rhetoric that was quite common in British-American life. In 1774, after visiting St. Mary's Catholic Church in Philadelphia, Adams wrote to Abigail:

This Afternoons Entertainment was to me, most awfull and affecting. The poor Wretches, fingering their Beads, chanting Latin, not a Word of which they understood, their Pater Nosters and Ave Maria's. Their holy Water—their Crossing themselves perpetually—their Bowing to the name of Jesus, wherever they hear it—their Bowings and Kneelings, and Genuflections before the Altar. The Dress of the Priest was rich with Lace—his Pulpit was Velvet and Gold. The Altar Piece was very rich—little Images and Crucifixes about Wax-Candles lighted up. But how shall I describe the Picture of our Saviour in a Frame of Marble over the Altar at full Length upon the Cross, in the Agonies, and the Blood dripping and streaming from his Wounds. . . . Here is every Thing which can lay hold of the Eye, Ear, and Imagination. Every Thing which can charm and bewitch the simple and ignorant. I wonder how Luther ever broke the spell.[20]

Adams believed that Catholics were being deceived by the teachings and rituals of their church. As a man deeply influenced by the Enlightenment, he could not tolerate any form of religion that seemed to contradict the dictates of reason. He had a particular contempt for those who spread the Catholic faith around the world, especially the Jesuits. When the Jesuit order was reconstituted by the Catholic Church in 1814, Adams was alarmed, writing to Thomas Jefferson, "If ever any Congregation of Men could merit, eternal Perdition on Earth and Hell . . . it is the Company of Loiola [Loyola]." He fully expected the Jesuits to come to America and influence political elections through the organization of Catholic voters.

In the political realm, Adams believed that "Liberty and Popery cannot live together." Catholicism was a tyrannical religious system that required its followers to pay ultimate homage to the pope. The Roman Catholic Church was the antithesis of liberty. Catholicism's religious authority in the Western world, including its "incomprehensible power of creating out of bread and wine the flesh and blood of God himself," kept "human nature chained fast for ages in cruel, shameful, and deplorable servitude to him [the pope], and his subordinate tyrants." Adams believed that Catholics were not permitted the freedom to read or interpret the Bible for themselves and were required to submit to a church hierarchy that claimed to hold the keys to eternal life. Catholicism was the established religion of some of the most tyrannical political regimes in Europe, especially France, England's most powerful military and economic rival. As

Adams put it, Catholicism and absolute monarchs had forged a "wicked confederacy" that held people in ignorance and stole their natural rights from them. A nation could never be built on principles of liberty and freedom when a large portion of the population maintained its highest allegiance to the Catholic Church.[21]

Adams's understanding of religious freedom was forged in the context of his anti-Catholicism. He believed that God, "in his benign Providence," had intervened in human history to topple the tyrannical hold that the Catholic Church had over the people of Europe. As Protestantism—a form of Christianity that gave people liberty to interpret the Bible for themselves—spread throughout the West, religious tyranny lost "strength and weight." The history lesson was clear. It was a natural love of liberty that led Puritans to flee to America in order to escape the Catholic-style tyranny imposed upon them by the seventeenth-century Anglican Church. In other words, the Church of England was a problem for Puritans because its leadership often behaved too much like Catholics.

In his pamphlet *A Dissertation on the Canon and Feudal Law* (1765), Adams applied this history lesson to the relationship between the colonies and the English Parliament, directly tying political freedom to religious freedom. He told his readers that "consenting to slavery is a sacrilegious breach of trust, as offensive in the sight of God as it is derogatory from our own honor or interest or happiness—and that God Almighty had promulgated from heaven, liberty, peace, and good-will to man."[22] God, Adams believed, was always on the side of freedom. Later in life he would speak more forcefully about this God-given right to religious freedom, asserting that "unlimited freedom of religion, consistent with morals and property is essential to the progress of society."[23] Religious establishments reeked of Catholic tyranny. When church and state were united in this way the loss of political liberty would soon follow.

Adams was a bit less strident in his criticism of Calvinism. He had much respect for the teachings of John Calvin as manifested in the New England Puritanism that informed his religious upbringing. Much about Adams's Puritan childhood transferred into his adult religious life. He was always aware of his imperfections and often saw the need to repent of his faults. As we will see below, he never abandoned a basic Calvinist belief in the providence of God. He was no deist. He believed in a God who played an active role in the lives of his human creation. He also thought that many of the original moral codes enforced by seventeenth-century Puritans in Massachusetts Bay Colony were still useful for fostering a virtuous society. And as he grew older he increasingly began to articulate a belief in a transcendent God who was mysterious and unknowable by mere mortals. In a letter to his granddaughter, Caroline de Windt, Adams described himself as a "Worm" who had few answers to the great questions of life: "The longer I live, the more I read, the more patiently I think, and the more anxiously I inquire, the less I seem to know." He told his grandson, George Washington Adams, that "the secrets of eternal wisdom are not to be fathomed by our narrow understandings."[24] These were not the words of a man who believed in the power of individuals to shape their own destinies or the power of reason to overcome all mystery. These were the words of a humble man who acknowledged the existence of a Being larger than himself and the limits that such a Being placed on his understanding.

In a letter to Presbyterian minister Samuel Miller, Adams would describe both his respect for Calvinism and his unwillingness to embrace its beliefs:

> I must be a very unnatural Son to entertain any prejudices against Calvinists or Calvinism, according to your confession of faith: for my Father & Mothers, my Uncles & Aunts, and all my predecessors from our common Ancestor who landed in this Country two hundred years ago . . . were of that persuasion. Indeed I have never known any better people than Calvinists. Nevertheless I must acknowledge that I can not class myself under that denomination.

It was the Calvinist doctrine of original sin and total depravity that made Adams particularly hostile to the religion of his youth. Adams could never reconcile his belief in the potential of human beings to perform benevolent actions with the Calvinist doctrine of original sin. He struggled with the Calvinist notion that humans were so "altogether malicious and malignant" that they were "destitute of benevolence" apart from a work of grace. He boldly declared that "there is no individual totally depraved." If Calvinism were true, then some of the greatest thinkers in the history of Western civilization, including Plato, Cicero, Tacitus, and Pliny, would be spending eternity "sweltering under the scalding drops of divine Vengeance."[25] Though Adams believed that human beings could and did sin against God, he also had too much faith in a loving God to believe that individuals pursuing a moral and benevolent life could be chosen to spend eternity in a perpetual state of punishment.

Religion, America, and the Public Good

Adams's devout Unitarianism deeply informed his understanding of the American Revolution. Like George Washington and many of the founders, he was a strong believer in God's providential care for the United States. Though Adams occasionally talked about God's providence as being "inscrutable" (usually after American losses on the battlefield), he was convinced that God was a patriot. As the Revolution got underway, he declared that the colonists "must depend upon Providence or We fail." "It is the Will of Heaven," he wrote, "that the two Countries [England and the United States] should be sundered forever."[26]

Adams always upheld a sense of "Reverence and Wonder" about the settlement of America. He fused his Enlightenment belief in human improvement with his providential understanding of the world. The United States of America was "the Opening of a grand scene and Design in Providence, for the Illumination of the Ignorant and the Emancipation of the slavish Part of Mankind all over the Earth." God was on the side of American progress. On one occasion, Adams admitted that such an appeal to Providence was "unfashionable" among educated and enlightened men like himself, but he remained enough of a Puritan at heart to continue "firmly" believing in it, regardless of what fashion dictated.[27]

Throughout his life Adams remained concerned with promoting a virtuous nation. The American Republic would only survive, he believed, if people acted in an ethical way that enabled them, at times, to place the interests of others over their own selfish needs and desires. Selfishness was at the heart of the British taxation policies during the years leading up to the American Revolution. The British, and particularly their tax collectors and colonial officials, were characterized by "Ambition and Avarice"—"Sins" that would eventually merit the "judgments of Heaven." Colonists, if they were not careful, could be tempted to commit the same public sins as the British. Adams lamented to Abigail that the people of America were more concerned about the "Mammon of Unrighteousness" than they were in cultivating the kind of patriotism needed for victory over British tyranny.[28] These calls for public virtue and righteousness were not uncommon during the American Revolution. Adams and many of his fellow founders merged traditional Christian teaching on sin with the political cause of revolution. If colonists were not virtuous and continued in their sin, God would not bless their pursuit of independence.

The family was at the heart of Adams's vision of a virtuous society. Mothers would play a vital role in instilling morality in the citizenry. Indeed, Adams believed that the "Manners of Women" were the "surest Criterion by which to determine whether a Republican Government is practicable." Adams suggested that previous attempts at republican government by the Greeks, Romans, Swiss, and Dutch all failed because these societies "lost the Modesty and Domestic Virtues of their Women." For Adams, "the foundations of national Morality must be laid in private Families."[29] Unless children were raised in a moral household, where ethics and religion were taught from an early age, there was nothing that schools or academies could do to foster the kind of virtue needed for a republic to survive. Adams's call for family values was not mere political rhetoric. He and Abigail went to great efforts to raise their children with a personal piety and a public spirit informed by morality and religion. Writing from Philadelphia during the meeting of the Second Continental Congress, John urged Abigail to "take care" of the spiritual and emotional needs of his sons: "Cultivate their Minds, inspire their little Hearts, raise their Wishes. Fix their Attention upon great and glorious Objects, root out every little Thing, weed out every Meanness, make them great and manly. Teach them to scorn Injustice, Ingratitude, Cowardice, and Falshood. Let them revere nothing but Religion, Morality, and Liberty."[30]

Adams was convinced that religion was the only true foundation of moral happiness in the American republic. "There is no such thing [morality]," Adams wrote, "without a supposition of a God. There is no right or wrong in the universe without the supposition of a moral government and an intellectual and moral governor." While serving as president he told the officers of a Massachusetts militia brigade, "Our Constitution was made only for a moral and religious people. It is wholly inadequate to the government of any other." In 1811 Benjamin Rush encouraged Adams to deliver a public address arguing that "the foundation of national happiness" could be found *"only* in religion." Adams never did deliver the speech. He feared that such an address might be interpreted by his enemies as an attempt to promote a "national establishment of Presbyterianism in America." But he did speculate on what he might say in such an address. Adams envisioned speaking about how "religion and virtue are the only foundations not only of republicanism and of all free government but of social felicity under all governments and in all combinations of human society." He recommended to his imagined audience "the sanctification of the Sabbath" and "a regular attendance of public worship as a means of moral instruction and social improvement."[31]

Adams never wavered in his conviction that government was responsible for promoting religion. During his presidency, at a time when the United States was engaged in a naval war with France, he announced that a day of "solemn humiliation, fasting, and prayer" be observed by all citizens of the nation, affirming that the "safety and prosperity" of the nation "ultimately and essentially depend on the protection and the blessing of Almighty God." He once again affirmed that "social happiness" could not be achieved or enjoyed without "morality and piety." On March 23, 1798, Americans were encouraged to abstain from their "customary worldly occupations" and "offer their devout addresses to the Father of Mercies," "acknowledge before God the manifold sins and transgressions with which we are justly chargeable as individuals and as a nation," and offer "sincere repentance and reformation which may afford us reason to hope for his inestimable favor and heavenly benediction."[32]

Many perceived Adams's call for a day of fasting and prayer to be little more than a political tool to win support for his own political party, the New England–concentrated Federalists. The Federalists believed that government had the responsibility of enforcing public morality rooted in the Christian faith. As we saw in chapter 9, Adams's home state of Massachusetts would continue until 1833 to support the Congregational Church as a means of maintaining moral order. Adams's call for a day of fasting and prayer was endorsed by the Presbyterian Church, a denomination that was suspected by many to have secret ambitions of creating a national religious establishment. The fast declaration was thus criticized by his Republican political enemies, including Thomas Jefferson, his eventual opponent in the next presidential election. According to Adams, American religious denominations and sects, especially those who guarded their religious liberties closely and tended to vote Republican, cried out: "Let us have Jefferson, Madison, Burr, anybody, whether they be philosophers, Deists, or even atheists, rather than a Presbyterian president." Adams was *not* a Presbyterian, but his firm belief that the president should promote religion and morality did not sit well with those Christians and others who feared that such government involvement in religious matters was the first step toward tyranny and the erosion of religious freedom. Adams would later write that his decision to call for a religious fast day may have cost him a victory in the 1800 presidential election.[33]

John Adams was a God-fearing man who should be commended by Christians for his attempts to live a life in accordance with the moral teachings of the Bible. He was a strong supporter of the idea that the success of the American Republic depended upon such teachings. He dreamed of a republic populated by individuals concerned less with their own selfish desires and more with the practice of virtues such as justice, charity, and forgiveness.

But Adams was also a man of his times. He showed little Christian tolerance for those with whom he disagreed, especially Catholics, Calvinists, and members of the clergy. As a product of New England liberalism, he had no patience for Christian beliefs such as the deity of Christ or, for that matter, any doctrine that could not be explained by reason. In the end, we might say that Adams did believe that the United States was a Christian nation, but only if we use the term to describe a moral system informed by the teachings of Jesus and a belief in a providential and unitary God who blesses America but who did not send his Son to become the Savior of the world.

Chapter Thirteen

Thomas Jefferson

Follower of Jesus

Thomas Jefferson could not have had a more traditional Anglican upbringing. His father, Peter Jefferson, was an Anglican vestryman, and young Thomas was schooled by Anglican ministers at the College of William and Mary. He was married in the Anglican Church and baptized his children as Anglicans. Jefferson maintained a lifelong fascination with religion. He read sermons and theological tracts. He corresponded on matters related to religion with some of the era's most prominent intellectuals. If the writing on his tombstone is any indication, Jefferson thought that one of his greatest accomplishments in life, in addition to his penning of the Declaration of Independence and founding the University of Virginia, was the authorship of the 1786 Virginia Statute for Religious Freedom. Jefferson biographer Edwin Gaustad has called him "the most self-consciously theological of all American presidents."[1]

Jefferson not only concerned himself with the ideas of religious thinkers and the relationship between Christianity and public life, but he also had a vibrant personal faith. He claimed to be a follower of the teachings of Jesus of Nazareth. His devotional life sustained him through times of crisis, including the death of his beloved wife and the loss of five of his children. His commonplace book, a book of thoughts and reflections, is filled with inspirational writings and his library contained volumes to aid him in religious meditation. As we will see below, Jefferson excerpted passages from the Gospels that would help him become a better follower of Jesus. The creation of this so-called Jefferson Bible, as Gaustad has shown, was not intended "to shock or offend," but was "for his assurance, for a more restful sleep at night and a more confident greeting of the mornings." For Jefferson, the moral teachings of Jesus represented the essence of Christianity. They should thus be read and practiced by all true believers.[2]

Jefferson was a follower of Jesus. But was he a Christian? If one's definition of Christianity is based solely on the moral teachings of Jesus as recorded in the Gospels, then Jefferson was a Christian. He was a member of the Anglican Church who tried, though not always perfectly succeeding, to live in accordance with what Jesus commanded. But if you measure Jefferson's beliefs against the history of orthodox Christian teaching, he falls well short. Like his political rival and later friendly correspondent John Adams, Jefferson fails the orthodoxy test. Indeed, he was probably the most skeptical of all the founders. Even as his life remained embedded in the Anglican culture of colonial and early national Virginia, he was a restless soul who never ceased to question the religious faith he inherited from childhood.

The Intelligent Creator

Since Jefferson was a product of the eighteenth-century Enlightenment, reason was central to his religious convictions. God had created every human being with the faculty of reason. The use of this faculty, Jefferson believed, was the only way to uncover religious truth: "Reason and free inquiry are the only effectual agents against error. Give a loose to them, they will support the true religion, by bringing every false one to their tribunal, to the test of their investigation." He told his nephew, Peter Carr, "Fix reason firmly in her seat, and call to her tribunal every fact, every opinion."[3] Jefferson thus rejected any doctrines that could not be explained by reason, including the incarnation, the deity of Christ, the atonement, and the resurrection. He thought that if men would "have the courage" to apply reason to their lives they would find that they "do not differ in religious opinions, as much as is supposed." Indeed, if everyone exercised their rational faculties, Jefferson predicted that Unitarianism would become the most prominent religion in the United States.[4]

Despite his skepticism about traditional Christian doctrines, Jefferson thought that it *was* rational to believe in a God who created the world. He was not an atheist; rather, he was convinced that any rational person would come to the conclusion that the universe had an intelligent "designer." In a revealing letter to John Adams, Jefferson wrote that it was "impossible for the human mind not to perceive and feel a conviction of design, consummate skill, and indefinite power in every atom of its composition." Unlike many of his deist friends, he did not believe that

God had removed himself from creation. Jefferson's God was active in sustaining the world. He governed the affairs of humankind by his providence.[5] Jefferson wrote about God's "superintending power to maintain the Universe in its course and order." God kept the stars, sun, and planets in place. Jefferson concluded, "So irresistible are these evidences of an intelligent and powerful Agent that, of the infinite numbers of men who have existed thro' all time, they have believed, in the proportion of a million at least to Unit, in the hypothesis of an eternal pre-existence of a creator, rather than in that of a self-existent Universe." He called this Creator and Sustainer of the universe "Nature's God"—a God who he believed was best portrayed in Psalm 148:

> Praise the Lord!
> Praise the Lord from the heavens, praise him in the heights!
> Praise him all his angels, praise him, all his host!
> Praise him, sun and moon, praise him, all you shining stars!
> Praise him, you highest heavens, and you waters above the heavens!
> Let them praise the name of the Lord!
> For he commanded and they were created.
> And he established them for ever and ever;
> He set a law which cannot pass away.[6]

Jefferson integrated science and creation in a way that moved him to praise.

Follower of Jesus

Jefferson's God, however, did not reveal himself to his human creation in the person of Jesus Christ. Unlike many Unitarians of his day, including Joseph Priestley, the English intellectual who influenced him on a host of religious matters, Jefferson did not believe that Jesus of Nazareth was sent by God to die and rise again for the sins of the world. On this point, Jefferson was a skeptic even by Unitarian standards. Priestley was not an orthodox Christian, but he worried about whether his friend from Virginia was truly saved.[7] Jefferson treated the teachings of Jesus as he would the teachings of any other ancient philosopher, but he did believe that Jesus' "system of morals" was "the most perfect and sublime that has ever been taught by man." "I am indeed," he wrote in 1803, "sincerely attached to his doctrines, in preference to all others." The teachings of Jesus could be universally applied to all humankind. They had the potential of gathering "all into one family, under the bonds of love, charity, peace, common wants, and common aids."[8]

Jefferson was convinced that his commitment to the moral system of Jesus made him a Christian. In 1816 he wrote, "I am a *real* Christian, that is to say, a disciple of the doctrines of Jesus." Two years later, he wrote that it is only in "getting back to the plain and unsophisticated precepts of Christ, that we become *real* Christians." Only true disciples would be permitted to enter into the "future state" that Jesus preached about in the Gospels. The afterlife offered an "incentive" to live ethically in this life.[9] On occasion Jefferson could sound like an evangelist. He believed that if the moral precepts of the gospel were preached in their purest form, "the whole civilized world would now have been Christian." His prayer was "Thy Kingdom come," and he had confidence that such a prayer would be answered. The kingdom of God was both possible and inevitable.[10]

Jefferson and His Bibles

Jefferson's commitment to a rational religion, and his dogged belief in the superiority of the teachings of Jesus, informed his views on the Bible. He did not believe that the Bible was the inspired Word of God. It was useful for moral improvement, but it should ultimately be read like any other great book. He told Peter Carr to read the Bible with a critical eye, "as you would Livy or Tacitus." When Carr began to study the Old Testament story in which Joshua asked God to command the sun to stand still so he could finish his battle with the Amorites (Joshua 10:1–15), his uncle informed him to read the passage in the way that any good astronomer would read it. Such a biblical story needed to be examined rationally, in accordance with the "law of probabilities." Jefferson was even harsher on the New Testament book of Revelation. He described the fantastic stories in this book as "the ravings of a Maniac, no more worthy, nor capable of explanation than the incoherences of our own nightly dreams." He concluded that "there is not coherence enough in them to countenance any suite of rational ideas."[11]

It was the Gospels—the teachings of Jesus of Nazareth—that drew Jefferson's attention more than any other books in the Bible. He had little respect, however, for the authors of Matthew, Mark, Luke, and John. He accused them of offering only fragments of Jesus' moral precepts. The Gospel authors had disfigured Jesus' true teachings with the "mysticisms of a Graecian Sophist."[12] And Jefferson did not stop there:

Among the sayings and discourses imputed to him [Jesus] by his biographers, I find many passages of fine imagination, correct morality, and of the most lovely benevolence: and others again of so much ignorance, so much absurdity, so much untruth, charlatanism, and imposture, as to pronounce it impossible that such contradictions should have proceeded from the same being. I separate therefore the gold from the dross: restore to him the former, and leave the latter to the stupidity of some and the roguery of others of the disciples. Of this band of dupes and imposters, Paul was the great Coryphaeus, and the first corrupter of the doctrines of Jesus.[13]

The four traditional Gospels and the other biblical books that explained the meaning of the Gospels (i.e., the Pauline Epistles) were corrupted by the authors' inclusion of irrational stories such as Jesus performing miracles, Jesus rising from the dead, and Jesus redeeming the sins of the world. Jefferson set out to correct this problem, devoting much of his intellectual energy to creating versions of the Gospels that did not obscure the true message of Jesus of Nazareth.

Jefferson produced two different versions of the Gospels. Neither of them contained stories from the life of Jesus that could be explained only supernaturally. Sometime in 1804, while serving his first term as president of the United States, Jefferson compiled a forty-six-page booklet that he called "The Philosophy of Jesus of Nazareth." The pamphlet was constructed by taking two copies of the New Testament and excerpting those passages that he believed best reflected the "pure" teachings of Jesus. Nine years later, he described the creation of this booklet to John Adams:

In extracting the pure principles which he [Jesus] taught, we should have to strip off the artificial vestments in which they have been muffled by priests, who have travestied them into various forms, as instruments of riches and power to them. . . . We must reduce our volume to the simple evangelists, select, even from them, the very words of Jesus, paring off the Amphibologisms into which they have been led by forgetting often, or not understanding, what had fallen from him, by giving their own misconception as his dicta, and expressing unintelligibly for others that they had not understood themselves. There will be found remaining the most sublime and benevolent code of morals which has ever been offered to man. I have performed this operation for my own use, by cutting verse by verse out of the printed book, and arranging, the matter which is evidently his, and which is as easily distinguishable as diamonds in a dunghill.[14]

About sixteen or seventeen years later, Jefferson produced a more sophisticated version of this project. The Jefferson Bible, which was published posthumously for the first time in 1895 under the title *The Life and Morals of Jesus of Nazareth*, was a testimony to Jefferson's profound intellectual skills. Jefferson's text was published in four columns. Each column was filled with his edited text in a different language—Greek, Latin, French, and English. Ample space was allotted for the Sermon on the Mount and other passages where Jesus expounded on matters related to personal and societal morality. The phrases and stories that Jefferson left out of his Bible are revealing. His account of Jesus' birth, for example, makes no reference to angels or prophecies. The words of Jesus that correlate with traditional Christian doctrines, such as the reference to him preaching "the baptism of repentance for the remission of sins," were omitted. All references to healings and other miracles, such as the turning of the water into wine at the wedding feast at Cana, were cut. The last verse in the Jefferson Bible reads: "There laid they Jesus, and they rolled a great stone to the door of the sepulcher, and departed." There is no mention of the resurrection.[15] In the end, the Jefferson Bible is perhaps our best guide to the rational religion of this follower of Jesus.

Jefferson believed that the authors of the Bible corrupted the message of Jesus, but so did the clergy who tried to interpret the Bible in the centuries that followed its original writing. He thought that the clergy, and the confessions and creeds of Christian orthodoxy that they promoted and preached, further diluted and disguised the true principles of Christianity. In this regard, Jefferson was a primitivist. He wanted to skip nearly two thousand years of Christian theological reflection and return to the undefiled teachings of Jesus as found in parts of the Gospels. As a result, Jefferson rarely passed up an opportunity to criticize the Christian clergy.[16] He described them as the "greatest obstacles to the advancement of the real doctrines of Jesus." He even went as far as to characterize them as the "real anti-Christ." He told Yale College president Ezra Stiles that "crazy theologists" took the teachings of a man who taught peace and harmony for all humankind and turned them into a "Babel of a religion" defined by schism and church controversy. Moreover, the clergy were corrupt. They used the teaching of Jesus to obtain wealth and power for themselves. They were hostile to liberty and often sided with despots, as he noted was the case in many of the nations of Europe.

Jefferson lamented that "I am sometimes more angry with them than is authorized by the blessed charities which he [Jesus] preached."[17]

Religious Freedom

Despite Jefferson's dislike of the clergy and the organized religion that they advanced, he dogmatically defended their right to practice it. More than any other founder, with perhaps the exception of James Madison, Jefferson championed freedom of religion. To defend such an idea in colonial Virginia made him a radical. Since the founding of the colony in 1607, the government of Virginia had supported the Church of England as its established church. This meant that all free inhabitants of the colony were required to pay taxes to help support the Anglican Church, whether their own religious beliefs and convictions conformed to the teachings of the church or not. By the eighteenth century the growing number of religious dissenters in Virginia—especially Baptists and Presbyterians—began to chafe under this religious establishment and the persecution that its defenders could dole out on those who did not conform. It was these dissenters, with the help of some prominent politicians like Jefferson and Madison, who consistently challenged Anglican authority in Virginia and led the successful movement for the disestablishment of the Church of England in the immediate aftermath of the American Revolution.[18]

In 1777 Jefferson came to the defense of these dissenters and anyone else whose beliefs did not fall in line with the teachings of Virginia's Anglican Church. In that year he composed a "Bill for Establishing Religious Freedom in Virginia." The bill, which was tabled by the Virginia General Assembly, protected all individuals from government coercion in matters of religion. It stated that

> no man shall be compelled to frequent or support any religious worship, place, or ministry whatsoever, nor shall be enforced, restrained, molested, or burthened in his body or goods, not shall otherwise suffer on account of his religious opinions or belief; but that all men shall be free to profess, and by argument to maintain, their opinion in matters of religion, and that the same shall in no wise diminish, enlarge, or affect their civil capacities.[19]

As we saw in chapter 9, it was not until 1786, after a few revisions, much debate, and some crafty legislative maneuvering on the part of Madison, that Jefferson's bill finally became law in the form of the Virginia Statute for Religious Freedom. The statute officially ended the religious establishment in Virginia and, unlike many other state constitutions, did not require officeholders to swear an oath professing a belief in Christianity.

Jefferson's views on religious freedom were rooted in his conviction that all human beings had been endowed by God with certain rights—including the right to worship in the way they saw fit without having to "furnish contributions of money for the propagation of opinions which he disbelieved and abhors." Indeed, "Almighty God hath created the mind free, and manifested his supreme will that free it shall remain by making it altogether insusceptible of restraint." Any attempt to undermine religious freedom was a "departure from the plan of the holy author of our religion, who being lord both of body and mind, yet chose not to propagate it by coercions on either, as was in his Almighty power to do, but to extend it by the influence of reason alone." God gave all human beings free will to make choices about matters of personal belief. It was the government's responsibility to respect these fundamental rights.[20] To deny religious freedom to individuals was a form of tyranny not unlike the tyranny enforced by the Christian clergy over their parishioners. In the Bill for Establishing Religious Freedom, Jefferson noted how religious and civil rulers had "assumed dominion over the faith of others, setting up their own opinions and modes of thinking as the only true and infallible, and as such endeavouring to impose them on others." These rulers "hath established and maintained false religions over the greatest part of the world and through all time."[21]

But just what were these "false religions" that Jefferson wrote about? Jefferson did not name them, but from his other writings on religion we can be rather sure of what he meant by them. First, as we have seen, Jefferson believed that a religion was false if its tenets did not conform to reason. The Bill for Establishing Religious Freedom may thus be read as yet another Jeffersonian attack on the kind of Christian institutions, led by power-hungry clergy, that he believed were corrupting the pure teachings of Jesus of Nazareth. Second, a religion was "false" when it was linked too closely to the state. Jefferson offered several candidates for this kind of "false religion." Certainly the Anglican Church in both England and Virginia qualified on this front. So did the Congregational religious establishments in New England. In an 1817 letter to John Adams, Jefferson commented on the breakup of the Congregational establishment in the state of Connecticut. He rejoiced at the news that Connecticut had finally retreated from the "Monkish darkness, bigotry, and abhorrence of those advances of the mind" that flowed directly from their religious establishment. Jefferson claimed to join Adams in "sincere congratulations that this den of the priesthood is at length broken up, and that a protestant popedom is no longer to disgrace the American history and character." He hoped that Massachusetts, which maintained a Congregational establishment until 1833, would follow suit.[22]

Following the ratification of the Constitution, which forbade a religious establishment on a national level, Jefferson kept a watchful eye out for "false religions" that he believed were trying to promote a Christian nation. "Presbyterians"—a name that Jefferson probably used as a general term to describe any and all Calvinists—drew his particular ire: "The Presbyterian clergy are the loudest, the most intolerant of all sects, the most tyrannical, and ambitious. . . . They pant to reestablish *by law* that holy inquisition, which they can now only infuse into *public opinion*." As a Virginian, Jefferson had seen this kind of religious establishment before. He knew, for example, that the Anglican/Episcopal Church in his home state harbored bitter feelings about the Virginia Statute for Religious Freedom. Jefferson also knew that Anglican clergy in Virginia and Congregationalist clergy in New England had "a very favorable hope of obtaining an establishment of a particular form of Christianity thro' the US." He was pleased, however, that the "returning good sense of our country threatens abortion to their hopes." Jefferson was determined to fight these attempts at establishing a Christian nation, noting in one of his most famous statements on religious freedom: "I have sworn upon the altar of god eternal hostility against every form of tyranny over the mind of man."[23]

The Dilemma of Slavery

As a follower of Jesus or, as Jefferson liked to put it, a "real Christian," the third president of the United States left a mixed legacy. Historian Mark Noll has suggested that many of Jefferson's political positions harmonized quite well with Christian ideals. For example, Jefferson acted with integrity when handling federal funds, he favored limited government, and during the impressment crisis with England in the early 1800s he did everything possible to avoid bringing the United States into a war. Of course, Jefferson's Statute for Religious Freedom comports well with the Christian belief in religious liberty rooted in the dignity of all human persons. These virtues, however, did not shield Jefferson from religious criticism. As we saw in chapter 10, Jefferson was attacked mercilessly by his Federalist opponents during the presidential election of 1800 because his religious views did not conform to prevailing views of Christian orthodoxy. Noll points to the irony behind these Federalist attacks. Jefferson was accused of being an unchristian presidential candidate by a Federalist party whose own candidate, John Adams, failed to conform his beliefs to many Christian doctrines as well. The Federalists were a party of big government, war, and religious establishments. Indeed, Noll is correct to remind us that "in American political history, those who use Christian language have in fact taken positions that accord well with Christian values—but not always, and never consistently."[24]

But we cannot let Jefferson off the hook too easily. Any treatment of his religious and moral life must examine his complicated relationship with the institution of black chattel slavery. On this front, Jefferson failed to live up to the "moral system" of Jesus of Nazareth that he captured so well in the Jefferson Bible. The author of the phrase "all men are created equal" and are "endowed by their Creator with certain unalienable Rights" failed to apply this principle to the nearly two hundred men and women in bondage at Monticello, Jefferson's Virginia plantation home. Jefferson knew that slavery was a morally unacceptable practice. He was aware of the contradictions between his advocacy for liberty and his practice of slaveholding. In *Notes on the State of Virginia*, the only book Jefferson published in his lifetime, he stated that Americans would face the wrath of God for their participation in this institution. When it came to slavery Jefferson seems to have abandoned whatever doubts he had about an angry Calvinist-style God who intervenes in human affairs:

> Indeed I tremble for my country when I reflect that God is just: that his justice cannot sleep for ever: that considering numbers, nature and natural means only, a revolution of the wheel of fortune, an exchange of situation, is among possible events: that it may become probable by supernatural interference! The Almighty has not attribute which can take side with us in such a contest.[25]

Jefferson was optimistic that slavery would not last much longer. With the help of God, this immoral institution would fade away: "The spirit of the master is abating, that of the slave rising from the dust, his condition mollifying, the way I hope preparing, under the auspices of heaven, for a total emancipation."[26] He made several efforts to assist the "auspices of heaven" in bringing the end of slavery in America. In 1769, as a new member of the Virginia House of Burgesses, he cosponsored a failed bill that encouraged slaveholders to emancipate their slaves. Seven years later, Jefferson used the Declaration of Independence to call for an end to the slave trade, accusing King George III of waging a "cruel war against human nature itself, violating its most sacred rights of life and liberty in the persons of a distant people who never offended him, captivating and carrying them into slavery in another hemisphere, or to incur miserable death in their transportation thither." The clause never made it into the final version of the Declaration. It was a victim of the protests of representatives from southern states (mostly South Carolina and Georgia) that were active participants and deeply invested in the slave trade. In 1783 Jefferson drafted a gradual emancipation program for the state of Virginia, but it was never brought before the General Assembly. Later that year, he wrote his "Plan of Government for the Western Territory," a proposal that would have banned slavery in Western settlements after 1800. It was rejected by Congress. Finally, in 1808 President Jefferson worked hard to bring an official end to the slave trade, thus fulfilling a promise that had been made twenty years earlier by the framers of the U.S. Constitution.[27]

Despite his attempts to end the spread of slavery, Jefferson also missed, or simply did not take, opportunities to close the door once and for all on this immoral institution. For example, Jefferson hesitated in distributing his *Notes on the State of Virginia* because he thought his antislavery comments might "produce an irritation" among his fellow slaveholders. His remarks have prompted historian David Brion Davis to wonder "how he expected to encourage the cause of emancipation without producing irritation!"[28] Part of the reason Jefferson was never able to free his own slaves was because to do so would have undermined the elaborate and luxurious lifestyle he had cultivated at Monticello. He went into debt in order to feed his desires for the material accoutrements of an English gentleman. Since slaves were a source of wealth and production on his plantation, he could not afford to free them. Instead, he often sold them in order to pay his bills.[29] Jefferson also failed to exert his influence to prohibit slavery in Louisiana Territory, the vast tract of land he purchased for the United States from France in 1803. The territory was originally planned as a region where small farmers could gain independence through landholding, but it quickly became fertile ground for the spread of slavery.[30]

Jefferson's understanding of the black race was another reason why he found emancipation to be such a difficult prospect. He believed that "blacks," whether "originally a distinct race, or made distinct by time and circumstances, are inferior to whites in the endowments both of body and mind."[31] Jefferson's views about the black race, which he claimed to be based upon his own scientific investigation, would today be cited as an ugly form of racism. He wrote that black slaves could not integrate into white society. If they ever were to be set free, they should be sent to live in their own colony in order to avoid their "deep rooted prejudices" against whites and their "ten thousand recollections . . . of the injuries they have sustained" through the experience of slavery. If freed slaves were left to live among whites they would create "convulsions" in society that might lead to the "extermination" of either the black race or the white race. In *Notes on the State of Virginia,* Jefferson concluded that blacks were inferior to whites because they smelled bad, had no "forethought," could not control their sexual desires, had "dull and tasteless" imaginations, were incapable of "uttering a thought above the level of plain narrative," and were ill-equipped to write good poetry (he especially indicted the great African American poet Phillis Wheatley, whose poems Jefferson believed were "below the dignity of criticism"). The inferiority of blacks, he believed, did not justify slavery; African Americans still deserved their natural rights. But Jefferson's racism, and the racism of virtually all slaveholders, served as a "powerful obstacle" to emancipation.[32]

Jefferson freed eight slaves in his life. All of them were related to Sally Hemings, the slave woman with whom he carried on a long-term sexual relationship after the death of his wife, Martha, in 1782. The nature of the relationship between Jefferson and Hemings has stirred much public debate, beginning in 1802 when James Callender, a disgruntled former Jefferson supporter, published an article in the Richmond *Recorder* claiming that the president had fathered Sally's son Tom, a young man who resembled Jefferson. In 1998 DNA evidence proved that a member of the Jefferson family fathered at least one of Hemings's sons. Historians continue to debate whether the father was Jefferson or one of his relatives who lived nearby, but many well-credentialed scholars, including Pulitzer Prize winner Annette Gordon-Reed, have suggested that Jefferson was probably the father of all six of Sally's children.[33] Evidence abounds that he was present at Monticello nine months before the births of all of them. Sally's son Madison claimed, in an 1873 interview, that his mother informed him that Jefferson was his father. And, as noted above, members of the Hemings family were the only slaves Jefferson ever emancipated.

To indict Jefferson as a moral failure on the issue of slavery is to indict an entire generation of founders, both northerners and southerners, for allowing this unchristian and immoral institution to flourish. It is easy to say that Jefferson was a man of his times and should not be condemned for his failures in the area of slavery. To his credit, he made several efforts to rid his country of the institution that he inherited. But other "men of the times"—George Washington, John Adams, Benjamin Franklin, and the Marquis de Lafayette—either freed their slaves upon their deaths or fought to end this institution. Jefferson was not one of them.

Thomas Jefferson deserves to be considered a great statesman. He wrote the Declaration of Independence with its strong championing of natural rights. He fought for religious freedom in Virginia based upon these God-given rights. These initiatives comport well with a Christian belief that all human beings, created by God to reflect his image, should be treated with dignity and respect. On the other hand, Jefferson devoted his life to the teachings of Jesus, but failed virtually every test of Christian orthodoxy. He spent a great deal of mental energy contemplating Jesus' "system of morality" as presented in the Gospels, but his biography reveals at least one glaring example—slavery—in which his rhetoric about being a "real Christian" did not match his behavior.

Chapter Fourteen

Benjamin Franklin

Ambitious Moralist

E zra Stiles, the Calvinist president of Yale College, was always curious about Benjamin Franklin's faith. In 1790 Stiles asked Franklin if he would be willing to put his religious beliefs down on paper. Franklin agreed to the request. He was nearing the end of his life (he would die six weeks later) and must have thought that it was as good a time as any to summarize the religious creed by which he tried to live. This is what he wrote to Stiles:

> Here is my Creed, I believe in one God, Creator of the Universe. That He governs it by his Providence. That he ought to be worshipped. That the most acceptable Service we render to him, is doing Good to his other Children. That the Soul of Man is immortal, and will be treated with Justice in another Life respecting its Conduct in this. These I take to be the fundamental Principles of all sound Religion, and I regard them as you do, in whatever Sect I meet with them.
>
> As for Jesus of Nazareth, my Opinion of whom you particularly desire, I think the system of Morals and his Religion as he left them to us, the best the World ever saw, or is likely to see; but I apprehend it has received various corrupting Changes, and I have, with most of the present Dissenters in England, some Doubts to his Divinity; tho' it is a Question I do not dogmatise upon, having never studied it, and think it needless to busy myself with it now, where I expect soon an Opportunity of knowing the Truth with less Trouble.[1]

The response was classic Franklin. It was witty and to the point. Religion was worthless unless it promoted virtuous behavior. Human beings

216

would be judged in the next life according to the good works they performed in this life. Jesus was the greatest moral teacher who ever lived, but he was not God.

There is much about Franklin's life that American Christians, or any American for that matter, will find attractive. His *Autobiography*, Franklin's most read and discussed book, extols the virtues of hard work, industry, self-improvement, education, and honesty. Franklin's phrase, "early to bed, early to rise, makes a man healthy, wealthy, and wise," is good advice. The man who wrote almanacs under the pseudonym "Poor Richard" was one of the wealthiest men in America. His list of philanthropic and civic contributions to Philadelphia and the world are well known. He invented things to make people's lives easier—bifocals, the modern stove, the catheter, swimming flippers, and the lightning rod, to name a few. Yet he refused to patent his inventions because he wanted them to benefit humankind. His civic organizations—hospitals, fire companies, libraries, and schools—brought improvement to society. Franklin practiced his religion well.

Franklin led an American life. His was the kind of rags-to-riches story that would later be described as "living the American Dream." Yet Christians must ask themselves just how far they are willing to embrace the religion of "making it." Franklin placed no limits on his life. Anything that held him back from his own improvement—whether it be his childhood Christianity or his commitment to his family—took a back seat to his quest for wealth, social prestige, and progress. For Christians, Franklin's legacy is a mixed one. Let us explore it more deeply.

A Puritan Childhood

Franklin was raised in a devout Puritan home. His father, Josiah, made candles and soap and was a member of Boston's Old South Church. Benjamin was raised on the teachings of New England Calvinism. God was sovereign. Human beings were separated from God because of their sin. But God, in his divine mercy, chose to offer salvation to some of humankind through the death and resurrection of his Son, Jesus Christ. Men and women were required to perform good works in the world, but any attempt at doing them without the aid of the Holy Spirit would be useless in the eyes of God. Josiah saw spiritual potential in his youngest son, Benjamin, and thus set him on a course toward the Congregational ministry. But when he could no longer pay the cost of Benjamin's schooling, Josiah was forced to apprentice him to his older brother James, a

Boston printer and the publisher of the *New England Courant*. Franklin would never escape the faith of his youth. The work ethic he would come to espouse was similar to the so-called Puritan work ethic that he learned growing up in New England, and he never seems to have fully relinquished a belief in the sovereignty of God over the world and its inhabitants.[2]

Was Franklin a Deist?

As a young boy, Franklin was an avid reader, from Bunyan's *Pilgrim's Progress* to *Plutarch's Lives* to his father's books on "polemic Divinity." When he was fifteen years old he read a series of lectures, published by the estate of British scientist Robert Boyle, designed to counter the influence of deism in English religious life. Deism was the belief that God created the world and then let it operate according to natural laws. Deists of the truest stripe believed that God did not intervene in the lives of his human creation. He did not perform miracles, answer prayer, or sustain the world by his providence. Religious belief was based on reason rather than divine revelation. Franklin wrote in his *Autobiography* that these lectures "wrought an Effect on me quite contrary to what was intended by them: For the Arguments of the Deists which were quoted to be refuted, appeared to me much Stronger than the Refutations." By reading the Boyle Lectures Franklin claimed to have become a "thorough Deist."[3]

Franklin's early commitment to deism, however, did not last very long. Historians interpret his flirtation with this worldview as little more than a form of youthful rebellion against the Calvinism of his Puritan upbringing. Though he would never return to the Calvinism of his childhood, the religion of his parents leavened much of his adult thinking.[4] Franklin's theological beliefs were based on what he called a "first Principle" or "the Existence of a Deity" as "the Creator of the Universe." This Creator-God possessed great wisdom, goodness, and power. The stars, the motion of the planets, the chemical makeup of the earth, and the "Structure of Animal Bodies of such an infinite variety" testified to an intelligent designer whose creation, when subjected to the "highest and most exquisite human Reason," was perfect. God not only created a perfect world, but he sustained it. Franklin was amazed, for example, at the way God created the stars and the planets, but he was even more amazed that God continued "to govern them in their greatest Velocity as they shall not flie off out of their appointed Bounds nor dash one against another, to their mutual Destruction."[5]

God sustained the world by his providence. Franklin put his faith in an active God who watched over his natural creation and could, on occasion, intervene in the lives of his human creation as well. Thirty-six years after he claimed to have embraced deism, Franklin sounded like anything but an adherent to this religious system: "Without the Belief of a Providence that takes Cognizance of, guards and guides and may favour particular Persons, there is no Motive to Worship a Deity, to fear its Displeasure, or to pray for its Protection."[6] Franklin believed that God requires worship, answers prayer, and intervenes in history to meet the needs of "particular Persons." As Franklin grew older his trust in divine providence grew stronger. In the *Autobiography* he claimed to "owe the mention'd Happiness of my past Life to His kind Providence, which led me to the Means I us'd and gave them Success."[7] In 1784 he professed his belief in a God who "abases the Proud and favours the Humble."[8] Four years later, in reflecting on the Constitutional Convention, he wrote:

> I beg I may not be understood to infer, that our General Convention was divinely inspired, when it form'd the new federal Constitution . . . yet I must own I have so much faith in the general Government of the world by *Providence*, that I can hardly conceive a Transaction of such momentous Importance to the Welfare of Millions now existing, and to exist in the Posterity of a great Nation, should be suffered to pass without being in some degree influenc'd, guided, and governed by that omnipotent, omnipresent, and beneficent Ruler, in whom all inferior Spirits live, and move, and have their Being.

Franklin thought that the United States was "influenced, guided, and governed" by God.[9]

Franklin believed in the power of prayer—both for himself and his nation. He wrote prayers for his own personal use and took the time to rewrite the Lord's Prayer so that it was more suitable to contemporary readers. In the *Autobiography* he records a prayer he wrote for the purpose of seeking the wisdom of God: "O Powerful Goodness! bountiful Father! merciful Guide! Increase in me that Wisdom which discovers my truest Interests; Strengthen my Resolutions to perform what that Wisdom dictates. Accept my kind Offices to thy other Children, as the only Return in my Power for thy continual Favours to me."[10] As we saw in chapter 10, Franklin's belief in the efficacy of petitioning God is evident from his call for prayer during the heated debates of the Constitutional Convention in the summer of 1787.[11]

A Religion of Virtue

Yet for all of his talk of God and his providence, Franklin's religious creed falls well short of orthodox Christianity. During the religious revivals of the 1740s known as the First Great Awakening, Franklin struck up a friendship with George Whitefield, the protagonist of the revivals and perhaps the most popular man in the British colonies. The relationship between Franklin and Whitefield was a mutually beneficial one. Franklin made money by printing Whitefield's sermons. And by having his sermons published, Whitefield spread the gospel message more effectively. Though they disagreed on the best way to promote virtue—Franklin through good works and Whitefield through converting as many as possible to the Christian gospel—they were brought together by their common longings for a moral society. Whitefield tried unsuccessfully to convert Franklin to Christianity. In 1764, after the evangelical fires of the Great Awakening had cooled, Franklin wrote to Whitefield, no doubt in response to one of Whitefield's evangelistic letters, to tell the preacher what he believed. "That Being [God] who gave me existence, and thro' almost threescore Years has been Continually showering his Favours upon me, can I doubt that he loves me?" Franklin went on to tell Whitefield about his views on the afterlife: "And if he loves me, can I doubt that he will go on to take care of me not only here but hereafter? This to some may seem Presumption; to me it appears the best grounded Hope: Hope of the Future; built on the Experience of the Past."[12]

Whitefield would have rejected much of what Franklin said in this letter about the afterlife. As an evangelical Christian he believed that human beings were saved by faith in the death, burial, and resurrection of Jesus Christ. Franklin's "hope" was a false one. Indeed, Franklin's view of the afterlife, which he summed up more succinctly as "the soul of Man is immortal and will be treated with Justice in another Life respecting its Conduct in this," departs significantly from traditional Christian views of salvation, evangelical or otherwise. Consider another version of his religious creed as recorded in the *Autobiography*:

> [I believe] That there is one God who made all things
> That he governs the World by his Providence
> That he ought to be worshipped by Adoration, Prayer, and
>   Thanksgiving
> But that the most acceptable Services of God is doing Good
>   to Man

That the Soul is immortal
And that God will certainly reward Virtue and punish Vice either
   here or hereafter.

Franklin's belief in God, Providence, worship, prayer, and doing good to one's fellow man are all compatible with Christian teaching. But they fail to address the supernatural aspects of Christianity, or those doctrines that believers are required to embrace by faith. Franklin's creed contains no reference to the deity of Christ, the Trinity, Christ's atonement of sins, the resurrection of the body, or the belief that one is truly saved by affirming such doctrines.[13]

Franklin's religious beliefs were less about Christian doctrine and more about virtue—moral behavior that serves the public good. He labored to instill virtue in his life, even going so far as to attempt "moral perfection" through the daily cultivation of temperance, silence, order, resolution, frugality, industry, sincerity, justice, moderation, cleanliness, tranquility, chastity, and humility.[14] He had little tolerance for the kind of theological squabbles often associated with organized Christianity and thought that debates over the meaning of Christian orthodoxy prevented clergy from preaching the true spirit of Christianity, namely loving one's neighbor and exercising virtue. Franklin told his brothers, Josiah and Abiah, that they would be examined in the afterlife not on what they thought, but on what they did. Referring to Matthew 25 he reminded them that "our Recommendation will not be that we said Lord, Lord, but that we did GOOD to our fellow Creatures." Franklin made this clear when he argued that a "virtuous Heretick shall be saved before a wicked Christian."[15]

Franklin's distinction between true religion and Christian orthodoxy is illustrated best in his attempt to defend clergyman Samuel Hemphill against the charges of heresy leveled by the Presbyterian Synod of Philadelphia. In 1734 the Presbyterian Church in Philadelphia—a church that Franklin often attended—installed Samuel Hemphill, a minister from Ireland, to assist its aging minister, Jedediah Andrews. Franklin was not a big fan of Andrews. He thought that the veteran minister was more concerned about turning his congregation into good Presbyterians than he was in leading them along the path of public virtue. Hemphill, who was popular among the congregation and, at least according to Franklin, a better preacher than Andrews, taught a moral message that was more akin to Franklin's convictions. Hemphill's moral sermons, however, got him in trouble with the synod. Andrews and others accused him of preaching unorthodox sermons that placed too much emphasis on human works as a means of salvation. When Andrews reported Hemphill to the synod, claiming that he was a heretic, Franklin came to the new minister's defense. He used his newspaper, *The Pennsylvania Gazette*, and his printing press to publish articles and pamphlets arguing that it was Hemphill, not Andrews or the synod, who was practicing true Christianity.[16]

Despite Franklin's vociferous defense, Hemphill was charged with heresy and removed from his position at the Philadelphia church. In arguing on behalf of Hemphill, Franklin made clear that "Morality or Virtue" is the ultimate end of true religion. "Faith" might aid a person in living a good life, but it is "only a Means to obtain that End." Hemphill, according to the synod, was not preaching the Protestant doctrine of salvation by faith alone. But according to Franklin, faith "can conduce nothing towards Salvation where it does not conduce to Virtue." He even made attempts to meet the Presbyterians on their own religious ground by appealing to the authority of the Bible on Hemphill's behalf: "St. James, in his second Chapter, is very zealous against these Cryers-up of Faith, and maintains that Faith without Virtue is useless, *Wilt thou know, O vain Man*, says he, *that Faith without Works is dead*; and, *shew me your Faith without your Works, and I will shew you mine by my Works*."[17] Four years later, in his popular *Poor Richard's Almanack*, Franklin made a similar argument: "Sin is not hurtful because it is forbidden but it is forbidden because it's hurtful. . . . Nor is a Duty beneficial because it is commanded, but it is commanded, because it's beneficial." Ultimately, Franklin believed that true religion could be found in any denomination that promoted the "Duties of morality," which he defined as feeding the hungry, clothing the naked, visiting the sick, and, in general, "Doing all the good that lies in our Power."[18]

This kind of morality made for a better, more humane, society. Civic life could not function without virtue. Franklin believed it was vital to sustaining a moral republic. Not everyone needed religion to be virtuous. There were some who could "live a virtuous life without the assistance afforded by Religion," especially those who had a "clear Perception of the Advantages and the Disadvantages of Vice" and possessed "Strength of Resolution sufficient" to resist "common Temptations." But most of the world, Franklin believed, was made up of "weak and ignorant Men and Women" who needed religion to "restrain them from Vice, and to retain them in the practice of it [virtue] till it becomes *habitual*." He was horrified by the thought of a world without religion: "If Men are so wicked as we now see them, *with Religion*," Franklin wrote, "what would they be if *without it*."[19]

Franklin's Failures

Despite Franklin's regular musings on the importance of moral improvement, he was a flawed man. On more than one occasion his behavior failed to conform to Christian ethics or the religion of virtue that he so firmly espoused. Franklin was fully aware of his faults. Indeed, his pursuit of self-improvement and moral perfection was often tempered by a belief similar to the Calvinist view of human nature that he had imbibed in his youth. Philosopher Kerry Walters has argued convincingly that Franklin maintained a pessimistic view of human reason and people's ability to make rational choices that contributed to the morality of society:

> The deep distrust of human reason birthed by his [Franklin's] boy-hood Calvinism and probably reinforced by his acquaintance with works such as de Mandeville's *Fable of the Bees* and Hobbes's *Leviathan*, preclude his sharing the deists' rather naive trust in rationality as a sufficient foundation for virtue. He knew too much about the way humans behaved—about the ways *he* behaved—in the absence of normative checks and balances. Reason did not and could not serve in this capacity because reason . . . is the slave of the passions and inclinations. . . . Humans are selfish, egoistic creatures, motivated always by the desire to aggrandize their own positions. Any program for moral improvement that idealistically denies rather than faces and works with this deep-seated wolfishness is doomed from the start.[20]

One of Franklin's well-documented flaws is that his family life was a mess. The Puritan beliefs that influenced his convictions about God and human beings did not translate into the way he conducted himself as a husband and a father. Part of the problem was that Franklin's strong appetite for the opposite sex often got the best of him. In the *Autobiography* he described his "hard-to-be-govern'd Passion of Youth" that had "hurried me frequently into Intrigues with low Women that fell in my Way, which were attended with some Expence & great Inconvenience." It was this "great Erratum" in his life that prompted him eventually to marry Deborah Read in 1730.[21] Benjamin and Deborah were wed in a common-law union (she was still legally married to her first husband, John Rogers, who abandoned her), and they would remain together for forty years. Deborah would become a trusted partner in Franklin's print shop—a "good help-meet," as he called her.

But upon his retirement in 1748, Franklin began his pursuit of a life of "publick affairs" and as a result things changed quickly in his relationship with Deborah.[22] In 1757 he was sent to London to represent the Pennsylvania Assembly and, with the exception of a two-year stint in Philadelphia between 1762 and 1764, would remain there for the rest of Deborah's life. Her health deteriorated while Benjamin was gone and she suffered from depression and a stroke, the latter of which she blamed on her husband "staying so much longer" in England. (Franklin never responded to the accusation.) In the meantime, Franklin's only daughter, Sally, was married in 1767. He made no effort to travel back to Philadelphia for the wedding, but did inform Deborah via letter to make sure she did not spend too much money on the reception.

Following Deborah's stroke, Franklin's letters home, which had always expressed love for his wife, became less personal and more focused on matters of business. Franklin and his associates in London made a few attempts to convince Deborah to come to England, but she always refused, citing her fear of water travel. It is more likely that Deborah declined these offers because she knew that she would only be in Benjamin's way. As the daughter of a Philadelphia carpenter, she was unfamiliar with the refined and courtly world of polite London and knew that if she did join her husband she would have been more of a hindrance to him (and perhaps even an embarrassment) than a "help-meet." In December 1774 Deborah suffered another stroke that resulted in her death five days later. Franklin remained in London. He would not return until months after his wife's death, and only then because the Continental Congress beckoned.[23]

Shortly before he met Deborah, Franklin had an illegitimate son, William, by an unknown woman. Benjamin doted over young William and included him in many of his activities in both Philadelphia and London (he addressed his *Autobiography* to him as well). But his relationship with his son soured when William, from his post as the royal governor of New Jersey, refused to support the American Revolution. When William was eventually arrested and imprisoned by the prorevolutionary New Jersey militia in 1776, Benjamin did nothing to help him. William made several efforts to reconcile with his father following the Revolution, but Benjamin rejected every one of them. "Nothing has ever hurt me so much and effected me with such keen Sensations," he wrote to William, "as to find my self deserted in old Age by my only Son; and not only deserted, but to find him taking up arms against me."[24] William's political sin against his father was unforgivable. Reconciliation was impossible. Franklin, the man of "publick affairs," would have certainly failed the "family values" test often applied to today's American politicians.

Some may also find disturbing Franklin's views on race, ethnicity, and American identity. Poor Richard was quite concerned, for example, about the large number of German immigrants arriving in Philadelphia and its hinterlands in the mid-eighteenth century. He asked why

> *Palatine Boors* be suffered to swarm into our settlements, and be herding together establish their languages and manners to exclusion of ours? Why should *Pennsylvania*, founded by the *English*, become a colony of *Aliens*, who will shortly be so numerous as to Germanize us instead of us Anglifying them, and will never adopt our language of customs, any more than they can acquire our complexion.[25]

Franklin's views here are not unlike those taken by some in today's contemporary debates over immigration in the United States—they fall well short of the Judeo-Christian idea of welcoming the stranger.

Despite Franklin's prominent role in the founding of the Pennsylvania Society for Promoting the Abolition of Slavery, he owned slaves for most of his life. One cannot ignore that Franklin, like many of the founders, profited from the institution of slavery. It would also not be much of a stretch to suggest that slavery aided him in his meteoric social rise. Franklin opposed the forced migration of slaves on the grounds that the presence of Africans in America would inevitably "darken" the white race. "Why increase the sons of *Africa*, by planting them in *America*, where we have so fair an opportunity, by excluding blacks and tawneys, of increasing the lovely white and red?" Franklin repudiated slavery later in life, but recent scholarship has argued that his reputation as an antislavery advocate may have been the result of early-nineteenth-century abolitionists using his name to support their cause.[26]

The Religion of the American Dream

To condemn Franklin for his lack of family values and his views on race, immigration, and slavery is a bit unfair. As we saw in the introduction to this book, one of the primary goals of history is to *understand* people in the past before we praise or condemn them. Family life in the eighteenth century differed from that in the twenty-first century. Franklin's decision to remain in England while Deborah toiled at home would not have been perceived to be as scandalous in early America as it might be today. His positions on race, slavery, and immigration, while appalling to most contemporary observers, were quite mainstream in Anglo-America. On the other hand, there were founders—such as John Adams—who did tend more closely and more Christianly to their family responsibilities. And others had a better track record on slavery than Franklin. In the end, he fails the orthodoxy test and would receive a below average grade on the orthopraxy test.

We must also remember that Franklin has a legacy. He put forth his story as a lesson for how to live an American life. His *Autobiography*, which went through twenty-two editions between 1794 and 1828 alone, has always taught Americans something about who they are, where they have been, and where they are going. Nineteenth-century schoolchildren read Franklin to learn American values. The *Autobiography* helped immigrants assimilate. According to Mark Twain, Franklin's moral lessons and pithy maxims "brought affliction to millions of boys . . . whose fathers had read Franklin's pernicious biography." Davy Crockett had a copy of the *Autobiography* in his pocket when he was killed at the Alamo.[27]

When Franklin is approached this way, the ideals that drive his story become quite familiar. Whatever moral criticism one might make of his family life fades behind the lavish praise heaped upon him for his peddling of the American Dream. Americans love Franklin because he teaches them how to "make it" in America. His *Way to Wealth*, a collection of wise sayings from his popular *Poor Richard's Almanac*, has appeared in 145 editions and has been translated into seven languages. Many still perceive it as one of America's great capitalist manifestos.[28] He presented himself as the quintessential member of the American middle class. His harshest critics described him, as Gordon Wood has summarized, as a model of "America's bourgeois complacency, its get-ahead materialism, its utilitarian obsession with success—the unimaginative superficiality and vulgarity of American culture that kills the soul."[29]

This, however, is only one side of Franklin's life. He was definitely concerned with making money, but his material pursuits were always balanced by civic responsibility and public service. For those who champion upward mobility, the pursuit of a comfortable life, and the importance of giving back to society, Franklin is a patron saint. The dark side of his economic acquisitiveness is balanced by his religion of virtue and his republican commitment to serving the common good. Franklin's community-centered ethic often washes clean any of the self-interested ambition he might have possessed. According to this view of Franklin, there is nothing wrong with making money, and lots of it, as long as one gives back to the community.[30]

In the end, Franklin's religion—both his stated views on orthodox Christianity and the American philosophy he helped to define—seldom fits comfortably with the teachings of Christianity. Franklin rejected most Christian doctrines in favor of a religion of virtue. Yet his most powerful legacy may be his commitment to the religion of ambition—the "making it" mentality that has always spoken powerfully to Americans. For Christians it is easy to condemn Franklin for his heterodox religious beliefs, but it is not always easy to recognize that Poor Richard and the "poor in spirit" might often find themselves at odds.

Chapter Fifteen

What about Witherspoon?

Three Orthodox Founders

John Witherspoon is a favorite among those who argue that America was founded as a Christian nation. The Presbyterian clergyman, president of the College of New Jersey at Princeton, and the only minister to sign the Declaration of Independence, is often invoked to counter historical accounts of the founders that highlight the non-Christian beliefs of men like Adams, Franklin, and Jefferson. David Barton cites Witherspoon extensively (28 times) in his defense of a Christian nation, *Original Intent*. On his WallBuilders Web site he describes Witherspoon as the "Billy Graham of his day." William J. Federer, the author of a book of founders' quotations popular with defenders of Christian America, writes that Witherspoon's "emphasis on biblical principles impacting government was tremendously felt in the Colonies during the foundation of America."[1]

Witherspoon was indeed a man of deep Christian piety and orthodox Christian faith. Christianity, as he understood it, influenced his decision to support the American Revolution and informed his vision of the American Republic. Witherspoon was not alone in his orthodox beliefs. Many of the founders shared a similar faith. Patrick Henry, Roger Sherman, and Elias Boudinot, to name a few, easily pass the orthodoxy test. But what role did these Christian statesman play during the American Revolution? How did their Christian convictions inform their politics? This chapter examines the evangelical impulse present at the American founding through a study of three of the most prominent and outspoken Christian revolutionaries: John Witherspoon, John Jay, and Samuel Adams.

John Witherspoon: Presbyterian Patriot

John Witherspoon was born in 1723 in Yester parish in the shire of East Lothian, Scotland, thus making him one of the few founders not born in the British North American colonies. The son of a Presbyterian clergyman and a clergyman's daughter, Witherspoon began his studies at Edinburgh University at the age of thirteen. He graduated with a master of arts in 1739 and then began his divinity training in preparation for a career as a Presbyterian minister. During his pastoral duties at Beith in Ayrshire and at Leigh Kirk in Paisley, Witherspoon became an outspoken voice of Presbyterian orthodoxy against the more theologically liberal Moderate Party in the Scottish kirk.

In 1767 he accepted the presidency of the College of New Jersey at Princeton. During his tenure at Princeton (1768–1794) Witherspoon brought the college curriculum more in line with the ideas of the British Enlightenment and trained a generation of young revolutionaries that included James Madison, Aaron Burr Jr., Philip Freneau, and Hugh Henry Brackenridge. Witherspoon became one of New Jersey's strongest voices for American independence and he was more than willing to use his pulpit to promote the cause. He served six years as a member of the Continental Congress (he was known for wearing his ministerial robe and bands to the meetings) and was appointed to more than one hundred committees, including the committees on war, finance, and foreign affairs. When Horace Walpole, a member of Parliament, wrote that "Cousin America has run off with a Presbyterian Parson," it is likely that he had Witherspoon in mind. In addition to his work as a member of the Continental Congress, Witherspoon signed the Articles of Confederation and was a representative to the New Jersey convention that ratified the U.S. Constitution.[2]

In the eighteenth century the ministers of the Church of Scotland were divided into two parties—the Popular Party and the Moderate Party. The members of the Popular Party stressed a strict adherence to the teachings of the Westminster Confession of Faith and tended to be evangelical in their theology. Ministers of this party preached the need for conversion and personal piety. The Moderates, on the other hand, were influenced by the moral teachings of the Scottish Enlightenment. They stressed morality over evangelical conversion and pursued refinement and gentility as a means of promoting a virtuous society. At the time that Witherspoon left Scotland for America in 1768, the Moderates held most of the important positions of power within the church.[3]

Witherspoon emerged as a leader of the Popular Party following the publication of *Ecclesiastical Characteristics, or the Arcana of Church Polity,* in 1753. In this satirical tract he criticized the Moderates (many of whom were his former classmates at Edinburgh) for being more concerned with morality, politeness, and "heathen writers" than they were with conversion, piety, and the teachings of Scripture and the Westminster Confession. Witherspoon attacked the Moderates with sermon after sermon exposing their failure to teach salvation by faith in Jesus Christ. He became part of a group of young evangelical Scots who prayed that God would revive his church through a spiritual awakening.[4]

Witherspoon's evangelical credentials were the primary reason that the trustees of the College of New Jersey at Princeton sought him out as their sixth president. Princeton was a bastion of evangelical Presbyterianism, and the trustees expected that Witherspoon would follow the legacy of previous Princeton presidents Jonathan Dickinson, Aaron Burr, Jonathan Edwards, Samuel Davies, and Samuel Finley. He did not disappoint. Upon his arrival in America Witherspoon continued to preach salvation through faith in Jesus Christ. He often reminded his students at Princeton that "religion is the grand concern to us all, as we are men;—whatever be our calling and profession, the salvation of our souls is the one thing needful." He told Princeton's class of 1775, "'Except a man be born again, he cannot enter the Kingdom of God.' True religion must arise from a clear and deep conviction of your lost state by nature and practice, and an unfeigned reliance on the pardoning mercy and sanctifying grace of God."[5]

Yet Witherspoon's Princeton curriculum also reflected significant changes in British Presbyterianism, particularly in its accommodation to the beliefs of the Enlightenment. Witherspoon's ethical beliefs were deeply influenced by what was called "The New Moral Philosophy." The leading advocate of this new approach to ethics was Francis Hutcheson, a professor of moral philosophy at the University of Glasgow. Hutcheson taught that all human beings had the potential to make good ethical choices by cultivating what he called the "moral sense." Similar to the conscience, the moral sense was instilled by God in all human beings. The moral sense was developed through education and the practice of sociability. In this sense, it was like an ethical muscle. During his years in Scotland, Witherspoon, ironically, criticized Hutcheson for teaching that there was a source of morality—the moral sense—that did not find its source in the Bible or a special infusion of God's grace. Yet, upon his arrival at Princeton, Witherspoon adopted much of Hutcheson's moral system.[6]

Witherspoon's decision to embrace the New Moral Philosophy of Hutcheson and others meant that he was now teaching his students that a moral life could be led without a conversion experience. One did not need the Holy Spirit to be virtuous. In the process, he was adopting a much more Enlightened, and much less Christian, view of ethics. Though Witherspoon believed that the moral sense (he preferred to call it the "conscience") would never lead one to act in such a way that contradicted the teachings of the Bible, he nevertheless affirmed the notion that all human beings could be moral by the very fact that they were all created with this ethical compass. Here Witherspoon parted ways with the third president of Princeton, Jonathan Edwards, who believed that "true virtue" could only come through God's grace as manifested in conversion.[7]

Witherspoon's moral convictions directly influenced his politics. His response to the American Revolution fused a traditional Calvinist belief in the providence of God with British political ideas that are often described as "Whig." Whig political thought focused predominantly on the protection of liberties and natural rights against tyrannical governments that had the potential of undermining them. Witherspoon, for example, taught his students that it was perfectly within their moral and natural rights to overthrow a government that was "found to be pernicious and destructive." Such revolutionary principles were drawn more from the teachings of John Locke than from the Christian tradition. In fact, Witherspoon's politics are no different than the politics of many of his fellow revolutionaries.[8]

In 1776, Witherspoon delivered and published one of the most cited sermons of his generation. "The Dominion of Providence over the Passions of Men"[9] reveals Witherspoon's confidence in being able to decipher the will of God as it related to the question of American independence. He wrote: "If your cause is just, if your principles are pure, and if your conduct is prudent, you need not fear the multitude of opposing hosts. If your cause is just—you may look with confidence to the Lord and intreat him to plead it as your own." In other words, if God is just, and Parliament and George III are acting toward the colonists in a way that is unjust, then God must be on the side of the American revolutionaries because he is always on the side of justice. By making this argument, Witherspoon was taking the popular political ideas of the age and baptizing them with his Calvinist belief in the sovereignty of God.

Once the Revolution was over—and Witherspoon was quite confident that it would end with colonial independence from England—then Americans needed to make sure that they maintained the kind of morality and religion necessary to secure God's continued blessing on their efforts at creating a new republic. He would affirm that the "best friend to American liberty" was the one "who is most sincere and active in promoting true and undefiled religion." In a 1782 thanksgiving sermon, Witherspoon was even more explicit about the necessity of religion to the moral fabric of the new American republic:

> Let us endeavour to bring into, and keep in credit and reputation, everything that may serve to give vigour to an equal republican constitution. Let us cherish a love of piety, order, industry, frugality. Let us check every disposition to luxury, effeminacy, and the pleasures of a dissipated life. . . . And in our families let us do the best by religious instruction, to sow the seeds which may bear fruit in the next generation. We are one of the body of confederated States. For many reasons I shall avoid making comparisons at present, but may venture to predict, that whatsoever State among us shall continue to make piety and virtue the standard of public honour, will enjoy the greatest inward peace, the greatest national happiness, and in every outward conflict will discover the greatest constitutional strength.[10]

Witherspoon thought that the pious practice of Christians contributed to a virtuous society. Indeed, he took this idea one step further, claiming that Christianity was the *best* source of producing the kind of virtue necessary to the survival of the American Republic. He also argued that the state, as theologian Gordon Tait has noted, "should give recognition and aid to Christianity *in general*, though not to particular denominations."[11]

As an evangelical, Witherspoon never ceased to believe that spiritual conversion was the only way to save one's soul. But when it came to promoting the public good and instilling virtues in the American people such as order, industry, and frugality, there was little difference between the morality that flowed from the lives of believers and the morality that all people could muster by following their moral sense. Witherspoon thus defended the right of all Americans to worship God according to their conscience, as long as their religion aided them in making contributions to the public good.[12]

Witherspoon's ideas about religion, revolution, and civic life are complicated. In his role as a minister, both in Scotland and America, he preached a clear evangelical message of salvation through faith in Jesus Christ's death, burial, and resurrection. Yet when it came to politics and morality Witherspoon was more secular than many of his contemporary defenders make him out to be. As historian Mark Noll has argued, "Witherspoon did not derive his politics from the Bible. He did not think the Christian God has a specific role to play in public life, where the rule of nature prevailed. And he did not worry about assuming an Enlightenment perspective on political matters."[13] While he believed that Christianity was the best way to promote a virtuous republic, and even felt that the government should privilege the Christian faith, he also taught that true virtue could stem from natural sources, namely the moral sense or conscience. Those who want to claim Witherspoon as a Christian statesman should thus proceed with caution.

John Jay: Christian Providentialist

Few statesmen were as active in American politics in the two decades following the American Revolution as John Jay. A prominent New York lawyer, Jay was a reluctant revolutionary. In 1774 he was elected to a New York committee formed to bring order to the mob violence practiced by some of the city's more radical patriots. As a delegate to the First Continental Congress, Jay believed the best way to deal with the British violation of colonial rights was to reach a peaceful accommodation with England. His spirit of reconciliation continued into the Second Continental Congress, when he supported John Dickinson's proposal to write the "Olive Branch Petition" as a last-ditch effort to avoid separation from the mother country.

Eventually Jay's views changed. By January 1776, when he realized that reconciliation would be impossible, he abandoned his moderate principles and turned his support toward the cause of independence. He returned home (his duties to the New York Provincial Congress meant that he would not be present in Philadelphia to sign the Declaration of Independence) and went to work drafting the New York Constitution (1777). Jay would eventually return to the Continental Congress and serve a short term as its president.

During the 1780s and 1790s Jay would play an important role in American foreign affairs, serving as a diplomat to Spain, England, and France. He was the secretary of foreign affairs under the Articles of Confederation. In 1795, as a special envoy to England, he hammered out what became known as "Jay's Treaty." At home he became a staunch supporter of the U.S. Constitution and was the author of five of the *Federalist Papers*. George Washington nominated Jay as the first chief justice of the Supreme Court in 1789, a position he held for six years before being elected governor of New York. In 1801 he retired from politics and became active in a host of Christian voluntary societies, including a stint as president of the American Bible Society (1821–1828).[14]

Jay was raised by Calvinist parents. His father descended from French Huguenots who fled France in the wake of the revocation of the Edict of Nantes, a decree that had protected the rights of French Protestants. John Jay's grandfather, Augustus Jay, was an elder in the French Reformed Church in New York City, but eventually joined the Anglican Trinity Church. Jay's father, Peter Jay, and later John himself, would be pillars of the Anglican community at Trinity. Peter Jay married Mary Van Cortlandt, a member of a prominent Dutch Reformed family in New York. John was born in 1745 and was baptized at Trinity Church. He remained connected to the church of his baptism through much of his life and would eventually serve it as a vestryman. When Trinity burned down in 1776, he lent the church £1200 to rebuild it. In the wake of the American Revolution he would play a significant role in the formation of the American Episcopal Church.[15]

Jay was an orthodox Christian. He readily affirmed that the "Christian dispensation" was the "only adequate plan" that had "ever appeared in the world" for breaching the gap, created by sin, between God and his human creation. He believed that the writers of the Bible were inspired by God. The Scriptures were the only source of a "Divine revelations and dispensations respecting the present and future state of mankind." Jay was unwilling to accept the authority of any Christian creedal statement unless it conformed to the teachings of the Bible.[16]

At times Jay argued on the basis of reason for the truth of Christianity. In 1796 he wrote, "I have been of [the] opinion that the Evidence of the Truth of Christianity requires only to be carefully examined to produce conviction in candid minds." Yet at other times he appealed to mystery. In a speech before the American Bible Society, Jay criticized religious commentators, many of whom had a "sincere desire to increase Christian knowledge," for penetrating too deeply into the recesses of "profound mysteries, and to dispel their obscurity by the light of reason." Jay said that such Christians "did not recollect that *no man can explain what no man can understand.* Those mysteries were revealed to our faith, to be believed on the credit of Divine testimony; and were not addressed to our mental abilities for explication."[17]

Jay also had an affinity for the study of biblical prophecy. John Adams, in a letter to Thomas Jefferson, worried that his son, John Quincy, would "retire like a Jay to study Prophecies to the End of his Life."[18] Jay's careful study of the Bible led him to believe that the twelve tribes would be restored to Israel and the tribe of Judah would convert to Christianity, thus ushering in the millennial return of Jesus Christ. He also compared Napoleon Bonaparte to King Nebuchadnezzar, the Babylonian king removed from power by the Hebrew God, as recorded in the Old Testament book of Daniel. Because of Napoleon's military aggression, Jay concluded that "Europe is a tempestuous and a raging ocean; and who can tell which of the governments afloat upon it will escape destruction or disaster?"[19]

Like most of the founders, Jay put his faith in an overruling Providence that governed the universe and the affairs of humans. He believed that God intervened in human affairs to accomplish his will. His view of Providence probably grew out of his upbringing in a household where Calvinist doctrine held sway.[20] He openly applied his view of Providence to the cause of the American Revolution and the success of the early American Republic. Writing to Jedidiah Morse in 1806, he offered his opinion about what a "proper history of the United States" might look like:

> A proper history of the United States would have much to recommend it: in some respects it would be singular, or unlike all others; it would develop the great plan of Providence, for causing this extensive part of our world to be discovered, and these "uttermost parts of the earth" to be gradually filled with civilized and *Christian* people and nations. The means or second causes by which this great plan has long been and still is accomplishing, are materials for history, of which the writer ought well to know the use and bearings and proper places. In my opinion, the historian, in the course of the work, is never to lose sight of that great plan.[21]

Jay regularly reminded New Yorkers that God was on the side of the American Revolution. In *Federalist* #2 he used Providence as part of his argument for the ratification of the Constitution, connecting national unity to God's plan for the United States.[22]

Jay affirmed the idea that America was a Christian nation. He believed that the United States should privilege Christianity (which Jay understood as Protestantism) over other religions. In another letter to Morse, Jay used the Bible to argue that Christians should not cast their votes for "*infidel* rulers." He justified his position by citing the words of the prophet Jehu to the Israelite king Jehoshaphat: "Shouldest thou help the ungodly, and love them that hate the Lord?"[23] He believed that the government should support days of fasting and prayer and enforce the Christian Sabbath. In his first year as governor of New York, Jay issued a Thanksgiving Day proclamation, an act that historian Jonathan Den Hartog has called an "unprecedented step" that was "unheard of in New York."[24] Jay was a firm believer in the idea that Christianity would promote the "general welfare" and public good of the United States. He thought that the Christian gospel should be taught in schools. He preached the necessity of Christian morality to republican virtue, and he believed that public Christianity was essential for bringing an end to the evils of slavery.[25]

Jay defended liberty of conscience in matters of religion. He affirmed that "rights of conscience" and "private judgment" are "by nature subject to no control but that of the Deity." He added, "Every man is permitted to consider, to adore, to worship his Creator in the manner most agreeable to conscience. No opinions are dictated, no rules of faith prescribed, no preference given to one sect to the prejudice of others." Jay did not fear that the Constitution's commitment to religious freedom would weaken the testimony of Christianity in American life. Though Christian faith was not supported by the "arm of the flesh," it "would not fall." Indeed, Jay believed that *real* Christians "will abstain from violating the Rights of others."[26]

While Jay believed that all Americans should have the right to worship God according to their consciences, he did not believe that the adherents of non-Protestant religious groups, especially Roman Catholics, should be involved in the political process. Jay's strong dislike of Catholics was probably rooted in some combination of his Huguenot upbringing, his interpretation of the Bible, and his belief that Catholics, because of their allegiance to papal authority, would not make good republican citizens. Like many Protestants of his day, Jay believed that the pope was the "great Antichrist mentioned in the Scriptures."[27] During the writing of the New York Constitution in 1777, he proposed an amendment forbidding Roman Catholics from owning land until they rejected the authority of "pope, priests or foreign authority" and the "dangerous and damnable doctrine, that the pope or any other earthly authority, have power to absolve men from sins or their obligation to the state of New York." The amendment was rejected, but it reveals Jay's fear that Catholics were incapable of giving their ultimate loyalty to the state. In the end, he was able to help pass an amendment to the Constitution requiring immigrants to "renounce all subjection to all and every foreign king, prince, potentate and state, in all matters, ecclesiastical as well as civil." As Den Hartog notes, Jay's hostility to Catholicism had logic to it: "if Catholics were opposed to liberty, were ruled authoritatively by foreign powers, and were hoping to enslave Protestant Americans, they could not be good republicans."[28]

Jay was undoubtedly a Christian nationalist. He believed that God had providentially brought the United States into existence and would continue to sustain it as long as the citizens of the nation practiced virtue rooted in Protestant piety. Following the election of Thomas Jefferson, Jay retired from political office, but continued to promote his Protestant nationalism through participation in voluntary societies such as the American Bible Society. He, perhaps more than any other founder, deserves the title "Christian statesman."

Samuel Adams: Puritan Republican

To quote historian Pauline Maier, Samuel Adams was the "American revolutionaries' American revolutionary." He doggedly challenged what he believed to be British tyranny and infused his revolutionary ideas with a healthy dose of Christianity and moral republicanism. In the fall of 1776 when Lord Richard Howe of the British navy tried to reconcile with the colonies to bring a peaceful end to the Revolutionary War, the admiral offered pardons to all American revolutionaries except the most incendiary of the bunch—Benjamin Franklin, Richard Henry Lee, John Adams, and Samuel Adams. Adams used his vocation as a politician to rail on England's unfair treatment of its American colonies, but he was also a moral reformer, spending his entire career attacking immorality, vice, and luxury in pursuit of his dream that America would become a "Christian Sparta."[29]

Adams was born in 1722 in Boston to devout Puritan parents. His father was a prominent layperson in the New South Church, and his mother nurtured him in Calvinist piety. Adams would remain a devout Christian his entire life. His parents sent him to Harvard to become a Congregationalist minister, but his true vocational interests lay in the fields of politics and business. During his years at Harvard, Adams developed an affinity for the ancient Greek and Roman writers, the teachings of John Locke, and the evangelical tracts of Jonathan Edwards. These works would become the intellectual foundation of his revolutionary political thought.[30]

Adams took a leadership role in the Boston town meetings that played an active part in the colonial opposition to the Sugar Act, Stamp Act, and Townshend duties. The popular perception of Adams as a rabble-rouser

Fig. 15.1   Samuel Adams, 1772. Despite his reputation as a firebrand, Samuel Adams was one of the most orthodox Christians among the Founding Fathers.

who incited mob violence as a leader of a group called the "Sons of Liberty" is not true. Adams was never directly connected to the Sons of Liberty. He actually denounced the rioting in the streets of Boston and the destruction of British property that often came with it.[31]

Adams did play an influential role in establishing Committees of Correspondence throughout British North America and probably played some part in the organization of the so-called Boston Tea Party. He was a member of the First and Second Continental Congresses and worked with his cousin, John Adams, in writing the Massachusetts Constitution of 1780. When the Constitutional Convention met in Philadelphia in the summer of 1787, Samuel Adams was skeptical. He did not think a strong federal government was needed and wondered if a union of the thirteen disparate states, with their different cultures and histories, was possible. In the end he agreed to support the Constitution, but throughout the 1790s he would affiliate himself with the Jeffersonian Republicans.[32]

Throughout his public career Samuel Adams never fully abandoned the Puritan values he learned growing up in Massachusetts Bay. He knew his Puritan history well, often appealing to New England founders such as John Bradford and John Winthrop—seventeenth-century religious dissenters who fled to America to escape English tyranny—as support for his resistance to English taxation schemes.[33] Like many of his Puritan forefathers, Adams believed that Massachusetts Bay had made a special covenant with God. The colony was God's new Israel. God would bless Massachusetts, and colonial society at large, if they remained virtuous, but he would punish them if they ceased devoting themselves to Christian morality. In the context of the American Revolution, Adams warned that God would discipline the colonies for their failure to resist British tyranny: "If heaven punishes Communities for their Vices," he wrote to his wife, Elizabeth, in 1776, "how sore must be the Punishment of that Community who thinks the Rights of human nature not worth struggling for and patiently submit to Tyranny."[34]

Adams filled his revolutionary rhetoric with Christian and biblical language. In 1771 he invoked the Old Testament story of Jeroboam, a ruler he described as a "perjur'd Traitor" whose sin led him to rebel "against God and *his Country.*" Adams used this story to illustrate his point that even "Kings and Governors" could commit treason against their own government. It was up to the good people of the colonies to stage a "glorious struggle in opposition to the lawless power" of these "Kings and Princes" who believed they were "authorized by God to *enslave* and *butcher* them!" By making sacrifices to foreign gods and drawing his people into such idolatry, Jeroboam was guilty of leading God's people into sin. Adams wondered if those ministers who supported the sin of English tyranny were not doing the same thing.[35] During the Stamp Act crisis he argued that submission to the slavery of English taxation only weakened the resolve of all good citizens, going as far as to suggest that failure to resist might lead to their "subjection to Satan."[36] In 1774 he prayed that "God would inspire" the Boston Committee of Correspondence with

"Wisdom & Fortitude" and thanked the "Supreme Being for the Salvation of our Country."[37]

Adams had no qualms about comparing British tyranny to the tyranny of "popery." His anti-Catholicism was strong. In 1768 he published a series of anti-Catholic articles in the *Boston Gazette* under the pseudonym "a Puritan." The articles were based on Adams's travels throughout eastern Massachusetts—a trip designed specifically for the purpose of sniffing out Catholicism wherever it reared its ugly head. His goal was to see if any "*romish* priests" were using their "*arts* and *tricks*" to draw people away from the "protestant cause." As a result of his tour he claimed "that much more is to be dreaded from the growth of POPERY in America, than from Stamp-Acts or *any other* Acts destructive of mens *civil* rights." Adams equated the religious practice of Catholics with that of Jeroboam. Both were guilty of the "*worshipping of graven images.*" He was consoled by the fact that "some of our Towns, maintain their integrity and show a laudable zeal against Popery." He was so proud of these anti-Catholic towns that he promised to publish a list of them so that they could be duly honored. Later, Adams would oppose the toleration of Catholics and their right to hold office in Massachusetts. Like John Jay, he believed that Catholicism was a false religion and its adherents were incapable of being good republican citizens because their primary loyalty was to the pope.[38]

Adams regularly employed the language of "Providence." Like Jay and Witherspoon, he believed that the Calvinist God was in control of all events and in the case of the American Revolution had taken the side of the colonists. In 1775 he wrote letters to Elizabeth claiming that "Righteous Heaven will surely smile on a Cause so righteous as ours is." Since the American cause was a just one, Adams assumed that it must have the support of God. He told Elizabeth that he was "so fully satisfied in the Justice of our Cause, that I can confidently as well as devoutly pray, that the righteous Disposer of all things would succeed in our Enterprises."[39] When Adams learned that Howe refused to grant him a pardon for his revolutionary agitation, he told Elizabeth: "I am animated with the full Perswasion that righteous Heaven will support the Americans if they preserve in their manly Struggles for their Liberty." Throughout the war, Adams monitored closely the performance of the Continental Army, offering providential spins to each battle, claiming that American military victories were the direct result of God's providential plan for the United States.[40]

Perhaps more than anything else, Adams was concerned with the moral character of the American people. In this sense he was a staunch believer in the ancient philosophy of republicanism. Adams believed, no doubt from his immersion in Greek and Roman literature, that republics survived only when their citizens sacrificed self-interest for the common good and lived upright and moral lives. There was no stronger advocate of this sort of self-sacrificial patriotism than Adams. He dreamed of a "*Christian* Sparta" where men would balance their freedom with virtue and moral behavior. He thanked God that he had backed the cause of American liberty, but wondered how long God would continue to bless a people who failed to live moral, frugal, and simple lives. He criticized America's sinful obsession with entertainment, luxury, "Assemblies and Balls," gambling, the latest fashions, the endless pursuit of wealth and economic gain (especially among officeholders), and other immoral diversions and "depravity of manners" that distracted ordinary people from practicing the kind of virtue necessary to sustain the Republic. He wondered if we "are arrivd to see such a Pitch of Levity & Dissipation as that the Idea of feasting shall extinguish every Spark of publick Virtue, and frustrate the Design of the most noble and useful Institution." He hoped for a moral reformation in America that would trigger those "Sobriety of Manners, that Temperance, Frugality, Fortitude and other manly Virtues which were once the Glory and Strength of my much lov'd native Town." Americans could not enjoy their liberty if they remained in such a "debauchd" state of moral affairs. As historian William Fowler has noted: "Adams's worldview was inimical to concepts of possessive individualism and extravagant consumption."[41]

For Adams the best way to achieve this kind of republic was through the promotion of religion. His Christian republicanism blended ancient views of a virtuous society with his Puritan convictions. This mix is clear from a 1776 letter to Boston selectman John Scollay:

> I have long been convincd that our Enemies have made it an Object, to eradicate from the Minds of the People in general a Sense of true Religion & Virtue, in hopes thereby the more easily to carry their Point of enslaving them. Indeed my Friend, this is a Subject so important in my Mind, that I know not how to leave it. Revelation assures us that "Righteousness exalteth a Nation"—Communities are dealt with in this World by the wise and just Ruler of the Universe. He rewards or punishes them according to their general Character. The diminution of publick Virtue is usually attended with that of publick Happiness, and the publick Liberty will not long survive the total Extinction of Morals. "The Roman Empire, says

the Historian, *must* have sunk, though the Goths had not invaded it. Why? Because the Roman Virtue was sunk." Could I be assured that America would remain virtuous, I would venture to defy the utmost Efforts of Enemies to subjugate her. You will allow me to remind you, that the Morals of that City which has born so great a Share of the American Contest, depend much upon the Vigilance of the respectable Body of Magistrates of which you are a Member.[42]

Samuel Adams knew his history well. It taught him that a corrupt society would eventually crumble under the weight of its own immorality.

Not all of the founders rejected orthodox doctrines such as the divinity of Jesus Christ or the Trinity. Witherspoon, Jay, and Adams were orthodox Christians who believed that Christianity was a major source of republican virtue. Their personal faith informed, in slightly different ways, their politics. All three of them believed that God was on the side of America. They all defended some version of religious liberty, but Jay and Adams refused to extend rights to Catholics. (Witherspoon would have probably taken the same view had he been in a position to aid in the formation of a state government.) And all three men blended their Christian convictions about societal happiness with more secular ideas. Witherspoon believed that the conscience was a source of virtue apart from God's grace. Jay wed his Calvinism with a belief in a strong national union. Adams blended his Puritan convictions with ancient republicanism. In the end, a close look at the beliefs of these statesmen reminds us that Christianity was present at the time of the American founding, but it often merged with other ideas that were compatible with, but not necessarily influenced by, Christianity.

Suggested Reading for Part Three

Adams, Dickinson W., ed. *Jefferson's Extracts from the Gospels*. Princeton: Princeton University Press, 1983.

Allen, Brooke. *Moral Minority: Our Skeptical Founding Fathers*. New York: Ivan Dee, 2006.

Diggins, John Patrick. *John Adams*. American Presidents Series. New York: Time Books, 2003.

Dreisbach, Daniel, Mark David Hall, and Jeffry Morrison, eds. *The Forgotten Founders on Religion and Public Life*. Notre Dame: University of Notre Dame Press, 2009.

Ellis, Joseph J. *American Sphinx: The Character of Thomas Jefferson*. 1997. Reprint, New York: Vintage, 1998.

Ellis, Joseph J. *His Excellency: George Washington*. 2004. Reprint, New York: Vintage, 2005.

Fowler, William M., Jr. *Samuel Adams: Radical Puritan*. New York: Longman, 1997.

Franklin, Benjamin. *The Autobiography and Other Writings*. Reprint, New York: Penguin, 1986.

Frazer, Gregg. *The Religious Beliefs of America's Founders: Reason, Revelation, and Revolution*. Lawrence: University of Kansas Press, 2012.

Gaustad, Edwin. *Sworn on the Altar of God: A Religious Biography of Thomas Jefferson*. Grand Rapids: Eerdmans, 1996.

Gordon-Reed, Annette. *Thomas Jefferson and Sally Hemings: An American Controversy*. Charlottesville: University Press of Virginia, 1997.

Grizzard, Frank E., Jr. *The Ways of Providence: Religion & George Washington*. Buena Vista, VA: Mariner, 2005.

Holmes, David L. *The Faiths of the Founding Fathers*. New York: Oxford University Press, 2006.

Huston, James H., ed. *The Founders on Religion*. Princeton: Princeton University Press, 2005.

Isaacson, Walter. *Benjamin Franklin: An American Life*. New York: Simon & Schuster, 2003.

Kennedy, Roger G. *Mr. Jefferson's Lost Cause: Land, Farmers, Slavery, and the Louisiana Purchase*. New York: Oxford University Press, 2003.

Longmore, Paul K. *The Invention of George Washington*. Berkeley: University of California Press, 1988.

McCullough, David. *John Adams*. New York: Simon & Schuster, 2001.

Morgan, Edmund. *Benjamin Franklin*. New Haven: Yale University Press, 2002.

Novak, Michael, and Jana Novak. *Washington's God: Religion, Liberty, and the Father of Our Country*. New York: Basic Books, 2006.

Onuf, Peter S., ed. *Jeffersonian Legacies*. Charlottesville: University Press of Virginia, 1993.

Smith, Gary Scott. *Faith and the Presidency: From George Washington to George W. Bush*. New York: Oxford University Press, 2006.

Stahr, Walter. *John Jay, Founding Father*. London: Hambledon & London, 2005.

Stoll, Ira. *Samuel Adams: A Life*. New York: Free Press, 2008.

Tait, Gordon L. *The Piety of John Witherspoon: Pew, Pulpit, and Public Forum*. Louisville: Geneva, 2001.

Thompson, Mary V. *"In the Hands of Good Providence": Religion in the Life of George Washington*. Charlottesville: University of Virginia Press, 2008.

Waldstreicher, David. *Runaway America: Benjamin Franklin, Slavery, and the American Revolution*. New York: Hill & Wang, 2004.

Walters, Kerry. *Benjamin Franklin and His Gods*. Urbana: University of Illinois Press, 1999.

Wood, Gordon. *The Americanization of Benjamin Franklin*. New York: Penguin, 2004.

Conclusion

In 2010 the political commentator Glenn Beck devoted an entire television program to a discussion of George Whitefield, the eighteenth-century evangelical revivalist and the precipitator of the event known as the First Great Awakening. Near the end of the show, Beck's conversation with his guests—two early American religious historians—turned to the topic of slavery. Beck wondered how Whitefield could inspire anti-slavery advocates in England such as John Newton, the author of the hymn "Amazing Grace," while at the same time owning slaves. Befuddled by this paradox, and clearly at a loss for words, Beck turned to the camera and said, "Sometimes history is a little complex."[1] Though Beck's use of history in his television and radio programs seldom reflects this kind of complexity, in this particular case he was absolutely right. Indeed, Beck's words about Whitefield, a man who may have inspired some of the American founders, go to the heart of what I have tried to accomplish in this book.

History is complex. Heroes sometimes do unheroic things. It is the responsibility of the historian to make every effort to explain the past in all its fullness. To do otherwise is not only to cease to be a historian, but to fail to act with integrity in interpreting the complexity of human activity in the world. Such a lesson applies to those who doggedly defend the notion that the United States was founded as a Christian nation, and those who doggedly defend the notion that the United States was founded as a secular nation. Historians will never achieve complete objectivity, but they should always strive to be truth tellers. Anything less is a moral failure—a failure to respect the complicated nature of the human condition as it has played out through time.

Having read this far, you know that this book never offers a definitive answer to the question I pose in its title: Was America founded as a Christian nation? I am sure some readers will be frustrated by this. As you have seen in the previous pages, the question cannot be answered with a simple yes or no. Instead, what I have tried to do in this primer is to give readers some things to think about, and perhaps to thoughtfully debate, whenever this historical question arises in their churches, schools, families, and places of employment. The issue of whether the United States is a Christian nation does not seem to be going away anytime soon.

What have we learned about the relationship between Christianity and the American founding? First, I have suggested that those who believe that the United States is a Christian nation have a good chunk of American history on their side. Throughout the nineteenth and twentieth centuries, and into the twenty-first century, there have always been believers who have tried to promote this idea. In the early nineteenth century, such a view was part of the cultural mainstream. Christians believed that they were living in a Christian nation. A close look at the historical record suggests that they were probably right. Though the Constitution would always prevent the United States from making Christianity its established faith, the religious culture of pre–Civil War America was shaped by evangelical Protestantism. It is even plausible to suggest that the Civil War was, at one level, a war over just what kind of Christian nation America would be. As the United States entered the twentieth century, the meaning of the phrase "Christian nation" continued to be contested. Conservative evangelicals and liberal Protestants fought diligently for what they believed to be the Christian soul of the nation. By the twentieth century, Catholics had provided their own vision of the United States as a Christian nation. Finally, in the wake of the turbulent 1960s and a series of Supreme Court decisions that seemed to be removing Christian values from the public square, the Christian Right emerged in American political culture and led the charge in forwarding the idea that the United States was founded as a Christian nation and should continue to be one.

Second, this book has turned to the period of the American Revolution to see if the claims of those who have thought that the United States was founded as a Christian nation can be supported with evidence from the eighteenth century. For example, it would be difficult to suggest, based upon the formal responses to British taxation between 1765 and 1774, that the leaders of the American Revolution were driven by overtly Christian values. Ministers used the Bible extensively to justify rebellion against England, but their interpretations of the Bible were more informed by the popular political ideas of the day than by sound theological reflection and exegesis. Though the Declaration of Independence refers to God multiple times, it cannot be called a "Christian document." The same might be said for the U.S. Constitution, which refers to God not at all. But when it comes to the individual states, today's defenders of Christian America have a compelling case. Nearly all of the state constitutions recognized God and Christianity, and many required officeholders to affirm Christian theology. Others maintained Christianity as the official and established state religion well into the nineteenth century.

Third, this book has explored the religious beliefs of some of the most prominent founders. As we have seen, the founders were an eclectic religious group. Some claimed to be Christians but rejected doctrines that are central to historic Christian orthodoxy, such as the inspiration of the Bible, the resurrection of Jesus Christ, or the Trinity. Others exemplified behavior that might lead one to question the depth of their Christian commitments. And others, as we saw in the last chapter, were devout believers who tried to bring their faith to bear on their vision for the new nation they helped to found. If there was one universal idea that all the founders believed about the relationship between religion and the new nation, it was that religion was necessary in order to sustain an ordered and virtuous republic.

In a sound-bite culture where public figures appeal to the past to score political points or advance a particular cultural agenda, it is my hope that this book might help Americans to think deeply about the role that Christianity played in the American founding. We owe it to ourselves to be informed citizens who can speak intelligently and thoughtfully about our nation's past.

Epilogue to the Revised Edition

Since *Was America Founded as a Christian Nation?* was published in 2011, the debate over the question in the title of my book has not waned. Politicians continue to appeal to the American founding to win political points in the present, and very few of them do it in a responsible way. I am writing this epilogue during the 2016 presidential primary season. In the fall of 2015 and into the early weeks of 2016, GOP candidates such as Ted Cruz, Ben Carson, Mike Huckabee (again!), John Kasich, Marco Rubio, and Rick Santorum have all invoked the founding fathers on religion, claimed that the United States has Judeo-Christian roots, or argued that the Declaration of Independence and the Constitution are Christian documents. David Barton, the Christian nationalist activist discussed in chapter four of this book, is directing a Ted Cruz super PAC. David Lane, the founder of a movement called The American Renewal Project, is trying to get five hundred pastors to run for political office. His model is the so-called "Black Robe Regiment," a name given to revolutionary-era pastors who used their pulpits to proclaim independence against Great Britain. The debate over the Christian character of the founding of the American republic continues to rage, but the last several years have witnessed at least two new developments on this front that are worth noting.

The first such development took place in the summer of 2012 with the publication of David Barton's book *The Jefferson Lies: Exposing the Myths You've Always Believed about Thomas Jefferson*. Barton's history of Jefferson challenged virtually everything that Jefferson scholars have said about the signer of the Declaration of Independence and the third president of the United States. These scholars, Barton argued, have portrayed Jefferson as an atheist, a racist, a bigot, and a slaveholder. In his attempt to rescue Jefferson from contemporary scholarship, Barton also pointed to the sinister "isms"—deconstructionism, poststructuralism, modernism, minimalism, and academic collectivism—behind these effort to discredit the Virginian.

In the end, Barton's Thomas Jefferson looked more like a twenty-first-century member of the Christian Right than a product of the eighteenth-century world in which he lived. He argued that Jefferson used federal funds to promote missions to native American tribes, rarely questioned the orthodox Christian beliefs of his time, rejected the idea of the "separation of church and state," did not have a child with his slave Sally Hemings, tried to establish a theological professorship at the public and nonsectarian University of Virginia, founded the Virginia Bible Society, and did not produce a version of the Gospels void of Jesus' miracles.[1]

The critical response to *The Jefferson Lies* was fast and furious. Jefferson scholars dismissed the book as little more than political propaganda. Evangelical historians also found Barton's portrayal of Thomas Jefferson to be unrecognizable. Martin Marty, doyen of American church historians, said that the book should be named *Barton's Lies about Jefferson*.[2] A group of African American pastors in Cincinnati criticized Barton for refusing to expose Jefferson as a racist and a slaveholder and petitioned Thomas Nelson to pull the book from publication.[3] But the strongest attack on Barton's work came from Warren Throckmorton and Michael Coulter, professors at Grove City College, a Christian college in western Pennsylvania. Throckmorton and Coulter published, first in e-book form and later in print, *Getting Jefferson Right: Fact-Checking Claims about Our Third President.* Throckmorton and Coulter never claimed to be historians (Throckmorton is a psychology professor and Coulter is a political scientist), but they did prove to be excellent fact-checkers. In a style that can only be described as "blow-by-blow," these scholars debunked virtually every claim that Barton made about Jefferson.[4]

Eventually the conservative evangelicals who supported Barton became concerned about the veracity and integrity of *The Jefferson Lies*. Jay Richards, a Christian philosopher and intelligent design advocate affiliated with the Discovery Institute, gathered together a team of conservative evangelical historians to evaluate the book. These historians found the book to be inadequate in its treatment of Jefferson and filled with historical errors of fact. In light of the committee's recommendation, Thomas Nelson publishers pulled the book from print. Throughout the entire ordeal, Barton defended his scholarship in *The Jefferson Lies* and seemed surprised that Thomas Nelson decided to remove it from print.[5] He pitched the book to other publishers, and it was eventually published again in fall of 2015 by the right-wing website World Net Daily.

Barton continues to deny that there is anything wrong with his research or his portrayal of Jefferson, and he gives his side of the story in the new edition. He claims that the book was rejected by Thomas Nelson because the evangelical publisher fell victim to a "scourge of 'political correct-ness.'"[6] In the wake of the controversy, Barton continues to promote the idea, through lectures, a radio show, and now a weekly television program, that the United States was founded as a Christian nation. He has also become more active in the political realm through his relation-ship with Ted Cruz. But his standing as an honest broker of the past has been discredited by nearly every evangelical historian in the country.

The second major development in the ongoing debate over the question of whether or not the United States was founded as a Christian nation is related to the recent conservative evangelical calls for religious liberty in the wake of two recent Supreme Court cases: Burwell v. Hobby Lobby (2014) and Obergfell v. Hodges (2015). In Burwell v. Hobby Lobby, the court ruled that a "closely held" for-profit corporation was exempt from providing contraceptives to its employees in accordance with the Afford-able Care Act (Obamacare) if the use of those contraceptives violated the religious beliefs of the owners. Hobby Lobby, a retail store specializing in arts and crafts, would not be required to provide contraceptive pills and intrauterine devices that prevented the implantation of a fertilized egg. When the court ruled that a corporation could claim a First Amend-ment right to religious liberty, it prompted other "closely-owned" busi-nesses to claim similar religious rights. In the wake of Burwell v. Hobby Lobby, Indiana passed the Religious Freedom Restoration Act (RFRA), which allowed individuals and companies to exercise religious freedom as a defense in legal proceedings. This was particularly the case in the wed-ding industry, where florists, bakers, photographers, and caterers who opposed gay marriage refused to render services to same-sex couples.

In Obergfell v. Hodges (2015), the court guaranteed the right of same sex couples to marry in accordance with the Fourteenth Amendment to the United States Constitution. Presidential candidate Mike Huckabee described the decision as an "out-of-control act of unconstitutional judi-cial tyranny." Ted Cruz advised individual states to ignore the decision. In Kentucky, Rowan County clerk Kim Davis refused to issue marriage licenses to same-sex couples because to do so would violate her con-science. When she was imprisoned for failing to uphold the newly estab-lished law, she quickly became a martyr (with the help of Huckabee and Cruz) for the cause of religious liberty.

Both of these Supreme Court cases signaled an obvious shift in the language and strategy of the Christian Right. Pleas to restore the United States to its Christian roots were replaced with impassioned defenses of religious liberty. For these conservative evangelicals, Burwell v. Hobby

Lobby was a victory for religious freedom. They could now turn their attention to defending the religious rights of other institutions—such as Christian colleges or the Little Sisters of the Poor, a Catholic religious organization for women that is also fighting the contraceptive mandates of the Affordable Care Act. Obergfell v. Hodges, however, was a tragic defeat for those who defended marriage as a sacred union between a man and a woman. Many conservatives saw the Obergfell decision as the ceremonial end of Christian culture in the United States. As we argued in the first chapter of this book, Americans had always seen themselves as living in a Christian nation until that idea became a contested one after the 1960s. For some, the legalization of same-sex marriage meant that America could no longer be considered a Christian nation. The contest for the soul of America was now over. The Christian nationalists had lost. The only appeal left was the First Amendment. If gay marriage was now the law of the land, then those who believed in an older, more traditional view of marriage needed to make sure that they would not be discriminated against for continuing to hold such a position.

As a result, GOP politicians and the leaders of the Christian Right began preaching the importance of religious liberty as an essential part of the American founding. In late 2015 Ted Cruz held religious freedom rallies around the country in which he argued that the Obama administration and the Supreme Court were persecuting Christians through the Affordable Care Act and the enforcement of Obergfell v. Hodges. He appealed to colonial America, a time when "brave men and women fleeing religious oppression" came to a "new world where they could seek and worship the Lord God almighty with all of their heart, mind, and soul—free of oppression from government."[7] Almost all of the GOP candidates running for president in 2016 defended Indiana's Religious Freedom Restoration Act. This use of religious freedom by conservative politicians and Christian cultural warriors appears to be little more than a clever new way of asserting Christian nationalism. As historian Benjamin Park has noted, "conservative appeals to religious freedom . . . are often not so much born of a desire for everyone to believe and practice as they wish, because that form of liberty would threaten America's righteousness and moral foundation; rather, they affirm an unspoken assumption that religious freedom is meant to guarantee the perpetuation of *true* belief and practice in the face of threatening opposition."[8]

Park's observations have played out in various ways among the Christian Right, but none more clearly than in the attempt to keep Muslims out of the United States in the wake of the tragic Paris attacks, carried out by members of ISIS in November 2015, and the subsequent efforts by some evangelicals to turn away Syrian refugees who are Muslim but to allow the entrance of Christian refugees. The implication of such a proposed policy is an obvious one: in a time of fear and the threat of terrorism on American shores, liberties, especially religious liberties, should be afforded only to Christians. This has put many on the Christian Right in the awkward and inconsistent position of having to defend liberties for themselves but deny the same religious freedom to those who do not conform to the slowly fading Christian nation to which they continue to cling. So far very few Christian Right defenders of religious liberty have come out strongly in support of the religious liberty of Muslims or other non-Christian groups.[9]

Historians are not prophets. We cannot predict the future. But we can make reasonable suggestions about the course of history based on what we know about the past. The idea that the United States was founded as a Christian nation will not go away any time soon. In fact, if history is indeed a guide, it may grow stronger in certain sectors of the population as a response to rapid social change. But as the United States becomes more diverse—both in terms of demographics and the ideas we as a nation are willing to welcome as part of our democratic life together—the idea that we are somehow a Christian nation or were founded as such is bound to lose traction and eventually disappear into the dustbin of history.

Notes

Preface to the First Edition

1. Vision Forum Ministries, "The Jamestown Quadricentennial," accessed Jan. 25, 2010, at http://www.visionforumministries.org/events/jq/001/vision.aspx.
2. House Resolution 888, accessed Jan. 25, 2010, at http://www.govtrack.us/congress/billtext.xpd?bill=hr110-888.
3. Mariah Blake, "Revisionaries: How a Group of Texas Conservatives Is Rewriting Your Kids' Textbooks," *Washington Monthly*, Jan.-Feb. 2010, accessed Jan. 25, 2010, at http://www.washingtonmonthly.com/features/2010/1001.blake.html.
4. Dan Gilgoff, "John McCain: Constitution Established a 'Christian Nation,'" accessed Jan. 25, 2010, at http://www.beliefnet.com/News/Politics/2007/06/John-Mccain-Constitution-Established-A-Christian-Nation.aspx; Huckabee Speech in Orlando, Florida, Oct. 21, 2007, accessed Jan. 25, 2010, at http://politifact.com/truth-o-meter/statements/2007/oct/23/mike-huckabee/1-out-of-56-equals-most-no-it-doesnt/.
5. "Evangelicals in America," *Time*, Feb. 7, 2005.
6. Mark Schwehn, *Exiles from Eden: Religion and the Academic Vocation in America* (New York: Oxford University Press, 1993), 49.

Introduction

1. Gordon Wood, *The Purpose of the Past: Reflections on the Uses of History* (New York: Penguin, 2008), 276.
2. Walt Whitman, *Leaves of Grass: The Poems of Walt Whitman* (London: Walter Scott, 1886), 102.
3. John Fea, *The Way of Improvement Leads Home: Philip Vickers Fithian and the Rural Enlightenment in Early America* (Philadelphia: University of Pennsylvania Press, 2008).
4. Peter C. Messer, *Stories of Independence: Identity, Ideology, and History in Eighteenth-Century America* (DeKalb: Northern Illinois University Press, 2005).
5. See, for example, Gary Nash, *History on Trial: Culture Wars and the Teaching of the Past* (New York: Vintage, 2000).

6. Thomas Andrews and Flannery Burke, "What Does It Mean to Think Historically?" *AHA Perspectives* 45: 1 (January 2007). Accessed at http://www.historians.org/Perspectives/issues/2007/0701/0701tea2.cfm.

7. John Tosh, *The Pursuit of History*, 4th ed. (New York: Longman, 2006), 12.

8. Quoted from Nash, *History on Trial*, 6.

9. Andrews and Burke, "What Does It Mean to Think Historically?"

10. Quoted from Gordon Wood, "Reading the Founders' Minds," *New York Review of Books* 54 (June 28, 2007).

11. Wood, *Purpose of the Past*, 308.

12. David Barton, *Original Intent: The Courts, the Constitution, & Religion*, 3rd ed. (Aledo, TX: WallBuilder, 2000), 5.

13. Sam Wineburg, *Historical Thinking and Other Unnatural Acts: Charting the Future of Teaching the Past* (Philadelphia: Temple University Press, 2001), 7.

14. Ibid., 24.

1. Evangelical America, 1789–1865

1. See, for example, Brooke Allen, "Our Godless Constitution," *The Nation* (Feb. 3, 2005); idem, accessed September 10, 2010, at www.thenation.com/article/our-godless-constitution?; "The Great Debate of Our Season," *Mother Jones* (December 2005), accessed September 10, 2010, at motherjones.com/politics/2005/12/great-debate/our-seaso1.

2. Thomas Kidd, *American Christians and Islam: Evangelical Culture and Muslims from the Colonial Period to the Age of Terrorism* (Princeton: Princeton University Press, 2008), 22–23.

3. These conclusions are based on the reading of hundreds of references to "Christian nation" in early-nineteenth-century print available through Google Books.

4. George Marsden describes a "massive evangelical consensus" in nineteenth-century America. See Marsden, *Reforming Fundamentalism: Fuller Seminary and the New Evangelicalism* (Grand Rapids: Eerdmans, 1988), 119.

5. The best treatment of this is Nathan Hatch, *The Democratization of American Christianity* (New Haven: Yale University Press, 1991).

6. Philip Schaff, *America: A Sketch of Its Political, Social, and Religious Character* (1855; repr., Cambridge: Belknap, 1961), 11, cited in Roger Finke and Rodney Stark, *The Churching of America, 1776–2005: Winners and Losers in Our Religious Economy*, 2nd ed. (New Brunswick, NJ: Rutgers University Press, 2005), 6.

7. Thomas Jefferson to Thomas Cooper, November 2, 1822, accessed at the University of Virginia Electronic Text Center, http://etext.virginia.edu/etcbin/toccer-new2?id=JefLett.sgm&images=images/modeng&data=/texts/english/modeng/parsed&tag=public&part=268&division=div1.

8. For an overview of the election see Edward J. Larson, *A Magnificent Catastrophe: The Tumultuous Election of 1800, America's First Presidential Campaign* (New York: Free Press, 2007).

9. William Linn, *Serious Considerations on the Election of a President* (Trenton: Sherman, Mersmon & Thomas, 1800), 4, 15, 16, 23.

10. Robert Baird, *The Progress and Prospects of Christianity in the United States of America* (London: Partridge and Oakey, 1851), 28.

11. The best treatment of the Whigs remains Daniel Walker Howe, *The Political Culture of the American Whigs* (Chicago: University of Chicago Press, 1984).
12. Lyman Beecher, *A Plea for the West* (Cincinnati: Truman & Smith, 1835), 189.
13. On the explosion of Christian print see Hatch, *Democratization of American Christianity*, 125–33.
14. Mercy Otis Warren, *History of the Rise, Progress and Termination of the American Revolution*, 2 vols. (1805; repr., Indianapolis: Liberty Fund, 1989), 97, 641, 505.
15. Ibid., vol. 2, 686.
16. Jonathan Tucker Boyd, "This Holy Hieroglyph: Providence and Historical Consciousness in George Bancroft's Historiography" (PhD diss., Johns Hopkins University, 1999), 105, 106, 110, 118–19.
17. Ibid., 206.
18. Charles A. Goodrich, *History of the United States* (Hartford: Barber & Robinson, 1823), 6.
19. J. Olney, *A History of the United States on a New Plan Adapted to the Capacity of Youth* (New Haven: Durrie & Peck, 1842), 266; William Grimshaw, *History of the United States*, 2nd ed. (Philadelphia: Benjamin Warner, 1821), 181, 189; Goodrich, *History of the United States*, 336.
20. Emma Willard, *History of the United States or Republic of America* (New York: Gallaher & White, 1826), 17.
21. Noah Webster, *History of the United States* (New Haven: Durrie & Peck, 1832), 9, 293–311.
22. Mason Locke Weems, *The Life of Washington: A New Edition with Primary Documents*, ed. Peter Onuf (Armonk, NY: M. E. Sharpe, 1996); Francois Furstenberg, *In the Name of the Father: Washington's Legacy, Slavery, and the Making of a Nation* (New York: Penguin, 2006), 123–26.
23. Weems, *Life of Washington*, 10–13. Justin J. Bollinger, "Mason Locke Weems, George Washington, and the Emergence of an 'Evangelical Nationalism' in the Early Nineteenth Century" (Senior honors thesis, Messiah College, May 2006).
24. Weems, *Life of Washington*, 10–13.
25. Mark A. Noll, *The Civil War as a Theological Crisis* (Chapel Hill: University of North Carolina Press, 2006).
26. For an introduction to the religious dimensions of Lincoln's second inaugural address see Ronald W. White, *Lincoln's Greatest Speech: The Second Inaugural* (New York: Simon & Schuster, 2002).
27. Rufus Choate, "American Nationality," July 5, 1858, in *The Works of Rufus Choate, with a Memoir of His Life* (Boston: Little, Brown, 1862), 436, 439.
28. Horace Bushnell, "Popular Government by Divine Right," November 24, 1864, in *"God Ordained This War": Sermons on the Sectional Crisis, 1830–1865*, ed. David B. Chesebrough (Columbia: University of South Carolina Press, 1991), quotation, 106; cf. 117; Albert Barnes, *The Love of Country* (Philadelphia: C. Sherman & Sons, 1861), 38–40.
29. John F. Bigelow, *The Hand of God in American History: A Discourse* (Burlington: W. H. & C. A. Hoyt, 1861), 6, 11–15, 17–23.
30. Francis Vinton, *The Christian Idea of Civil Government* (New York: George F. Nesbitt, 1861), 3, 11; Bushnell, "Popular Government," 121; E. E. Adams, *A Sermon Delivered in the North Broad Street Presbyterian Church* (Philadelphia: Henry B. Ashmead, 1861), 3.

31. Barnes, *Love of Country*, 45.
32. Chesebrough, *God Ordained This War*, 85–86.
33. Finney, "Lectures on Systematic Theology," cited in *God Ordained This War*, ed. Chesebrough, 58; Eddy, *Secession: Shall it Be Peace or War?* quoted in *God Ordained This War*, ed. Chesebrough, 59.
34. Debby Applegate, *The Most Famous Man in America: The Biography of Henry Ward Beecher* (New York: Doubleday, 2006).
35. Henry Ward Beecher, "National Injustice and Penalty," in *Freedom and War: Discourses on Topics Suggested by the Times* (Boston: Ticknor and Fields, 1863), 318.
36. What follows draws heavily from Mark A. Noll, *America's God: From Jonathan Edwards to Abraham Lincoln* (New York: Oxford University Press, 2002), 426–38.
37. Adams, *Sermon*, 6; Bigelow, *Hand of God*, 35, 42.
38. "Constitution of the Confederate States of America, March 11, 1861," accessed at Yale Law School Avalon Project, http://avalon.law.yale.edu/19th_century/csa_csa.asp.
39. Benjamin Morgan Palmer, *National Responsibility Before God*, June 13, 1861, in *God Ordained This War*, ed. Chesebrough, 207–9.
40. Mitchell Snay, *Gospel of Disunion: Religion and Separatism in the Antebellum South* (1993; repr., Chapel Hill: University of North Carolina Press, 1997), 190–93.
41. Drew Gilpin Faust, *The Creation of Confederate Nationalism: Ideology and Identity in the Civil War South* (Baton Rouge: Louisiana State University Press, 1988), 27, 29.
42. Harry S. Stout, *Upon the Altar of the Nation: A Moral History of the Civil War* (New York: Viking, 2006), 47–48.
43. Much has been written about the Southern defense of slavery, and it is not my intention to go into full detail describing the intricate ways in which Southern leaders defended slavery, but a few basic points are worth mentioning here. A few helpful books on this topic are Eugene Genovese and Elizabeth Fox-Genovese, *The Mind of the Master Class: History and Faith in the Southern Slaveholders' Worldview* (New York: Cambridge University Press, 2005); Charles Irons, *The Origins of Proslavery Christianity: White and Black Evangelicals in Colonial and Antebellum Virginia* (Chapel Hill: University of North Carolina Press, 2008); Stephen R. Haynes, *Noah's Curse: The Biblical Justification of American Slavery* (New York: Oxford University Press, 2002).
44. Thomas R. Dew, "An Essay on Slavery" (1832), in *The Pro-Slavery Argument: As Maintained by the Most Distinguished Writers of the Southern States* (Charleston: Walker, Richards, 1852), 451–62, accessed at http://www.wwnorton.com/college/history/archive/resources/documents/ch15_03.htm.
45. Robert L. Dabney, *A Defence of Virginia: and Through Her, of the South* (New York: E. J. Hale & Son, 1867), 203–4.
46. William Lloyd Garrison, *The Liberator* (1849), quoted in Mark A. Noll, *One Nation Under God? Christian Faith and Political Action in America* (San Francisco: Harper & Row, 1988), 125.
47. James H. Thornwell, "The Rights and the Duties of Masters," May 26, 1850, in *God Ordained This War*, ed. Chesebrough, 177–78; Stephen Elliott, "Ezra's Dilemma," August 21, 1863, in *God Ordained This War*, ed. Chesebrough, 253; W. T. Hamilton, *Duties of Masters and Slaves* (1844), quoted in *God Ordained This War*, ed. Chesebrough, 146.
48. Benjamin Morgan Palmer, "Slavery a Divine Trust: Duty of the South to Preserve and Perpetuate It" (1861), quoted in *God Ordained This War*, ed. Chesebrough, 146; Dabney, *Defence of Virginia*, 281, 169.

2. Evangelicals, Liberals, and Christian America, 1865–1925

1. George Duffield Jr., *The God of Our Fathers* (Philadelphia: T.B. Pugh, 1861), 19.
2. The National Association to Secure the Religious Amendment of the Constitution of the United States, *Proceedings of the National Convention to Secure the Religious Amendment of the Constitution of the United States*, (Philadelphia: James B. Rogers Co., 1872), 14.
3. *Proceedings of the National Convention*, 4–8.
4. Ibid., 13.
5. Ibid., 72, 75.
6. Ibid., 17–18.
7. Ibid., 84.
8. Ibid., 1, 60.
9. Isaac Kramnick and R. Laurence Moore, *The Godless Constitution: The Case Against Religious Correctness* (New York: Norton, 1996), 145–48.
10. Theodore Woolsey, "The Relations of Constitution and Government in the United States to Religion," in *History, Essays, Orations, and Other Documents of the Sixth General Conference of the Evangelical Alliance*, ed. Philip Schaff and Irenaeus Prime (New York: Harper and Brothers, 1874), 523; William F. Warren, "American Infidelity; Its Factors and Phases," in *History, Essays, Orations*, ed. Schaff and Prime, 249.
11. George P. Fisher, "Protestantism, Romanism, and Modern Civilization," in *History, Essays, Orations*, ed. Schaff and Prime, 461–66.
12. William H. Allen, "The Labor Question," in *History, Essays, Orations*, ed. Schaff and Prime, 670–74.
13. Reverend Mark Hopkins, "The Sabbath Made for Man—His Consequent Right to Legislation for Serving Its Ends," in *History, Essays, Orations*, ed. Schaff and Prime, 540–44.
14. Reverend Henry A. Nelson, "Intemperance and Its Suppression," in *History, Essays, Orations*, ed. Schaff and Prime, 689–94.
15. Ibid.
16. George M. Marsden, *Fundamentalism and American Culture: The Shaping of Twentieth-Century Evangelicalism: 1870–1925* (New York: Oxford University Press, 1980), 66–67.
17. Dwight Lyman Moody and W. H. Daniels, *Moody: His Words, Work, and Workers* (Chicago: Walden, 1877), 476.
18. Ibid., 132; Michael Kazin, *A Godly Hero: The Life of William Jennings Bryan* (New York: Knopf, 2006).
19. Cited in John Fea, "The Town That Billy Sunday Could Not Shut Down: Prohibition and Sunday's Chicago Crusade of 1918," *Illinois Historical Journal* 87 (1994): 250.
20. Cited in Roger A. Bruns, *Preacher: Billy Sunday and Big-Time American Evangelism* (New York: Norton, 1992), 177.
21. Fea, "The Town That Billy Sunday Could Not Shut Down," 242–58.
22. Marsden, *Fundamentalism and American Culture*, quotation, 142; see also 149–53.
23. Marsden, *Understanding Evangelicalism and Fundamentalism* (Grand Rapids: Eerdmans, 1991), 1–2.
24. Marsden, *Fundamentalism and American Culture*, 206.
25. Ibid., 184–88. For a good overview of the Scopes trial see Edward J. Larson, *Summer for the Gods: The Scopes Trial and America's Continuing Debate over Science* (New York: Basic Books, 1997).

26. William R. Hutchison, *The Modernist Impulse in American Protestantism* (Cambridge: Harvard University Press, 1976), 2.

27. Henry Ward Beecher, "The Tendencies of American Progress" (1871), in *God's New Israel: Religious Interpretations of American Destiny*, ed. Conrad Cherry, rev. ed. (Chapel Hill: University of North Carolina Press, 1998), 235–48.

28. William Lawrence, "The Relation of Wealth to Morals" (1901), in *God's New Israel*, ed. Cherry, 249–59.

29. Susan Curtis, *A Consuming Faith: The Social Gospel and Modern American Culture* (Baltimore: Johns Hopkins University Press, 1991), 2, 3.

30. Robert T. Handy, *A Christian America: Protestant Hopes and Historical Realities*, 2nd ed. (New York: Oxford University Press, 1984), 140, 144.

31. All three quotes come from ibid., 144, 145.

32. Charles S. Macfarland, ed., *Christian Cooperation and World Redemption* (New York: Federal Council of the Churches of Christ in America, 1917), 48.

33. Ibid., 50; Handy, *Christian America*, 148–49.

34. Curtis, *Consuming Faith*, 154.

35. Richard M. Gamble, *The War for Righteousness: Progressive Christianity, the Great War, and the Rise of the Messianic Nation* (Wilmington, DE: ISI Books, 2003), 159, 176.

36. P. C. Kemeny, *Princeton in the Nation's Service: Religious Ideals and Educational Practice, 1868–1928* (New York: Oxford University Press, 1998).

37. Ronald J. Pestritto, *Woodrow Wilson and the Roots of Modern Liberalism* (Lanham, MD: Rowman & Littlefield, 2005), 40–43.

38. Gamble, *War for Righteousness*, 56, 130, quotation on 143.

39. *Church of the Holy Trinity v. United States*, 143 U.S. 457 (1892), accessed at http://supreme.justia.com/us/143/457/case.html.

40. David J. Brewer, *The United States: A Christian Nation* (Philadelphia: John C. Winston, 1905), 11–45. This section largely follows the argument of Hugh Heclo, "Is America a Christian Nation?" *Political Science Quarterly* 122 (2007): 61–63.

3. Christian America in a Modern Age, 1925–1980

1. This section draws heavily from Joel Carpenter, *Revive Us Again: The Reawakening of American Fundamentalism* (New York: Oxford University Press, 1997).

2. John Fea, "Power from on High in an Age of Ecclesiastical Impotence: The 'Enduement of the Holy Spirit' in American Fundamentalist Thought, 1880–1936," *Fides et Historia* 26 (1994): 26–27.

3. Carpenter, *Revive Us Again*, 149; Isaac Kramnick and R. Laurence Moore, *The Godless Constitution: The Case Against Religious Correctness* (New York: Norton, 1997), 148.

4. William Martin, *A Prophet with Honor: The Billy Graham Story* (New York: William Morrow, 1991), 91, 101, 115–16; Carpenter, *Revive Us Again*, 221–22.

5. Carpenter, *Revive Us Again*, 157–58, 187–88. The idea of "custodianship" comes from Grant Wacker, "Uneasy in Zion: Evangelicals in Postmodern Society," in *Evangelicalism and Modern America*, ed. George Marsden (Grand Rapids: Eerdmans, 1984), 17–28. On Fuller Seminary and neo-evangelicalism see Marsden, *Reforming Fundamentalism: Fuller Seminary and the New Evangelicalism* (Grand Rapids: Eerdmans, 1995).

6. Carpenter, *Revive Us Again*, 31. See also Robert T. Handy, "The American Religious Depression, 1925–1935," *Church History* 29 (1960): 3–16.

7. For example, Handy, "American Religious Depression."

8. Charles Clayton Morrison, "The Protestant Situation," *Christian Century* 63 (April 10, 1946): 458–60.

9. Charles Clayton Morrison, "Protestantism and the Public School," *Christian Century* 63 (April 17, 1946): 490–93; Morrison, "Protestantism and Science," *Christian Century* 63 (April 24, 1946): 524–27; Morrison, "Protestantism and Commercialized Entertainment," *Christian Century* 63 (May 1, 1946): 553–56.

10. Morrison, "The Protestant Task," *Christian Century* 63 (May 15, 1946): 618–21.

11. Morrison, "Protestantism, Thou Ailest, Here, and Here!" *Christian Century* 63 (May 22, 1946): 650–53; Morrison, "Protestant Localism," *Christian Century* 63 (May 29, 1946): 686–89; Morrison, "Protestant Misuse of the Bible," *Christian Century* 63 (June 5, 1946): 712–15; Morrison, "The Concept of an Ecumenical Protestantism," *Christian Century* (June 26, 1946): 801–4; Morrison, "Protestantism and the Lordship of Christ," *Christian Century* (July 3, 1946): 832–35.

12. "Longinqua: Encyclical of Pope Leo XIII on Catholicism in the United States," January 6, 1895, accessed on February 22, 2010, at http://www.vatican.va/holy_father/leo_xiii/encyclicals/documents/hf_l-xiii_enc_06011895_longinqua_en.html.

13. "Longinqua," paragraph 13.

14. "Longinqua," paragraph 21, 22.

15. Jay P. Dolan, *The American Catholic Experience: A History from Colonial Times to the Present* (New York: Doubleday, 1985), 351–52; see also Patrick W. Carey, *Catholics in America: A History* (Westport, CT: Praeger, 2004), 93–95.

16. Harold E. Fey, "Can Catholicism Win America," *Christian Century* 61 (Nov. 29, 1944), 1378–80; "Catholicism Comes to Middletown," *Christian Century* 61 (Dec. 6, 1944): 1409–11; "Catholicism and the Negro," *Christian Century* 61 (Dec. 20, 1944): 1476–79; "Catholicism and the Worker," *Christian Century* 61 (Dec. 27, 1944): 1498–1500; "Catholicism Fights Communism," *Christian Century* 62 (Jan. 3, 1945): 13–15; "Catholicism Invades Rural America," *Christian Century* 62 (Jan. 10, 1945): 44–47; "The Center of Catholic Power," *Christian Century* 62 (Jan. 17, 1945): 74–76. For a helpful introduction to twentieth-century American fears of Catholicism see John T. McGreevy, *Catholicism and American Freedom: A History* (New York: Norton, 2003).

17. Quoted in Robert Wuthnow, *The Restructuring of American Religion* (Princeton: Princeton University Press, 1988), 67.

18. James Hudnut-Beumler, *Looking for God in the Suburbs: The Religion of the American Dream and Its Critics, 1945–1965* (New Brunswick, NJ: Rutgers University Press, 1994), 31–37.

19. This paragraph draws heavily from Wuthnow, *Restructuring of American Religion*, 74, 81, 138, 142, 143, 176, 182–83.

20. House Joint Resolution 244, *Congressional Record*, House, Feb. 12, 1954, p. 1700.

21. Hudnut-Beumler, *Looking for God*, 50–51; Will Herberg, *Protestant, Catholic, Jew: An Essay in American Religious Sociology* (New York: Doubleday Anchor, 1960).

22. David Chappell, *A Stone of Hope: Prophetic Religion and the Death of Jim Crow* (Chapel Hill: University of North Carolina Press, 2004).

23. Martin Luther King Jr., *Letter from a Birmingham Jail* (Chicago: Christian Century, 1963).

24. I am following the argument here of Randall Balmer, *Thy Kingdom Come: An Evangelical's Lament* (New York: Basic Books, 2006), 13–17.

25. See Barry Hankins, *Francis Schaeffer and the Shaping of Evangelical America* (Grand Rapids: Eerdmans, 2008), 175–77, 180–91, 198–202.

26. Jerry Falwell, *Listen, America!* (New York: Doubleday, 1980), 24–50. For a more extensive view of Falwell's understanding of American history see Ed Dobson, Ed Hindson, and Jerry Falwell, *The Fundamentalist Phenomenon: The Resurgence of Conservative Christianity* (Grand Rapids: Baker, 1981), 27–149.

27. Hankins, *Francis Schaeffer*, 192–200, 209–27; Mark A. Noll, Nathan O. Hatch, and George M. Marsden, *The Search for Christian America*, 2nd ed. (Colorado Springs: Helmers & Howard, 1989).

4. History for the Faithful: The Contemporary Defenders of Christian America

1. WallBuilders Web site: http://www.wallbuilders.com.

2. Peter Marshall and David Manuel, *The Light and the Glory* (Old Tappan, NJ: Revell, 1977), 22.

3. Bush, first inaugural address, Jan. 20, 2001. The quote comes from a letter written in 1776 from Virginia statesman John Page to Thomas Jefferson. It draws upon several biblical passages, including Nahum 1:3 and Exodus 23:20–21.

4. David Fischer, "Teaching God's Providence in History," in Edward M. Panosian, ed., *The Providence of God in History* (Greenville, SC: Bob Jones University Press, 1996).

5. Rachel C. Larson, Pamela B. Creason, and Michael D. Matthews, *The American Republic for Christian Schools*, 2nd ed. (Greenville, SC: Bob Jones University Press, 2000), ix.

6. David Barton, *Original Intent: The Courts, the Constitution, & Religion*, 3rd ed. (Aledo, TX: WallBuilder, 2000), 333; Marshall and Manuel, *The Light and the Glory*, 19.

7. John Winthrop, "A Modell of Christian Charity," sermon, 1630, in *Collections of the Massachusetts Historical Society* (Boston 1838), 3rd ser. 7:31–48.

8. Michael R. Lowman et al., *United States History in Christian Perspective: Heritage of Freedom* (Pensacola: A Beka Books, 1992),104; Tim LaHaye, *Faith of Our Founding Fathers* (Green Forest, AR: Master Books, 1990), 65; D. James Kennedy with Jerry Newcombe, *What if America Were a Christian Nation Again?* (Nashville: Nelson, 2003), 10.

9. Larson, *American Republic*, 19, 89.

10. Marshall and Manuel, *The Light and the Glory*, 18, 49, 51–58, 73.

11. Kennedy, *What if America*, 11–12.

12. Marshall and Manuel, *The Light and the Glory*, 191; Lowman, *United States History*, 34, 35, 37.

13. Marshall and Manuel, *The Light and the Glory*, 116; Kennedy, *What if America*, 14; Mark A. Beliles and Stephen K. McDowell, *America's Providential History* (Charlottesville, VA: Providence Foundation, 1989), 58, 73.

14. Marshall and Manuel, *The Light and the Glory*, 191–203. Not all of the advocates of a providential view of American history are this harsh. At least one textbook praises the colony of Rhode Island—the place where Williams and Hutchinson both ended up after being expelled from Massachusetts Bay—as God's evidence to the world that "true Biblical Christianity can thrive without government assistance" (Lowman, *United States History*, 39).

15. Marshall and Manuel, *The Light and the Glory*, 270; Larson, *American Republic*, 89; Beliles and McDowell, *America's Providential History*, 147–48.

16. Marshall and Manuel, *The Light and the Glory*, 79; Timothy Keesee and Mark Sidwell, *United States History for Christian Schools* (Greenville, SC: Bob Jones University Press,

2001), 35; Gary DeMar, *America's Christian Heritage* (Nashville: Broadman & Holman, 2003), 13.

17. Marshall and Manuel, *The Light and the Glory*, 120; Lowman, *United States History*, 33–37.

18. Marshall and Manuel, *The Light and the Glory*, 246, 251, 254–55; Lowman, *United States History*, 72, 76, 78, 82; Beliles and McDowell, *America's Providential History*, 127.

19. This definition of the "Founding Fathers" comes from Barton, *Original Intent*, 124.

20. Ibid., 123; cf. also Kennedy, *What if America*, 4–5.

21. LaHaye, *Faith of Our Founding Fathers*, xi, 30, 110, 137; Lowman, *United States History*, 112, 126–27; William J. Federer, *America's God and Country: Encyclopedia of Quotations* (St. Louis: Amerisearch, 2000). The unconfirmed quotes can be found at Barton's WallBuilders Web site: http://www.wallbuilders.com/LIBissuesArticles .asp?id=126.

22. Barton, *Original Intent*, 32, 319–30; LaHaye, *Faith of Our Founding Fathers*, 123; Kennedy, *What if America*, 59–61.

23. Marshall and Manuel, *The Light and the Glory*, 344; LaHaye, *Faith of Our Founding Fathers*, 71; Lowman, *United States History*, 104, 128–29.

24. Barton, *Original Intent*, 13; LaHaye, *Faith of Our Founding Fathers*, 192; Kennedy, *What if America*, 44.

25. Barton, *Original Intent*, 24, 31 (italics added in Story quotation); see also 33, 35; DeMar, *America's Christian Heritage*, 36, 63.

26. Barton, *Original Intent*, 24, 25, 29, 31–32, 48, 202, 210; DeMar, *America's Christian Heritage*, 35, 64.

27. Barton, *Original Intent*, 279; cf. also 122, 280–81, 284; DeMar, *America's Christian Heritage*, 82.

28. Barton, *Original Intent*, 5, 316.

29. LaHaye, *Faith of Our Founding Fathers*, 1, 3, 4, 5, 6; DeMar, *America's Christian Heritage*, 81–83; Beliles and McDowell, *America's Providential History*, 5.

5. Were the British Colonies Christian Societies?

1. D. James Kennedy with Jerry Newcombe, *What if America Were a Christian Nation Again?* (Nashville: Nelson, 2003), 10; Vision Forum Jamestown Quadricentennial Web site, http://www.visionforumministries.org/events/jq/.

2. "The First Charter of Virginia; April 10, 1606," Yale Law School: The Avalon Project. http//Avalon.law.yale.edu/17th_century/va01.asp

3. Richard Hildreth, *The History of the United States of America: From the discovery of the continent to the organization of government under the federal Constitution, 1497–1789*, Vol. 1 (New York: Harper and Brothers, 1854), 96.

4. Lyon Gardiner Tyler, ed., *Narratives of Early Virginia, 1606–1625* (New York: Barnes & Noble, 1907, reprint 1957), 271–273.

5. William Waller Hening, ed., *Hening's Statutes at Large*, March 1623–4, vol. 1, 122 accessed at http//vagenweb.org/hening/ on September 9, 2010. 1:122–24.

6. Ibid., 144, 269, 277, 341–42, 532–33.

7. Ibid., 155–56 (punishments).

8. Ibid., 157.

9. Edward L. Bond, "Source of Knowledge, Source of Power: The Supernatural World of English Virginia, 1607–1624," *Virginia Magazine of History and Biography* 108, no. 2 (2000): 105–38.

10. Alexander Brown, *The Genesis of the United States*, 2 vols. (Boston, 1890), 1:506–7, quoted in T. H. Breen, "Looking Out for Number One: Conflicting Cultural Values in Early Seventeenth-Century Virginia," *South Atlantic Quarterly* 78 (1979): 345.
11. Breen, "Looking Out for Number One," 346–51.
12. Alan Taylor, *American Colonies: The Settling of North America* (New York: Penguin, 2001), 142; Breen, "Looking Out for Number One," 348.
13. Edmund Morgan, *American Slavery, American Freedom: The Ordeal of Colonial Virginia* (New York: Norton, 1975).
14. On the "Great Puritan Migration" see David Cressy, *Coming Over: Migration and Communication Between England and New England in the Seventeenth Century* (New York: Cambridge University Press, 1987); and Virginia DeJohn Anderson, *New England's Generation: The Great Migration and the Formation of Society and Culture in the Seventeenth Century* (New York: Cambridge University Press, 1992).
15. Edmund Morgan, *Visible Saints: The History of Puritan Idea* (Ithaca, NY: Cornell University Press, 1965).
16. David D. Hall, *Worlds of Wonder, Days of Judgment: Popular Religious Belief in Early New England* (Cambridge: Harvard University Press, 1990).
17. For a good biography of Williams see Edwin Gaustad, *Roger Williams* (New York: Oxford University Press, 2005).
18. For a fine biography of Hutchinson see Timothy D. Hall, *Anne Hutchinson: Puritan Prophet* (Saddle River, NJ: Prentice-Hall, 2009).
19. Cited in Paul S. Boyer et al., *The Enduring Vision: A History of the American People*, 6th ed. (Boston: Houghton-Mifflin, 2008), 68.
20. My thinking in this paragraph has been informed by the chapter "America's 'Christian' Origins: Puritan New England as a Case Study," in Mark A. Noll, Nathan O. Hatch, and George M. Marsden, *The Search for Christian America*, 2nd ed. (Colorado Springs: Helmers & Howard, 1989), 43–46.

6. Christianity and the Coming of the American Revolution

1. For a discussion of these developments see Timothy H. Breen, *The Marketplace of Revolution: How Consumer Politics Shaped American Independence* (New York: Oxford University Press, 2004).
2. My discussion of the rights of Englishmen comes from the English Bill of Rights (1689), accessed on March 5, 2010, at http://avalon.law.yale.edu/17th_century/england.asp; Gordon Wood, "This Land Is Your Land," *New York Review*, Feb. 3, 1983, cited in Mark A. Noll, Nathan O. Hatch, and George Marsden, *The Search for Christian America*, 2nd ed. (Colorado Springs: Helmers & Howard, 1989), 96.
3. Thomas K. Curry, *The First Freedoms: Church and State in America to the Passage of the First Amendment* (New York: Oxford University Press, 1986).
4. Quoted in Breen, *Marketplace of Revolution*, 91.
5. John M. Murrin, "A Roof Without Walls: The Dilemma of American National Identity," in *Beyond Confederation: Origins of the Constitution and American Identity*, ed. Richard Beeman, Stephen Botein, and Edward Carter II (Chapel Hill: University of North Carolina Press, 1987), 333–48.
6. Peter D. G. Thomas, "The Grenville Program, 1763–1765," in *The Blackwell Encyclopedia of the American Revolution*, ed. Jack P. Greene and J. R. Pole (Cambridge, MA: Blackwell, 1991), 107–12.

7. Virginia Resolves, May 29, 1765, http://www.constitution.org/bcp/vir_res1765.htm.

8. "The Declaration of Rights of the Stamp Act Congress," Oct. 19, 1765, accessed March 16, 2010, at http://www.constitution.org/bcp/dor_sac.htm.

9. For a good introduction to the violence in response to the Stamp Act see Gary B. Nash, *The Unknown American Revolution: The Unruly Birth of Democracy and the Struggle to Create America* (New York: Viking, 2005).

10. Stamp Act Congress, *Proceedings of the Congress at New York* (Annapolis: Jonas Green, 1766), 15.

11. John Dickinson, *Letters from a Farmer in Pennsylvania* (Philadelphia: David Hall and William Sellers, 1768). The four references to "God" can be found on pp. 7, 15, 38, 70.

12. Massachusetts Circular Letter, Feb. 11, 1768, http://www.historycentral.com/documents/MassCircular.html.

13. David L. Ammerman, "The Tea Crisis and Its Consequences Through 1775," in *Blackwell Encyclopedia of the American Revolution*, ed. Greene and Pole, 198–99.

14. The text of the Suffolk Resolves can be found at http://en.wikipedia.org/wiki/Suffolk_Resolves#Full_Text.

15. Declaration and Resolves of the First Continental Congress, Oct. 14, 1774, http://avalon.law.yale.edu/18th_century/resolves.asp.

16. "The Association Read and Signed," Oct. 20, 1774, http://colet.uchicago.edu/cgi-bin/amarch/getdoc.pl?/projects/artflb/databases/efts/AmArch/IMAGE/.1072.

17. Donald S. Lutz, "The Relative Influence of European Writers on Late Eighteenth-Century American Political Thought," *American Political Science Review* 78 (March 1984): 190.

7. The Revolutionary Pulpit

1. John Allen, *An Oration upon the Beauties of Liberty* (1773), in *Political Sermons of the American Founding Era, 1730–1805*, ed. Ellis Sandoz (Indianapolis: Liberty Fund, 1991), 315–18, 320–24.

2. Enoch Green, "Upon His Appointment as Chaplain of the New Jersey Militia," manuscript sermon, 1776, Firestone Library, Dept. of Rare Books and Special Collections, Princeton University, Princeton, NJ; Enoch Green, manuscript sermon, Titus 2:14, Presbyterian Historical Society, Philadelphia.

3. Abraham Keteltas, *God Arising and Pleading His People's Cause* (1777), in *Political Sermons*, ed. Sandoz, 584–99, 603.

4. Samuel Sherwood, *The Church's Flight into the Wilderness: An Address on the Times* (New York: S. Loudon, 1776), 36, 9, 10.

5. Ibid., 10–11.

6. Ibid., 18, 25, 49.

7. Mark A. Noll, Nathan O. Hatch, and George M. Marsden, *The Search for Christian America*, 2nd ed. (Colorado Springs: Helmers & Howard, 1989), 81.

8. Jonathan Boucher, *A View of the Causes and Consequences of the American Revolution; in Thirteen Discourses* (1797; repr., New York: Russell & Russell, 1967), 500.

9. David Jones, *Defensive War in a Just Cause Sinless* (Philadelphia: Henry Miller, 1775), 6.

10. John Carmichael, *A Self-Defensive War Lawful* (Philadelphia: John Dean, 1775), 8–9.

11. Jones, *Defensive War*, 8–10.

12. Carmichael, *Self-Defensive War Lawful*, 15–16, 17.

13. Jonathan Boucher, "Discourse X. ON the Character of Ahitophel," in *View of Causes*, 422–23.

14. Samuel Seabury, *St. Peter's Exhortation to Fear God and Honor the King* (New York: H. Gaine, 1777), 5–6.

15. Charles Inglis, *The Duty of Honouring the King, Explained and Recommended* (New York: Hugh Gaine, 1780), 10.

16. Seabury, *St. Peter's Exhortation*, 5–6, 12.

17. Inglis, *Duty of Honouring the King*, 11.

18. Jonathan Mayhew, *A Discourse Concerning Unlimited Submission and Non-Resistance to the Higher Powers* (Boston: D. Fowle and D. Gookin, 1750). For the Adams quote, see John Adams, *The Works of John Adams*, ed. Charles Francis Adams (Boston: Little, Brown, and Company, 1850–1856), 10 vols., 10:301, cited in C. H. Van Tyne, "The Influence of the Clergy and of Religious and Sectarian Forces on the American Revolution," *American Historical Review* 19 (October 1913): 50.

19. Mayhew, *Discourse Concerning Unlimited Submission*, 18, 21, 23, 24, 30, 44, 45. See Steven M. Dworetz, *The Unvarnished Doctrine: Locke, Liberalism, and the American Revolution* (Durham: Duke University Press, 1994), 160.

20. On the "liberal" interpretations of Romans 13 and 1 Peter 2:13–17 see Dworetz, *Unvarnished Doctrine*, 155–72.

21. Ibid., 155.

22. John Calvin, "Civil Government," *Institutes of the Christian Religion* 4.20.27, quoted in Gregg Frazer, "The Political Theology of the American Founding" (PhD diss., Claremont Graduate University, 2004), 359–360.

23. Frazer, "Political Theology," 359–61.

24. A search of "Augustine" or "Aquinas" in Charles Evans's Early American Imprint Collection reveals that these Christian thinkers were never employed in relation to war in any published political or religious pamphlet published between 1765 and 1783.

25. Noll et al., *Search for Christian America*, 95–97; Noll, "Was the American Revolutionary War Justified?" *Christianity Today* 43, no. 2 (1999): 70.

26. Carmichael, *Self-Defensive War Lawful*, 21–24.

27. John Wesley, "Some Observations on Liberty" (1776), in *Political Writings of John Wesley*, ed. Graham Maddox (Bristol: Thoemmes, 1998), 54–57, 73–74, 81–83.

28. Noll, "Was the Revolutionary War Justified?" 70.

29. Ibid., 81–85.

8. Nature's God: Is the Declaration of Independence a Christian Document?

1. Letter from John Adams to Abigail Adams, 16 September 1774 [electronic edition], *Adams Family Papers: An Electronic Archive*, Massachusetts Historical Society, http://www.masshist.org/digitaladams.

2. Letter from John Adams to Abigail Adams, 16 September 1774 [electronic edition], *Adams Family Papers: An Electronic Archive*, Massachusetts Historical Society, http://www.masshist.org/digitaladams.

3. Quoted in *Washington at Valley Forge Together with the Duché Correspondence* (Philadelphia: J. M. Butler, 1858), 49–50.

4. Derek Davis, *Religion and the Continental Congress, 1774–1789: Contributions to Original Intent* (New York: Oxford University Press, 2000), 26, 59.

5. *Journals of the Continental Congress*, May 8, 1778, accessed from American Memory Web site, Library of Congress, www.memory.loc.gov.

6. *Journals of the Continental Congress*, December 7, 1776, accessed from American Memory Web site, Library of Congress, www.memory.loc.gov; *Journals of the Continental Congress*, May 8, 1779, accessed from American Memory Web site, Library of Congress, www.memory.loc.gov; *Journals of the Continental Congress*, Oct. 30, 1778, accessed from American Memory Web site, Library of Congress, www.memory.loc.gov; *Journals of the Continental Congress*, March 15, 1782, accessed from American Memory Web site, Library of Congress, www.memory.loc.gov.

7. *Journals of the Continental Congress*, May 8, 1778, accessed from American Memory Web site, Library of Congress, www.memory.loc.gov; *Journals of the Continental Congress*, October 30,1778, accessed from American Memory Web site, Library of Congress, www.memory.loc.gov.

8. *Journals of the Continental Congress*, July 6, 1775, accessed from American Memory Web site, Library of Congress, www.memory.loc.gov.

9. *Journals of the Continental Congress*, June 12, 1775, accessed from American Memory Web site, Library of Congress, www.memory.loc.gov.

10. *Journals of the Continental Congress*, March 29, 1779, accessed from American Memory Web site, Library of Congress, www.memory.loc.gov; *Journals of the Continental Congress*, March 11, 1780, accessed from American Memory Web site, Library of Congress, www.memory.loc.gov.

11. *Journals of the Continental Congress*, March 16, 1776, accessed from American Memory Web site, Library of Congress, www.memory.loc.gov.

12. *Journals of the Continental Congress*, March 29, 1779, accessed from American Memory Web site, Library of Congress, www.memory.loc.gov.

13. *Journals of the Continental Congress*, March 16, 1776, accessed from American Memory Web site, Library of Congress, www.memory.loc.gov.

14. *Journals of the Continental Congress*, March 20, 1781, accessed from American Memory Web site, Library of Congress, www.memory.loc.gov.

15. *Journals of the Continental Congress*, June 12, 1775, accessed from American Memory Web site, Library of Congress, www.memory.loc.gov.

16. *Journals of the Continental Congress*, March 29, 1776, accessed from American Memory Web site, Library of Congress, www.memory.loc.gov.

17. *Journals of the Continental Congress*, March 19, 1782, accessed from American Memory Web site, Library of Congress, www.memory.loc.gov.

18. *Journals of the Continental Congress*, March 11, 1780, accessed from American Memory Web site, Library of Congress, www.memory.loc.gov.

19. *Journals of the Continental Congress*, October 26, 1781, accessed from American Memory Web site, Library of Congress, www.memory.loc.gov.

20. *Journals of the Continental Congress*, October 26, 1781, accessed from American Memory Web site, Library of Congress, www.memory.loc.gov.

21. Davis, *Religion and the Continental Congress*, 75–76, 80.

22. Ibid., 144–46; *Journals of the Continental Congress*, September 12, 1782, accessed from American Memory Web site, Library of Congress, www.memory.loc.gov.

23. Gary T. Amos, *Defending the Declaration: How the Bible and Christianity Influenced the Writing of the Declaration of Independence* (Brentwood: Wolgemuth & Hyatt, 1989), 22.

24. David Armitage, *The Declaration of Independence: A Global History* (Cambridge: Harvard University Press, 2007), 18, 63–65, 113; Pauline Maier, *American Scripture: Making the Declaration of Independence* (New York: Knopf, 1997), xvii, 167; Barry Alan Shain, *The Myth of American Individualism: The Protestant Origins of American Political Thought* (Princeton: Princeton University Press, 1994), 246–47.
25. Thomas Jefferson to Henry Lee, May 8, 1825, quoted in Shain, *Myth of American Individualism*, 247.
26. John Adams, *A Collection of State-Papers Relative to the Acknowledgement of the Sovereignty [sic] of the United States of America* (The Hague, 1782); and John Quincy Adams, *An Address Delivered at the Request of the Committee of Arrangements for Celebrating the Anniversary of Independence, at the City of Washington on the Fourth of July 1821* (Cambridge, 1821), quoted in Armitage, *Declaration of Independence*, 66–67.
27. Abraham Lincoln, "Speech at Springfield, Illinois, June 26, 1857," quoted in Armitage, *Declaration of Independence*, 26.
28. Armitage, *Declaration of Independence*, 63–64.
29. Maier, *American Scripture*, 189–206.
30. Davis, *Religion and the Continental Congress*, 102.

9. Religion in the Critical Period

1. For a discussion of religion and the Articles of Confederation see Derek Davis, *Religion and the Continental Congress, 1774–1789: Contributions to Original Intent* (New York: Oxford University Press, 2000), 157–63.
2. Virginia Declaration of Rights, June 12, 1776, accessed at Yale University Avalon Project, http://avalon.law.yale.edu/18th_century/virginia.asp.
3. Virginia Constitution, June 29, 1776, accessed at University of Chicago Press Web edition of *The Founders Constitution*, ed. Philip B. Kurland and Ralph Lerner, http://press-pubs.uchicago.edu/founders/documents/v1ch1s4.html.
4. Edwin Gaustad, *Sworn on the Altar of God: A Religious Biography of Thomas Jefferson* (Grand Rapids: Eerdmans, 1996), 51–52.
5. Patrick Henry, "A Bill for Establishing a Provision for Teachers of the Christian Religion," January, 1784, accessed at http://www.beliefnet.com/resourcelib/docs/122/A_Bill_Establishing_A_Provision_for_Teachers_of_the_Christia_1.html.
6. Ibid.
7. David Barton, *Original Intent: The Courts, the Constitution, & Religion*, 3rd ed. (Aledo, TX: WallBuilder, 2000), 24.
8. For a helpful summation of Madison's notes during this debate see Steven Waldman, *Founding Faith: Providence, Politics, and the Birth of Religious Freedom in America* (New York: Random House, 2008), 116–18.
9. James Madison, "Memorial and Remonstrance Against Religious Assessments," June 20, 1785, accessed at http://www.beliefnet.com/resourcelib/docs/13/Memorial_and_Remonstrance_against_Religious_Assessments_1p.html.
10. Waldman, *Founding Faith*, 121–22, 191.
11. Gaustad, *Sworn*, 63–67.
12. "A Bill for Establishing Religious Freedom in Virginia," 1786, in *The Sacred Rights of Conscience: Selected Readings on Religious Liberty and Church-State Relations in the American Founding*, ed. Daniel Dreisbach and Mark David Hall (Indianapolis: Liberty Fund, 2009), 250–51.

13. Massachusetts Constitution, January 1780, accessed at http://www.beliefnet.com/resourcelib/docs/33/Massachusetts_Constitution_of_1780_1.html. For a short overview of the religion clauses in the Constitution see John Witte Jr., "'A Most Mild and Equitable Establishment of Religion': John Adams and the Massachusetts Experiment," in *Religion and the New Republic: Faith in the Founding of America*, ed. James H. Hutson (Lanham, MD: Rowman & Littlefield, 2000), 1–40.

14. Massachusetts Constitution, January 1780, accessed at http://www.beliefnet.com/resourcelib/docs/33/Massachusetts_Constitution_of_1780_1.html; see Witte, "Most Mild," 2. The Congregational establishment in Massachusetts would be eliminated by constitutional amendment in 1833.

15. "Fundamental Orders of 1638." The Avalon Project. Yale Law School accessed at http://avalon.law.yale.edu/17th_century/order.asp

16. Philip Hamburger, *Separation of Church and State* (Cambridge: Harvard University Press, 2002), 144–45.

17. Edwin Gaustad, *Faith of Our Fathers: Religion and the New Nation* (San Francisco: Harper & Row, 1987), 173–74.

18. Ibid., 169–70, 167–68; *Laws of the State of New York Passed in the First Session of the Senate and Assembly of the Said State, Beginning the Tenth Day of September 1777 . . .* (Albany: Weed, Parsons, 1886), 1:13.

19. Gaustad, *Faith of Our Fathers*, 162, 164, 168–69, 170–72.

20. Ibid., 161, 162.

21. 1818 Constitution of the State of Connecticut, accessed at http://www.ct.gov/sots/cwp/view.asp?A=3188&Q=392280.

22. For an extensive discussion of this process see William McLoughlin, *New England Dissent: Baptists and the Separation of Church and State*, 2 vols. (Cambridge: Harvard University Press, 1971), 2:1205–62.

23. Gaustad, *Faith of Our Fathers*, 164–65, 172, 174, 172–73, 163; Vermont Constitution of 1793, accessed at http://www.vtcommons.org/files/VTcon93.pdf.

10. A "Godless Constitution"?

1. *The Liberator*, Feb. 3, 1843, cited in Walter M. Merrill, ed., *The Letters of William Lloyd Garrison*, vol. 3: *No Union with Slaveholders, 1841–1849* (Cambridge: Harvard University Press, 1973), 118.

2. William Lloyd Garrison, "On the Constitution and the Union," *The Liberator*, Dec. 29, 1832, accessed at http://fair-use.org/the-liberator/1832/12/29/on-the-constitution-and-the-union; William Lloyd Garrison to Samuel J. May, July 17, 1845, in *No Union with Slaveholders*, ed. Merrill, 303.

3. Gordon Wood, *The Creation of the American Republic, 1776–1787* (Chapel Hill: University of North Carolina Press, 1969), 467.

4. For the "secular" view see Isaac Kramnick and R. Laurence Moore, *The Godless Constitution: The Case Against Religious Correctness* (New York: Norton, 1996). For the "federalist" position see the works of Daniel Dreisbach, especially "A Godless Constitution? A Response to Kramnick and Moore," 1997, accessed at http://www.wallbuilders.com/LIBissuesArticles.asp?id=84.

5. For the debates in Congress I have consulted: *The Records of the Federal Convention of 1787*, ed. Max Farrand (New Haven: Yale University Press, 1911), accessed at the Library of Congress American Memory Project, http://memory.loc.gov/ammem/

amlaw/lwfr.html; and Edward J. Larson and Michael P. Winship, eds., *The Constitutional Convention: A Narrative History from the Notes of James Madison* (New York: Modern Library, 2005).

6. *Records*, June 28, 1787, ed. Farrand, accessed at the Library of Congress American Memory Project, http://memory.loc.gov/ammem/amlaw/lwfr.html, 1:450–52.

7. *Federalist Papers* #37 (1788), cited in *The Sacred Right of Conscience: Selected Readers on Religious Liberty and Church-State Relations in the American Founding*, ed. Daniel L. Dreisbach and Mark David Hall (Indianapolis: Liberty Fund, 2009), 351.

8. *Records*, June 28, 1787, ed. Farrand, 1:452, accessed at the Library of Congress American Memory Project, http://memory.loc.gov/ammem/amlaw/lwfr.html.

9. Akhil Reed Amar, *America's Constitution: A Biography* (New York: Random House, 2005), 166.

10. Ibid., 91.

11. Ibid., 89.

12. Mark A. Noll, George M. Marsden, and Nathan O. Hatch, *The Search for Christian America*, expanded ed. (Colorado Springs: Helmers & Howard, 1989), 100–101.

13. John Murrin, "A Roof Without Walls: The Dilemma of American National Identity," in *Beyond Confederation: Origins of the Constitution and American Identity*, ed. Richard Beeman, Stephen Botein, and Edward C. Carter II (Chapel Hill: University of North Carolina Press, 1987), 333–48.

14. *Federalist* #2.

15. *Federalist* #39, 60.

16. John Murrin, "Religion and Politics in America from the First Settlements to the Civil War," in *Religion and Politics in America: From the Colonial Period to the Present*, ed. Mark A. Noll (New York: Oxford University Press, 1990), 31. An interesting discussion of the issues is found in John Patrick Diggins, *The Lost Soul of American Politics: Virtue, Self-Interest, and the Foundations of Liberalism* (New York: Harper-Collins, 1984), 74–85. On Witherspoon's influence on Madison see Jeffry H. Morrison, *John Witherspoon and the Founding of the American Republic* (Notre Dame: University of Notre Dame Press, 2005), 39–43.

17. Isaac Kramnick and R. Laurence Moore, *The Godless Constitution: The Case Against Religious Correctness* (New York: Norton, 1996), 38–40.

18. Luther Martin, "The Genuine Information Delivered the Legislature of the State of Maryland Relative to the Proceedings of the General Convention Lately Held at Philadelphia," in *The Complete Anti-Federalist*, vol. 2: *Objections of Non-Signers of the Constitution, and Major Series of Essays at the Outset*, ed. Herbert J. Storing (Chicago: University of Chicago Press, 1981), 75.

19. Aristocrotis, "The Government of Nature Delineated or an Exact Picture of the New Federal Constitution," 1788, in *Complete Anti-Federalist*, vol. 3: *Pennsylvania*, ed. Storing, 205–6.

20. *Complete Anti-Federalist*, vol. 4: *Massachusetts and New England*, ed. Storing, 4:193, 232, 242.

21. Cited in Kramnick and Moore, *The Godless Constitution*, 33.

22. Charles Turner, "Speech in the Massachusetts Ratifying Convention," Feb. 5, 1788, in *Complete Anti-Federalists*, vol. 4, ed. Storing, 219–21.

23. "Letters by David," March 7, 1788, in *Complete Anti-Federalist*, vol. 4, ed. Storing, 246–48.

24. Daniel Dreisbach, *Thomas Jefferson and the Wall of Separation between Church and State* (New York: New York University Press, 2002), 60.

25. Edwin Gaustad, *Faith of Our Founders: Religion and the New Nation* (New York: Harper & Row, 1987), 161–74.

26. Jefferson to Samuel Miller, Jan. 23, 1808, accessed at "The Thomas Jefferson Papers," Library of Congress, http://hdl.loc.gov/loc.mss/mtj.mtj.mtjbib018142.

27. Jefferson, second inaugural address, March 4, 1805, accessed at Yale Law School Avalon Project, http://avalon.law.yale.edu/19th_century/jefinau2.asp.

28. "Letters of Centinel," Dec. 22, 1787, in *Complete Anti-Federalist*, vol. 2, ed. Storing, 152; "Essays of an Old Whig," n.d., in *Complete Anti-Federalist*, vol. 3, ed. Storing, 35–36; "Essays by Philadelphiensis, II," November 1787–April 1788, in *Complete Anti-Federalist*, vol. 3, ed. Storing, 107–8; "Address by Sydney," June 13, 14, 1788, in *Complete Anti-Federalist*, vol. 6: *New York, and Conclusion*, ed. Storing, 119.

29. Jefferson to Danbury Baptist Association, Jan. 1, 1802 (final version), cited in Dreisbach, *Thomas Jefferson*, 148.

30. For an introduction to this issue see James H. Hutson, "Thomas Jefferson's Letter to the Danbury Baptists: A Controversy Rejoined," *William and Mary Quarterly*, 3rd series, 61 (October 1999): 775–90.

31. Dreisbach, *Thomas Jefferson*, 33.

32. Address of the Danbury Baptist Association to Jefferson, October 1801, cited in Dreisbach, *Thomas Jefferson*, 142–43.

33. Hutson, "Thomas Jefferson's Letter to the Danbury Baptists," 780–81.

34. Ibid., 783–84.

35. Ibid., 788–90.

36. Dreisbach, *Thomas Jefferson*, 55–70, 95–106.

11. Did George Washington Pray at Valley Forge?

1. George Washington to John Bannister, April 21, 1778, quoted in Joseph J. Ellis, *His Excellency: George Washington* (New York: Vintage, 2005), 112.

2. Mason Locke Weems, *The Life of Washington: A New Edition with Primary Documents*, ed. Peter S. Onuf (Armonk, NY: M. E. Sharpe, 1996), 146–47.

3. Francois Furstenberg, *In The Name of the Father: Washington's Legacy, Slavery, and the Making of a Nation* (New York: Penguin, 2006), 123; Gary Scott Smith, *Faith and the Presidency: From George Washington to George W. Bush* (New York: Oxford University Press, 2006), 24.

4. Frank E. Grizzard Jr., *The Ways of Providence: Religion & George Washington* (Buena Vista, VA: Mariner, 2005).

5. Timothy Dwight, "Discourse Delivered at New Haven, Feb. 22, 1800," quoted in Gerald F. Kahler, *The Long Farewell: Americans Mourn the Death of George Washington* (Charlottesville: University of Virginia Press, 2008), 63; Stanley Griswold, "A Funeral Eulogium, Pronounced at New Milford, on the Twenty-second of February, 1800," quoted in Kahler, *Long Farewell*, 63.

6. Thomas Jefferson Diary, Feb. 1, 1800, in *The Complete Thomas Jefferson*, ed. Saul K. Padover (New York: Duell, Sloan & Pierce, 1973), 1279.

7. Tim F. LaHaye, *The Faith of Our Founding Fathers* (Green Forest, AR: Master Books, 1990), 110; Peter Lillback, *Sacred Fire* (Bryn Mawr, PA: Providence Forum, 2006), 26–27; Ellis, *His Excellency*, 45; Edwin S. Gaustad, *Faith of Our Founders: Religion and the*

New Nation (New York: Harper & Row, 1987), 77; Brooke Allen, *Moral Minority: Our Skeptical Founding Fathers* (New York: Ivan Dee, 2006), 28.

8. Lillback, *Sacred Fire*, 27.

9. Smith, *Faith and the Presidency*, 22.

10. Lillback, *Sacred Fire*, 579; Gregg Frazer, "The Political Theology of the American Founding" (PhD diss., Claremont University Graduate School, 2004), 168.

11. Michael and Jana Novak, *Washington's God: Religion, Liberty, and the Father of Our Country* (New York: Basic Books, 2006), 178–79; Smith, *Faith and the Presidency*, 30.

12. Novak and Novak, *Washington's God*, 178–79; also 78–79.

13. George Washington to John Augustine Washington, July 18, 1755, quoted in Novak and Novak, *Washington's God*, 56; Samuel Davies, *Religion and Patriotism the Constituents of a Good Soldier* (Philadelphia, 1755), 8–9.

14. Washington to John Augustine Washington, Oct. 18, 1777, quoted in Novak and Novak, *Washington's God*, 185–86.

15. General Orders, Oct. 18, 1777, quoted in Steven Waldman, *Founding Faith: How Our Founding Fathers Forged a Radical New Approach to Religious Liberty* (New York: Random House, 2008), 69.

16. Washington's first inaugural address, April 30, 1789, accessed Jan. 25, 2010, at http://www.loc.gov/rr/program/bib/ourdocs/inaugural.html.

17. Mary V. Thompson, *"In the Hands of a Good Providence": Religion in the Life of George Washington* (Charlottesville: University of Virginia Press, 2008), 16–29.

18. Ibid., 53, 57; David L. Holmes, *The Faiths of the Founding Fathers* (New York: Oxford University Press, 2006), 61.

19. Paul K. Longmore, *The Invention of George Washington* (Berkeley: University of California Press, 1988), 115, 118, 130; Thompson, *In the Hands*, 59.

20. Thompson, *In the Hands*, 41, 80.

21. Allen, *Moral Minority*, 28–29.

22. Longmore, *Invention of George Washington*, 87.

23. On Anglican piety see Edward L. Bond, *Damned Souls in a Tobacco Colony* (Macon, GA: Mercer University Press, 2001); John K. Nelson, *A Blessed Company: Parishes, Parsons, and Parishioners in Anglican Virginia, 1690–1776* (Chapel Hill: University of North Carolina Press, 2001).

24. Cited in Paul Boller, *George Washington and Religion* (Dallas: Southern Methodist University Press, 1953), 94.

25. Letter from Washington to the General Assembly of the Presbyterian Church, New York, 1789, cited in Grizzard, *Ways of Providence*, 33; cf. Gaustad, *Faith of Our Founders*, 76–77.

26. Washington to Delaware chiefs, May 12, 1779, in *George Washington: A Collection*, ed. W. B. Allen (Indianapolis: Liberty Fund, 1988), 45.

27. Washington, "Circular to the States," June 8, 1783, accessed Jan. 25, 2010, at http://www.loc.gov/teachers/classroommaterials/presentationsandactivities/presentations/timeline/amrev/peace/circular.html.

28. Jeffry H. Morrison, *The Political Philosophy of George Washington* (Baltimore: Johns Hopkins University Press, 2009), 144; Lillback, *Sacred Fire*, 305–14, 317–18, 321–22, 325–28.

29. Reverend Bird Wilson, *Memoir of the Life of the Right Reverend William White, D.D.* (Philadelphia: J. Kay Jr. and Brother, 1839), 193; Marshall, *Life of Washington*, quoted in Thompson, *In the Hands*, 3; Samuel Langdon to Washington, July 8, 1789, quoted in Smith, *Faith and the Presidency*, 33.

30. Ellis, *His Excellency*, 269; *The Life of Samuel Miller*, quoted in Boller, *George Washington and Religion*, 89.

31. George Washington to the Marquis de Lafayette, Aug. 15, 1787, quoted in Frazer, "Political Theology," 172.

32. Thompson, *In the Hands*, 50–51, 93.

33. Letter from Nelly Custis Lewis to Jared Sparks, Feb. 26, 1833, cited in Grizzard, *Ways of Providence*, 48–49; Thompson, *In the Hands*, 93, 94.

34. Washington Diary, June 1, 1774, cited in Longmore, *Invention of George Washington*, 116.

35. Thompson, *In the Hands*, 33–34.

36. Smith, *Faith and the Presidency*, 39.

37. Thompson, *In the Hands*, 77–78; Bird Wilson, *Memoir of the Life of the Right Reverend William White, D.D. Bishop of The Protestant Episcopal Church in the State of Pennsylvania* (Philadelphia: J. Kay Jr. and Brother, 1839), 197.

38. Quoted in William B. Sprague, *Annals of the American Pulpit* (New York, 1859), 5:394, cited in Boller, *George Washington and Religion*, 33.

39. Thompson, *In the Hands*, 75–77; Holmes, *Faiths of the Founding Fathers*, 63.

40. Thompson, *In the Hands*, 80–81.

41. Holmes, *Faiths of the Founding Fathers*, 66.

42. Thompson, *In the Hands*, 42.

43. George Washington, Farewell Address, 1796, accessed Jan. 25, 2010, at Yale Law School Avalon Project: http://avalon.law.yale.edu/18th_century/washing.asp.

44. Quoted in Novak and Novak, *Washington's God*, 89, 90.

45. Washington to the General Assembly of the Presbyterian Church, May 1789, quoted in Grizzard, *Ways of Providence*, 33–34.

46. Washington to Roman Catholics in America United States of America, March 1790, quoted in Grizzard, *Ways of Providence*, 37.

47. Washington to the Philadelphia Protestant Clergy, March 3, 1797, quoted in Grizzard, *Ways of Providence*, 46.

48. Washington to the Hebrew Congregation in Newport, Rhode Island, Aug. 18, 1790, quoted in Grizzard, *Ways of Providence*, 42. Washington is referring to Micah 4:4.

49. Washington to The New Church in Baltimore, Maryland, Jan. 27, 1793, quoted in Grizzard, *Ways of Providence*, 44.

50. Washington to the United Baptist Churches of Virginia, New York, May 1789, quoted in Grizzard, *Ways of Providence*, 32.

51. Boller, *George Washington and Religion*, 126–27.

52. Waldman, *Founding Faith*, 65.

53. For a brief discussion see Smith, *Faith and the Presidency*, 49.

12. John Adams: Devout Unitarian

1. John Adams to Benjamin Rush, Aug. 28, 1811, in *The Spur of Fame: Dialogues of John Adams and Benjamin Rush, 1805–1813*, ed. John A. Schutz and Douglass Adair (Indianapolis: Liberty Fund, 1966), 209.

2. John Adams Diary, Feb. 22, 1756, in John Adams Diary 1, 18 November 1755–29 August 1756 [electronic edition], *Adams Family Papers: An Electronic Archive*, Massachusetts Historical Society. http://www.masshist.org/digitaladams/.

3. John Adams to Abigail Adams, 1 July 1774 [electronic edition], *Adams Family Papers: An Electronic Archive*, Massachusetts Historical Society. http://www.masshist.org/

digitaladams/; John Adams autobiography, part 1, "John Adams," through 1776, sheet 16 of 53 [electronic edition], ibid.; John Adams to Abigail Adams, 8 May 1775, ibid.; "Father": ibid., 15 April 1776; John Adams autobiography, part 1, "John Adams," through 1776, sheet 16 of 53, ibid.

4. Adams to Abigail Adams, 2 June 1777, ibid.; ibid., 3 June 1778, 8 September 1777; ibid., 13 April 1777; John Adams to John Quincy Adams, 16 June 1816, Adams Papers (microfilm), reel 432, Library of Congress, cited in *The Founders on Religion*, ed. James H. Hutson (Princeton: Princeton University Press, 2005), 49; John Adams to Thomas Jefferson, April 19, 1817, in *The Adams-Jefferson Letters*, ed. Lester J. Cappon (1959; repr., Chapel Hill: University of North Carolina Press, 1987), 509; John Adams to Caroline de Windt, Jan. 24, 1820, Adams Papers (microfilm), reel 124, Library of Congress, cited in *Founders on Religion*, ed. Hutson, 49.

5. John Adams to Abigail Adams, 28 January 1799, in *Adams Family Papers: Electronic Archive*.

6. John Adams diary, July 26, 1796, in John Adams diary 46, various loose folded sheets, 6 August 1787–10 September 1796 (with gaps), 2 July–21 August, in *Adams Family Papers: Electronic Archive*.

7. John Adams to Abigail Adams, 27 October 1799, in *Adams Family Papers: Electronic Archive*.

8. Adams to Benjamin Rush, Feb. 1, 1810, in *Spur of Fame*, ed. Schutz and Adair, 176.

9. Adams to Thomas Jefferson, Nov. 4, 1816, in *Adams-Jefferson Letters*, ed. Cappon, 494.

10. Adams to Jefferson, July 16, 1813, in *Adams-Jefferson Letters*, ed. Cappon, 359–60; John Adams to John Quincy Adams, March 28, 1816, Adams Papers (microfilm), reel 430, Library of Congress, cited in *Founders on Religion*, ed. Hutson, 121; Adams Diary, Feb. 13, 1756, in John Adams diary 1, 18 November 1755–29 August 1756, in *Adams Family Papers: Electronic Archive*.

11. Edwin Gaustad, *Faith of Our Fathers: Religion and the New Nation* (San Francisco: Harper & Row, 1987), 90.

12. See Daniel Walker Howe, *The Unitarian Conscience: Harvard Moral Philosophy, 1805–1861* (Cambridge: Harvard University Press, 1970).

13. Adams to Jedidiah Morse, May 15, 1815, in Adams Papers (microfilm), reel 122, Library of Congress, cited in *Founders on Religion*, ed. Hutson, 220; March 28, 1816, in *Founders on Religion*, ed. Hutson, 220–21.

14. Adams Autobiography, November 30, 1804, in John Adams autobiography, part I, "John Adams," through 1776 sheet 3 of 53, 1751–1755 [electronic version], *Adams Family Papers: Electronic Archive*.

15. John Adams, Diary, Feb. 18, 1756, in John Adams Diary 1, 18 November 1755–29 August 1756, *Adams Family Papers: Electronic Archive*.

16. Adams to Jefferson, May 18, 1817, in *Adams-Jefferson Letters*, ed. Cappon, 2:515.

17. John Adams, *Governor Winthrop to Governor Bradford*, Feb. 9 and 16, 1767, no. II, in *The Revolutionary Writings of John Adams*, ed. C. Bradley Thompson (Indianapolis: Liberty Fund, 2000), 62;

18. John Adams to Louisa Catherine Adams, Jan. 3, 1818, Adams Papers (microfilm), reel 442, Library of Congress, cited in *Founders on Religion*, ed. Hutson, 79

19. John Adams to John Quincy Adams, May 10, 1816, Adams Papers (microfilm), reel 431, Library of Congress, cited in *Founders on Religion*, ed. Hutson, 189.

20. John Adams to Abigail Adams, Oct. 9, 1774, *Adams Family Papers: Electronic Archive*.

21. Adams to Jefferson, May 16, 1816, in *Adams-Jefferson Letters*, ed. Cappon, 474; John Adams to Louisa Catherine Adams, May 17, 1821, Adams Papers (microfilm), reel 451, Library of Congress, cited in *Founders on Religion*, ed. Hutson, 41; Adams, *A Dissertation on the Canon and Feudal Law*, 1765, in *Revolutionary Writings of John Adams*, ed. Thompson, 22–24.

22. Adams, *Dissertation on the Canon*, in *Revolutionary Writings of John Adams*, ed. Thompson, 22–24, 33.

23. Adams to Francis van der Kemp, Oct. 2, 1818, Adams Papers (microfilm), reel 123, Library of Congress, cited in *Founders on Religion*, ed. Hutson, 1344; Adams to van der Kemp, June 5, 1812, cited in *Founders on Religion*, ed. Hutson, 158.

24. John Adams to Abigail Adams, Oct. 27, 1799, *Adams Family Papers: Electronic Archive*; John Adams to John Quincy Adams, June 16, 1816, Adams Papers (microfilm), reel 432, Library of Congress, cited in *Founders on Religion*, ed. Hutson, 49; Adams to Caroline de Windt, Jan. 24, 1820, Adams Papers (microfilm), reel 124, Library of Congress, cited in *Founders on Religion*, ed. Hutson, 49; John Adams to George Washington Adams, Feb. 10, 1822, Adams Papers (microfilm), reel 454, Library of Congress, cited in *Founders on Religion*, ed. Hutson, 49; John Adams to John Quincy Adams, March 11, 1813, Adams Papers (microfilm), reel 415, Library of Congress, cited in *Founders on Religion*, ed. Hutson, 73.

25. Adams to Samuel Miller, July 8, 1820, Adams Papers (microfilm), reel 450, Library of Congress, cited in *Founders on Religion*, ed. Hutson, 38; Adams to Francis van der Kemp, March 9, 1806, reel 118, Library of Congress, cited in *Founders on Religion*, ed. Hutson, 200; Adams to Jefferson, April 19, 1817, in *Adams-Jefferson Letters*, ed. Cappon, 509; John Adams to John Quincy Adams, March 28, 1816, Adams Papers (microfilm), reel 430, cited in *Founders on Religion*, ed. Hutson, 220–21.

26. John Adams to Abigail Adams, Sept. 4, 1776, *Adams Family Papers: Electronic Archive*; John Adams to Abigail Adams, May 8, 1775, *Adams Family Papers: Electronic Archive*; John Adams to Abigail Adams, July 3, 1776, *Adams Family Papers: Electronic Archive*.

27. John Adams Diary 10, 24 January–21 February 1765, August 1765, *Adams Family Papers: Electronic Archive*; John Adams to Abigail Adams, July 3, 1776, *Adams Family Papers: Electronic Archive*.

28. John Adams to Abigail Adams, July 5–6, 1774, in *Adams Family Papers: Electronic Archive*; John Adams to Abigail Adams, Oct. 8, 1776, *Adams Family Papers: Electronic Archive*.

29. John Adams autobiography, June 2, 1778, in John Adams Autobiography, part 2, "Travels and Negotiations," 1777–1778, sheet 27 of 37, 30 May–3 June 1778, *Adams Family Papers: Electronic Archive*.

30. John Adams to Abigail Adams, April 15, 1776, *Adams Family Papers: Electronic Archive*.

31. Adams, marginal note in Condorcet's *Outlines of an Historical View of the Progress of the Human Mind*, cited in *Founders on Religion*, ed. Hutson, 146; Adams to the Officers of the First Brigade of the 3rd Division of the Massachusetts Militia, Oct. 11, 1798, Adams Papers (microfilm), reel 119, Library of Congress, cited in *Founders on Religion*, ed. Hutson, 76; Benjamin Rush to Adams, Aug. 20, 1811, cited in *Spur of Fame*, ed. Schutz and Adair, 205–6; Adams to Rush, Aug. 28, 1811, cited in *Spur of Fame*, ed. Schutz and Adair, 208, 209.

32. John Adams, Proclamation of Day of Fasting, Humiliation, and Prayer, March 23, 1798, accessed Sept. 3, 2009, from the Web site of the University of Virginia's Miller Center for Public Affairs, http://millercenter.org/scripps/archive/speeches/detail/3942.

Though Adams promulgated the speech, it was written by Presbyterian minister Ashbel Green, who was serving as the chaplain of the U.S. House of Representatives. Thanks to Jonathan Den Hartog for bringing this to my attention.
33. Adams to Rush, Aug. 28, 1811, cited in *Spur of Fame*, ed. Schutz and Adair, 208, 209; Adams to Rush, June 12, 1812, cited in *Spur of Fame*, ed. Schutz and Adair, 244; Rush to Adams, June 27, 1812, cited in *Spur of Fame*, ed. Schutz and Adair, 247.

13. Thomas Jefferson: Follower of Jesus

1. Edwin Gaustad, *Sworn on the Altar of God: A Religious Biography of Thomas Jefferson* (Grand Rapids: Eerdmans, 1996), xiii.
2. Paul Conkin, "The Religious Pilgrimage of Thomas Jefferson," in *Jeffersonian Legacies*, ed. Peter S. Onuf (Charlottesville: University Press of Virginia, 1993), 27; Gaustad, *Sworn*, 131.
3. Thomas Jefferson, *Notes on the State of Virginia, 1781*, ed. William Peden (Chapel Hill: University of North Carolina Press, 1955), 159–60, cited in *The Founders on Religion: A Book of Quotations*, ed. James H. Hutson (Princeton: Princeton University Press, 2005), 187; Jefferson to Peter Carr, Aug. 10, 1787, in *The Papers of Thomas Jefferson*, ed. Julian P. Boyd et al., 36 vols. (Princeton: Princeton University Press, 1950–2009), 12:15–17, cited in *Founders on Religion*, ed. Hutson, 187; Jefferson to William Carver, Dec. 4, 1823, Jefferson Papers, Library of Congress, cited in *Founders on Religion*, ed. Hutson, 188.
4. Jefferson to John Adams, Aug. 22, 1813, in *The Adams-Jefferson Letters*, ed. Lester J. Cappon (1959; repr., Chapel Hill: University of North Carolina Press, 1987), 367–68; Jefferson to Benjamin Waterhouse, June 26, 1822, in *Jefferson's Extracts from the Gospels*, ed. Dickinson W. Adams (Princeton: Princeton University Press, 1983), 406, cited in *Founders on Religion*, ed. Hutson, 221.
5. On Providence see Jefferson's reference to the doctrine in Declaration of Independence ("on the protection of divine Providence") and his first inaugural address, March 4, 1801 ("acknowledging and adoring an overruling Providence"). Also Jefferson to David Barrow, May 1, 1815, Jefferson Papers, Library of Congress, cited in *Founders on Religion*, ed. Hutson, 180.
6. Jefferson to John Adams, April 11, 1823, in *Adams-Jefferson Letters*, ed. Cappon, 592; Gaustad, *Sworn*, 36–38; Steven Waldman, *Founding Faith: Providence, Politics, and the Birth of Religious Freedom in America* (New York: Random House, 2008), 83–84.
7. Conkin, "Religious Pilgrimage," 34.
8. Jefferson, "Syllabus of an Estimate of the Merit of the Doctrines of Jesus, Compared with Those of Others," April 23, 1803, in *Jefferson's Extracts*, ed. Adams, 332–34, cited in *Founders on Religion*, ed. Hutson, 123–25; Jefferson to Benjamin Rush, April 21, 1803, in *Jefferson's Extracts*, ed. Adams, 331, cited in *Founders on Religion*, ed. Hutson, 123.
9. Jefferson to Charles Thomson, Jan. 9, 1816, in *Jefferson's Extracts*, ed. Adams, 365, cited in *Founders on Religion*, ed. Hutson, 58; Jefferson to Salma Hale, July 26, 1818, in *Jefferson's Extracts*, ed. Adams, 385, cited in *Founders on Religion*, ed. Hutson, 58; Jefferson, "Syllabus of an Estimate of the Merit of the Doctrines of Jesus, Compared with Those of Others," April 23, 1803, in *Jefferson's Extracts*, ed. Adams, 332–34, cited in *Founders on Religion*, ed. Hutson, 123–25.
10. Jefferson to Benjamin Waterhouse, June 26, 1822, in *Jefferson's Extracts*, ed. Adams, 405, cited in *Founders on Religion*, ed. Hutson, 58; Jefferson to Waterhouse, Oct. 15,

1822, Jefferson Papers, Library of Congress, cited in *Founders on Religion*, ed. Hutson, 58–59.

11. Jefferson to Peter Carr, Aug. 10, 1787, in *Papers of Thomas Jefferson*, ed. Boyd, 12:15–16, cited in *Founders on Religion*, ed. Hutson, 29; Jefferson to Alexander Smyth, Jan. 17, 1825, in *Jeffersonian Extracts*, ed. Adams, 415–16, cited in *Founders on Religion*, ed. Hutson, 175.

12. Jefferson, "Syllabus of an Estimate of the Merit of the Doctrines of Jesus, Compared with Those of Others," April 23, 1803, in *Jefferson's Extracts*, ed. Adams, 332–34, cited in *Founders on Religion*, ed. Hutson, 123–25.

13. Jefferson to William Short, April 13, 1820, in *Jefferson's Extracts*, ed. Adams, 392, cited in *Founders on Religion*, ed. Hutson, 157–58.

14. Jefferson to John Adams, Oct. 12, 1813, in *Adams-Jefferson Letters*, ed. Cappon, 383–84; Gaustad, *Sworn*, 119.

15. For the text and a thorough analysis of the Jefferson Bible, see Adams, ed., *Jefferson's Extracts*. Also Gaustad, *Sworn*, 126.

16. See, for example, Jefferson to Benjamin Waterhouse, Oct. 15, 1822, Jefferson Papers, Library of Congress, cited in *Founders on Religion*, ed. Hutson, 58–59. Also Gaustad, *Sworn*, 145.

17. Jefferson to Thomas Baldwin, Jan. 19, 1810, in *Jefferson's Extracts*, ed. Adams, 345; Jefferson to Horatio Spofford, March 17, 1814, Jefferson Papers, Library of Congress, cited in *Founders on Religion*, ed. Hutson, 68; Jefferson to Ezra Stiles, June 25, 1819, in *Jefferson's Extracts*, ed. Adams, 387.

18. The best treatment on these matters remains Thomas E. Buckley, *Church and State in Revolutionary Virginia, 1776–1787* (Charlottesville: University of Virginia Press, 1977).

19. Jefferson, "A Bill for Establishing Religious Freedom," 1777, in *Papers of Thomas Jefferson*, ed. Boyd, 2:545–46.

20. Ibid.

21. Ibid.

22. Jefferson to John Adams, May 5, 1817, in *Adams-Jefferson Letters*, ed. Cappon, 512.

23. Jefferson to William Short, April 13, 1820, in *Jefferson's Extracts*, ed. Adams, 393; Jefferson to Benjamin Rush, Sept. 23, 1800, in *Jefferson's Extracts*, ed. Adams, 320.

24. Mark Noll, *One Nation Under God: Christian Faith and Political Action in America* (San Francisco: Harper & Row, 1988), 83–88.

25. Jefferson, *Notes on the State of Virginia* (1781), ed. William Peden (1955 repr., Chapel Hill: University of North Carolina Press, 1982), 1664.

26. Jefferson, *Notes on the State of Virginia* (1781), 163.

27. For a helpful overview of Jefferson's attempt so end slavery and the slave trade see Paul Finkelman, "Jefferson and Slavery: 'Treason Against the Hope of the World,'" in *Jeffersonian Legacies*, ed. Onuf, 181–224.

28. David Brion Davis, quoted in Finkelman, "Jefferson and Slavery," 182.

29. Finkelman, "Jefferson and Slavery," 183.

30. Ibid., 202; Roger G. Kennedy, *Mr. Jefferson's Lost Cause: Land, Farmers, Slavery, and the Louisiana Purchase* (New York: Oxford University Press, 2003).

31. Jefferson, *Notes*, ed. Peden, 143.

32. Ibid., 138–43.

33. Annette Gordon-Reed, *Thomas Jefferson and Sally Hemings: An American Controversy* (Charlottesville: University Press of Virginia, 1997).

14. Benjamin Franklin: Ambitious Moralist

1. Franklin to Ezra Stiles, March 9, 1790, accessed at http://www.beliefnet.com/resourcelib/docs/44/Letter_from_Benjamin_Franklin_to_Ezra_Stiles_1.html
2. For a good discussion of the ways in which Franklin continued to be subtly influenced by Calvinism, see Kerry Walters, *Benjamin Franklin and His Gods* (Urbana: University of Illinois Press, 1999).
3. Ibid., 32.
4. Ibid., 39.
5. Franklin, "On the Providence of God in the Government of the World," 1732, in *The Papers of Benjamin Franklin*, ed. Leonard W. Labaree, 37 vols. (New Haven: Yale University Press, 1959–2003), 1:265–66, cited in *The Founders on Religion*, ed. James H. Hutson (Princeton: Princeton University Press, 2005), 107–8.
6. Franklin to unknown recipient, Dec. 14, 1757, in *Papers*, ed. Labaree, 7:294, cited in *Founders on Religion*, ed. Hutson, 178.
7. Franklin, *Autobiography*, cited in *Founders on Religion*, ed. Hutson, 178.
8. Franklin to William Stahan, Aug. 19, 1784, in *Writings*, ed. Smyth, 9:262, cited in *Founders on Religion*, ed. Hutson, 178–79.
9. Franklin, "A Comparison of the Conduct of Ancient Jews and Anti-Federalists in the United States of America," 1788, cited in *Founders on Religion*, ed. Hutson, 76–77; Walters, *Benjamin Franklin and His Gods*, 107–8.
10. Franklin, *Autobiography*, 166; cf. Franklin, "New Version of the Lord's Prayer," in *Papers*, ed. Labaree, 15:301–3, cited in *Founders on Religion*, ed. Huston, 166–69.
11. See chapter 10.
12. Franklin to George Whitefield, June 9, 1764, in *Papers*, ed. Labaree, 11:231–32, cited in *Founders on Religion*, ed. Hutson, 7. On the relationship between Franklin and Whitefield see Harry S. Stout, *The Divine Dramatist: George Whitefield and the Rise of Modern Evangelicalism* (Grand Rapids: Eerdmans, 1991), 229.
13. Franklin to Ezra Stiles, March 9, 1790, Franklin Papers, Library of Congress, cited in *Founders on Religion*, ed. Huston, 8; Franklin, *The Autobiography of Benjamin Franklin*, ed. Leonard W. Labaree (New Haven: Yale University Press, 1964), 153.
14. Franklin, *Autobiography*, 82.
15. Franklin, "Proposals Relating to the Education of Youth in Pennsylvania," 1749, in *Papers*, ed. Labaree, 3:413, cited in *Founders on Religion*, ed. Hutson, 57; Franklin to Josiah and Abiah Franklin, April 13, 1738, in *Papers*, ed. Labaree, 2:204, cited in *Founders on Religion*, ed. Hutson, 79–80; Franklin, "Dialogue Between Two Presbyterians," April 10, 1735, in *Papers*, ed. Labaree, 2:33.
16. For an overview of the Hemphill affair see Melvin H. Buxbaum, *Benjamin Franklin and the Zealous Presbyterians* (University Park: Pennsylvania State University Press, 1975).
17. Franklin, "Dialogue Between Two Presbyterians," April 10, 1737, in *Papers*, ed. Labaree, 2:30.
18. Franklin, *Poor Richard's Almanack*, 1739, cited in Edmund Morgan, *Benjamin Franklin* (New Haven: Yale University Press, 2002), 19; Walters, *Benjamin Franklin*, 85.
19. Franklin to unknown recipient, Dec. 14, 1757, in *Papers*, ed. Labaree, 7:294–95.
20. Walters, *Benjamin Franklin*, 125–26.
21. Franklin, *Autobiography*, 68.

22. On Franklin's relationship with Deborah see Sheila Skemp, "Family Partnerships: The Working Wife, Honoring Deborah Franklin," in *Benjamin Franklin and Women*, ed. Larry Tise (University Park: Pennsylvania State University Press, 2000), 19–36.

23. Ibid.; Gordon Wood, *The Americanization of Benjamin Franklin* (New York: Penguin, 2004), 89–90, 132; Walter Isaacson, *Benjamin Franklin: An American Life* (New York: Simon & Schuster, 2003), 179, 239–40, 282–83; Morgan, *Benjamin Franklin*, 112.

24. Quoted in Wood, *Americanization of Benjamin Franklin*, 163.

25. Franklin, *Observations Concerning the Increase of Mankind, Peopling of Countries, & c.* (Tarrytown, NY: William Abbatt, 1918), cited in *Major Problems in American Immigrations and Ethnic History*, ed. John Gjerde (Boston: Houghton-Mifflin, 1998), 72–73.

26. Franklin, *Observations Concerning the Increase*, 73; David Waldstreicher, *Runaway America: Benjamin Franklin, Slavery, and the American Revolution* (New York: Hill & Wang, 2004).

27. Twain, "The Late Benjamin Franklin" (1870), in *Mark Twain: Collected Tales, Sketches, Speeches & Essays, 1852–1890* (New York: Library of America, 1992); Wood, *Americanization of Benjamin Franklin*, 3.

28. Isaacson, *Benjamin Franklin*, 100.

29. Wood, *Americanization of Benjamin Franklin*, 5.

30. For this view of Franklin see Robert Wuthnow, *Poor Richard's Principle: Recovering the American Dream through the Moral Dimensions of Work, Business, & Money* (Princeton: Princeton University Press, 1996), 4, 59–60.

15. What about Witherspoon? Three Orthodox Founders

1. David Barton, *Original Intent: The Courts, the Constitution, & Religion*, 3rd ed. (Aledo, TX: WallBuilder, 2000); Barton, "Should Christians—Or Ministers—Run for Office," Wall Builders Web site, accessed February 1, 2010, at http://www.wallbuilders.com/LIBissuesArticles.asp?id=77; William J. Federer, *America's God and Country* (St. Louis: Amerisearch, 2000), 702.

2. The best biography of Witherspoon remains Varnum L. Collins, *President Witherspoon: A Biography*, 2 vols. (Princeton: Princeton University Press, 1925). Also see Jeffry Morrison, *John Witherspoon and the Founding of the American Republic* (Notre Dame, IN: University of Notre Dame Press, 2005); Gordon L. Tait, *The Piety of John Witherspoon: Pew, Pulpit, and Public Forum* (Louisville: Geneva, 2001); and Ned C. Landsman, "Witherspoon and the Problem of Provincial Identity in Scottish Evangelical Culture," in *Scotland and America in the Age of the Enlightenment*, ed. Richard B. Sher and Jeffrey R. Smitten (Princeton: Princeton University Press, 1990), 29–45.

3. Tait, *Piety of John Witherspoon*, 7–9.

4. Landsman, "Witherspoon," 33–35; Tait, *Piety of John Witherspoon*, 12.

5. Witherspoon, "Lectures on Divinity I," quoted in Morrison, *John Witherspoon*, 28; Witherspoon, "An Address to the Senior Class, 1775," quoted in Tait, *Piety of John Witherspoon*, 185.

6. John Fea, *The Way of Improvement Leads Home: Philip Vickers Fithian and the Rural Enlightenment in Early America* (Philadelphia: University of Pennsylvania Press, 2008), 70.

7. Ibid., 70–71.

8. Ibid., 137.

9. Ibid., 139.
10. Witherspoon, "Thanksgiving Sermon, 1782," quoted in Morrison, *John Witherspoon*, 29.
11. Tait, *Piety of John Witherspoon*, 164–65, 167.
12. Fea, *Way of Improvement*, 140; Tait, *Piety of John Witherspoon*, 167.
13. Mark A. Noll, George M. Marsden, and Nathan O. Hatch, *The Search for Christian America*, expanded ed. (Colorado Springs: Helmers & Howard, 1989), 91.
14. The most recent biography of Jay is Walter Stahr, *John Jay* (New York: Continuum, 2006).
15. Patricia Bonomi, "John Jay, Religion, and the State," *New York History* 81 (2000): 11–12; Stahr, *John Jay*, 232–36.
16. John Jay to Lindley Murray, Aug. 22, 1794, quoted in *The Founders on Religion: A Book of Quotations*, ed. James H. Hutson (Princeton: Princeton University Press, 2005), 202–3; Bonomi, "John Jay," 10; Jay to the American Bible Society, May 12, 1825, quoted in *Founders on Religion*, ed. Hutson, 24–25; Jay to Samuel Miller, Feb. 18, 1822, Jay Papers (online edition), Columbia University Library, quoted in *Founders on Religion*, ed. Hutson, 80. The best overall treatment of Jay's religious beliefs is Jonathan Den Hartog, "John Jay and the 'Great Plan of Providence,'" in *The Forgotten Founders on Religion and Public Life*, ed. Daniel Dreisbach, Mark David Hall, and Jeffry Morrison (Notre Dame: University of Notre Dame Press, 2009), 145–70.
17. Jay to Uzal Ogden, Feb. 14, 1796, Jay Papers (online edition), Columbia University Library, quoted in *Founders on Religion*, ed. Hutson, 57; Jay to the American Bible Society, May 12, 1824, quoted in *Founders on Religion*, ed. Hutson, 187.
18. John Adams to Thomas Jefferson, July 16, 1813, in *The Adams-Jefferson Letters*, ed. Lester J. Cappon (Chapel Hill: University of North Carolina Press, 1959), 360.
19. Jay to the American Bible Society, May 8, 1823, quoted in *Founders on Religion*, ed. Hutson, 129–30; cf. Bonomi, "John Jay," 10.
20. Den Hartog, "John Jay," 145–46, 154.
21. Jay to Jedidiah Morse, Aug. 16, 1806, quoted in *Founders on Religion*, ed. Hutson, 179.
22. Den Hartog, "John Jay," 156–58.
23. Jay to Jedidiah Morse, Jan. 1, 1813, quoted in *Founders on Religion*, ed. Hutson, 60. The Old Testament passage is 2 Chronicles 19:2.
24. Den Hartog, "John Jay," 163.
25. Jay to Noah Worcester, June 21, 1819, Jay Papers (online edition), Columbia University Library, quoted in *Founders on Religion*, ed. Hutson, 96; Den Hartog, "John Jay," 156, 164.
26. Jay, "Charge to the Ulster County Grand Jury," Sept. 9, 1777, quoted in *Founders on Religion*, ed. Hutson, 135; Jay to John Murray Jr., Oct. 12, 1816, quoted in *Founders on Religion*, ed. Hutson, 197.
27. Jay to Jedidiah Morse, Sept. 4, 1798, Jay Papers (online edition), Columbia University Library, quoted in *Founders on Religion*, ed. Hutson, 43.
28. Bonomi, "John Jay," 13, 15; Den Hartog, "John Jay," 155.
29. Pauline Maier, *The Old Revolutionaries: Political Lives in the Age of Samuel Adams* (New York: Knopf, 1980), 50.

30. Gary Scott Smith, "Samuel Adams: America's Puritan Revolutionary," in *Forgotten Founders*, ed. Dreisbach et al., 45; William M. Fowler Jr., *Samuel Adams: Radical Puritan* (New York: Longman, 1997), 20, 27–29.
31. This is the argument of Maier, *Old Revolutionaries*, 27.
32. Fowler, *Samuel Adams*, 167–72.
33. Maier, *Old Revolutionaries*, 42; Ira Stoll, *Samuel Adams: A Life* (New York: Free Press, 2008), 61.
34. Samuel Adams to Elizabeth Adams, Dec. 19, 1776, in *The Writings of Samuel Adams*, ed. Harry Alonzo Cushing, 4 vols. (New York: Putnam, 1904–1908), 3:326–27; Smith, "Samuel Adams," 51, 53.
35. Samuel Adams (writing as "Candidus"), *Boston Gazette*, Nov. 11, 1771, in *Writings*, ed. Cushing, 2:268–74.
36. Samuel Adams (writing as "a Puritan"), *Boston Gazette*, April 11, 1768, in *Writings*, 1:203.
37. Samuel Adams to the Committee of Correspondence of Boston, Sept. 14, 1774, in *Writings*, 3:154–55.
38. Samuel Adams (writing as "a Puritan"), *Boston Gazette*, April 4 and 11, 1768, in *Writings*, 1:201–7; Smith, "Samuel Adams," 48.
39. Samuel Adams to Elizabeth Adams, Nov. 7, 1775, in *Writings*, 3:239–40; Samuel Adams to Elizabeth Adams, Oct. 20, 1775, in *Writings*, 3:227–28.
40. Samuel Adams to Elizabeth Adams, Nov. 29, 1776, in *Writings*, 3:320–21; Smith, "Samuel Adams," 54.
41. Adams to John Scollay, December 30, 1780, in *Writings*, 4:236–39; Samuel Adams to Elizabeth Adams, Sept. 28, 1778, in *Writings*, 4:65; Adams to Samuel Philips Savage, Oct. 6, 1778, in *Writings*, 4:67–68; Adams to John Langdon, Aug. 7, 1777, in *Writings*, 3:401–3; Fowler, *Samuel Adams*, 96.
42. Adams to John Scollay, April 30, 1776, in *Writings*, 3:285–88.

Conclusion

1. This episode of the Glenn Beck Show can be watched on YouTube at http://www.youtube.com/watch?v=1CGbDRNmKLI.

Epilogue to the Revised Edition

1. David Barton, *The Jefferson Lies: Exposing the Myths You've Always Believed about Thomas Jefferson* (Nashville: Thomas Nelson, Inc., 2012).
2. Martin Marty, "David Barton's Jefferson," https://divinity.uchicago.edu/sightings/david-bartons-jefferson-martin-e-marty.
3. Bob Allen, "Pastors Call for Thomas Nelson Boycott," *Baptist News Global*, August 7, 2012, https://baptistnews.com/culture/media-and-arts/item/7687-pastors-call-for-thomas-nelson-boycott.
4. Warren Throckmorton and Michael Coulter, *Getting Jefferson Right: Fact Checking Claims about Our Third President* (Union Grove, WI: Salem Grove Press, 2012).
5. Thomas Kidd, "Lost Confidence," *World*, August 9, 2012, http://www.worldmag.com/2012/08/lost_confidence.
6. WND Books, promotional website for *The Jefferson Lies*, accessed January 12, 2016, http://wndbooks.wnd.com/the-jefferson-lies/.

7. Ted Cruz Campaign Website, accessed January 12, 2016, https://www.tedcruz.org/l/defend-religious-liberty/.

8. Benjamin E. Park, "Kim Davis and the Anxieties of Christian America," *Religion & Politics*, September 16, 2015, http://religionandpolitics.org/2015/09/16/kim-davis-and-the-anxieties-of-christian-america/.

9. John Fea, "Do GOP Candidates Want Religious Freedom or the Closing of Mosques? They Can't Have Both," *History News Network*, December 3, 2015, http://historynews-network.org/article/161373.

Index

Numbers in *italics* indicate figures.